Contending Voices

Biographical Explorations of the American Past

Volume I: To 1877

FOURTH EDITION

JOHN HOLLITZ
College of Southern Nevada

CENGAGE
Learning·

Australia • Brazil • Mexico • Singapore • United Kingdom • United States

CENGAGE
Learning

Contending Voices: Biographical Explorations of the American Past, Volume I: To 1877,
Fourth Edition
John Hollitz

Product Director: Paul Banks

Product Manager: Clint Attebery

Content Developer: Cara Swan

Product Assistant: Andrew Newton

Marketing Manager: Kyle Zimmerman

IP Analyst: Alexandra Ricciardi

IP Project Manager: Betsy Hathaway

Manufacturing Planner: Sandee Milewski

Art and Design Direction, Production Management, and Composition: Lumina Datamatics, Inc.

Cover Image: © North Wind Picture Archives/Alamy Stock Photo

For product information and technology assistance, contact us at **Cengage Learning Customer & Sales Support, 1-800-354-9706**

For permission to use material from this text or product, submit all requests online at **www.cengage.com/permissions**. Further permissions questions can be emailed to **permissionrequest@cengage.com.**

Library of Congress Control Number: 2015948750

Student Edition:
ISBN: 978-1-305-65593-5

Cengage Learning
20 Channel Center Street
Boston, MA 02210
USA

Cengage Learning is a leading provider of customized learning solutions with employees residing in nearly 40 different countries and sales in more than 125 countries around the world. Find your local representative at **www.cengage.com**.

Cengage Learning products are represented in Canada by Nelson Education, Ltd.

To learn more about Cengage Learning Solutions, visit **www.cengage.com.**

Purchase any of our products at your local college store or at our preferred online store **www.cengagebrain.com.**

Printed in the United States of America
Print Number: 01   Print Year: 2015

Contents

PREFACE   viii

1   The Cross and the Sword in Spain's New World: Bartolomé de Las Casas and Hernán Cortés   1

SOURCE 1: *Las Casas Describes Spanish Atrocities* (1552)   11

SOURCE 2: *Cortés Describes the Aztecs* (1519, 1520)   12

SOURCE 3: *An Aztec View of the Temple Massacre* (ca. 1550)   14

SOURCE 4: *Cortés Defends* Encomiendas (1522)   14

SOURCE 5: *Las Casas Attacks Conversion by Conquest* (1537)   15

SOURCE 6: *Las Casas Attacks* Encomiendas (1542)   17

2   Revolt on the Virginia Frontier: Nathaniel Bacon and William Berkeley   19

SOURCE 1: *Frontier Planters Appeal to Governor William Berkeley* (Spring 1676)   29

SOURCE 2: William Berkeley, *"Declaration and Remonstrance"* (May 1676)   30

SOURCE 3: *A Summary of the June Assembly's Laws* (1676)   31

SOURCE 4: *Bacon's Manifesto* (July 1676)   31

SOURCE 5: *Grievances Submitted to the King's Commissioners* (1677)   32

3 Faith and Reason in an Age of Enlightenment: Jonathan Edwards and Benjamin Franklin   35

SOURCE 1: *Jonathan Edwards Accepts God's Sovereignty* (ca. 1740)   47

SOURCE 2: *Jonathan Edwards's Resolutions for Self-Improvement* (1723)   48

SOURCE 3: *Benjamin Franklin, "First Principles"* (1728)   49

SOURCE 4: *Benjamin Franklin's Moral Improvement Project* (1791)   50

SOURCE 5: *Benjamin Franklin on the Great Awakening* (1791)   53

SOURCE 6: *Jonathan Edwards, "Sinners in the Hands of an Angry God"* (1741)   54

4 The Price of Patriotism: Jonathan Sewall and John Adams   57

SOURCE 1: *"Instructions of the Town of Braintree to the Representative"* (1765)   67

SOURCE 2: *Jonathan Sewall Offers a Defense of British Authority* (1771)   68

SOURCE 3: *Jonathan Sewall on the Revolutionary Threat* (1775)   69

SOURCE 4: John Adams, *"Novanglus"* (1775)   70

5 The Conflict over the Constitution: Patrick Henry and James Madison   73

SOURCE 1: Mercy Otis Warren, *"Observations on the New Constitution"* (1788)   82

SOURCE 2: James Madison, *"The Federalist No. 10"* (1788)   83

SOURCE 3: Patrick Henry, *Speech to the Virginia Convention* (June 4, 1788)   84

SOURCE 4: Patrick Henry, *Speech to the Virginia Convention* (June 5, 1788)   85

SOURCE 5: James Madison, *"The Federalist No. 39"* (1788)   86

6 Political Conflict in the Early Republic: Benjamin Franklin Bache and Alexander Hamilton   89

SOURCE 1: Alexander Hamilton, *"To the People of the United States"* (1794)   99

SOURCE 2: *Benjamin Bache on Hamilton and the Whiskey Rebellion* (1794)   100

SOURCE 3: Alexander Hamilton, *"The French Revolution"* (1794)   102

SOURCE 4: *Resolutions of the Pennsylvania Democratic Society* (1794)   103

SOURCE 5: *Hamilton Defends Jay's Treaty* (1795)   104

SOURCE 6: *Benjamin Bache Assaults Jay's Treaty* (1795)   106

7   Resistance and Western Expansion: Tecumseh and William Henry Harrison   109

SOURCE 1: Thomas Jefferson, *Letter to William Henry Harrison* (1803)   117

SOURCE 2: William Henry Harrison, *Letter to William Eustis, Secretary of War* (1809)   118

SOURCE 3: William Henry Harrison, *A Discourse on the Aborigines of the Ohio Valley* (1839)   119

SOURCE 4: Tecumseh, *Speech to Harrison at Vincennes* (1810)   120

SOURCE 5: Tecumseh, *"Sleep Not Longer, O Choctaws and Chickasaws"* (1811)   121

8   The Fruits of the Factory System: Sarah Bagley and Nathan Appleton   124

SOURCE 1: Nathan Appleton, *"The Introduction of the Power Loom, and Origin of Lowell"* (1858)   135

SOURCE 2: *Regulations of the Appleton Company* (1833)   136

SOURCE 3: Sarah Bagley, *"The Pleasures of Factory Life"* (1840)   137

SOURCE 4: Sarah Bagley, *"Voluntary?"* (1845)   138

SOURCE 5: Nathan Appleton, *"Labor, Its Relations, in Europe and the United States, Compared"* (1844)   138

9   Politics, Morality, and Race in the Abolitionist Crusade: William Lloyd Garrison and Frederick Douglass   141

SOURCE 1: *Detail of* Liberator *Masthead* (1831)   152

SOURCE 2: *Garrison Announces His New Reform Policy* (1837)   153

SOURCE 3: *Douglass Recounts His Life as a Slave* (1845)   154

SOURCE 4: *Garrison Announces "No Union with Slaveholders"* (1844)   156

SOURCE 5: *Frederick Douglass Responds to William Lloyd Garrison* (1853)   157

SOURCE 6: Frederick Douglass, *"The Meaning of July Fourth for the Negro"* (1852)   158

10 The Feminine Sphere in Antebellum Society: Catharine Beecher and Elizabeth Cady Stanton   161

SOURCE 1: *"Differences Between the Sexes"* (1835)   174

SOURCE 2: *Catharine Beecher on Women's Proper Place* (1837)   175

SOURCE 3: Catharine Beecher, *A Treatise on Domestic Economy* (1841)   176

SOURCE 4: *Elizabeth Cady Stanton Addresses the Seneca Falls Convention* (1848)   177

SOURCE 5: *Elizabeth Cady Stanton Answers the Critics of Woman's Rights* (1848)   179

11 Manifest Destiny and Conquest: Thomas Larkin and Juan Bautista Alvarado   182

SOURCE 1: *Richard Henry Dana Assesses the Californios* (1840)   192

SOURCE 2: *Thomas Larkin on the Situation in California* (1845)   193

SOURCE 3: *Juan Bautista Alvarado on the Conquest of California* (1876)   194

SOURCE 4: *Vigilante Justice in Los Angeles* (1857)   195

12 The South and the Slavery Debate: Hinton Rowan Helper and George Fitzhugh   198

SOURCE 1: George Fitzhugh, *Slavery Justified* (1850)   207

SOURCE 2: George Fitzhugh, *Cannibals All!* (1857)   208

SOURCE 3: *Hinton Rowan Helper on Chinese Immigrants* (1855)   210

SOURCE 4: Hinton Rowan Helper, *The Impending Crisis of the South* (1857)   211

SOURCE 5: Emily Burke, *Reminiscences of Georgia* (1850)   213

13 Yankees and "Border Ruffians" in "Bleeding Kansas": Sara Robinson and David Atchison   216

SOURCE 1: John C. Calhoun, *"Address to the People of the Southern States"* (1849)   227

SOURCE 2: *Report of the Committee to Investigate the Troubles in Kansas* (1856)   228

SOURCE 3: *Sara Robinson on "Bleeding Kansas"* (1856)   229

SOURCE 4: *Sara Robinson on the "Sack" of Lawrence* (1856)   230

SOURCE 5: *David Atchison on the "Abolitionist" Threat* (1856)   231

14 Mr. Lincoln's War: Clement Vallandigham and Benjamin Wade 234

SOURCE 1: *Benjamin Wade Assaults a Southern Colleague* (1854) 244

SOURCE 2: Abraham Lincoln, *Letter to Horace Greeley* (1862) 245

SOURCE 3: Benjamin Wade and Henry Davis, *The Wade-Davis Manifesto* (1864) 246

SOURCE 4: Clement Vallandigham, *"The Great Civil War in America"* (1863) 247

SOURCE 5: *Scene of New York City Draft Rioters Lynching an African American* (1863) 248

SOURCE 6: *Clement Vallandigham Attacks Benjamin Wade* (1862) 249

15 Race and Redemption in the Reconstructed South: Robert Smalls and Wade Hampton 252

SOURCE 1: Zion Presbyterian Church, *"Memorial to the Senate and House of Representatives"* (1865) 264

SOURCE 2: *Wade Hampton Protests to the President* (1866) 265

SOURCE 3: *A Northerner Assesses Southern Attitudes* (1866) 267

SOURCE 4: *Wade Hampton Testifies Before a Congressional Committee* (1871) 269

SOURCE 5: *Representative Robert Smalls Protests the Withdrawal of Federal Troops* (1876) 273

SOURCE 6: *Instructions to Red Shirts* (1876) 275

Preface

The encouraging reception from students and instructors to the previous editions of *Contending Voices: Biographical Explorations of the American Past* has led me to create a fourth edition. As before, this book uses paired biographies to bring alive the debates and disagreements that have shaped American history. It is based on the assumption that students find history more engaging when they realize that it is full of conflict. Through biography, individual men and women emerge from the tangle of events, dates, and facts that often make history so challenging for students.

Following the organization of most survey texts, each chapter examines two individuals who stood on different sides of an important issue. Their stories, combined with a small set of primary sources in each chapter, show students how individuals—from the pre-English settlement of the New World to the present—influenced their times and were influenced by them. At the same time, the book's biographical approach naturally incorporates political, social, economic, cultural, religious, and diplomatic histories while underscoring the diversity of those who shaped the past. This biographical approach highlights competing perspectives, prompting students to think about issues from multiple viewpoints. The biographical essays that introduce the Sources were written with these pedagogical goals in mind.

Although students will encounter familiar names in these pages, many of the thirty individuals in each of *Contending Voices'* two volumes rarely appear in survey texts. All of them, however, addressed significant events and issues of their times. In Volume I, sixteenth-century *conquistador* Hernán Cortés and Dominican priest Bartolomé de Las Casas contest the fate of Native Americans. In the seventeenth century, the pitched battles between Governor William Berkeley and rebel Nathaniel Bacon reveal forces shaping early Virginia. Other chapters illuminate the American Revolution, the ratification of the Constitution, and political conflict between Federalists and Republicans in the 1790s. Later, the life-and-death conflict between William Henry Harrison and Tecumseh reflects the larger struggle between whites and Indians sparked by westward expansion in the early nineteenth century. In the same period, chapters pairing union organizer Sarah Bagley with industrialist Nathan Appleton and Governor Juan Bautista Alvarado of Mexican California with merchant Thomas Larkin focus on the rise of the factory system and Manifest Destiny. At mid-century, George Fitzhugh and Hinton Rowan Helper debate slavery's impact on the South and reveal deep fears at the heart of a growing sectional conflict. Still later, antiwar Democrat Clement Vallandigham and radical Republican Benjamin Wade demonstrate the limits of dissent during the Civil War.

New biographies in Volume I include New England minister Jonathan Edwards and Benjamin Franklin, who highlight the conflict between faith and reason in the eighteenth-century colonies.

Volume II offers a similar diversity of individuals and topics. The new biographies in Volume II feature the Sioux chief Sitting Bull and Indian education advocate Richard Henry Pratt, who battled in the late nineteenth century to define the place of Native Americans in American society, and John D. Rockefeller and Ida Tarbell, who clashed in the early twentieth century over the power exercised by Rockefeller's Standard Oil trust.

In the early twentieth century, antiwar critic Randolph Bourne and war propagandist George Creel further illuminate aspects of progressive reform as well as the new power of advertising and the effects of World War I on American society. Japanese-American internee Harry Ueno and internment director Dillon Myer illustrate the experience of Japanese relocation during World War II. Later battles are brought to life in chapters pairing civil rights activist Fannie Lou Hamer with black leader Roy Wilkins; women's rights champion Betty Friedan with feminist Gloria Steinem; and Interior Secretary James Watt with novelist Edward Abbey. They illustrate the challenges confronting the civil rights, women's, and environmental movements and the conflicts dividing them. Finally, Richard Clarke and John Yoo, two officials in the administration of George W. Bush, illuminate the sharp and ongoing differences arising out of the "war on terror" after the September 11, 2001, attacks on the United States.

While permitting easy access to often unfamiliar topics, *Contending Voices* is also designed to build students' critical thinking skills. Each chapter begins with a brief essay providing an introduction to the lives and ideas of the two individuals who held conflicting views on an important issue. The essay does not offer a complete accounting of subjects' lives—an impossible task—but focuses instead on aspects that illuminate the chapter's main topic. Each essay begins with a short vignette designed to capture the reader's attention and includes a running glossary, which defines terms that may be unfamiliar to many survey students. A set of four to seven primary sources illustrating and amplifying the chapter's central themes follows each essay. These sources demonstrate the variety of sources historians use to understand the past and reflect another premise behind this book—that the best way for students to learn history is to explore it themselves. Their explorations are assisted by a brief set of Questions to Consider following the primary sources. In addition, references to each primary source appear in the essays, helping to integrate the primary and secondary material. A brief introduction to each primary source also aids student analysis. Finally, a brief Further Reading section contains both biographical and general works that will help interested students explore each chapter topic further.

Many people made valuable contributions to these volumes. At the College of Southern Nevada (CSN), Charles Okeke offered welcome encouragement, while administrative assistants Alaina Priscu and Terresa Waters provided technical assistance. CSN Interlibrary Loan librarian Marion Martin and library assistant Jessica Caseman cheerfully and efficiently tracked down the needed material. At Cengage Learning, Clint Attebery and Tonya Lobato oversaw the revision process, and Cara Swan brought a keen eye to the manuscript and offered numerous helpful suggestions throughout the revision process. Margaret Bridges carefully guided the manuscript through the production phase.

Numerous colleagues around the country reviewed these chapters and offered many useful ideas, suggestions, and criticisms. These volumes benefited greatly from their efforts. They include Ginette Aley, University of Southern Indiana; Daniel Ashyk, Cleveland State University; Matthew Bloom, Bowling Green State University; Michelle Brattain, Georgia State University; John Bullion, University of Missouri-Columbia; Larissa Fergeson, Longwood University; James Paradis, Arcadia University; Stephen Shwiff, University of Texas-San Antonio; and Timothy Thurber, Virginia Commonwealth University.

As always, my biggest debt is to Patty. Once again, this book is dedicated to her.

—J.H.

1

The Cross and the Sword in Spain's New World: Bartolomé de Las Casas and Hernán Cortés

The pulse of the sixty-six-year-old Bartolomé de Las Casas quickened as he stepped into the court of King Charles I of Spain in 1540. The Catholic friar could not suppress his nervous anticipation. After all, he carried to Charles a story of bloody conquest and naked exploitation that the monarch would surely find shocking. In the half century since Columbus's voyage of discovery in 1492, Spanish conquerors claimed vast portions of the New World and put millions of its native inhabitants under Spain's yoke. Las Casas knew that none of these men figured more prominently in Spain's conquest than Hernán Cortés. In 1519, the young conquistador marched fewer than six hundred Spanish soldiers into the Aztec Empire in central Mexico and took it over. In little time, the area represented the heart of Spain's vast empire in the New World. Las Casas was aware that Cortés and other conquerors brought great wealth and glory to His Majesty's realm. Yet he believed that there was much more to the story of Spain's conquest of the New World.

Las Casas was no stranger to the New World. After arriving in the West Indies in 1502, he lived there on and off for the next four decades. He sought passage to the Indies to make his fortune and along with many other Spaniards secured the right to control the labor of numerous Indians for his own benefit. As a young colonist, he seemed destined to live as a prosperous West Indian planter. Life in the New World took a strange turn, though. Less than a decade after his arrival there, Las Casas heard the call of the priesthood. Then a few years after his ordination, he heeded another call. Increasingly troubled by the cruelty of many Spaniards toward the Indians, Las Casas denounced the system by which his countrymen held many native people and renounced

Bartolomé de Las Casas   Hernán Cortés

his own grant of Indian laborers. Then he proceeded to make it his life's work to defend the Indians and challenge the Spaniards' treatment of them.

Now as he stepped into the royal court, he was ready to lay before his king the gruesome details of the Spanish extermination of the Indians and the conquistadors' brutal rule over the survivors. Among the "tyrants" he singled out was the founder of New Spain, Hernán Cortés. Impressed as Cortés was by the way the Aztecs lived, Mexico's conqueror had no doubt that they should be converted by the sword and then be made to serve his—and his nation's—ends. After conquering the Aztecs, Cortés grew rich and powerful from his exploitation of Native American labor, inspiring other Spaniards to conquer millions more Indians. The conquistadors exacted an awful price from their victims, and now Las Casas pleaded with the Spanish king to take control of the Indians away from these greedy men. As he stood in His Majesty's court, he believed that the fate of the New World's native population was at stake.

"THE INDIANS HAVE SLAIN LAS CASAS!"

Bartolomé de Las Casas's connections to the New World and its native inhabitants began almost as soon as Spain's encounter with them. Las Casas was born in 1474 in the southwestern Spanish town of Seville. The son of a merchant who had fallen on hard times, Bartolomé was eighteen years old in 1493 when he witnessed Columbus's triumphant procession through the streets of his hometown after the latter had returned from his first voyage to the New World. Later that same year, Las Casas's father and uncle shipped out with Columbus on his second voyage and were among the first colonists to settle in Hispaniola.* When Bartolomé's father returned to Spain in 1498, he brought along a present for his son: a Taino Indian servant from Hispaniola. We do not know the young man's reaction to this gift, but his imagination must have been fired by tales of Columbus's adventures.

In 1502, when he was twenty-eight, Las Casas sailed with his father to the West Indies. With a university education in Latin, he was qualified to hold the position of *doctrinero*, or teacher of Christian doctrine. As such, he would earn an ample salary and was able to acquire property. As soon as Las Casas's ship reached Santo Domingo,* he discovered that there were plenty of opportunities to do just that. He immediately heard the news that gold had been discovered on the island and that a war with the Tainos had produced a large number of slaves to mine it. Years before, the Tainos had impressed Columbus with their meekness and hospitality. It had not taken long, however, for friendly relations between the Spaniards and Tainos to descend into a nightmare of slaughter and enslavement.

Here and elsewhere in the West Indies, Columbus had set in motion a series of events that would have devastating consequences for the New World's native peoples. Periodically, his men kidnapped Tainos "to learn the secrets of the land." In 1494, Columbus dispatched his first human cargo from the New World to be sold at the slave market in Seville. Later that year, his men launched a savage attack on the Tainos that resulted in the destruction of villages, the killing of countless people, and the shipment of five hundred more slaves to Spain. By the time Las Casas arrived in Hispaniola, many Tainos were working as forced laborers for the Spaniards in the mines and fields.

These practices may shock modern sensibilities, but they reflected the attitudes of Spanish culture at the time. Unlike most of Europe, southern Spain had not done away with slavery by the late fifteenth century. That area had been a stronghold of the Moors—Muslims from North Africa who had invaded Spain in the eighth century and occupied parts of it until the late fifteenth century. The Spaniards viewed the invaders as infidels—that is, non-Christians—and as such inferior. They applied the same views to the native inhabitants of the Caribbean islands. To the Spaniards, these people—living without cities, clothes, private property, or any concept of economically productive work—appeared utterly irresponsible and uncivilized. Moreover, as Christians, the Spaniards saw these strangers who worshiped numerous gods as heathens.

By the late fifteenth century, the Spaniards, who viewed Africans in the same way, began to import African slaves to the West Indies to replace the native workers who had succumbed to Old World diseases and Spanish cruelty. In the fifty years following Columbus's arrival, the Indian population fell by perhaps 90 percent. In the fifteenth century alone, Spanish and Portuguese slave traders shipped as many as a quarter of a million Africans to the West Indies to fill this void.

As Las Casas settled down in the West Indies, he gave no indication that he disagreed with the Spaniards' attitudes toward the Indians. Shortly after arriving there, he helped to suppress several Indian uprisings and was rewarded with an *encomienda*—a grant of land and the native people living on it. **[See Source 1.]** In theory, the *encomenderos*—the recipients of these grants—were responsible for the protection of the people entrusted to them and for their introduction to Christianity. But in reality, the *encomienda* system was nothing more than slavery. Ambitious and energetic, Las Casas had few qualms about this

---

Hispaniola: The island east of Cuba that is now occupied by Haiti and the Dominican Republic.

Santo Domingo: A seaport and the principal Spanish settlement on Hispaniola.

arrangement. In fact, when a group of Dominican* friars arrived on Hispaniola in 1510, Las Casas was unmoved by their arguments against the colonists' mistreatment of the Indians.

Even Las Casas's decision to become a priest the same year did not lead immediately to his rejection of the *encomienda* system. In early 1512, he joined an expedition led by a military adventurer named Diego Velásquez who was already engaged in the conquest of the neighboring island of Cuba. Serving as chaplain, he witnessed the slaughter of hundreds of Indians that, he said, left "a stream of blood running … as if a great number of cows had perished." Las Casas attempted to stop the massacre, but without success. Afterward, however, he accepted an *encomienda* on Cuba, where he prospered by farming and raising cattle.

Within a few years, Las Casas began to have doubts about the treatment of the native people. The turning point came as he was preparing a sermon after discussing the plight of the Indians with some Dominicans who shared his concerns. As he thumbed through the Bible, his eyes fell on this passage: "Tainted his gifts who offers in sacrifice ill-gotten goods." Las Casas was unable to get these words out of his mind, and he finally concluded that everything done to the people of the West Indies was "unjust and tyrannical." Committed now to giving up his own Indian slaves, he soon delivered his first sermon denouncing the treatment of the islanders.

In fact, the Indians posed a thorny problem for Spanish Christians. Like the Moors, the New World's natives were outsiders captured in battle. Unlike the Moors, they were not stubborn infidels, but people capable of salvation. At the same time, Indian labor was the key to extracting the New World's wealth. Indeed, making the natives economically productive was essential to "civilizing" them. In 1512, King Ferdinand had called a group of jurists and theologians together to consider what to do about the Indians. The group called for the teaching of Christian doctrine to the native people, but it also offered Ferdinand a powerful justification for Indian service. Because of their "natural lack of understanding," the Indians were unable to rule themselves. They could not be considered slaves, but for their own good, they would have to "work for those who govern them."

Shortly thereafter, Ferdinand issued the Laws of Burgos, the first royal confirmation of the *encomienda* system. These laws contained provisions to prevent the abuse of Indian laborers, but those provisions were largely ignored. Spain was a poor country, and the impoverished Spanish crown had an obvious interest in the gold mines of the West Indies. Moreover, numerous royal officials had a vested interest in the *encomienda* system. Indeed, Ferdinand was the largest holder of Indians in the New World. Thus the Laws of Burgos salved Spanish consciences, but wealth continued to flow out of the West Indies, and the natives continued to die in the mines and fields.

In contrast to most of his countrymen, Las Casas believed that the Indians, despite their primitive mode of living, were rational beings with "excellent, subtle, and very capable minds." Like other clerics, he never doubted the need to save the Indians by making them economically productive. But he also knew that their way of life poorly fitted them for servitude. Slavery did not "civilize" the Indians; it killed them. They could be converted and civilized only through "love and tenderness." Determined to see the *encomienda* system destroyed, Las Casas returned to Spain in 1515 and gained an audience with Ferdinand. Within weeks, however, Ferdinand was dead. When Las Casas then took his case to officials in charge of Spanish affairs in the New World, he got the cold shoulder.

In response, Las Casas devised a remarkable plan to save the people of the New World by scrapping the *encomienda* system. Under his plan, the Indians would live in their own villages, learn to govern themselves, and claim a share of the profits of their

---

Dominican: A member of a Catholic religious order founded in the thirteenth century.

labor. They would also be treated in a humane manner, although they would continue to work for the Spanish settlers and produce revenue for the Crown. For Hispaniola, where the native population had already been largely destroyed, he proposed an alternative plan. Spanish peasants would be sent to the island to work alongside, and eventually intermarry with, the surviving Indians. Las Casas endorsed the importation of African slaves to do heavy labor and to compensate the colonists who had lost their *encomiendas*. He seemed to have few qualms about enslaving Africans, perhaps because he believed that Africans could better endure the rigors of slavery, or perhaps because Africans were more "outlandish" to him than the Native Americans he was so eager to save. Las Casas presented his plan to Francisco Jiménez, the cardinal of Spain and the regent* of the young King Charles I.* In response to Las Casas's proposals, Jiménez named him "Protector of the Indians," and royal authorities issued orders granting free passage and land to Spanish peasants who immigrated to the West Indies. Las Casas soon learned, however, that the great landowners in Spain had no desire to lose their tenants.

Forced to abandon his plan, Las Casas developed an even grander scheme to save the Indians. Battling colonial agents at court for a year, he finally secured a grant of land running about eight hundred miles along the coast of Venezuela. Only a few missionaries had penetrated the area, and thus the native inhabitants had been spared the fate of the Tainos. Under Las Casas's plan, the Indians would be converted and live in towns. He knew that any successful effort to save the Indians had to profit the Spaniards, so he promised to the Crown handsome revenues resulting from the production of gold and various trade items.

Las Casas's model community was doomed to failure, however. When he set sail from Spain in 1520, he was accompanied by seventy condemned men escaping punishment. Shortly after he arrived in Venezuela, he sailed to Santo Domingo in an attempt to stop Spanish slave traders' continued attacks on the Indians there. A few days after he left Venezuela, the Indians killed several Spaniards and burned a monastery. When his ship landed at the wrong end of Hispaniola, he was forced to walk across the island to Santo Domingo. As he walked, people told him the news from Venezuela: "The Indians … have slain the cleric Bartolomé de Las Casas and all his household!"

Las Casas was stunned. He had compromised his principles, he believed, when he threw in with the Spaniards, who were interested only in money. Taking the news from Venezuela as "a divine judgment," and no longer confident that he had been chosen to save the Indians, he decided to turn his back on the world. In 1522, he entered the Dominican monastery in Santo Domingo and the next year took his vows as a Dominican friar. To "all appearances," as Las Casas himself put it, for the next eleven years he "slept." As he dozed off, Hernán Cortés was putting millions of Indians under Spain's yoke.

"A VAST MULTITUDE OF CORPSES"

Hernán Cortés was a restless man of action. Born in Medellín* in 1485, the son of an army commander, young Hernán was sent off to study Latin and law at the same university attended by Las Casas. Two years later, at the age of sixteen, he returned to

---

Regent: An individual appointed to rule in a monarchy when the sovereign is too young or otherwise unable to govern. The appointment of a cardinal to this position indicates that church and state were inseparable in sixteenth-century Spain.

Charles I: The grandson of Ferdinand and Isabella. Because his mother was insane and his father had died, Charles inherited the Spanish throne while still a boy.

Medellín: A town in southwestern Spain.

Medellín, convinced that his future lay in the military. In 1504, still only nineteen, Cortés sailed for the West Indies, landing in Santo Domingo. Soon after his arrival, like Las Casas, he participated in an expedition under the command of Diego Velásquez to crush an Indian revolt. He distinguished himself in the fighting and, again like Las Casas, was rewarded with an *encomienda*. For six years, he enjoyed life as a planter. Then in 1511, he accompanied Velásquez's expedition to conquer Cuba—the same expedition that left Las Casas shocked by the carnage he witnessed. Rewarded with another *encomienda*, Cortés settled in the seaport of Santiago, in southwestern Cuba.

In the years since Columbus's first voyage to the New World, the Spaniards had seized control of the West Indies, visited Florida, and probed the coasts of Central and South America. Strangely, however, they had never sailed due west from Cuba. Then in 1517, an expedition in search of more Indians to work Cuba's mines and fields did just that, landing on the Yucatán, a peninsula extending northward into the Caribbean Sea from southern Mexico. When the expedition returned to Cuba the following year with gold and other treasure, Velásquez immediately outfitted another group, which returned with still more gold and the knowledge that the Yucatán was not, as previously thought, an island. Determined to discover what lay to the north of this peninsula, Velásquez turned to Cortés to lead a third expedition. The restless *encomendero* seized the opportunity. To finance the voyage, he borrowed heavily and even pledged his *encomienda* as collateral.

Cortés set sail in early 1519 with an armada of 11 ships carrying 553 soldiers, 4 cannons, and a banner that read, "Friends, let us follow the cross with true faith, with which we will conquer." His orders were to explore further, rescue any Spaniards captured by the Indians during the earlier expeditions, find any gold and silver he could, and colonize the area if conditions were favorable. The fleet made its way to Cozumel, an island off the northeastern tip of the Yucatán. There Cortés encountered people living very differently from the primitive West Indians. For the first time, he saw native cities and evidence of a highly organized society. These Indians were descendants of the Mayas, who had built a complex civilization in southern Mexico and Guatemala between the sixth and tenth centuries. Like other Mesoamerican[*] peoples, the Mayas built stone structures, lived in cities, and used sophisticated agricultural techniques. They also worshiped numerous gods and practiced human sacrifice, both of which were shocking and incomprehensible to the Spaniards. Although he was no priest, Cortés took his Catholic faith seriously. The product of a militantly religious society, he was driven by his duty as a Christian warrior to bring these heathens to God. After entering one blood-splattered temple, for example, he smashed the idols inside, erected a cross, and ordered a priest to say Mass. Before his conquest was over, he would strike down many more Native American idols.

Sailing on, Cortés's party soon landed near the mouth of the Tabasco River on the Gulf of Mexico. When the native Tabascans gave the Spaniards a hostile reception, the Spaniards brought their horses and superior arms to bear, killing more than eight hundred Tabascans. The Indians then presented Cortés with gold and twenty young women. One of the women spoke Mayan and Nahuatl, the Aztec language. Named Malinche, she had been born into a noble Aztec family. After her father died, her mother remarried and bore a son. To make sure this son received his inheritance, her mother and stepfather sold Malinche into slavery. Now handed over by the Tabascans, she soon became Cortés's faithful helper and lover. She also played another important role, translating

---

[*]*Mesoamerican:* The term applied to the Native Americans, including the Mayas and Aztecs, who lived in present-day Mexico and Central America.

Nahuatl into Mayan, which a priest rescued from the Yucatán then translated into Spanish. Cortés now had the means to communicate with the emperor of Mexico.

As the expedition continued along the coast, Cortés heard tales of a magnificent kingdom in the interior. Anchoring at the site of modern-day Veracruz, he soon received a chief bearing gifts of gold from the Aztec emperor, Montezuma II. The Aztec leader had already heard about the battle with the Tabascans and no doubt wanted to learn more about these newcomers, their strange animals, and their weapons that made a deafening roar. Cortés told the emissary that he represented a great monarch on the other side of the ocean, information that confirmed an important Aztec myth. The Aztecs believed that a white-skinned, bearded god named Quetzalcoatl had founded the Indian race and then sailed away to the east, promising to return and reestablish his rule. The Aztec emperor may or may not have believed this myth, but he surely did not want to give up his power. The ambassador told Cortés that Montezuma did not want to see him. Cortés was undeterred. If he returned to Cuba without enough gold to pay for the voyage, he would lose his *encomienda*. Facing disgrace and financial ruin, he knew there was no turning back. After executing two conspirators who wished to head home, he had his men unload all the ships' provisions; then he ordered the vessels burned. Without the possibility of retreat, the choice was now simple: the conquest of Montezuma's empire or death.

In this desperate hour, messengers arrived from the chief of the Totonacs, another Mesoamerican people who had recently been defeated by Montezuma's warriors. Cortés was encouraged by evidence of dissension among the Indians. In August 1519, the Spaniards set off with thirteen hundred Totonac warriors for Tenochtitlán,[*] the capital of the Aztec Empire. It was an arduous and bloody trek. More than two hundred miles lay between the coast and the heart of Montezuma's empire on Mexico's central plateau. Getting there required a climb to more than seven thousand three hundred feet above sea level. Along the way, the expedition came under attack by the Tlaxcalans, another people in central Mexico subject to Aztec rule. Overwhelmed by the Spaniards' superior arms, the Tlaxcalans decided to join the invaders.

By the time Cortés marched into the Aztec religious center of Cholula, about sixty miles southeast of Tenochtitlán, his army had swollen to six thousand men. They were met by more than twenty thousand people. Warned by Malinche that the Cholulans were planning an ambush, Cortés struck first. With the aid of their Tlaxcalan allies, the Spaniards fell on the Cholulans and slaughtered them. Two days later, six thousand men, women, and children lay dead. Cortés pressed on to Tenochtitlán, arriving at its outskirts in early November.

Realizing that he could not prevent the Spaniards from entering his domain, Montezuma invited the visitors into the city. The capital of an empire numbering perhaps sixteen million people, Tenochtitlán was an awesome sight. With some three hundred thousand residents, it was larger than any city the Spaniards had ever seen. In many ways, it was also the most sophisticated. Built on an island in Lake Texcoco, it was supplied with water by an aqueduct linked to the mainland. People and goods entered the city across three viaducts, each fortified with drawbridges. Its plaza, the site of a weekly market, could accommodate sixty thousand people. In short, Tenochtitlán was the creation of a highly organized civilization. Dominated by pyramids that seemed to touch the sky, it amazed even the hard-bitten Spanish soldiers. Montezuma's gifts of gold, silver, and jewels had the same impact.

The emperor no doubt hoped that the Spaniards would be impressed by his power and generosity and then depart. Cortés had no intention of leaving, however. The Aztecs

---

[*]*Tenochtitlán:* Pronounced "the-noach-*tee*-tlan," the city was built on the site of present-day Mexico City.

astounded Cortés with their magnificent achievements and highly organized social structure, which was similar to that of Spain. But in Cortés's eyes, they were still barbarians. In every town on their trek to Tenochtitlán, his men had seen temples where humans were sacrificed to appease the unpredictable gods. In the Aztec capital, Montezuma took Cortés to the top of the highest pyramid, the temple of the war god Huitzilopochtli, where Cortés saw a fearsome idol covered with dried human blood. Witness to such sights, Cortés never doubted that the Aztecs were heathens—or the justice of bringing them to God by the sword. **[See Source 2.]**

Not intimidated by Montezuma's power, Cortés seized the emperor and held him hostage. He justified the action by claiming that some Spaniards left in defense of Veracruz had been killed by Montezuma's men. Cortés detained the emperor for five months, while the Spaniards studied the Aztecs and surveyed their empire. Then he ordered Montezuma to gather his nobles and announce that he was submitting to the Spanish monarch. As tribute, the Spanish took huge quantities of gold objects. It seemed that Cortés had accomplished the unthinkable: the peaceful conquest of the Aztec Empire.

The Aztecs began to grow restless, however, and Cortés received word that a Spanish fleet had arrived at Veracruz with orders from Diego Velásquez to return to Cuba immediately. Leaving a small force in the Aztec capital, Cortés returned to the coast to persuade this force to join him. While he was away, more than six hundred Aztec nobles and some three thousand spectators assembled in Tenochtitlán's temple area for sacred dances. Fearing an insurrection, Spanish troops fell on the crowd. When they were finished, the courtyard was littered with bodies, and the leading Aztec nobles had been wiped out. **[See Source 3.]**

When Cortés returned from the coast, the Aztecs were up in arms. Desperate, he forced Montezuma to appear before his people and plead for peace. But the move backfired. Many Aztecs, disillusioned with the emperor's apparent cowardice, turned on Montezuma with stones and arrows, fatally wounding him. With his valuable hostage lost, Cortés retreated. As the Spaniards tried to escape, the Aztecs, led by Montezuma's brother Cuitlahuac, attacked. Bogged down by gold and other loot, the Spaniards lost 450 men, 4,000 Indian confederates, and dozens of horses. In the confusion of battle, they also lost much of their treasure.

Cortés barely escaped, but the Aztecs had not seen the last of him. The invaders returned to their Tlaxcalan allies, who had amassed a force of one hundred fifty thousand. They marched back to Tenochtitlán, slaughtering all who resisted. As smallpox raged through the empire, killing Cuitlahuac, Cortés and his army laid siege to the capital. When the Aztecs continued to hold out, Cortés decided that the only way to defeat them was to systematically destroy the city. With the assistance of his Indian allies, the Spaniards laid waste to Tenochtitlán. The siege and campaign of destruction lasted for seventy-five days. When it was over in August 1521, the Aztecs had lost perhaps one hundred forty thousand people. Their once magnificent capital was reduced to rubble, and its streets and canals were littered with "a vast multitude of corpses."

The victorious Spaniards were quickly disappointed, however. Searching for more Aztec wealth, they found little. Even torturing Cuitlahuac's twenty-three-year-old successor, the last Aztec emperor, produced no treasure. Frustrated in his hopes for immediate riches, Cortés organized expeditions to the outer reaches of the Aztec domain, speeding the Spanish discovery of more Mexican territory and the founding of new cities. In short order, all of the Aztec Empire was under Cortés's command. The decimation of the Aztec lords and priests, who were often burned at the stake, hastened the consolidation of Spanish control. Accustomed to authoritarian rule, the surviving Indians quietly submitted to their new masters.

The outlines of a new society quickly emerged from the ashes of the old. One characteristic—a racially mixed population—began to appear when Malinche presented Cortés with a son shortly after the conquest. Because most of the early Spanish immigrants to Mexico were male, sexual liaisons and sometimes even marriages between Spaniards and Native American women were common. In time, many more *mestizos* (mixed-blood children) were born. Just as Mexico City was built on the site of the destroyed Aztec capital, the new society was based on the exploitation of Indian labor. Like Mexico City, the *encomiendas*, which Cortés generously distributed to himself and his officers, were a symbol of one culture's conquest of another. **[See Source 4.]** His own grants included twenty-two towns and perhaps as many as ninety thousand Indian vassals. Appointed governor of New Spain in 1522, Cortés lived regally. "I did not come here," he declared, "to till the land like a peasant."

A "TYRANNICAL PESTILENCE"

As Cortés built New Spain, Bartolomé de Las Casas studied and contemplated behind monastery walls. After eleven years in retreat, he was ready to resume his role as "Protector of the Indians." Turning to Central America, he founded a Dominican monastery in Nicaragua in 1534. After attacking the Spanish governor's efforts to conquer the Indians there, he left to evangelize the people of Guatemala. As three military expeditions had failed to convert them, Guatemala's governor granted Las Casas permission to use peaceful means instead. When his efforts began to bear fruit, he published *The Only Method of Attracting All People to the True Faith* (1537), an assault on the assumption of Cortés and other conquistadors that the Indians could not be converted unless conquered. **[See Source 5.]**

His confidence restored, Las Casas again took up his fight against the *encomienda* system. After winning an audience with King Charles in 1540, Las Casas read at court his account of Spanish atrocities against the Indians. Determined to shock the king, he related revolting details of the Spaniards' "murder and destruction" of the Indians and the "tyrannical pestilence" introduced among them. Then he called on Charles to take the revolutionary step of abolishing the *encomienda* system, the very basis of Spanish control of the Indians. **[See Source 6.]** In 1542, Charles responded by issuing the New Laws, which prohibited the enslavement of any more Indians, stripped officials of their *encomiendas*, and transferred other *encomiendas* to the Crown upon the death of their owners. Indians would be emancipated from the plantations and set on the path to freedom.

Getting the New Laws on the books was one thing, but enforcing them was quite another. When Las Casas returned to the New World, he encountered the wrath of Spanish settlers. When he arrived in southern Mexico, where church officials had offered him a bishopric[*], local *encomenderos* were up in arms over the New Laws, and colonial officials refused to enforce them. So he set off again for Spain. On his way, he visited Mexico City, where he defended the New Laws and denounced the *encomienda* system before political authorities and fellow bishops. Word of his actions reached Spain, and in 1547 officials there rebuked him. Las Casas refused to back down, and the New Laws stayed on the books.

By that time, the man directly responsible for the virtual enslavement of New Spain's Indians had suffered a reversal of fortune. Cortés's fabulous success in Mexico had sparked tremendous interest in New Spain. On the heels of his conquest came an influx of settlers, many of whom also were anxious to make their fortunes. They came

---

[*]*Bishopric*: The office of a bishop.

to develop Mexico rather than merely loot it. That required administrators and politicians rather than soldiers. As conquest gave way to settlement, Cortés was pushed aside. He faced constant challenges to his authority and was accused of hiding part of Montezuma's treasure and defrauding the Crown of its revenue. Under a cloud, Cortés was stripped of his governorship.

Playing on Cortés's love of conquest, Charles named him governor of the lands of the "Southern Sea"—the Pacific Ocean. Cortés outfitted several expeditions to explore the Pacific and search for a strait connecting it and the Caribbean. Little came of these voyages, although he did discover a sea between lower California and Mexico, which he named for himself. When he traveled to Spain to ask Charles to protect his remaining military power, he was met with indifference. Worn down by his struggle with Spanish authorities, he decided to stay in Spain and settle his "account with God." Although there is no evidence that he ever regretted his conquest of the Aztecs, he told Charles in 1544 that "it is better to lose my fortune than my soul." He never returned to the New World and in 1547 died at the age of sixty-two.

By then, other conquistadors had set off in search of more Native American empires. In 1531, Francisco Pizarro and several hundred Spanish soldiers marched into the Inca Empire high in the Andes mountains along the west coast of South America. Conquering and enslaving the Incas, Pizarro and his men seized a mother lode of gold and silver. A little later, other military expeditions probed north from New Spain. In the early 1540s, Francisco Coronado searched futilely for fabled cities of gold in what would later be the southwestern United States. At about the same time, Hernando de Soto traveled into the Mississippi Valley. Inspired by Cortés's success, these men helped Spain forge the richest European empire by the beginning of the seventeenth century. They also provided later English settlers in the New World a vivid example of the relationship between wealth and labor exploitation.

Cortés played a large role in defining the nature of the Spanish experience in the New World. By imposing the *encomienda* system on New Spain, he sealed the fate of millions of Indians. True, the passage of the New Laws—and Las Casas's successful efforts to keep them on the books—led to a decline of the *encomienda* system in the seventeenth century. But a new system of labor exploitation soon arose. *Haciendas* (large estates) came to be worked by Indians who were free and entitled to wages for their labor. In reality, these *peóns*, or farm workers, quickly fell into debt and became debt slaves. The Catholic Church, New Spain's largest landowner by the seventeenth century, supported this system of debt peonage. As Indians became tied to the land, it was easier for clerics to see them as inferior dependents. Meanwhile, black slavery continued for several centuries as well, but only on a small scale compared to that in the West Indies and other areas of the New World. Most of New Spain's black slaves were imported in the sixteenth century and were absorbed into the larger Native American population. Indian debt peonage remained the dominant form of labor exploitation for generations.

Cortés's legacy was visible even in New Spain's remote borderlands. By the time the Spaniards settled in Mexico's far northern frontier at the end of the sixteenth century, their attitudes toward the Indians were already fixed. The consequences for the Indians were much the same as they had been farther south. In New Mexico, colonized by Spaniards in 1598, the Pueblo Indians rose up in revolt in 1680 against the exploitation of their labor and efforts to wipe out their religion. When Spanish authorities regained control twelve years later, they were less zealous in fighting the Indians' culture. Nevertheless, the Indians remained in a subservient position. In California, colonized in 1769, the Indians were virtually enslaved by the missionaries there. In fact, wherever the Spaniards settled, their assumptions about the Indians' inferiority reinforced the basic Spanish need for labor. It was a powerful combination. The belief of Las Casas and a few other sixteenth-century clerics that Native Americans could be fully integrated into Spanish colonial society was no match for it.

Las Casas continued to struggle against Spanish policies in the New World for the rest of his life. Convinced that his most important work could be done at court in Spain, he resigned his New World bishopric in 1550 and moved to a Dominican monastery in his homeland. There he fought Spanish injustices against Native Americans and Africans with his pen. Las Casas had by then changed his views about African slavery. He knew that thousands of black slaves had been imported into the New World, but not one Indian had been freed as a result. He realized that the Africans' enslavement "was as unjust as the Indians'," but the Indians' fate still troubled him more. In 1552, he published his *Very Brief Account of the Destruction of the Indies* and two years later completed a sweeping *History of the Indies*. Both books recounted in gruesome detail Spanish atrocities in the West Indies and Cortés's brutal conquest of Mexico.

Eventually translated into many languages, these books had a huge impact on history. In particular, they laid the foundation for the long-standing "Black Legend" that the Spaniards had the bloodiest hands of all the Europeans in the New World. Often embraced by later English and American historians to exonerate English settlers, this legend was a gross distortion. The English, of course, amassed their own bloody record against the Indians. Moreover, the Spaniards often mixed with the Indians, as Cortés's union with Malinche demonstrates. By contrast, the English violently dispossessed the Indians of their land and pushed them away from areas of European settlement.

For all his work to save the Indians, Las Casas had a greater impact on Spain's image in the New World than on the native peoples themselves. In fact, he regretted until he died that he had not done more to affect their fate. Surely, he had had little influence on Cortés, who had established a colony with millions of Indians in bondage. Long after Las Casas died, though, his writings did have an influence on how later generations viewed Mexico's conqueror. Although Las Casas could not see the conquest of the New World as the native peoples did, he did see those events through sympathetic eyes. Thus he left enduring images that made it easier for later historians to question the more traditional views of the conquest. If Cortés prevailed over the Indians, Las Casas in the end prevailed over him.

• PRIMARY SOURCES •

Source 1: *Las Casas Describes Spanish Atrocities* (1552)

In this account, Las Casas describes the Spanish attacks on the natives of Hispaniola (present-day Haiti and the Dominican Republic). As you read this source, keep in mind his actions in the West Indies after initially settling there. Do you think it was such scenes as Las Casas describes here or other factors that turned him against the Spanish treatment of the Indians?

The Christians, with their horses and swords and lances, began to slaughter and practise strange cruelty among them. They penetrated into the country and spared neither children nor the aged, nor pregnant women, nor those in child labour, all of whom they ran through the body and lacerated, as though they were assaulting so many lambs herded in their sheepfold.

SOURCE: Bartolome de las Casas, *A Brief Account of the Destruction of the Indies* (www.gutenberg.org/ebooks/20321), pp. 267–268.

They made bets as to who would slit a man in two, or cut off his head at one blow: or they opened up his bowels. They tore the babes from their mothers' breast by the feet, and dashed their heads against the rocks. Others they seized by the shoulders and threw into the rivers, laughing and joking, and when they fell into the water they exclaimed: "boil body of so and so!" They spitted the bodies of other babes, together with their mothers and all who were before them, on their swords.

They made a gallows just high enough for the feet to nearly touch the ground, and by thirteens, in honour and reverence of our Redeemer and the twelve Apostles, they put wood underneath and, with fire, they burned the Indians alive.

They wrapped the bodies of others entirely in dry straw, binding them in it and setting fire to it; and so they burned them. They cut off the hands of all they wished to take alive, made them carry them fastened on to them, and said: "Go and carry letters": that is; take the news to those who have fled to the mountains.

They generally killed the lords and nobles in the following way. They made wooden gridirons of stakes, bound them upon them, and made a slow fire beneath: thus the victims gave up the spirit by degrees, emitting cries of despair in their torture.

I once saw that they had four or five of the chief lords stretched on the gridirons to burn them, and I think also there were two or three pairs of gridirons, where they were burning others; and because they cried aloud and annoyed the captain or prevented him sleeping, he commanded that they should strangle them: the officer who was burning them was worse than a hangman and did not wish to suffocate them, but with his own hands he gagged them, so that they should not make themselves heard, and he stirred up the fire, until they roasted slowly, according to his pleasure. I know his name, and knew also his relations in Seville. I saw all the above things and numberless others.

Source 2:   *Cortés Describes the Aztecs* (1519, 1520)

In letters to King Charles I, Hernán Cortés described the religious practices of the Indians along the Gulf of Mexico and among the Aztecs. He also discussed the Aztec capital of Tenochtitlán. In this selection, how does Cortés portray Aztec civilization? What rationale does he offer for the conquest of the Indians?

There are some large towns and well laid out. The houses in those parts where there is stone are of masonry and mortar and the rooms are small and low in the Moorish fashion. In those parts where there is no stone they make their houses of adobes, which are whitewashed and the roofs covered with straw. There are houses belonging to certain men of rank which are very cool and have many rooms, for we have seen as many as five courtyards in a single house, and the rooms around them very well laid out, each man having a private room. Inside there are also wells and water tanks and rooms for slaves and servants of which they have many.... [T]he temples where they are kept are the largest and the best and the finest built of all the buildings found in the towns; and they are much adorned with rich hanging cloths and featherwork and other fineries.

Each day before beginning any sort of work they burn incense in these temples and sometimes sacrifice their own persons, some cutting their tongues, others their ears, while there are some who stab their bodies with knives. All the blood which flows from them they offer to those idols, sprinkling it in all parts of the temple, or sometimes throwing it

SOURCE: From HERNANDO CORTES: LETTERS FROM MEXICO by Hernando Cortes, edited by Anthony Pagden, translated by Anthony Pagden, translation copyright © 1971 by Anthony Pagden. Used by permission of Viking Books, an imprint of Penguin Publishing Group, a division of Penguin Random House LLC.

into the air or performing many other ceremonies, so that nothing is begun without sacrifice having first been made. They have a most horrid and abominable custom which truly ought to be punished and which until now we have seen in no other part, and this is that, whenever they wish to ask something of the idols, in order that their plea may find more acceptance, they take many girls and boys and even adults, and in the presence of the idols they open their chests while they are still alive and take out their hearts and entrails and burn them before the idols, offering the smoke as sacrifice. Some of us have seen this, and they say it is the most terrible and frightful thing they have ever witnessed.

This these Indians do so frequently that, as we have been informed, and, in part, have seen from our own experience during the short while we have been here, not one year passes in which they do not kill and sacrifice some fifty persons in each temple; and this is done and held as customary from the island of Cozumel to this land where we now have settled. Your Majesties may be most certain that, as this land seems to us to be very large, and to have many temples in it, not one year has passed, as far as we have been able to discover, in which three or four thousand souls have not been sacrificed in this manner. Let Your Royal Highnesses consider, therefore, whether they should not put an end to such evil practices, for certainly Our Lord God would be well pleased if by the hand of Your Royal Highnesses these people were initiated and instructed in our Holy Catholic Faith, and the devotion, trust and hope which they have in these their idols were transferred to the divine power of God; for it is certain that if they were to worship the true God with such fervor, faith and diligence, they would perform many miracles….

This city* has many squares where trading is done and markets are held continuously. There is also one square twice as big as that of Salamanca,* with arcades all around, where more than sixty thousand people come each day to buy and sell, and where every kind of merchandise produced in these lands is found; provisions as well as ornaments of gold and silver, lead, brass, copper, tin, stones, shells, bones, and feathers. They also sell lime, hewn and unhewn stone, adobe bricks, tiles, and cut and uncut woods of various kinds….

There are in the city many large and beautiful houses, and the reason for this is that all the chiefs of the land, who are Mutezuma's vassals, have houses in the city and live there for part of the year; and in addition there are many rich citizens who likewise have very good houses. All these houses have very large and very good rooms and also very pleasant gardens of various sorts of flowers both on the upper and lower floors.

Along one of the causeways to this great city run two aqueducts made of mortar. Each one is two paces wide and some six feet deep, and along one of them a stream of very good fresh water, as wide as a man's body, flows into the heart of the city and from this they all drink. The other, which is empty, is used when they wish to clean the first channel. Where the aqueducts cross the bridges, the water passes along some channels which are as wide as an ox; and so they serve the whole city….

… The people of this city are dressed with more elegance and are more courtly in their bearing than those of the other cities and provinces, and because Mutezuma and all those chieftains, his vassals, are always coming to the city, the people have more manners and politeness in all matters. Yet so as not to tire Your Highness with the description of the things of this city (although I would not complete it so briefly), I will say only that these people live almost like those in Spain, and in as much harmony and order as there, and considering that they are barbarous and so far from the knowledge of God and cut off from all civilized nations, it is truly remarkable to see what they have achieved in all things.

---

*Tenochtitlán
*Salamanca: A prominent city in northwestern Spain.

Source 3:   *An Aztec View of the Temple Massacre* (ca. 1550)

This picture is an adaptation of an Aztec rendering of the massacre of Aztec nobles in the temple at Tenochtitlán made shortly after the Spanish conquest. What does this Aztec view emphasize?

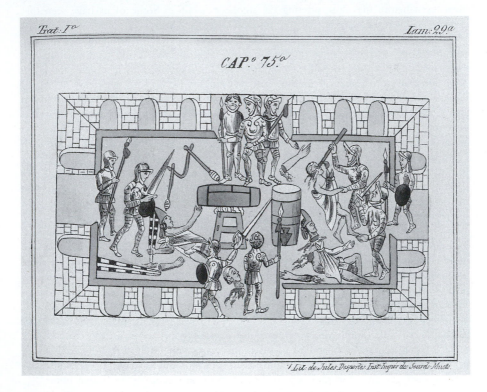

Source 4:   *Cortés Defends* Encomiendas (1522)

In this letter to King Charles, Hernán Cortés defends holding the Indians in encomiendas. On what grounds does he do so? How would you compare the views expressed here regarding the Indians with those in Source 2? Considering Cortés's experience in the New World, how were the views expressed here in his own interest?

In a letter of mine I informed Your Majesty how the natives of these parts are of much greater intelligence than those of the other islands; indeed, they appeared to us to possess

SOURCE 3: Cap 75, illustration from 'Historia de las Indias de Nueva Espana y islas de tierra firme', with plate by Jules Desportes, Mexico, 1867–80 (colour litho), Duran, Diego (16th century) (after)/Private Collection/Bridgeman Images.

SOURCE 4: From Hernan Cortes, LETTERS FROM MEXICO (New York: Grossman Publishers, 1971), pp. 279–280; translated and edited by A. R. l Pagden.

such understanding as is sufficient for an ordinary citizen to conduct himself in a civilized country. It seemed to me, therefore, a serious matter at this time to compel them to serve the Spaniards as the natives of the other islands do; yet if this were not done, the conquerors and settlers of these parts would not be able to maintain themselves. In order therefore to avoid enslaving these Indians, and at the same time to provide the Spaniards with their needs, it seemed to me that Your Majesty should command that from the income which belongs to Your Majesty here we should obtain assistance for the expenses and maintenance of the settlers; and in this matter Your Majesty should decree as You saw most fitting to Your service. Since then, however, I have been almost forced to deliver the chieftains and other natives of these parts to the Spaniards in recognition of the services they have rendered to Your Majesty, because Your Majesty's expenses have been continuous and considerable, and we ought rather to try by every means to increase Royal revenues than to give cause for spending them; also we have been at war for a long time and have all contracted debts thereby and find ourselves in difficulties. Furthermore, on account of the inevitable delay in ascertaining Your Majesty's commands on this matter, and because I was so pressed by Your Majesty's officials and the other Spaniards, I could not in any way avoid it. So until some new order is made, or this one confirmed, the aforementioned chieftains and natives will serve the Spaniards with whom they have been deposited in all they may require in their affairs. This conclusion was reached on the advice of persons who have considerable knowledge and experience in this land; moreover, nothing better or more convenient could be devised either for the maintenance of the Spaniards or for the safety and good treatment of the Indians; of all this the representatives who are now leaving New Spain will give a more detailed account to Your Majesty. Your Majesty's farms and estates have been established in the cities and provinces which seem the best and most suitable. I entreat Your Majesty to approve this and command how You may best be served in these matters.

Source 5:   *Las Casas Attacks Conversion by Conquest* (1537)

In The Only Method of Attracting All People to the True Faith, *published in 1537, Bartolomé de Las Casas argues against the conquistadors' method of converting the Indians to Christianity through conquest. What assumptions does Las Casas make about the natives? How do they compare to Cortés's assumptions?*

Then too there exist extraordinary kingdoms among our Indians who live in the regions west and south from us. There are large groupings of human beings who live according to a political and a social order. There are large cities, there are kings, judges, laws, all within civilizations where commerce occurs, buying and selling and lending and all the other dealings proper to the law of nations. That is to say, their republics are properly set up, they are seriously run according to a fine body of law, there is religion, there are institutions. And our Indians cultivate friendship and they live in lifegiving ways in large cities. They manage their affairs in them with goodness and equity, affairs of peace as well as war. They run their governments according to laws that are often superior to our own....

SOURCE: BARTOLOME DE LAS CASAS, The Only Way (Mahwah, N.J.: Paulist Press, 1992), pp. 64–65, 68, 117, 118–119; edited by Helen Rand Parish, translated by Francis Patick Sullivan, S.J. Reprinted by permission of Paulist Press via the Copyright Clearance Center.

The quality of their minds is seen finally in superb artifacts, finely, beautifully fashioned, fashioned by hand. They are so skilled in the practical arts that their reputation should place them well ahead of the rest of the known world, and rightly so. The practical things these people make are striking for their art and elegance, utensils that are charmingly done, feather work, lace work. Mind does this. The practical arts result from a basic power of mind—a power we define as knowledge of how to do things the right way, a planning power that guides the various decisions the artisan makes so he acts in an ordered and economical fashion and does not err as he thinks his way along....

And in the liberal and allied arts, to date, these people offer no less an indication of sound intelligence. They make objects that are high art and with a genius that awes everyone. The genius of an artist shows in the art work. It is as the poet says: "The work applauds its maker." Prosper remarks in one of his *Epigrams:* "It must be so, that an author shows in the fine things he has written. They sing praise to their maker."

The Indians are highly skilled also in the arts we educate ourselves to, the Indians we have taught thus far: grammar, logic. And they charm the ear of an audience with every kind of music, remarkable beauty. Their handwriting is skillful and lovely, such that one cannot tell often if the letters are handwritten or printed.... I have seen all this with my own eyes, touched it with my own hands, heard it with my own ears, over the long time I passed among those peoples....

One way, one way only, of teaching a living faith, to everyone, everywhere, always, was set by Divine Providence: the way that wins the mind with reasons, that wins the will with gentleness, with invitation. It has to fit all people on earth, no distinction made for sect, for error, even for evil....

The opposite way would clearly be this: If a group whose duty it was to preach the gospel to pagans, or to send them preachers, decided it would be quicker and better done if they subjected pagans willy-nilly to Christian political power. Once the pagans were beaten, they could be preached to without trouble. And they would not be coerced into belief. The preaching would appeal to their minds and draw them gently once the conquest had removed their political defenses.

No pagan in his right mind, especially a pagan prince, would surrender to political control by a Christian people or a Christian prince. There would have to be war.

War brings with it cannon lire, surprise attacks, shore raids that are lawless and blind, violence, riots, scandals, corpses, carnage, butchery, robbery, looting, parent split from child, child from parent, slavery, the ruin of states and kingdoms, of lords and local rulers, the devastation of cities and towns and people without number. War fills here and there and everywhere with tears, with sobs, with keening over every pitiful spectacle possible....

The next step is to see how opposed to the peaceful way of preaching the faith, how utterly opposed the violent way is. It is the dead opposite, the reverse of preaching the faith and drawing people gently into the flock of Christ, of reaching the goal God wants from the preaching, honor for the divine name, change of heart and eternal life for the human soul. The proof runs this way:

... A rational creature is born with a free will and therefore must be treated as free, must be drawn, led, moved toward what is good gently, gently, without pressure, delicately. Now take pagans who have just been subjected to the horrors of war: they are crushed; they are bleak; they are helpless; they despair of their lost children, their lost homes, their lost liberty; they curse their evil luck. How could they possibly want to hear what we would want to teach them about faith, religion, justice, truth? How could they possibly accept such teaching? Again, if a kind man makes many friends, and a violent man forces quarrels and quarrels create enemies (Proverbs 15:18; 10:12), what about words and deeds that are cutting and harsh and cruel and acid to the core—how many enemies will they create? And men gone mad in war, how much violence, how much hatred will they engender?

Conclusion: A creature with a mind and will has to be drawn through its own nature to what is good—i.e., to belief, to religion—drawn gently, without pressure, respectfully. If such a being is driven against its nature by the dogs of war, if it is forced by brutal means, by cruel, heartless, vicious, violent means, it is inevitable that such means, in essence unnatural and inhuman, will produce unnatural, inhuman effects, i.e., people who are deaf to the faith, or who despise what they hear of it. They may be forced to listen, but not forced to agree to what they hear. And that is belief, to accept willingly an understanding of the faith. No one believes without choosing to. Just as sense creates sense, nonsense creates nonsense. If sense is the cause of sense, nonsense is the cause of nonsense. Contrary causes produce contrary effects.

Source 6:   *Las Casas Attacks* Encomiendas (1542)

In this memorial delivered to King Charles, Las Casas calls for the elimination of the encomienda system. On what grounds does he attack the system? How does his argument against encomiendas compare to Cortés's argument for keeping them?

Since the purpose of the dominion of Your Majesty over those peoples is the preaching and establishing of the faith among them, and their conversion and knowledge of Christ, this and no other ..., Your Majesty is therefore obliged to remove all obstacles that can hinder the attainment of this purpose.... But one of the greatest obstacles and impediments that there has been until now ... has been for the Christians to hold them in encomiendas. The same and much worse could be said if they were given to the Christians as vassals. As proof of this we give three reasons.

The first, which has been manifest to everyone, is the great greed and avarice of the Spaniards, because of which they neither wish nor permit the religious to enter the towns of Indians entrusted to them. For they say they receive chiefly two injuries from this. One, that ... when the religious preach to the Indians, the Spaniards lose them ... because of the Indians' being idle and not going to work on the estates. And it has happened that there were Indians in a church listening to a sermon and the religious preaching to them, and a Spaniard entered before all and took fifty or a hundred of them whom he needed to carry loads from his estate. And because they did not wish to go, he gave them kicks and blows with a stick in spite of them and the religious, scandalizing all the people there and hindering the salvation of both Spaniards and Indians.

The other injury which they say they receive is that after the Indians have been instructed and made Christians, they become babblers; they know more than they knew, and because of that the Spaniards cannot profit so much by them thenceforth as before.... Spaniards who hold Indians in encomiendas and wish to keep them as vassals usually ... say and argue ... that if the Indians are taken away from them the Spaniards will be unable to live in the land. They say that if the Indians remain by themselves, Your Majesty's dominion over them and, consequently, the Catholic faith, would be endangered ... and they would go to hell as they were accustomed to before the Christians entered among them, etc....

SOURCE: From BARTOLOME DE LAS CASAS: A SELECTION OF HIS WRITINGS by Bartoleme De Las Casas, translated by George Sanderlin, published by Alfred A. Knopf, a division of Random House, Inc.

But to be good Christians, all should feel that even though it were possible for Your Majesty to lose his entire royal dominion and for the Indians never to become Christians, if the opposite could not take place without their death and total destruction, as has happened until now, it would not be unfitting for Your Majesty to cease to be their lord and for them never to become Christians.

QUESTIONS TO CONSIDER

1.   How would you compare Las Casas's and Cortés's attitudes about Native Americans, their cultures, and their conversion to Christianity? What assumptions shaped their conclusions? Which sources are the most revealing of those attitudes and assumptions?

2.   What does the life of Cortés demonstrate about the forces behind the Spanish conquest of the Native Americans and the factors that influenced their fate? In particular, what was the role played by the Spanish crown, to which both Las Casas and Cortés appealed, in shaping the Indians' fate?

3.   What does Las Casas's life reveal about the alternative possibilities regarding the fate of the Native Americans and the forces working against their realization? What was his influence regarding the fate of the Indians?

4.   In their writings, Las Casas and Cortés emphasize different aspects of life in the New World. Citing specific sources, how would you compare those accounts?

FOR FURTHER READING

Patricia de Fuentes, ed., *The Conquistadors* (New York: Orion Press, 1963), provides firsthand Spanish accounts of the conquest of Mexico.

Ross Hassig, *Mexico and the Spanish Conquest* (London: Longman, 1994), offers a concise treatment of Cortés's conquest of the Aztecs.

Peggy K. Liss, *Mexico Under Spain, 1521–1556* (Chicago: University of Chicago Press, 1975), is a brief analysis of the early years of Spanish rule in Mexico and the emergence of a new type of society there.

Richard Lee Marks, *Cortés: The Great Adventurer and the Fate of Aztec Mexico* (New York: Alfred A. Knopf, 1993), offers an engaging account of Cortés's life and his conquest of Mexico.

Hugh Thomas, *Rivers of Gold: The Rise of the Spanish Empire, From Columbus to Magellan* (New York: Random House, 2004), places Cortés and Las Casas against the broader backdrop of Spanish global conquest.

Henry Raup Wagner, *The Life and Writings of Bartolomé de Las Casas* (Albuquerque: University of New Mexico Press, 1967), is a thorough and carefully researched discussion of Las Casas's career as "Protector of the Indians."

2

Revolt on the Virginia Frontier: Nathaniel Bacon and William Berkeley

As he paused just outside of Jamestown, Virginia, Nathaniel Bacon was in no mood to be denied. The twenty-nine-year-old planter stood accused by his own cousin, Governor William Berkeley, of slaughtering Indians. Declared an outlaw, Bacon was determined to fight back. He would wrest from Berkeley a military commission allowing him to wage indiscriminate war on the "savages." Backing Bacon were six hundred well-armed and angry colonists. Four hundred of them were on foot, too poor to afford a horse. At two o'clock in the afternoon on June 23, 1676, Bacon's men marched into Jamestown. Within a half hour, this "scum of the country," as one observer called them, had secured control of the capital.

Now Bacon would get what he wanted. Flanked by two musket-wielding columns, he marched up to the statehouse door. "God damn my blood, I came for my commission, and a commission I will have before I go," he shouted. Undaunted by Bacon's show of force, the seventy-year-old Berkeley flew out of the statehouse and confronted his young cousin. "Here! Shoot me … shoot," he screamed as he ripped open his shirt. Again Bacon demanded a commission as "general of all forces in Virginia against the Indians." When the enraged governor replied that he would rather see his own hand cut off, Bacon's men responded with shouts of "We will have it." Then they turned their guns on the legislators who had crowded at the windows to witness the confrontation outside. "Damn my blood, I'll kill the governor, council[,] assembly[,] and all," Bacon shouted.

Bacon's threat had the desired effect. One frightened legislator waved a handkerchief and shouted back, "You shall have it. You shall have it." The assembly quickly persuaded Berkeley to grant Bacon his military command. Three days later, Bacon left Jamestown with his commission and his army. Yet the governor's problems with Bacon

Nathaniel Bacon

William Berkeley

and his followers were not over. In the following months, Bacon's men waged brutal war against the Indians, turned their guns on Berkeley's government, forced it to flee Jamestown, and burned the colony's capital to the ground. Not until early 1677 did Berkeley's forces stamp out the uprising that came to bear Bacon's name. But Bacon's Rebellion had vividly demonstrated that not all was well in Virginia.

"AMBITIOUS AND ARROGANT"

Nathaniel Bacon and William Berkeley shared more than family ties—and hot blood. As sons of prominent English families, both had received an elite education and sought personal advancement in Virginia. Yet the two men arrived in the colony under very different circumstances: One brought the blessings of the king, while the other carried the burden of his own family's rejection.

William Berkeley was born in 1606 into a family with long influence at the English court. After receiving degrees from Oxford, he followed his family's footsteps to the Privy Council, a body of close advisers appointed by the monarch, where he became a favorite of Charles I.* As the author of several plays and pamphlets, the young courtier made a mark with his pen and polish. Eventually, however, the colonies came to play the key role in Berkeley's advance, as they often did in the lives of younger sons whose older brothers inherited family estates. (In William's family, John, first Lord Berkeley of Stratton, was the favored son.) William was appointed commissioner of Canadian affairs in 1632 and governor of Virginia nine years later.

When Berkeley arrived in Virginia in 1642, he promptly won the support of the colony's important planters, who were alarmed about talk in Parliament of reviving the

---

*Charles I: The king of England from 1625 to 1649.

defunct Virginia Company.* Such a move would jeopardize property titles established after the company's demise in 1624. When Berkeley landed with assurances that the company would not be restored, the grateful assembly presented him with two houses and an orchard. His reputation rose even higher when he met a threat to the colony from the Powhatan Indians, who had dealt the fatal blow to the Virginia Company when they attacked the colonists in 1622. In 1644, they struck again, leaving five hundred settlers dead. In response, Berkeley led a military force to the frontier, crushed the Powhatans' resistance, and extracted a treaty that ended hostilities on the frontier for a generation.

Berkeley proved no less popular with royal officials. A staunch supporter of the monarchy, he shared with other seventeenth-century aristocrats a disdain for commoners and once boasted that Virginia had neither free schools nor printing presses. Thus when the English Civil War* broke out in 1642 between Oliver Cromwell's parliamentary forces and the supporters of King Charles, Berkeley stood behind the Crown and even provided refuge for royalists during the war. Although he had to surrender his power when Cromwell's fleet sailed up the James River to Jamestown, his loyalty to the king paid off. Living quietly for seven years at Green Spring Manor outside Jamestown, Berkeley watched from afar as the government in England established by Cromwell eventually collapsed. Then shortly after the monarchy was restored in 1660, he found himself back in the statehouse when Charles II named him governor.

With the support of other prominent planters, Berkeley quickly reestablished his political hold. Like the governor, many of his supporters were the second sons of wealthy English families. Often holding choice seats in the colony's government, they were also eager to claim what they regarded as their rightful inheritance. Some of them, such as Virginia secretary Thomas Ludwell, were related by marriage to the governor, who had solidified his own position through matrimony as well. (After arriving in Virginia, Berkeley had won the hand of Frances Culpeper, whose family owned vast tracts in the colony.) Once established in the colony, these members of Virginia's landed gentry expected to be treated with proper deference, and they recommended the colony enthusiastically to prospective settlers. As Berkeley himself noted, "A small sum of money will enable a younger brother to erect a flowering family in the New World."

Whereas Berkeley had found a place for himself in Virginia, newcomer Nathaniel Bacon found prospects there far less to his liking. Born in 1647, the only son of an English gentleman, Bacon grew up on his father's estate, Freestone Hall, surrounded by vast fields and woodlands. He attended Cambridge University and then continued his education back at home under the guidance of a private tutor. After a three-year grand tour of the continent, Bacon returned to Cambridge, where he was granted a master's degree in 1668. Following the path trod by numerous forebears, he read law at the Inns of Court.* By 1670, the young esquire had returned home and married Elizabeth Duke, the daughter of a Suffolk squire.

Virginia Company: A joint-stock company founded by London merchants in 1606 to plant settlements in the New World. The company was responsible for establishing Jamestown in 1607.

English Civil War: The war (1642–1649) fought between the Puritan-dominated forces raised by Parliament and the supporters of royal authority. It ended with the execution of Charles I, the triumph of Oliver Cromwell, and the establishment of a commonwealth.

Inns of Court: The London legal societies that had the exclusive right to allow individuals to practice law.

There seemed to be more to Bacon's makeup, however, than good breeding and a fancy education. In England, many who knew him came to doubt his character. His tutor acknowledged his "quick wit" but also concluded that he was "impatient of labor." Bacon's father-in-law was so dismayed at his daughter's choice that he disinherited her and would never speak to her again. Bacon also disappointed his own father, who had been forced to withdraw him from Cambridge for "having broken into some extravagances." Later, when the young spendthrift was caught defrauding another young man of his inheritance, Bacon's father gave him eighteen hundred pounds and packed him off to Virginia.

When the tall, thin, dark-haired Bacon arrived in Virginia in 1674, his youthful indiscretions were thousands of miles behind him. With Elizabeth, a daughter, and his father's largesse in hand, he was graciously received by Governor Berkeley and by another cousin, Nathaniel Bacon Sr. With the assistance of his namesake, who sat on the governor's council, Bacon was soon established as a frontier planter. Claiming that he had "always been delighted in solitude," Bacon used his endowment to purchase Curles Neck, a plantation forty miles up the James River in Henrico County. He took up residence there and began planting tobacco. He also bought another tract twenty miles farther upriver at the Fall Line,* which he placed in charge of an overseer. Altogether, Bacon owned more than twelve hundred acres. In addition, Berkeley granted him a seat on his council and a license to trade with the Indians. Though exiled in disgrace, Bacon had made an astonishing recovery in a remarkably short time.

Yet the frontier, which provided Bacon with solitude and a measure of prosperity, would bring him little peace. He was not there long before older residents began to accuse him of "despising the wisest of his neighbors for their ignorance." The young man, they said, was "ambitious and arrogant," possessing a "dangerous hidden pride of heart." In addition, festering social and economic problems were about to erupt, thrusting Bacon into a life-and-death struggle.

"A SAD DILEMMA"

Relying on the labor of indentured servants, many of Virginia's planters had made handsome profits during the colony's early tobacco boom. By the time Bacon arrived, however, the days of getting rich quick by growing tobacco were over. After selling as high as twenty-seven pence a pound in 1618, tobacco had fallen in price to a penny a pound by 1630 and would never rise much above two and a half pence for the rest of the century. Virginians had been too successful in producing the leafy plant. Yet low prices had not stopped the colony's growth or, until the middle of the century, posed a threat to its stability. Even after the boom, immigrants continued to arrive, drawn by the dream of getting rich by planting tobacco. Many of these newcomers—mostly young men—arrived as servants, usually indentured for four years in exchange for passage across the Atlantic. Although approximately two thousand African slaves lived in Virginia by the 1670s, cheaper servants provided the main source of labor in the tobacco fields. With land easy to secure in the colony's early years, they could look forward to joining

---

*Fall Line: The line marking the waterfalls of nearly parallel rivers. The falls limited navigation and thus posed a significant barrier to settlement for much of the seventeenth century. In this case, it refers specifically to the Appomattox, James, Rappahannock, and Potomac Rivers.

the ranks of the planters. In time, some former servants would even come to control the labor of others and begin to prosper.

By the mid-seventeenth century, the number of servants who became freemen began to grow. Earlier, servants were lucky if they survived their terms of indenture. By the 1650s, however, Virginians began to live longer, thanks perhaps to healthier diets. Though still often overworked and abused by masters, more servants lived to become freemen. Mostly, of course, they planted tobacco, further depressing its price. They also competed for good tobacco land. Virginia had abundant uncultivated land, but prominent planters had secured much of the choice tidewater* land, often through their connections to the government. In fact, many were members of the "Green Spring faction," as Berkeley's influential supporters came to be known. By the 1660s, freemen who wished to plant found themselves facing a difficult choice. They could move to the frontier, where it was often impossible to ship tobacco to market and the danger of Indian attack was ever present. Or they could rent land from one of Virginia's big landowners. Many naturally chose the safety of settled areas. Though surrounded by vast stretches of uncultivated land, perhaps a third of the free adult males now worked as tenants for the colony's big planters or moved from place to place as vagrants. In 1670, the assembly declared these landless freemen ineligible to vote. In effect, an artificial scarcity of land had created a pool of poor—and powerless—workers.

Making matters worse, Virginians faced a crushing annual poll tax of as much as two hundred pounds of tobacco, export taxes, and customs duties. The taxes helped fill the king's coffers, but they also paid for generous perquisites of office in Virginia. From the governor and legislators to clerks of the county courts, officeholders rewarded themselves handsomely. Governor Berkeley's salary was an astonishing twelve hundred pounds sterling—more than the average freeman could hope to see in a lifetime. In addition, he took two hundred pounds of tobacco for every marriage license issued, 350 pounds annually from every tavern, and an annual tribute of beaver pelts from the colony's subject Indians, as well as payoffs from licensed fur traders. Meanwhile, the Speaker and clerk of the House of Burgesses were awarded as much as twenty thousand pounds of tobacco each for every session of the legislature. As making money by planting tobacco grew more difficult, the colony's government became the way to wealth in Virginia. Yet participation in the government was beyond the reach of former servants. Not a single servant who arrived in Virginia after 1640 was elected to the House of Burgesses, much less appointed to the governor's council.

In the years before Bacon's Rebellion, discontent boiled to the surface of Virginia society. In 1661, servants rebelled in protest against their treatment. Though confined to one county and quickly suppressed, that uprising was followed two years later by the revelation of a plot among servants in another county. "Consider us," Berkeley told the king, "as a people press'd at our backes with Indians, [and] in our Bowills with our servants." Free Virginians, moreover, could be just as unruly, and the governor had to put down two small insurrections of freemen in 1674. To be sure, full-scale armed revolt was unlikely because settlers were spread over the land, separated by rivers and forests. Still, when war erupted, the colony mustered large numbers of armed men, and that could be dangerous. When the governor gathered a force in 1673 to prevent a Dutch invasion of the colony, he observed that one-third of the defenders were poor or indebted freemen who would just as soon join the Dutch "in hopes of bettering their condition by sharing the plunder

---

Tidewater: The low, coastal areas east of the Fall Line whose rivers and streams were affected by tidal movements.

of the country with them." As Berkeley would soon learn, an armed force raised to defend the colony from a different threat could be even more dangerous.

About the same time Bacon took up residence in Virginia, trouble was stirring on the colony's frontier. In the three decades following the Powhatans' failed uprising in 1644, the Pamunkey, Appomattox, Chickahominy, and other tribes lived peacefully under the sovereignty of the English king. The Indians, Berkeley boasted, "are absolutely subjected, so that there is no fear of them." The continuing growth of the English population in Virginia, however, threatened to change that. By 1670, maybe forty thousand English and four thousand subject Indians made Virginia their home. As the settlers' numbers grew, so did encroachment on Indian lands near the Fall Line.

The result by 1675 was rapidly escalating violence. In July of that year, some thirty Virginians responded with a violent outburst to the murder of a white settler by a Doeg Indian. First they killed eleven Doegs. Then they surrounded a cabin sheltering more frightened Indians and gunned them down when they attempted to flee. Fourteen bodies lay around the cabin by the time the men realized that the victims were friendly Susquehannas. Later that summer, a thousand armed Virginians descended on the Susquehannas. The Virginians were convinced that the Susquehannas, the most powerful tribe along the Fall Line, were sheltering other Indian marauders. The Susquehannas denied any involvement in the recent attacks. They blamed them on the Senecas, one of the Iroquois tribes that had squeezed the Susquehannas from the interior, just as the English now pressed them from the other direction. But their denials fell on deaf ears. Surrounding a fort sheltering about a hundred Susquehannas, the Virginians grabbed five chiefs who ventured out to ask the reason for the armed force. The Virginians led the chiefs away and murdered them. The rest of the Susquehannas eventually slipped out of the besieged fort at night, killing ten Virginians in their escape. In early 1676, the Susquehannas, still furious about the murder of their chiefs, launched a raid near the falls of the Potomac and Rappahannock Rivers, leaving sixty settlers dead. Confronted with rising danger on the frontier, white settlers demanded that the governor respond with armed force. **[See Source 1.]**

Berkeley was in a bind. As governor, he was responsible for maintaining order in the colony so that Virginians could continue to produce tobacco revenue for the Crown. He was also charged with overseeing the lucrative fur trade. Peaceful relations with the Indians were in both his and the colony's best interests, and he was livid about the murder of the Susquehanna chiefs. "If they had come to treat in peace," he declared, "they ought to have gone in peace." He was also well aware of the dangers of sending a force of armed Virginians to the frontier, given the recent indiscriminate attacks against the Indians. Thus the governor sought a solution that addressed the frontier dwellers' concerns without needlessly provoking the Indians.

Berkeley's answer became evident when he convened the assembly in March 1676. The representatives promptly declared war on "all such Indians who ... shall be discovered to have committed murders ... and depredations." It also moved to restrain vigilante action on the frontier, passing a bill authorizing a string of forts to be built along the Fall Line. The forts would be manned not by frontiersmen, but by men from more secure parts of the colony. They would be commanded by officers reporting directly to the governor. In addition, the assembly forbade trade with the Indians, even by those with licenses. "Sad experience," it declared, had demonstrated that traders had broken the law by providing guns and powder to the Indians. From now on, commissions for trade with the Indians would be granted by the governor's appointees on the county courts. While issuing harsh words against the Indians, the legislature had actually exercised a restraining hand on white settlers.

Frontiersmen reacted angrily to the new laws. The forts would require new taxes at a time when tobacco prices were low and many planters were already in dire financial straits.

Moreover, they charged, the forts would be placed too far apart to prevent Indian raids. The Indians could easily penetrate a stationary defense and attack exposed plantations at will. The frontier planters could not legally raise their own force to repel the Indian threat, but if they did not take action, they left themselves exposed to "the merciless power of a most bloody and barbarous enemy." It was, they protested, "a sad dilemma."

Fed by growing suspicion about Berkeley's motives and increasing doubts about the loyalty of any Indians, rumors spread up and down the Fall Line: Building forts was intended only to reward Berkeley's cronies with contracts. Berkeley's friends were selling arms to hostile Indians. Virginia's Indians were paying tribute to other tribes two hundred to three hundred miles away to unite with them. And as the Indian uprising known as King Philip's War raged in New England, some Virginians even began to dread a "general combination of all [tribes] from New England hither."

In an atmosphere of growing fear and frustration, Bacon emerged to lead the fight against the Indians. The impetuous young planter had already run afoul of Berkeley's Indian policy. When Bacon saw fit to seize some Appomattox Indians the previous fall for allegedly stealing corn, the governor condemned his "rash[,] heady action." Now Bacon, who recently lost an overseer in a Susquehanna attack and had just begun a trading business, scorned Berkeley's plan for frontier defense. He accused the governor of excluding settlers from the Indian trade only to reward his "favorites." Although Bacon had little in common with Virginia's freemen, he shared with them a feeling that an inside group was reaping rewards at the expense of others.

He was not the only socially prominent newcomer to conclude that he had been treated unfairly. Richard Lawrence, an Oxford graduate; William Drummond, former governor of Carolina; and Giles Bland, whose family claimed extensive landholdings in Virginia, all had had run-ins with Berkeley or his officials. When Bland had arrived in 1671 to take over as customs collector, for instance, Berkeley's secretary Thomas Ludwell had dismissed him as a "puppy and Sonn of a whore." Feeling similarly excluded from Berkeley's ruling circle, Bacon paid a visit in April 1676 to a force of backcountry volunteers at the urging of several other planters. Denouncing the governor as "negligent, wicked, treacherous, and incapable," Bacon took unauthorized command of the force, promising to bear all the costs of the campaign against the Indians. The lives of the frontier inhabitants, he declared, had been "wretchedly sacrificed," and he resolved to risk his "life and fortune" in their defense.

Bacon's new position provoked a speedy response from Berkeley, who warned Bacon not to mutiny and ordered him to Jamestown. Bacon refused to go and instead requested that Berkeley entrust him "with the country's safety" by granting him a commission for command of the volunteers. When Berkeley denied the commission, Bacon issued his "Appeal of the Volunteers to all well minded and charitable people." Because "wrongs and violences" had been "cunningly" committed by several Indian tribes, he declared, it was very difficult to distinguish from which tribes "the said wrongs did proceed." As Bacon and his men mobilized for their first campaign, it would soon become clear just how little use they had for making distinctions between friendly and unfriendly Indians.

"SO GLORIOUS A CAUSE"

In May 1676, Bacon and several hundred of his followers set out to solve Virginia's Indian problem. In search of the Susquehannas, they marched about eighty miles southwest from the James River through thick forests to a fort belonging to the Occaneechees, a friendly tribe living near the present border of Virginia and North Carolina. Encamped near the Occaneechees, they found what they were looking for: a party of Susquehannas, refugees from the Virginians' attack on their fort to the north. When the Susquehannas sought the Occaneechees' aid, they instead alerted the Virginians to their new neighbors' whereabouts. After providing Bacon's exhausted force with food and shelter, the Occaneechees offered to attack the Susquehannas themselves. Bacon and his men were only too willing to have the Occaneechees do their fighting for them. When the Occaneechees returned victorious, however, the Virginians were far less willing to show their gratitude. Bacon demanded that they turn over their plunder, including Indians from other tribes who had been held prisoner by the Susquehannas. After the Occaneechees refused, Bacon's men turned their guns on them. In a fight that lasted through the night, the Virginians poured fire into the Occaneechee fort. They also fell upon men, women, and children left outside and, according to one of Bacon's men, "disarmed and destroyed them all." The next morning, Bacon's force headed home, leaving more than a hundred Indians dead.

By taking action against the Occaneechees, Bacon had openly defied the king's representative in Virginia. Governor Berkeley had more on his mind, though, than respect for royal authority. Bacon's command of an unauthorized army could have dangerous social consequences in the kind of society Virginia had become. In fact, Bacon's army looked a lot like the force of poor freemen that Berkeley had raised only three years earlier to defend the colony from a Dutch invasion. As Berkeley favorite Philip Ludwell said, Bacon's men were "Rabble of the basest sort." Thus while Bacon busied himself killing the Occaneechees, Berkeley moved swiftly to suppress growing discontent with his own policies. First he publicly denounced Bacon and removed him from his council. Then he moved to shore up his support by calling for the new assembly to be elected by all freemen, not just property holders. "All persons are to have liberty," declared Berkeley, "freely to present to [the assembly] all such complaints as they or any other have against me as governor." In addition, Berkeley demonstrated a newfound determination to kill Indians—or at least to make a show of it. Upon hearing reports that subject Indians had attacked colonists, he led a force to the frontier. On the way, he stopped at Curles Neck, where he told Elizabeth Bacon that her husband "would most certainly hang" upon his return from the Occaneechee campaign. In fact, Berkeley had no desire either to kill Indians or to execute Bacon. After several fruitless weeks on the upper James River, Berkeley and his men returned to Jamestown and awaited the convening of the new assembly. When Bacon's bedraggled force emerged from the forest, Berkeley hinted that he would pardon Bacon and offered to let him travel to England to state his case directly to King Charles II. **[See Source 2.]**

Bacon not only rejected Berkeley's offer but also refused to apologize for actions "in so glorious a cause as the country's defense." He was buoyed by his success against the Indians and by the fact that Henrico County voters had just elected him to the new assembly. In June 1676, he arrived in Jamestown to take his seat in the assembly and demand his military commission once again. When Bacon concluded that staying in the capital was too risky and headed back upriver, Berkeley sent an armed ship after him. The next time Bacon stepped ashore at Jamestown, he was a prisoner. "Now I behold the greatest rebel that ever was in Virginia," exclaimed the triumphant governor. After Bacon signed a written confession of his transgressions, Berkeley presented him to the assembly. In a show of public submission, the young rebel dropped to his knees before the governor, who proclaimed, "God forgive you! I forgive you!" Berkeley then took the further precaution of placing Bacon back on his council, removing a potentially troublesome voice from the assembly. Bacon had no choice but to head back to Curles Neck a few days later.

The governor had outmaneuvered Bacon. The conditions that led to Bacon's rise, however, had not gone away. Nor had Bacon's popular support, which was reflected in the new assembly. What came to be known as Bacon's Assembly passed numerous laws to pacify disgruntled Virginians. **[See Source 3.]** It also abandoned Berkeley's plan for a string of frontier forts. Instead, it authorized a force of a thousand men, commanded by Bacon, to conduct war against hostile Indians. Soldiers would be paid up to 2,250 pounds of tobacco each and would "have benefit of all the plunder" taken from the Indians. To quell the possibility of open revolt, the assembly had handed Virginia's restless freemen a few reforms and the promise of greater action against the Indians.

At the same time, Berkeley moved to reinforce his own position by lecturing the assembly on the injustice of indiscriminate attacks on the Indians. As a result, the legislature refused to endorse an all-out war against the Indians. Rather, it declared that only Indians who left their lands without the permission of Virginia's authorities would be considered enemies. Berkeley challenged the representatives to find fault with him. Then he extracted a resolution from them that "humbly intreat[ed] and request[ed] his honor that he will please still to continue [as] our Governor."

Although the legislature reiterated its support for the governor, it also gave Bacon the encouragement he needed to challenge Berkeley for a second time. Perhaps driven by a sense of power as champion of the people, Bacon was determined to claim the commission supported by the legislature. With it, he would lead the campaign against the Indians. For the second time in a month, he set out for Jamestown. This time, however, he was accompanied by a force of six hundred men.

"THAT NAKED COUNTRY"

On June 23, 1676, Bacon and his army arrived in Jamestown. After the dramatic confrontation with the governor outside the assembly door, Bacon finally got his commission. He and his followers were no longer rebels but legitimate soldiers. The commander and his force, soon to number thirteen hundred men, quickly began to help themselves to supplies from plantations near Jamestown. Berkeley responded to Bacon's freebooting by rescinding his commission and raising a force of twelve hundred men to march against him. When the soldiers learned that they were marching against Bacon rather than the Indians, however, they refused to fight. Seizing the opportunity, Bacon led his men toward Jamestown. Berkeley once again declared Bacon a rebel—and then fled with five of his supporters across the Chesapeake to Virginia's Eastern Shore.

Setting up camp in the tiny settlement of Middle Plantation (later the site of Williamsburg), Bacon was joined by Richard Lawrence and William Drummond. At the end of July, he issued a "manifesto" defending his actions. **[See Source 4.]** He also summoned other prominent Virginians to Middle Plantation. At first, they balked when Bacon proposed that they swear an oath not to aid Berkeley and to fight any royal forces sent from England to assist the governor. That would be treason. In the end, though, they observed that "every magistrate that hath loyally declared his dissent against [Bacon's] … monstrous proceedings is threatened with the plundering and pulling down [of] their houses." Rather than be plundered, they hedged their bets and signed Bacon's oath. Meanwhile, other prominent planters abandoned their plantations and headed to Berkeley's refuge on the Eastern Shore.

Through the remainder of the summer and into the early fall, Virginia was plunged into civil war as Bacon's and Berkeley's forces clashed. Bacon saw to it that his men plundered the Indians as well. Marching a detachment of troops to the backcountry, he came across the peaceful Pamunkeys, killed some, and took forty-five others prisoner. Meanwhile, Giles Bland set out with three hundred men to capture Berkeley on the Eastern Shore, only to be taken prisoner himself. Heartened by this turn of events,

Berkeley went on the offensive. To attract support, the governor offered the plunder from the plantations of those who signed Bacon's oath. He also offered freedom to servants who supported him. Though fearful of insurrection by the "rabble," Berkeley was desperate. When he sailed back to Jamestown in early September, however, few servants had rallied to his cause. By contrast, Bacon quickly gained volunteers as he marched toward Jamestown with his Indian captives in tow. He also offered freedom to the servants and slaves of Berkeley's loyalists, a move that led hundreds of blacks to join Bacon's ranks.

By the time he arrived in Jamestown, Bacon's force greatly outnumbered Berkeley's. Nonetheless, Bacon took the precaution of rounding up the wives of prominent Berkeley supporters from nearby plantations, including the wife of his cousin Nathaniel Bacon Sr. While his men dug in just outside Jamestown's palisade, Bacon placed the women on his fortifications to prevent a premature attack by Berkeley's men. When the governor's force launched an unsuccessful attack after Bacon had removed his female captives from danger, Bacon's men opened their guns on Jamestown. The next morning, after Berkeley and his force had retreated to nearby ships, Bacon and his men entered the deserted capital. Berkeley's forces still controlled the waters around Jamestown, however, and a loyalist force raised in Virginia's northern counties was marching south. Bacon realized that he could not hold the capital. Before withdrawing from Jamestown, he and his men torched twenty-five houses (five of them owned by Berkeley), the statehouse, the church, and outlying residences. After pillaging Berkeley's Green Spring plantation, they retreated across the York River to Gloucester County, not far from Yorktown. There Bacon continued to plunder plantations, try opponents, and imprison them.

By early October, the tide had turned against Bacon and his men. Berkeley had dispatched a message to the king, and Bacon and his men now faced the prospect of fighting royal reinforcements. When he asked his followers to swear an oath declaring Berkeley a traitor and vowing to fight the king's forces, they refused. When he delivered an appeal to the residents of the Eastern Shore to seize the "abominable Juggler" Berkeley and his "ring leaders," it had no impact. Meanwhile, Bacon had fallen ill. Weakened by his military exploits, he was afflicted with lice and dysentery. According to one witness, as Bacon lay near death at a Gloucester plantation, "the swarms of vermin that bred in his body he could not destroy but by throwing his shirts into the fire as often as he shifted himself." On October 26, 1676, he died. In the following months, the rebellious mood of Bacon's followers began to expire as well. Armed ships arrived from England, quashing resistance up and down the York and James Rivers. On the south bank of the York, Berkeley's rejuvenated troops found an armed force of four hundred black slaves and white freemen. Most were persuaded to surrender, but eighty blacks and twenty whites refused to lay down their arms until they were confronted with the thirty guns of the ship *Concord*. The slaves were quickly returned to their masters.

At the end of January 1677, a three-man royal commission sent to investigate the situation in the colony and to restore order arrived with a thousand troops. By the time it landed, Berkeley had already begun to crack down with trials of Bacon's prominent supporters. Giles Bland, William Drummond, and twenty-one others were convicted of treason and hanged. "That old fool," observed Charles II, "has hanged more men in that naked country than I did for the murder of my father." Berkeley regretted that he was unable to hang Bacon as well. Perhaps he found consolation in stripping the dead rebel's estate from Elizabeth Bacon. Under orders from Charles II, Berkeley returned to England in May to provide an account of Virginia's recent troubles. Two months later, he died.

By then, the royal commissioners had found much in Berkeley's Virginia to dismay them, especially the continued looting by the governor's forces. Noting the "sullen and obstinate" character of the colonists, the commissioners encouraged them to communicate their "pressures or grievances." Virginians responded in force. [See Source 5.] Yet the commissioners did not exonerate Bacon. Instead, they condemned the "inconsiderate sort of men who so rashly and causelessly cry up a war, and seem to wish and aim at an utter extirpation of the Indians." Like Charles II, the commissioners were mostly concerned that Virginians get back to the business of producing tobacco, which did so much to swell the royal coffers.

Bacon's Rebellion thus produced a new administration in Virginia but no major reforms in the colony's government or society. Nonetheless, this uprising was a crucial event in reshaping early Virginia. Prior to 1676, the colony was a social pressure cooker characterized by exploitation of the many and aggrandizement by the few. In 1676, the pressure cooker exploded. Bacon's Rebellion demonstrated to prominent Virginians the dangers of relying on laborers who could turn into unruly neighbors. In the years after the rebellion, these planters turned to another form of labor exploitation, relying increasingly on slaves rather than servants to wrest wealth from the land. Indeed, by the end of the seventeenth century, the place of Virginia's landed gentry had been firmly secured by its control of a slave-labor force that grew nearly sixfold from the eve of Bacon's Rebellion to the turn of the eighteenth century.

Moreover, Virginians had learned that conflicts among white colonists could be defused by rallying them against others. On the eve of the Occaneechee campaign, Bacon informed Berkeley that the colonists' protest against taxes and the governor's plan for frontier forts had "been suppressed" because the "discourse and earnestness of the people [was] against the Indians." Hatred of an "inferior" race, in other words, was a powerful force to unite whites and subdue social discontent. Thus even before the colony's black population exploded at the end of the seventeenth century, Virginia's planter elite knew how to unite freemen of all ranks against those at the bottom of society and thereby dampen resentment against those at the top. In the end, Bacon's Rebellion helped teach Virginia's ruling class how to keep poor whites and black slaves in their place.

•PRIMARY SOURCES•

Source 1:   *Frontier Planters Appeal to Governor William Berkeley* (Spring 1676)

What does this petition reveal about the attitude of Virginia's frontiersmen toward authority? How do you think the petitioners' economic or social class may have influenced their attitude?

To the Right Honorable Sir William Berkeley Knight governor Capt. General of Virginia: The humble petition of the poor distressed subjects in the upper parts of [the] James River in Virginia humbly complain[s] that the Indians hath already most

SOURCE: Reprinted In Warren M. Billings, ed., *The Old Dominion in the Seventeenth Century: A Documentary History of Virginia, 1606–1689* (Chapel Hill: University of North Carolina Press, 1975), p. 267; originally from Colonial Office 1/36, fol. 139, Public Record Office. On occasion, minor changes have been made to spelling and punctuation for the convenience of modern readers.

barbarously and inhumanly taken and murdered several of our brethren and put them to most cruel torture by burning of them alive and by cruel torturing of them which makes our hearts ready to bleed to hear. And we the poor subjects are in daily danger of losing our lives by the heathen in so much that we are all afraid of going about our domestic affairs. Wherefore we most humbly request that your gracious Honor would be pleased to grant us a commission and to make choice of commissioned officers to lead this party now ready to take arms in defense of our lives and estates which without speedy prevention lie liable to the injury of such insulting enemies. Not that your petitioners desire to make any disturbance or put the country to any charge. Wherefore we humbly plead your Honor's speedy answer for we are informed that the Indians daily approach our habitations and we your petitioners as in duty bound shall ever pray.

Source 2:   William Berkeley, "Declaration and Remonstrance" (May 1676)

Governor Berkeley issued this statement after Bacon's campaign against the Occaneechees. How does he try to gain Virginians' support against Bacon? Do you think Berkeley's and Bacon's relationship as cousins influenced the argument or tone of this statement?

Now my friends I have lived amongst you four and thirty years as uncorrupt and diligent as ever [a] governor was. Bacon is a man of two years amongst you. His person and qualities [are] unknown to most of you.... This very action wherein he so much boasted was ... foolishly and, as I am informed, treacherously carried to the dishonor of the English nation. Yet in it he lost more men than I did in three wars and by the Grace of God [I] will put myself to the same dangers and troubles again when I have brought Bacon to acknowledge the laws are above him. And I doubt not by the assistance of God to have better success than Mr. Bacon has had. The reason of my hopes are that I will take counsel of wiser men than myself. But Mr. Bacon has none about him but the lowest of the people.

Yet I must further enlarge that I cannot without your help do anything in this but die in the defense of my King, his laws, and subjects which I will cheerfully do though alone I do it. And considering my poor fortunes I cannot leave my poor wife and friends a better legacy than by dying for the King and you, for his sacred majesty will easily distinguish between Mr. Bacon's actions and mine....

Now after all this, if Mr. Bacon can show me precedent or example where such actings in any nation whatsoever was approved of, I will mediate with the King and you for a pardon and excuse for him. But I can show him a hundred examples where brave and great men have been put to death for gaining victories against the command of their superiors.

Your incessant Servant
William Berkeley

SOURCE: Reprinted in Warren M. Billings, ed., *The Old Dominion in the Seventeenth Century: A Documentary History of Virginia, 1606–1689* (Chapel Hill: University of North Carolina Press, 1975), pp. 271–272; originally from Henry Coventry Papers, LXXVII, fols. 157–158, Estate of the Marquis of Bath, Longleat, Warminster, Wiltshire, England. On occasion, minor changes have been made to spelling and punctuation for the convenience of modern readers.

Source 3:   *A Summary of the June Assembly's Laws* (1676)

The assembly of June 1676, often called Bacon's Assembly because most of the burgesses (representatives) were Bacon's supporters, passed a number of reforms. What do these laws reveal about the causes of their discontent? What changes did these laws make in the government?

ACT I. *An act for carrying on a warre against the barbarous Indians.*
Declared war against enemy Indians and ordered the raising of a thousand troops. Bacon was named "generall and commander in cheife of the force raised."

ACT II. *An act concerning Indian trade and traders.*
Prohibited all trade with the Indians, except for "friendly Indians."

ACT III. *An act concerning Indian lands deserted.*
Lands deserted by the Indians reverted to the colony; these lands were to "dispose to the use of the publique towards defraying the charge of this warr."

ACT IV. *An act for suppressing of tumults, routs, etc.*
Every officer and magistrate was authorized to suppress unlawfull "routs, riotts and tumults."

ACT V. *An act for the regulateing of officers and offices.*
Prohibited sheriffs from holding office "more than one year successively," abolished plural officeholding, regulated fees, and denied office to anyone not a resident of the colony for at least three years....

ACT VII. *An act enabling freemen to vote for burgesses and preventing false returnes of burgesses.*
Repealed an act of 1670 that had restricted the franchise to freeholders and imposed a stiff fine on any sheriff who made a false election return....

ACT XII. *Councellors and Ministers families to pay levies, and money allowed them.*
Removed tax exempt status of conciliar and ministerial families; gave councillors a fixed salary....

ACT XIX. *An act of general pardon and oblivion.*
Pardoned all "treasons, misprison of treasons, murders, fellonies, offences, crimes, contempts and misdemeanors" committed between March 1 and June 25, 1676.

Source 4:   *Bacon's Manifesto* (July 1676)

How does the tone of Bacon's Manifesto differ from that of the frontier petition? How do you account for the difference? What does Bacon's attack on Governor Berkeley's government reveal about his motives? How does Bacon justify his attacks on the Indians?

SOURCE 3: Reprinted in Warren M. Billings, ed., *The Old Dominion in the Seventeenth Century: A Documentary History of Virginia, 1606–1689* (Chapel Hill: University of North Carolina Press, 1975), pp. 274–275; originally from William Waller Hening, ed., *The Statutes at Large: Being a Collection of All the Laws of Virginia from the First Session of the Legislature, in the Year 1619* (Richmond, New York, and Philadelphia, 1809–1823), II, pp. 341–365.

SOURCE 4: Reprinted in Warren M. Billings, ed., *The Old Dominion in the Seventeenth Century: A Documentary History of Virginia, 1606–1689* (Chapel Hill: University of North Carolina Press, 1975), pp. 278, 279. On occasion, minor changes have been made to spelling and punctuation for the convenience of modern readers.

[S]ince we cannot in our hearts find one single spot of rebellion or treason or that we have in any manner aimed at subverting the settled government … let truth be told and all the world know the real foundations of [our] pretended guilt…. [L]et us trace these men in authority and favor to whose hand the dispensation of the country's wealth has been committed. Let us observe the sudden rise of their estates compared with the quality in which they first entered this country or the reputation they have held here amongst wise and discerning men…. Let us consider their sudden advancement and let us also consider whether any public work for our safety and defense … [is] in any [way] adequate to our vast charge. Now let us compare these things together and see what sponges have sucked up the public treasure and whether it hath not been privately contrived away by unworthy favorites and juggling parasites whose tottering fortunes have been repaired and supported at the public charge….

Another main article of our guilt is our open and manifest aversion of all, not only the foreign but the protected and darling Indians. This we are informed is rebellion … whereas we do declare and can prove that they have been for these many years enemies to the King and country, robbers and thieves and invaders of his Majesty's right and our interest and estates, but yet have by persons in authority been defended and protected even against his majesty's loyal subjects….

Another main article of our guilt is our design not only to ruin and extirpate all Indians in general but all manner of trade and commerce with them…. Since the right honorable … Governor hath been pleased by his commission to warrant this trade, who dare oppose it?

Source 5: *Grievances Submitted to the King's Commissioners (1677)*

What do these grievances from one Virginia county reveal about the situation in the colony before Bacon's Rebellion? Do they reflect only a desire to complain about conditions in Virginia?

Whereas His Majesty's Commissioners … have commanded us the subscribers, in the behalf of Gloucester County to give in our grievances: in obedience thereunto, we have drawn up our Grievances, and they are as follows.

1. Whereas about 17 years since there was a tax laid upon tobacco shipped in this county of 2 shillings per hogshead by act of [the] assembly, under pretense of defraying the public charge of the county … in order to [prevent] other public taxes…. The county levies hath notwithstanding this tax been ever since as great or more than before. Therefore they humbly conceive the said tax of 2 shillings per hogshead to be a grievance, unless it may be employed as pretended when first raised….

3. That within this 14 or 15 months, it is conceived [that] there hath been near 300 Christian persons barbarously murdered by the Indians. And after the murder of several

SOURCE: "Grievances Submitted to the King's Commissioners (1677)" from Warren M. Billings, ed., THE OLD DOMINION IN THE SEVENTEENTH CENTURY: A DOCUMENTARY HISTORY OF VIRGINIA, 1606–1689 (Chapel Hill: University of North Carolina Press, 1975), pp. 280–282; originally from Colonial Office 1/39, 244, Public Record Office.

numbers of the said persons, the assembly (called for that purpose) ordered 500 men to be raised against the said murderers, by whom forts were erected. We were informed that the commanders of the said soldiers had order not to molest an Indian unless they knew them to be the murderers or began to act in a hostile way first. [Such] leniency, we humbly conceive, gave the Indians encouragement to persist in their bloody practice and was occasion in part of the people arming themselves without command from their superiors in a rebellious manner, with whom the rebel Bacon, having before by extravagancy lost his fortunes, takes the opportunity and joins. And being amongst them reputed a wit, was adhered to by the rest ... after he had illegally obtained a commission, which was published as legally obtained in the several counties by consent of the grand assembly.... Many people were ignorantly deluded and drawn into his party that thought of no other design than the Indian war. Most of [these] persons, though never so innocent, are persecuted with rigor ... which, with the ill-management of this war at first, we complain of as grievances.

4. That whereas there were several grievances presented to the assembly in June last, in order to prevent many exorbitant fees and other disorders in government, upon which many good laws were consented to, and agreed upon by that grand assembly before the rebel Bacon came to interrupt the said assembly. We beg that those good and wholesome laws may be confirmed by this assembly.

5. We complain that since the late rebellion the rebels have taken and plundered diverse good subjects' estates. We beg that this assembly will take some course that right owners may be empowered to be revested in all that was so taken from them....

6. We complain that some particular persons near about the governor have obtained commission to plunder and destroy the rebels, which they have made use of to the imprisonment of the persons and rifling their estates, and converting them to their own uses....

9. Whereas by the too frequent assemblies and high charges of the burgesses, the county is exposed to a great charge which we do complain [of] as a grievance.

QUESTIONS TO CONSIDER

1. One historian has remarked that Bacon's Rebellion was "a rebellion with abundant causes but without a cause." Do you agree? What were the causes of Bacon's Rebellion? Did Nathaniel Bacon have a cause? Did William Berkeley?

2. What do the essay and sources reveal about Bacon's motivation in challenging royal authority in Virginia? What do the actions of Bacon and Berkeley reveal about the difficulty of establishing the motives of people in the past?

3. In the early twentieth century, many historians saw Bacon's Rebellion as a precursor of the American Revolution: an attempt to overthrow a repressive royal government and establish a more democratic society. Later historians have argued that Bacon was no democrat and that this episode's significance is what it reveals about the evolution of Virginia society in the seventeenth century. What do you think is the significance of Bacon's Rebellion? How did it reflect tensions in Virginia related to economic or social class? What economic, social, or political changes did this rebellion bring to the colony?

4.   On the basis of the information in this chapter's sources, would you have moved to Virginia as an indentured servant in the third quarter of the seventeenth century? Would you have sided with Bacon's or Berkeley's forces in 1676?

FOR FURTHER READING

Warren M. Billings, *Sir William Berkeley and the Forging of Colonial Virginia* (Baton Rouge: Louisiana State University Press, 2004), provides a recent biography that explores Berkeley's role in early Virginia.

David W. Galenson, *White Servitude in Colonial America: An Economic Analysis* (Cambridge: Cambridge University Press, 1981), discusses the nature of indentured servitude in the colonies and its role in the colonial economy.

Edmund S. Morgan, *American Slavery American Freedom: The Ordeal of Colonial Virginia* (New York: W. W. Norton & Company, 1975), sees Bacon's Rebellion as a pivotal event in Virginia's evolution toward a society dominated by race-based slavery.

James D. Rice, *Tales from a Revolution: Bacon's Rebellion and the Transformation of Early America* (New York: Oxford University Press, 2012), provides a brief, engaging account of Bacon's Rebellion and its impact.

Wilcomb E. Washburn, *The Governor and the Rebel: A History of Bacon's Rebellion in Virginia* (Chapel Hill: University of North Carolina Press, 1957), offers a sympathetic view of Governor Berkeley as a defender of the Indians and portrays Bacon as their aggressive, ambitious, and unscrupulous enemy.

Stephen S. Webb, *1676: The End of American Independence* (New York: Alfred A Knopf, 1984), places Bacon against the backdrop of England's civil war and argues that his rebellion was a revolt against post-Restoration Stuart despotism.

3

Faith and Reason in an Age of Enlightenment: Jonathan Edwards and Benjamin Franklin

Jonathan Edwards took to the pulpit on the early spring Sunday in 1737 as he had so many times and peered over his flock. Packed in pews below and in the gallery above, Edwards's faithful congregants eyed an imposing presence. Standing more than six feet tall with a towering intellect to match, their minister was responsible for a remarkable religious revival that had warmed their own Northampton and other western Massachusetts towns only two years before. As he stood before his congregation, however, Edwards believed that the "lively spirit in religion" had burned out. In fact, he may have thought it fitting that this winter had brought such bitter cold.

Neither the minister nor anyone in the assembled crowd knew what the winter chill had in fact done to their old church structure—or what they were about to witness as a result. As the rickety building heaved atop the frozen ground, the joists holding the packed gallery in place had been nearly separated from their supports. Just as Edwards began his sermon, the crowded upper level split in half. With the sound "like an amazing clap of thunder," the gallery crashed down, taking with it those who sat there, mostly women and children, and burying scores of worshipers under shattered timbers below. Edwards's words were suddenly drowned out by the painful shrieks and cries of the multitude. It was impossible not to conclude, as Edwards later reported, "that great numbers must instantly be crushed to death or dashed in pieces." As parishioners dug out the buried victims, however, they discovered that miraculously not one had been killed. No one had suffered even a broken bone.

Spiritual heirs of their seventeenth-century Puritan forebearers, Edwards and his congregants saw the hand of God in dramatic events, be they earthquakes, lightning strikes, or collapsed church balconies. Theirs was no remote God, but rather an

North Wind Picture Archives/AP Images

North Wind Picture Archives

Jonathan Edwards   Benjamin Franklin

immediate and active participant in human affairs who frequently and directly intervened in people's lives, sometimes in powerful and frightening ways. It was only natural, then, to seek meaning in these events. With this "dangerous and surprising" accident, Edwards believed, God had delivered a powerful rebuke to his lax congregation so that they might "praise his name for so wonderful … a preservation."

Edwards's conclusion about this near catastrophe cut to the heart of his lifelong struggle with the world. The Northampton minister mounted nothing less than an all-out defense of seventeenth-century Puritanism in a new century of slackening religious zeal and revolutionary ideas. As no other religious figure in his time, Jonathan Edwards reaffirmed old doctrines of mankind's utter depravity and the individual's absolute dependence on God. In doing so, he created some of the most memorable images—both vivid and horrifying—to remind audiences of the terrifying and awesome power of God in human affairs. Edwards's battle was, in its way, heroic. After all, he chose to resist the intellectual, social, and cultural tides of the eighteenth century. In defending seventeenth-century Puritan doctrine in a new era, he would stake a claim as the greatest theologian to rise from colonial American soil and one of the most prominent in American history. More immediately, he helped spur an emotional counter-reaction in the early 1740s known as the Great Awakening—an outpouring of religious fervor, repentance, and conversion in the 1740s on a scale previously unseen in American society.

As his contemporary Benjamin Franklin—another son of Puritan New England—could have told Edwards, however, it was a battle he was unlikely to win. As Franklin surely sensed, colonial life had changed in important ways since the seventeenth century.

In fact, Franklin's own life reflected those changes. The stern, angry God of orthodox Puritanism appealed to fewer people in each generation, including Franklin, who turned his back on Puritan Boston for good as a mere lad. Franklin's life would amply demonstrate the appeal of a new "enlightened" conception of the world that attracted many educated and influential colonists. In the new scheme, a benign God had created an orderly universe that operated according to certain "natural laws." Reason and science promised to reveal its workings, and salvation was to be found in the works of man—in ordering one's life and society according to the same laws of nature. Franklin's differences with Edwards were not personal. In fact, the two men never knew one another. Yet they stood opposed, one man resisting the currents of his time, and the other carried by them to wide fame and worldly success. For us, they remain powerful representatives of two opposing world views that contended for mastery of an age.

"THE GLORIOUS MAJESTY AND GRACE OF GOD"

Compared to Benjamin Franklin's, Jonathan Edwards's life appears quite dull. Foremost, he was a man of books. The provincial minister traveled little and preferred his own or his family's company to that of others. Often withdrawn, he frequently rose at four and spent thirteen hours a day in his study. Breaks came in the form of long, solitary walks in nature. At the same time, Edwards's interior life was far from ordinary. As he contemplated the awesome power of God, he summoned a powerful mind to defend traditional Puritan doctrines. In an age of individual rights and empowerment, though, Edwards's rigid views would stir a rebellion in his own church that revealed how far many Americans had moved from traditional assumptions about authority and older beliefs about the inability of individuals to control their own fate. Rejected by his congregation, he was exiled to the Massachusetts frontier, where he spent years ministering to the Native Americans. All the while, he continued his long argument against almost every new eighteenth-century assumption about God and the universe.

If Edwards was ill-suited for his age, his early life perfectly prepared him for his calling. Born in 1703 in the village of East Windsor, Connecticut, he was the son of a Harvard graduate and Congregational* minister, and grandson of the highly respected Solomon Stoddard, who ministered to the congregation at Northampton for fifty-seven years. His early schooling was at home under the watchful eyes of his father and mother. In the pious and strict Edwards household, education and religion came naturally. His father introduced him to Latin at age six and Greek a little later. At age eight, young Edwards reported his first religious experience, after which he became greatly concerned about his salvation and often discussed with his father the state of their souls. He later reported that he and some other young boys built "a booth in a swamp," where he spent "much time in religious conversation." Growing up the only boy among ten sisters, young Jonathan spent much time alone. At such times, his thoughts often turned to God. Sometimes, he reported later, a "sweet sense of divine things" struck him. Once, contemplating the clouds and sky as he walked alone in his father's pasture, he was overcome with "a sense of the glorious majesty and grace of God."

*Congregational: The denomination of the New England Puritan church characterized by a form of organization in which individual congregations chose their own ministers and were not subject to the control of a higher church body.

Edwards continued his education and spiritual development at Yale College in preparation for the ministry. He enrolled at thirteen—the usual age in those years—already studious, serious-minded, and respectful of authority. He stood apart from his classmates, wanting nothing to do with their college pranks. Instead, he wrote to his father about the "Preciousness" of his time and expressed "great Content" at the rector's strictness. He also reported that he was "perfectly free" of his fellow students' vandalism, card-laying, theft, and other "monstrous improprieties." His unhappy relationship with fellow students was revealed when he noted that, "There has no new quarrels broke out betwixt me and any of the scholars."

More important, as he focused on his studies, Edwards discovered Isaac Newton, John Locke, and other great Enlightenment* thinkers. Their work had laid the foundation for the new understanding of the cosmos: an orderly and reasonable universe based on knowable laws and presided over by a remote God. That view, of course, threatened to undermine the Puritan conception of the world. Yet Edwards was hardly won over. Instead, he would enlist Enlightenment concepts to support Puritan orthodoxy.* From Locke's argument that ideas arise only from our direct sensations, for instance, Edwards concluded that understanding through the senses was the only source of religious authority. In other words, reason had little to do with religious experience. Likewise, in the cause and effect of Newtonian physics, Edwards found a secure place for a sovereign God. Newton concluded, for example, that gravity (the cause of which he could not explain) is inherent in matter, but was not the cause of an object's mass. Newton's unexplained cause was, for Edwards, a manifestation of God's power. He went on to conclude that salvation, too, was caused by a force other than "works" or even faith. The cause was God's grace. In other words, human effort to gain salvation was in vain. Good works or faith might be effects of salvation, but never the cause of it. That was God's alone to give.

Edwards's God dispensed grace in what seemed an arbitrary fashion. Yet Puritans rarely fell into a fatalistic malaise. As if to confirm to themselves or others evidence of their own salvation, they characteristically lived orderly, self-disciplined, upright lives, and worked hard at their "callings." Edwards was no exception. A diligent student, he graduated from Yale at the top of his class and then stayed for two years of graduate studies in divinity. It was a natural choice. During his Yale years, Edwards had a conversion experience that led to "new dispositions" and a "new sense of things." Everything in nature, including once-terrifying thunderstorms, now filled him with a sense of the "sweet glory of god." **[See Source 1.]** In 1722, he secured the pulpit of a small congregation in New York. There, in an exercise in self-discipline, Edwards drew up thirty-four resolutions (later expanded to seventy) concerning control over his spiritual life. It was, as he later put it, an effort to be "a complete Christian." **[See Source 2.]** At the same time, however, his old disposition and inability to relate well to others were apparently undiminished and eight months later he stepped down from the pulpit.

He was not away from his calling for long. After returning to Yale to pursue further study, he was called back to the ministry in 1727. This time, he was the assistant

---

Enlightenment: A philosophical movement in the seventeenth and eighteenth centuries that assumed a universe governed by certain knowable laws. Enlightenment thinkers emphasized human reason rather than revelation as the source of knowledge and refused to accept ideas on faith alone.

Puritan orthodoxy: A set of beliefs conforming to the teachings of the sixteenth-century theologian John Calvin. Orthodox Puritans emphasized salvation at God's hand for only a few people and the doctrine of predestination—the belief that an individual's salvation is determined long before birth.

pastor and eventual successor to his grandfather, the venerable Solomon Stoddard in Northampton. Stoddard, well known throughout New England, had served his church since 1672. Only five months into his new position, Edwards further reinforced his connection to New England's ministerial elite by marrying Sarah Pierrepont, the seventeen-year-old daughter of a founder of Yale College and the leading minister in New Haven, Connecticut. It was apparently a good match. The gracious Sarah was a diligent housekeeper and would bear eleven children.[*] For the next twenty-three years, Edwards ministered to his Northampton church. For more than twenty of them, after Stoddard died in 1729, he served as its pastor. There he waged battle against the popular doctrine of "works," the idea that individuals could achieve salvation through their own free will. In time, though, the unbending Edwards demonstrated how ill-suited he was to an age of individual rights and optimism about human progress.

"LIVE IN ALL RESPECTS LIKE
A RATIONAL CREATURE"

Jonathan Edwards and Benjamin Franklin, the defender of a stern Puritan God and the exemplar of Enlightenment assumptions and virtues, actually shared much in common. Both were towering figures of their times who rose from nowhere. At the same time, the roots of each reached well into the soil of Puritan New England. While Puritanism was the very core of Edwards's life, it also left its clear mark on Franklin. As one biographer put it, Franklin embodied the "Protestant ethic divorced from dogma." In their own way, they shared an earnest desire to lead a virtuous life. Likewise, each maintained a sense of wonderment about the workings of nature. Yet, in outlook, temperament, beliefs, and social attitudes, they could not have been more different. The differences were crucial. Just as Edwards proved out of sync with his times, Franklin would seem perfectly in step with his.

Franklin imbibed Puritan attitudes early on. He was born in 1706 one of the seventeen children of a Boston candle maker. His father Josiah had migrated from England in 1683. As with many migrating Puritans, he left as much for financial as spiritual reasons. A craftsman who worked hard at his calling, he wanted to improve his lot in life. Josiah reflected the Puritan belief that salvation and material success were not necessarily at odds. In fact, young Benjamin so often heard his father quote the Bible passage, "Seest thou a man diligent in his calling, he shall stand before Kings" that he had the words "Diligence in thy calling" inscribed on Josiah's gravestone. Benjamin absorbed that same diligence as well as a keen appreciation for thrift. Once, intrigued by another boy's whistle, young Benjamin gave the boy all the coins in his pocket for it, only to be told by his siblings that he had dearly overpaid. That knowledge, he later confessed, pained him more than any pleasure he gained from the whistle. Sounding a frequent refrain later in life, he concluded that "industry and frugality" are "the means of procuring wealth and thereby securing virtue."

Those Puritan virtues were perfectly suited to a thriving commercial society filled with merchants, tradesmen, and farmers. They are associated with Franklin to this day.

---

[*]*Edwards-Pierrepont families:* One of Edwards's daughters would go on to marry Aaron Burr, the president of the College of New Jersey—now Princeton University. In the early nineteenth century, the couple's son and Burr's namesake would mortally wound Alexander Hamilton in a duel. [See Chapter 6.] Later in the same century, the Wall Street banking colossus John Pierrepont (J.P.) Morgan traced his ancestry to Sarah's father.

So, too, is the idea of the "self-made man." Franklin, of course, would become one—in many later observers' eyes, his country's first. It was not formal education that earned him this distinction. Josiah intended to tithe to God young Benjamin—his tenth child—by having him study for the ministry at Harvard College. The boy was enrolled at Boston Latin School, but a year later Josiah pulled him out. Family finances may have been the reason or maybe Benjamin's temperament. The young boy, not especially pious or reverent, but plenty skeptical, mischievous, and unimpressed by authority, was clearly ill-suited for the ministry. So after an additional year of writing and arithmetic instruction at another academy, Benjamin's schooling stopped. Instead he went to work in his father's shop and two years later was apprenticed for more than nine years to his older brother James, a printer. In both shops and those of other Boston tradesmen, Franklin came to appreciate craft work and the apron-clad men who did it. Working for James, he also won a way to express himself. After his brother launched a newspaper, Benjamin—self taught and still in his teens—wrote a series of imaginative essays published in the paper. In them, he introduced the character of Silence Dogood, a rural widow, to voice his own views. Though rough, the essays demonstrated a folksy, home-spun humor—the same qualities found in much of his later writing.

Denied much formal education, Franklin revealed in the Dogood essays that he had found other opportunities to learn. Specifically, he had come to appreciate books. He pulled them from his father's modest shelf: Plutarch's Lives, a classical demonstration of how individual effort could change the course of history for the better, Englishman Daniel Defoe's An Essay upon Projects (1697), a set of proposals for economic and social improvement, and Cotton Mather's Essays to Do Good (1710), in which the eminent Boston minister pointed to the power of individuals working through voluntary associations to reform—and redeem—society. One of his favorites, though, was John Bunyan's Pilgrim's Progress (1678), the tale of a man named Christian determined to reach the Celestial City. As revealed in the title, its theme was progress of individuals as they overcome adversity and gained knowledge and wisdom. From his reading, Franklin came to see people's lives shaped by their own efforts, not by some fixed and impersonal forces. That view, of course, did not fit well with the Puritan belief in predestination and mankind's depravity. At the same time, though, he embraced another aspect of Puritanism—the commitment to build a strong community that ran from Mather back to John Winthrop's vision of a "City Upon a Hill." Joining diligence and thrift to that obligation, Franklin could easily reconcile doing well and doing good.

Never a loner, Franklin rarely had difficulty making friends. At a young age, he realized that being argumentative and dogmatic—"disputatious," as he called it—was "a very bad habit." He learned instead to be the "humbler enquirer"—a remarkable insight for such a young person. Practicing the art of gentle, reasonable persuasion throughout his life no doubt made it easier to do well and good as he mixed with a wide range of people from the streets of Boston or Philadelphia to the halls of power. Getting along with his brother was another matter. Subjected to James's beatings, Benjamin yearned for his independence. When the Massachusetts General Court forbade James from publishing his newspaper after he penned an attack on religion, he evaded the ban by pretending to turn the paper over to Benjamin. He also discharged the boy from his apprenticeship to make the transfer appear legitimate. When he had Benjamin sign a new, secret apprenticeship agreement, the boy had his opening. He shrewdly realized that James would never try to enforce the new agreement, revealing that James still owned the paper. Two months later, the seventeen-year-old Benjamin was gone. Such "harsh and tyrannical treatment," Franklin later reflected, left him "with that aversion to arbitrary power" that stayed with him his entire life.

Ten days after leaving Boston, Franklin entered Philadelphia. Decades later in his autobiography, he recounted the now-famous scene. He walked from the wharf up Chestnut Street, tired, hungry, and dirty, with a bread roll under each arm and a couple of coins in his pocket. It may have seemed an unpromising beginning in his new home, but in Philadelphia, Franklin found a congenial environment for his talents and temperament. With two thousand residents, the bustling commercial center was second only to Boston in size and on its way to becoming the colonies' biggest town. Simple in dress, egalitarian, and tolerant of others, its Quaker* founders had created an unpretentious and open community. Like Franklin, the Quakers—and later German and Scottish immigrants—were industrious and thrifty.

Franklin quickly landed on his feet. The day after walking off the wharf, he found work in a printer's shop. Just as quickly, the affable newcomer made friends. Soon he was the center of a group of other young tradesmen. He also came to know Sir William Keith, Pennsylvania's governor. Keith had marched into the printer's shop where Franklin worked after reading a letter he had written extolling the virtues of Philadelphia. Keith was so impressed that someone so young had penned this message that he promised to help Franklin set up his own shop. Keith arranged to have Franklin travel to London to purchase printing equipment, but he realized once there that the governor's promise to finance his purchases was hollow. Making the best of the situation, Franklin found work in two of London finest printing houses.

While there, he also furthered his education. Exposed to Enlightenment tracts as a printer, Franklin proved a receptive student. He was especially drawn to deism,* the conception of God as a remote but benign Creator of the universe. In a "dissertation" written in London in 1725, he declared that "the arguments of the deists … appeared to me much stronger" than the Calvinist doctrine of man's absolute dependence on God for salvation. He concluded that "all creatures must be equally esteemed by the Creator" and knowledge of God and the universe were to be gained from the scientific study of nature, not divine revelation. Less interested in metaphysical concepts than practical impact, Franklin in time realized that religious belief was actually useful in promoting morality and good behavior, while the deist belief in a benevolent but remote God was not very useful because it could undermine both. Still, the Calvinist concept of salvation through God's grace rather than good works was not beneficial either. God, Franklin finally concluded, was actually served by the useful or good works people performed to improve society and to help others—the ultimate purpose of religion. "I firmly believe," he declared, "[that] [H]e delights to see me Virtuous." **[See Source 3.]**

Returning to Philadelphia in 1726, Franklin was ready to lead a practical, useful life—one devoted to the pursuit of worldly success, scientific study, and good works. On the voyage back, he wrote down resolutions regarding his own conduct that he might "live in all respects like a rational creature." He vowed that he would be "extremely frugal," "aim at sincerity in every word and action," apply himself "industriously" to his business, and "to speak ill of no man whatsoever." He returned to a job the same printer's shop, but soon left to start a shop of his own. He also started a club of

---

Quakers: An offshoot of the English Protestant reformation founded by George Fox in the late 1640s, Quakers preached that salvation was open to everyone, believed in religious toleration, practiced pacifism.

Deism: An Enlightenment creed that reason applied to nature—not revelation—was the means to discover God. Deists often perceived the universe in mechanical terms with a Creator who had set it in operation and then withdrawn from active intervention in people's lives.

other young tradesmen called the Junto, widening at once his social and business connections. Guided by his hand, members discussed current issues, philosophical questions, and methods for self-improvement: "Hath you heard of any citizen's thriving well, and by what means?" for instance, or "What unhappy effects of intemperance have you lately observed or heard? Of imprudence? Of passion? Or of any other vice or folly?" About the same time, Franklin began a "bold and arduous" quest for his own moral perfection. First, he listed twelve virtues (later expanded to thirteen when a Quaker acquaintance suggested he had omitted humility from his list). In a notebook, he allotted one page for each virtue and created a grid on each to track his efforts. To aid him in practicing order, a virtue he found particularly vexing, he also devoted a page to outline his daily activities so that "every part of my business should have its allotted time." **[See Source 4.]**

Unlike Edwards's resolutions to be a "complete Christian," here were virtues intended for worldly success. In fact, as he practiced the diligence he preached, Franklin and his business thrived. He was careful not only to be industrious and frugal, but "to avoid all appearances of the contrary." And, of no small importance, he took a helpmate. Franklin had encountered Deborah Read the first time he walked into Philadelphia from the wharf six years before. Theirs was a practical union, seemingly born more out of pragmatic considerations than intense feelings. (About the same time he had taken custody of a boy he had fathered out of wedlock—a nagging reminder of his own imprudence.) Industrious and thrifty, Deborah helped out in the shop, took care of the accounts, and bore him two children.* Meanwhile, Franklin was an energetic competitor. He launched a newspaper, the *Pennsylvania Gazette*, and in time he drove two competing papers out of business as well as the print shop of his old boss. He also printed his own essays. One of his first was a call for the colony to print more paper money, which Franklin believed would increase wages and spur trade. In due course, the legislature awarded him a contract to print additional currency. It was not the last time Franklin would merge the pursuit of public interest and his own profit. As he put it, it was "another advantage gained by my ability to write."

That ability gained him greater success—and increasing renown. The best example of that was *Poor Richard's Almanac*. Here, as in the earlier Silence Dogood essays, Franklin employed fictional characters, Poor Richard Saunders and Bridget, his nagging wife. Through them, he conveyed his own views and pricked pretension and snobbery with wit and folk humor. Sprinkled through each edition were also homey—now famous—maxims:

> Early to bed, early to rise, makes a man healthy, wealthy and wise…
> He that lies down with dogs shall rise up with fleas…
> Haste makes waste…
> Search others for their virtues, thy self for thy vices…
> No gains without pains…
> God helps them that help themselves.

Started in 1732, *Poor Richard's Almanac* sold ten thousand copies a year. Later, Franklin created another character named Father Abraham, who summarized Richard's adages regarding diligence and thrift. Published as *The Way to Wealth*, it was reprinted in nearly

---

Franklin Children: Franklin's daughter Sarah would marry Richard Bache. Their son, Benjamin Franklin Bache, would follow his famous grandfather's footsteps as a newspaper publisher and become an unwavering foe of the Federalist Party. [See Chapter 6.]

one hundred editions in numerous languages and ranks as one of the most famous books to emerge from the colonies. Poor Richard promoted virtue and he made Franklin rich.

Franklin reminded readers that industry and frugality were the means to procure wealth and thereby secure virtue. Still a young man, he now found himself in a secure position to promote civic virtue—to do good. Evidence of his civic engagement and good works was soon evident all around his adopted town. He started a subscription library, an outgrowth of the Junto library created from members' own books and the first in the colonies. Libraries, he later noted, "made the common tradesmen and farmers as intelligent as most gentlemen from other countries." To help ensure public safety, he pushed for a tax to support watchmen or constables, who finally took to Philadelphia's streets in 1752 after the Pennsylvania legislature approved Franklin's plan.

Likewise, he proposed the creation of a volunteer fire company. Created in 1736, it proved so popular that other fire companies soon sprang up around the town. He promoted the creation of an academy, which in time would become the University of Pennsylvania. Finally, he proposed to create a society "for promoting useful knowledge" among the American colonies. The result was the American Philosophical Society, the oldest learned society in America. As a Junto on a far larger scale, it would concern itself with diverse fields, from anthropology and history to medicine and physics. Like his other projects, this one was desirable because it would be useful for the general improvement of society. As he argued in his proposal for this society, it would conduct "all philosophical experiments that let light into the nature of things, tend to increase the power of man over matter, and multiply the conveniences or pleasures of life."

"SOME LOATHSOME INSECT OVER THE FIRE"

As Benjamin Franklin contemplated ever more projects for social improvement in Philadelphia, Jonathan Edwards was just starting his duties as minister in Northampton. He had taken on a difficult assignment. By the late colonial period, New England's population had increased and land, once relatively abundant, had become increasingly difficult for young men to secure, often delaying marriage and creating discontent. Compared to the days of the Puritan founders, many people had strayed from the church and fewer still were willing or able to stand for church membership by attesting to the experience of grace. Worse, ministers were no longer the respected authorities in their communities, but often criticized and sometimes even ridiculed. No wonder Edwards and other ministers complained about declining religious zeal! In Northampton, Edwards's grandfather Solomon Stoddard had adjusted to the reality of declining religious enthusiasm. In the face of sagging church membership, he opened the sacrament of the Lord's Supper to any person of good character, rather than only those who could prove their conversion. Viewing this sacrament as a "converting ordinance," Stoddard boldly broadened the prerequisites of church membership that had existed since the founding of Puritan Massachusetts. In his eighties, Stoddard was esteemed in his church and community; young Edwards, also concerned about slackening zeal, had no interest in making adjustments to social realities.

Taking over from Stoddard, Edwards enjoyed success at first. In the mid-1730s, he stoked an outburst of religious enthusiasm with powerful images of God's absolute power and the base sinfulness of mankind. He accused stunned congregants, for instance, of "wallowing in sensual filthiness" and declared that God viewed each of them as "a wretched, despicable creature; a worm … a vile insect." His emotional sermons had a remarkable impact. In one year, about three hundred converts joined his church. Even

Edwards was amazed. Not only were people "seized with a deep concern about their eternal salvation," he said, but the fervor had ended "differences" between ministers and their parishioners. Edwards's revival spread out of Northampton to some thirty towns in the Connecticut River Valley, but it soon spent itself. By 1737, when he published his *Faithful Narrative of the Surprising Work of God*, an account of the remarkable awakening, it was already over.

Revival preaching was just getting started, however. The same year, a young English minister named George Whitefield (pronounced "Whitfield") arrived in the colonies. With a booming voice and an impressive oratorical skill, he could leave crowds weeping and shouting. When Whitefield preached in Philadelphia, the ever-curious Franklin turned out to get a glimpse of the sensational preacher, although he almost seemed more interested in calculating the size of Whitefield's audience than in his message. Whitefield, and other revival preachers like the fiery Gilbert Tennent of Pennsylvania and the raucous James Davenport of New York sparked the "Great Awakening," an outpouring of religious fervor in the early 1740s extending from New England to the Carolinas. As an amazed Franklin noted after observing Whitefield, "It seem'd as if all the world were growing religious." **[See Source 5.]**

Emotion had played little role in the cerebral Puritanism of the seventeenth century. Likewise, the Calvinist doctrine of salvation by God's grace had little to do with Enlightenment rationalism in the eighteenth century. For Calvinists like Edwards, the benign rational universe of deism was absurd given God's absolute sovereignty and man's utter depravity. For rationalists like Franklin, the idea of salvation divorced from good works or merit seemed equally absurd.

In the Awakening, however, Edwards would marshal both emotion and Enlightenment thought in an unwavering defense of salvation by God's grace alone. They came together in what he called "experimental" religion. Edwards believed that people must have a personal experience with religion—an emotional response that made it "experimental." He would create that emotional experience in defense of a sovereign Calvinist God, drawing from Locke's assertion that ideas arose only from sensations. Edwards would enlist people's senses with the most vivid, sensational images to emerge during the Great Awakening. In Enfield, Connecticut, in 1741, he preached "Sinners in the Hands of an Angry God," the best-known sermon of the Awakening and now one of the most famous in American history. Here he pictured a sovereign God holding the sinner over the pit of hell by a mere thread like "some loathsome insect over the fire … ten thousand times more abominable in his eyes, than the most hateful venomous serpent is in ours." **[See Source 6.]** Edwards saw nothing especially harsh in the sermon, but others did. Before Edwards could finish, people were moaning and crying out. According to one observer, "there was such a breathing of distress, and weeping" that Edwards had to ask for silence so he could finish his words.

Within a year after Edwards delivered his famous sermon, a reaction had set in against the itinerant preaching, mass conversions, and hysterical outbursts associated with the Awakening. Those defending these practices were so-called New Lights; those opposed were "Old Lights." Despite the obvious emotions his sermons could elicit, Edwards did not consider himself a New Light. Yet he published a defense of the Awakening, arguing that it had a positive impact by calling people to God's "moral commands of self-denial, righteousness, meekness, and Christian love." When he read that passage in Philadelphia, Benjamin Franklin took it to support his own view that people needed to show their religion in deeds. Edwards's defense of emotional preaching, however, was rooted in Calvinist doctrine, not its usefulness for promoting morality in society. In fact, he missed the larger meaning of the Awakening as a social phenomenon. It appealed not to the comfortable and educated, but more often to those who were dispossessed and the struggling—people who were more interested in a religion of the heart than the head. They were also uninspired by a doctrine suggesting that they had no control over their salvation—the very doctrine of grace that Edwards used emotional religion to defend.

Just how much Edwards was out of step with his flock—and out of tune with his times—became very evident as the Awakening's embers died down. To people who wanted a more easygoing religion, Edwards continued to preach relentlessly against the doctrine of "works"—the belief that human action could affect one's salvation. Then in 1748 he also rejected Solomon Stoddard's compromise admitting to the Lord's Supper—and thus church membership—not just the converted but those who had hoped for it. Worse, he proceeded to preach several sermons on the subject despite the instructions of a church committee that he not do so. The austere and bookish Edwards had no feel for the people before whom he stood. With the glow of the revivals now dimmed, his rigid views and detached personality stood out. In 1750, after a nasty struggle, he was dismissed by his congregation. A bitter Edwards accepted a position sixty miles to the west in Stockbridge, Massachusetts, as missionary to the Indians, where he stayed for seven years. Though overqualified, unhappy, and ill-suited for the mission, he could take solace in his belief expressed years earlier that "this life ought to be so spent by us, as to only be a journey or pilgrimage towards heaven."

"THIS IS AN AGE OF EXPERIMENTS"

Late in life, Benjamin Franklin wrote in his autobiography that he lived "in an age of experiments." Edwards, who called on "experimental religion" in a defense of a theology that proclaimed the individual's helplessness in the face of God, might have agreed. Franklin, of course, had something far different in mind—the scientific experimentation of his time, much of it his own. Driven by an intense curiosity, his experiments reflected the Enlightenment assumption that the application of human reason rather than divine revelation was the key to unlocking the mysteries and order of the universe. Moreover, he pursued them to promote the welfare and happiness of mankind.

Little interested in theory, Franklin kept his eye fixed on finding solutions to everyday problems, whether protecting buildings in thunderstorms or venting smoke from a fire. The best known example of this practical bent was his experimentation with lightning. Before Edwards had accepted lightning and thunder as an indication of the "majestic and awful voice" of God, he was terrified by them. Franklin, on the other hand, saw lightning as a natural phenomenon waiting to be explained in concrete, scientific terms—and then tamed. He suspected that water vapor in clouds could be electrically charged and that in a storm tall objects on the ground would attract an electrical discharge in the form of a lightning bolt. His experiments, which famously included flying a kite during a thunderstorm, demonstrated that the discharge from the cloud (transferred to the key at the bottom of his kite string) had the same properties as the electricity generated in his own lab. He put that realization to good use, designing a useful device—the lightning rod—to protect tall structures from this destructive force of nature and then convinced residents of Philadelphia to install two of them on tall buildings. As word of Franklin's invention spread from America to Europe, some commentators expressed outrage that people felt compelled to protect themselves in this way from the voice of God. Dismissing such complaints, Franklin declared thunder to be "no more supernatural than rain." The lightning rod, of course, quickly spread as people realized the benefit of Franklin's invention. Franklin's curiosity and his practical experimentation did not end there, however. He would go on, for instance, to develop a urinary catheter, the first in America. He also used his knowledge of convection to design a stove that, built into a fireplace, permitted the smoke to rise up the chimney. Though ultimately built somewhat differently in the future, such stoves would bear his name.

Franklin performed many of his experiments in the 1740s. He could pursue them even more after he retired in 1748 at the age of forty-two. Financially secure, he turned over the day-to-day operation of his printing business to a foreman. Aside from his experiments, he said, he would now have time to read and study and to interact "with ingenious and worthy" individuals. Unfortunately, Jonathan Edwards would not be similarly blessed. His exile on the Massachusetts frontier ended in 1757 when he was awarded the presidency of the College of New Jersey (later Princeton University), an indication of the respect he had earned from his impressive body of theological writings. By the next year, though, he was dead, the victim of smallpox. His passing at age fifty-five was barely noticed in the colonial press. Ironically, the longest tribute was published in Franklin's newspaper, the *Gazette*.

Meanwhile, nearly half of Franklin's life still lay ahead of him. So were some of his biggest contributions to his society—and nation—as a politician, diplomat, and statesman. Often, the same Enlightenment assumptions reflected in his experiments and inventions informed these activities as well. The Enlightenment faith in the power of individuals to unlock and control the secrets of nature was liberating. Truth was no longer revealed, handed down from higher authority. So, too, political power was not to be exercised from above. Government legitimately arose from politically equal citizens, capable of governing themselves. Tyranny arose from political inequality, dogma, and inherited power. Franklin was no political theorist, but he knew from his own experience what individuals freed from political oppression, superstition, and tradition could accomplish by working together. At the same time, he was no revolutionary. Like many Enlightenment thinkers who perceived an orderly universe that ran according to certain natural laws, Franklin believed in an orderly society. Yet he also had an aversion to the abuse of power. He never forgot his treatment as a boy at the hands of his tyrannical brother James and remained sensitive his entire life to oppressive government.

Though Franklin came around only slowly to the idea of American independence, his political and diplomatic career amply reflected his egalitarianism, his faith in the abilities of common citizens, and his distrust of authority. As a member of the Pennsylvania legislature in the 1750s, he naturally became an opponent of the Penns, the colony's proprietors. He would go on to serve as a colonial diplomat in London, a delegate to the Continental Congress and the committee to draft the Declaration of Independence, and as an American envoy to France. There he helped to forge a French alliance with the United States in the Revolutionary War and negotiate a treaty with Britain at its end. With his wit, charm, and famous fur cap, Franklin could easily play for his French hosts the archetypal American—the product of an environment in which talents mattered more than birth and ordinary citizens could rise to defy kings.

Franklin's long career ended when he died in 1790, but only after further public service, including at the Constitutional Convention in Philadelphia in 1787. There, the delegates launched yet another eighteenth-century experiment—a government of citizens. His final essay, finished just before he died, was "An Address to the Public from the Pennsylvania Society for Promoting the Abolition of Slavery." After his death, Franklin would take his place in the pantheon of Founding Fathers. Remembered today as a scientist, statesman, and self-made man, he is the most approachable of the Founders. Jonathan Edwards, by contrast, is mostly forgotten. When remembered, he appears remote, dour, and pessimistic. Unlike Franklin, he seems not quite American.

• PRIMARY SOURCES •

Source 1: *Jonathan Edwards Accepts God's Sovereignty* (ca. 1740)

In his "Personal Narrative," written around 1740 and first published in 1765, Edwards relates his acceptance of God's absolute sovereignty in the universe. As would Benjamin Franklin in his work, he reveals in this document a close attention to nature. What does he see in it? What do these passages reveal about Edwards's outlook regarding the goal of life?

From my childhood up, my mind had been full of objections against the doctrine of God's sovereignty, in choosing whom he would to eternal life, and rejecting whom he pleased; leaving them eternally to perish, and be everlastingly tormented in hell. It used to appear like a horrible doctrine to me. But I remember the time very well, when I seemed to be convinced, and fully satisfied, as to this sovereignty of God, and his justice in thus eternally disposing of men, according to his sovereign pleasure. But I never could give an account how, or by what means, I was thus convinced, not in the least imagining at the time, nor a long time after, that there was any extraordinary influence of God's Spirit in it; but only that now I saw further, and my reason apprehended the justice and reasonableness of it. However, my mind rested in it; and it put an end to all those cavils and objections. And there has been a wonderful alteration in my mind, with respect to the doctrine of God's sovereignty, from that day to this; so that I scarce ever have found so much as the rising of an objection against it, in the most absolute sense, in God's showing mercy to whom he will show mercy, and hardening whom he will. God's absolute sovereignty and justice, with respect to salvation and damnation, is what my mind seems to rest assured of, as much as of any thing that I see with my eyes; at least it is so at times. But I have often, since that first conviction, had quite another kind of sense of God's sovereignty that I had then. I have often since had not only a conviction, but a delightful conviction. The doctrine has very often appeared exceeding pleasant, bright, and sweet Absolute sovereignty is what I love to ascribe to God. But my first conviction was not so....

After this my sense of divine things gradually increased, and became more and more lively, and had more of that inward sweetness. The appearance of every thing was altered; there seemed to be, as it were, a calm, sweet cast, or appearance of divine glory, in almost every thing. God's excellency, his wisdom, his purity and love, seemed to appear in every thing; in the sun, and moon, and stars; in the clouds and blue sky; in the grass, flowers, trees; in the water, and all nature; which used greatly to fix my mind. I often used to sit and view the moon for continuance; and in the day spent much time in viewing the clouds and sky, to behold the sweet glory of God in these things; in the mean time, singing forth, with a low voice, my contemplations of the Creator and Redeemer. And scarce any thing, among all the works of nature, was so sweet to me as thunder and lightning; formerly, nothing had been so terrible to me. Before, I used to be uncommonly terrified with thunder, and to be struck with terror when I saw a thunder storm rising; but now, on the contrary, it rejoiced me. I felt God, so to speak, at the first appearance of a thunder storm; and used to take the opportunity, at such times, to fix myself in order to view the clouds and see the lightnings play, and hear the majestic and awful voice of God's thunder, which oftentimes was exceedingly entertaining, leading me to sweet contemplations of my great and glorious God. While thus engaged, it always seemed natural to me to sing, or chant forth my meditations; or, to speak my thoughts in soliloquies with a singing voice....

SOURCE: Harold P. Simonson, ed., Selected Writings of *Jonathan Edwards* (New York: Frederick Ungar Publishing Co., 1970), pp. 28–29, 31–32, 34–35; originally from *The Works of President Edwards* (New York, 1869).

Holiness, as I then wrote down some of my contemplations on it, appeared to me to be of a sweet, pleasant, charming, serene, calm nature; which brought an inexpressible purity, brightness, peacefulness and ravishment to the soul. In other words, that it made the soul like a field or garden of God, with all manner of pleasant flowers; all pleasant, delightful, and undisturbed; enjoying a sweet calm, and the gentle vivifying beams of the sun. The soul of a true Christian, as I then wrote my meditations, appeared like such a little white flower as we see in the spring of the year; low and humble on the ground, opening its bosom to receive the pleasant beams of the sun's glory; rejoicing as it were in a calm rapture; diffusing around a sweet fragrancy; standing peacefully and lovingly, in the midst of other flowers round about; all in like manner opening their bosoms, to drink in the light of the sun. There was no part of creature holiness, that I had so great a sense of its loveliness, as humility, brokenness of heart, and poverty of spirit; and there was nothing that I so earnestly longed for. My heart panted after this, to lie low before God, as in the dust; that I might be nothing, and that God might be ALL, that I might become as a little child....

... My heart was knit in affection to those in whom were appearances of true piety; and I could bear the thoughts of no other companions but such as were holy, and the disciples of the blessed Jesus. I had great longings for the advancement of Christ's kingdom in the world; and my secret prayer used to be, in great part, taken up in praying for it.

Source 2: *Jonathan Edwards's Resolutions for Self-Improvement* (1723)

As a young man, Edwards drew up a list of sixty-nine resolutions for self-improvement. What appears to be Edwards's primary aim in these resolutions? How do they reveal his Calvinist beliefs?

1. *Resolved*, That I *will do whatsoever* I think to be most to the glory of God, and my own good, profit, and pleasure, in the whole of my duration; without any consideration of the time, whether now, or never so many myriads of ages hence. *Resolved*, to do whatever I think to be my *duty*, and most for the good and advantage of mankind in general. *Resolved*, so to do, whatever *difficulties* I meet with, how many soever, and how great soever.

2. *Resolved*, To be continually endeavouring to find out some *new contrivance* and invention to promote the fore-mentioned things.

5 *Resolved*, Never to lose one moment of time, but to improve it in the most profitable way I possibly can.

8. *Resolved*, To act in all respects, both speaking and doing, as if nobody had been so vile as I, and as if I had committed the same sins, or had the same infirmities or failings, as others; and that I will let the knowledge of their failings promote nothing but shame in myself, and prove only an occasion of my confessing my own sins and misery of God.

13 *Resolved*, To be endeavouring to find out fit objects of charity and liberality.

20 *Resolved*, To maintain the strictest temperance, in eating and drinking.

41 *Resolved*, To ask myself, at the end of every day, week, month and year, wherein I could possibly, in any respect, have done better. *Jan*.11, 1723.

44. *Resolved*, That no other end but religion shall have any influence at all on any of my actions; and that no action shall be, in the least circumstance, any otherwise than the religious end will carry it.

Source: Alfred Owen Aldridge, *Jonathan Edwards* (New York: Washington Square Press, 1964), pp. 14, 15; M. X. Lesser, *Jonathan Edwards* (Boston: Twayne Publishers, 1988), p. 5; originally from Sereno Edwards Dwight, *Life of President Edwards* (New York: S. Converse, 1829).

45. *Resolved*, Never to allow any pleasure or grief, joy or sorrow, nor any affection at all, nor any degree of affection, nor any circumstance relating to it, but what helps religion.

69 *Resolved,* Always to do that, which I shall wish I had done when I see others do it. *Aug.* 11, 1723.

Source 3: *Benjamin Franklin, "First Principles"* (1728)

In this statement written when he was still a young man, Franklin set forth his religious beliefs. How would you describe his conception of God? How do you think it might have reinforced an impulse to perform "good works"?

I believe there is one supreme, most perfect Being, Author and Father of the Gods themselves. For I believe that Man is not the most perfect Being but one, rather that as there are many Degrees of Beings his Inferiors, so there are many Degrees of Beings superior to him.

Also, when I stretch my Imagination thro' and beyond our System of Planets, beyond the visible fix'd Stars themselves, into that Space that is every Way infinite, and conceive it fill'd with Suns like ours, each with a Chorus of Worlds forever moving round him, then this little Ball on which we move, seems, even in my narrow Imagination, to be almost Nothing, and myself less than nothing, and of no sort of Consequence.

When I think thus, I imagine it great Vanity in me to support, that the *Supremely Perfect* does in the least regard such an inconsiderable Nothing as Man. More especially, since it is impossible for me to have any positive clear idea of that which is infinite and incomprehensible, I cannot conceive otherwise than that he *the Infinite Father* expects on requires no Worship or Praise from us but that he is even infinitely above it.

But, since there is in all men something like a natural principle, which inclines them to DEVOTION, or the worship of some unseen Power;

And since Men and endued with Reason superior to all other Animals, that we are in our world acquainted with;

Therefore I think it seems required of me, and my Duty as a Man, to pay Divine Regards of SOMETHING.

I conceive then, that the INFINITE has created many beings or Gods, vastly superior to Man, who can better conceive his Perfections than we, and return him a more rational and glorious Praise.

As, among men, the Praise of the Ignorant or of Children is not regarded by the ingenious Painter or Architect, who is rather honour'd and pleas'd with the approbation of Wise Men & Artists.

It may be that these created Gods and immortal, or it may be that after many Ages, they are changed, and others Supply their Places.

Howbeit, I conceive that each of these is exceeding wise and good, and very powerful; and that Each has made for himself one glorious sun, attended with a beautiful and admirable System of Planets.

It is that particular Wise and good God, who is the author and owner of our System, that I propose for the object of my praise and adoration.

SOURCE: L. Jesse Lemisch, ed., *Benjamin Franklin: The Autobiography and Other Writings* (New York: New American Library, Inc., 1961), pp. 326–328; originally from Albert Henry Smyth, ed., *The Writings of Benjamin Franklin: Collected and Edited with a Life and Introduction*, 10 vols. (New York: 1905–1907).

For I conceive that he has in himself some of those Passions he has planted in us, and that, since he has given us Reason whereby we are capable of observing his Wisdom in the Creation, he is not above caring for us, being pleas'd with our Praise, and offended when we slight Him, or neglect his Glory.

I conceive for many Reasons, that he is a *good Being;* and as I should be happy to have so, wise good, and powerful as Being my Friend, let me consider in what manner I shall make myself most acceptable to him.

Next to the Praise resulting from and due to his Wisdom, I believe he is pleas'd and delights in the Happiness of those he has created; and since without Virtue Man can have no Happiness in this World, I firmly believe he delights to see me Virtuous, because he is pleased when he sees Me Happy.

And since he has created may Things, which seem purely design'd for the Delight of Man, I believe he is not offended, when he sees his Children solace themselves in any manner of pleasant exercises and Innocent Delights, and I think no Pleasure innocent, that is to Man hurtful.

I *love* him therefore for his Goodness, and I *adore* him for his wisdom.

Let me then not fail to praise my God continually, for it is his Due, and it is all I can return for his may Favours and great Goodness to me, and let me resolve to be virtuous, that I may be happy, that I may please Him, who is delighted to see me happy. Amen!

Source 4: *Benjamin Franklin's Moral Improvement Project (1791)*

Franklin's autobiography, first published in 1791, detailed his efforts as a young man to attain moral perfection. How do these resolutions compare to those of Jonathan Edwards, written about the same time? How do they reflect Franklin's Puritan upbringing?

In the various enumerations of the moral virtues I had met with in my reading, I found the catalogue more or less numerous, as different writers included more or fewer ideas under the same name. Temperance, for example, was by some confined to eating and drinking, while by others it was extended to mean the moderating every other pleasure, appetite, inclination, or passion, bodily or mental, even to our avarice and ambition. I propos'd to myself, for the sake of clearness, to use rather more names, with fewer ideas annex'd to each, than a few names with more ideas; and I included under thirteen names of virtues all that at that time occurr'd to me as necessary or desirable, and annexed to each a short precept, which fully express'd the extent I gave to its meaning.

These names of virtues, with their precepts, were:

1. TEMPERANCE. Eat not to dullness; drink not to elevation.
2. SILENCE. Speak not but what may benefit others or yourself; avoid trifling conversation.
3. ORDER. Let all your things have their places; let each part of your business have its time.
4. RESOLUTION. Resolve to perform what you ought; perform without fail what you resolve.
5. FRUGALITY. Make no expense but to do good to others or yourself; i.e., waste nothing.
6. INDUSTRY. Lose no time; be always employ'd in something useful; cut off all unnecessary actions.

SOURCE: *Benjamin Franklin*, The Autobiography of Benjamin Franklin with introduction and notes edited by Charles W. Eliot (Hazleton, Penn.: The Pennsylvania State University), pp. 77–78, 79–80, 81.

7. SINCERITY. Use no hurtful deceit; think innocently and justly, and, if you speak, speak accordingly.
8. JUSTICE. Wrong none by doing injuries, or omitting the benefits that are your duty.
9. MODERATION. Avoid extreams; forbear resenting injuries so much as you think they deserve.
10. CLEANLINESS. Tolerate no uncleanliness in body, cloaths, or habitation.
11. TRANQUILLITY. Be not disturbed at trifles, or at accidents common or unavoidable.
12. CHASTITY. Rarely use venery but for health or offspring, never to dulness, weakness, or the injury of your own or another's peace or reputation.
13. HUMILITY. Imitate Jesus and Socrates.

My intention being to acquire the habitude of all these virtues, I judg'd it would be well not to distract my attention by attempting the whole at once, but to fix it on one of them at a time; and, when I should be master of that, then to proceed to another, and so on, till I should have gone thro' the thirteen; and, as the previous acquisition of some might facilitate the acquisition of certain others, I arrang'd them with that view, as they stand above....

I made a little book, in which I allotted a page for each of the virtues. I rul'd each page with red ink, so as to have seven columns, one for each day of the week, marking each column with a letter for the day. I cross'd these columns with thirteen red lines, marking the beginning of each line with the first letter of one of the virtues, on which line, and in its proper column, I might mark, by a little black spot, every fault I found upon examination to have been committed respecting that virtue upon that day.

I determined to give a week's strict attention to each of the virtues successively. Thus, in the first week, my great guard was to avoid every the least offence against Temperance, leaving the other virtues to their ordinary chance, only marking every evening the faults of the day. Thus, if in the first week I could keep my first line, marked T, clear of spots, I suppos'd the habit of that virtue so much strengthen'd and its opposite weaken'd, that I might venture extending my attention to include the next, and for the following week keep both lines clear of spots. Proceeding thus to the last, I could go thro' a course compleat in thirteen weeks, and four courses in a year....

FORM OF THE PAGES EAT NOT TO DULNESS; DRINK NOT TO ELEVATION.

	S.	M.	T.	W.	T.	F.	S.
T.							
S.	★	★		★		★	
O.	★★	★	★		★	★	★
R.			★			★	
F.		★			★		
I.			★				
S.							
J.							
M.							
C.							
T.							
C.							
H.							

The precept of Order requiring that every part of my business should have its allot-ted time, one page in my little book contain'd the following scheme of employment for the twenty-four hours of a natural day:

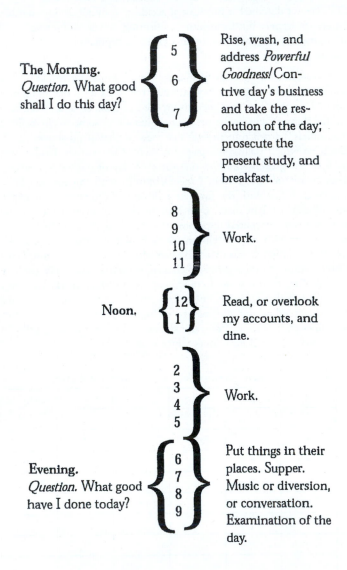

The Morning.
Question. What good shall I do this day?

5
6
7

Rise, wash, and address *Powerful Goodness!* Con-trive day's business and take the res-olution of the day; prosecute the present study, and breakfast.

8
9
10
11

Work.

Noon.

12
1

Read, or overlook my accounts, and dine.

2
3
4
5

Work.

Evening.
Question. What good have I done today?

6
7
8
9

Put things in their places. Supper. Music or diversion, or conversation. Examination of the day.

Source 5:   Benjamin Franklin on the Great Awakening (1791)

Franklin observed, and later befriended, the English itinerant preacher George Whitefield when he came to Philadelphia during the Great Awakening. Like Edwards, Franklin counted himself one of Whitefield's supporters. On what grounds does he support the preacher?

In 1739 arrived among us from Ireland the Reverend Mr. Whitefield, who had made himself remarkable there as an itinerant preacher. He was at first permitted to preach in some of our churches; but the clergy, taking a dislike to him, soon refus'd him their pulpits, and he was oblig'd to preach in the fields. The multitudes of all sects and denominations that attended his sermons were enormous, and it was matter of speculation to me, who was one of the number, to observe the extraordinary influence of his oratory on his hearers, and bow much they admir'd and respected him, notwithstanding his common abuse of them, by assuring them that they were naturally half beasts and half devils. It was wonderful to see the change soon made in the manners of our inhabitants. From being thoughtless or indifferent about religion, it seem'd as if all the world were growing religious, so that one could not walk thro' the town in an evening without hearing psalms sung in different families of every street....

Mr. Whitefield, in leaving us, went preaching all the way thro' the colonies to Georgia. The settlement of that province had lately been begun, but, instead of being made with hardy, industrious husbandmen, accustomed to labor, the only people fit for such an enterprise, it was with families of broken shop-keepers and other insolvent debtors, many of indolent and idle habits, taken out of the jails, who, being set down in the woods, unqualified for clearing land, and unable to endure the hardships of a new settlement, perished in numbers, leaving many helpless children unprovided for. The sight of their miserable situation inspir'd the benevolent heart of Mr. Whitefield with the idea of building an Orphan House there, in which they might be supported and educated. Returning northward, he preach'd up this charity, and made large collections, for his eloquence had a wonderful power over the hearts and purses of his hearers, of which I myself was an instance.

I did not disapprove of the design, but, as Georgia was then destitute of materials and workmen, and it was proposed to send them from Philadelphia at a great expense, I thought it would have been better to have built the house here, and brought the children to it. This I advis'd; but he was resolute in his first project, rejected my counsel, and I therefore refus'd to contribute. I happened soon after to attend one of his sermons, in the course of which I perceived he intended to finish with a collection, and I silently resolved he should get nothing from me, I had in my pocket a handful of copper money, three or four silver dollars, and five pistoles in gold. As he proceeded I began to soften, and concluded to give the coppers. Another stroke of his oratory made me asham'd of that, and determin'd me to give the silver; and he finish'd so admirably, that I empty'd my pocket wholly into the collector's dish, gold and all....

SOURCE: *Benjamin Franklin*, The Autobiography of Benjamin Franklin with introduction and notes edited by Charles W. Eliot (Hazleton, Penn.: The Pennsylvania State University), pp. 97, 98–100.

The following instance will show something of the terms on which we stood. Upon one of his arrivals from England at Boston, he wrote to me that he should come soon to Philadelphia, but knew not where he could lodge when there.... My answer was, "You know my house; if you can make shift with its scanty accommodations, you will be most heartily welcome." He reply'd, that if I made that kind offer for Christ's sake, I should not miss of a reward. And I returned, "Don't let me be mistaken; it was not for Christ's sake, but for your sake." One of our common acquaintance jocosely remark'd, that, knowing it to be the custom of the saints, when they received any favour, to shift the burden of the obligation from off their own shoulders, and place it in heaven, I had contriv'd to fix it on earth....

He had a loud and clear voice, and articulated his words and sentences so perfectly, that he might be heard and understood at a great distance, especially as his auditories, however numerous, observ'd the most exact silence. He preach'd one evening from the top of the Court-house steps, which are in the middle of Market-street, and on the west side of Second-street, which crosses it at right angles. Both streets were fill'd with his hearers to a considerable distance. Being among the hindmost in Market-street, I had the curiosity to learn how far he could be heard, by retiring backwards down the street towards the river; and I found his voice distinct till I came near Front-street, when some noise in that street obscur'd it. Imagining then a semi-circle, of which my distance should be the radius, and that it were fill'd with auditors, to each of whom I allow'd two square feet, I computed that he might well be heard by more than thirty thousand.

Source 6:   Jonathan Edwards, "Sinners in the Hands of an Angry God" (1741)

In this now-famous sermon delivered during the Great Awakening, Edwards presented his most vivid and memorable view of God. How does his conception of God differ from that of Benjamin Franklin? Why do you think this sermon was so effective in moving those who heard it?

There is nothing that keeps wicked men at any one moment out of hell, but the mere pleasure of God.

By the mere pleasure of God, I mean his sovereign pleasure, his arbitrary will, restrained by no obligation, hindered by no manner of difficulty, any more than if nothing else but God's mere will had in the least degree or in any respect whatsoever, any hand in the preservation of wicked men one moment.

The truth of this observation may appear by the following considerations.

1. There is no want of power in God to cast wicked men into hell at any moment. Men's hands cannot be strong when God rises up: the strongest have no power to resist him, nor can any deliver out of his hands.

He is not only able to cast wicked men into hell, but he can most easily do it. Sometimes an earthly prince meets with a great deal of difficulty to subdue a rebel, that has found means to fortify himself, and has made himself strong by the number of his followers. But it is not so with God. There is no fortress that is any defence against the power of God. Though hand join in hand, and vast multitudes of God's enemies combine and associate themselves, they

SOURCE: Harold P. Simonson, ed., Selected Writings of *Jonathan Edwards* (New York: Frederick Ungar Publishing Co., 1970), pp. 97–99; originally from *The Works of President Edwards* (New York, 1869).

are easily broken in pieces: they are as great heaps of light chaff before the whirlwind; or large quantities of dry stubble before devouring flames. We find it easy to tread on and crush a worm that we see crawling on the earth; so it is easy for us to cut or singe a slender thread that any thing hangs by; thus easy is it for God, when he pleases, to cast his enemies down to hell. What are we, that we should think to stand before him, at whose rebuke the earth trembles, and before whom the rocks are thrown down!

2. They deserve to be cast into hell; so that divine justice never stands in the way, it makes no objection against God's using his power at any moment to destroy them. Yea, on the contrary, justice calls aloud for an infinite punishment of their sins. Divine justice says of the tree that brings forth such grapes of Sodom, "Cut it down, why cumbereth it the ground?" Luke xiii. 7. The sword of divine justice is every moment brandished over their heads, and it is nothing but the hand of arbitrary mercy, and God's mere will, that holds it back.

3. They are already under a sentence of condemnation to hell. They do not only justly deserve to be cast down thither, but the sentence of the law of God, that eternal and immutable rule of righteousness that God has fixed between him and mankind, is gone out against them; and stands against them; so that they are bound over already to hell: John iii. 18, "He that believeth not is condemned already." So that every unconverted man properly belongs to hell; that is his place; from thence he is: John viii. 23, "Ye are from beneath:" and thither he is bound; it is the place that justice, and God's word, and the sentence of his unchangeable law, assign to him.

4. They are now the objects of that very same anger and wrath of God, that is expressed in the torments of hell: and the reason why they do not go down to hell at each moment, is not because God, in whose power they are, is not then very angry with them; as angry, as he is with many of those miserable creatures that he is now tormenting in hell, and do there feel and bear the fierceness of his wrath. Yea, God is a great deal more angry with great numbers that are now on earth; yea, doubtless, with many that are now in this congregation, that, it may be, are at ease and quiet, than he is with many of those that are now in the flames of hell.

So that it is not because God is unmindful of their wickedness, and does not resent it, that he does not let loose his hand and cut them off. God is not altogether such a one as themselves, though they may imagine him to be so. The wrath of God burns against them; their damnation does not slumber; the pit is prepared; the fire is made ready; the furnace is now hot; ready to receive them; the flames do now rage and glow. The glittering sword is whet, and held over them, and the pit hath opened her mouth under them.

QUESTIONS TO CONSIDER

1. How would you compare Jonathan Edwards's and Benjamin Franklin's personalities or temperaments, religious beliefs, and attitudes toward life? Which of these factors in the case of each man seemed to be most decisive in shaping his life and career?

2. The work of Jonathan Edwards and Benjamin Franklin reflected both Puritanism and Enlightenment thought. How did these two influences shape the life and outlook of each man? How are those influences revealed in the primary sources in this chapter?

3. If Edwards and Franklin were representatives of two conflicting world views, how would you define those views? How do the lives of Edwards and Franklin reflect

the important changes in eighteenth-century colonial society, religion, or thought, related to these differing world views? Did Edwards, Franklin, or something else, ultimately "win" this conflict?

4. "Morality or Virtue is the End," Franklin once declared. "Faith only a means to obtain that End." How did Franklin's work and his writings reflect that conviction? What do you think Jonathan Edwards would have said to Franklin in response? How did Edwards's work and writings reflect his views about this assertion?

5. Jonathan Edwards defended a fearsome Calvinist theology in the eighteenth century. At the same time, Benjamin Franklin promoted an optimistic view about human progress and a benign view of the universe. Today, Franklin is remembered by many; Jonathan Edwards is not. Do you think the explanation for that lies with them, their own times, or ours?

FOR FURTHER READING

Alfred Owen Aldridge, *Jonathan Edwards* (New York: Washington Square Press, 1964), remains an excellent overview and critical assessment of Edwards, his life, and work.

Walter Isaacson, *Benjamin Franklin: An American Life* (New York: Simon & Schuster, 2003), presents a highly readable introduction to Franklin's life and times and highlights his differences with Jonathan Edwards.

Leonard Labaree, ed., *The Autobiography of Benjamin Franklin* (New Haven: Yale University Press, 1964), an American classic, offers readers a fascinating glimpse of Franklin through his own eyes.

M. X. Lesser, *Jonathan Edwards* (Boston: Twayne Publishers, 1988), is a brief introduction to Edwards's life, writings, and theology.

Henry F. May, *The Enlightenment in America* (New York: Oxford University Press, 1976), offers an assessment of the religious and intellectual changes in eighteenth-century America.

Edmund S. Morgan, *Benjamin Franklin* (New Haven: Yale University Press, 2002), provides a relatively brief and very accessible account of Franklin's life.

4

The Price of Patriotism: Jonathan Sewall and John Adams

As Jonathan Sewall strolled toward the hilltop overlooking Maine's sparkling Casco Bay, he had more on his mind than an early-morning view of the island-dotted Atlantic inlet. On this midsummer morning in 1774, he had asked John Adams to walk with him in a desperate attempt to save his friend from folly. Relations between Great Britain and the American colonies were approaching a dangerous point, and Adams had just been elected a delegate to the Continental Congress. Sewall was determined that Adams not serve. As they walked, Sewall reminded Adams that taking a seat in Philadelphia would be an act of rebellion against His Majesty's government. Adams's brilliant legal career would face certain ruin. "Great Britain is determined in her system," he declared. "Her power is irresistible and will be destructive to you if you persevere in opposition to her designs."

Adams considered Sewall his best friend but was unmoved by his pleas. "I will sink or swim, live or die, survive or perish with my country—that is my unalterable determination," he replied. When Sewall persisted, Adams declared, "I see we must part, and with bleeding heart I say, I fear forever." Adams was wrong. Thirteen years later, he met up with his old friend in London. By that time, the United States had won its independence from Britain, and Adams had won the gratitude of the new nation for his service to it. He had sat in the First and Second Continental Congresses, negotiated the treaty ending the Revolution, and served as minister to Great Britain. The two men talked for several hours, and Sewall observed that their conversation was just what might be expected "at the meeting of two old sincere friends after a long separation."

Nonetheless, for Sewall, the meeting could not have been easy. Adams had already secured an honored place as one of his country's founding fathers, while Sewall remained

The Boston Massacre

John Adams

an outcast. He longed for his beloved Massachusetts, his brilliant legal career was over, and his mental state had deteriorated along with his fortunes. To be sure, Adams had made great personal sacrifices to serve his nation. Yet he had also led a full and rewarding life—a testament to the possibilities presented by his country's creation. Like Adams, Sewall had made an irrevocable commitment to *his* country. He chose to "sink or swim" with Great Britain, becoming at once an articulate defender of the Loyalist position and a prominent target of patriot wrath. As a result, he enjoyed neither honor nor fame, and he stands today as a reminder of the hopes and fears that motivated the Loyalists and the enormous toll this position exacted.

"A BRILLIANT IMAGINATION"

"The childhood shows the man, as morning shows the day," wrote the Puritan poet John Milton. Jonathan Sewall was not born a Loyalist, but his sympathies seemed to arise naturally from his early years. The product of an old and distinguished New England family, he would be well served by family and social connections. When his merchant father died bankrupt in 1731, three years after Jonathan was born, young Sewall would be provided for by more successful relatives. The pastor of Sewall's exclusive Brattle Street Church in Boston saw to it that his wealthy parishioners opened their pocketbooks to pay for the boy's schooling. His uncle Stephen Sewall, chief justice of the Massachusetts Superior (supreme) Court, also helped out. When Jonathan turned fifteen, Justice Sewall reached into his purse and sent Jonathan to Harvard. After Jonathan graduated and took up teaching, a distant relative opened his Salem home and library to the young schoolmaster, and there he studied law. Several years later, his benefactor introduced him to Chambers Russell, a judge and colleague of Stephen Sewall's. Russell took the young man into his Charlestown home and tutored him further in the law. Russell was wealthy and well connected, sat in the Massachusetts assembly, and commanded the deference and respect of his fellow citizens. Sewall could not have found a better mentor.

By the time Russell died in 1766, Sewall had already taken over his Charlestown law practice. The next year, he was sworn in before the Massachusetts bar and set up his own practice. For much of the next decade, Sewall busied himself with petty squabbles over land, livestock, debts, and thefts. To secure additional cases, he followed the superior court as it sat in various counties throughout the year. The frequent travel was compensated by the opportunity to mix with other attorneys, including a fellow Harvard graduate named John Adams.

Although Sewall was lighthearted and Adams serious and introspective, the two men struck up a friendship sustained by the frequent exchange of letters. Adams found much to like in his friend: "a lively wit, a pleasing humor, a brilliant imagination, [and] great subtlety of reasoning." The mundane cases in both the superior and lower courts also gave Sewall the opportunity to master the intricacies of the law and hone his courtroom manner. He had "a soft, smooth, insinuating eloquence," Adams noted, "which ... gave him as much power over [a jury] as any lawyer ought ever to have." Sewall's talents were also noticed by Edmund Trowbridge, the attorney general of Massachusetts. Eventually, Trowbridge made Sewall his junior partner, passing along wealthy clients to his young protégé. Through him, Sewall gained entry into the highest circles in the colony.

In time, personal loyalty led to service for men in power. Sewall's attachments were evident when an influenza epidemic swept Boston in 1760, claiming the life of Stephen Sewall. A battle for the justice's empty court seat between speaker of the assembly James Otis Jr. and Lieutenant Governor Thomas Hutchinson quickly ensued. When Governor Francis Bernard chose Hutchinson, prominent merchants saw the appointment as an attempt by Bernard to gain control of the court at a crucial time. Several years earlier, the royal governor had introduced writs of assistance, which allowed customs officials to board ships and enter buildings and merchants' houses to search for smuggled goods, even without evidence that contraband might be held there. Smuggling was widespread on Boston's wharves, but the writs gave customs officials sweeping power. Outraged Massachusetts merchants had hired Otis to defend them against rummaging officials. Otis denounced the warrants as an assault on the traditional rights of privacy guaranteed by the British constitution. Hutchinson's elevation to the superior court, however, ensured that the issue would be decided in favor of the administration.

Although many Massachusetts lawyers sided with Otis, Jonathan Sewall did not. Chambers Russell and Edmund Trowbridge were friends of Hutchinson and supporters of Governor Bernard, who had just named Sewall justice of the peace for Middlesex County. In addition, when Sewall turned to Otis for assistance in settling his uncle's debt-ridden estate, the legislature refused to help. When the divide between Governor Bernard and the legislature deepened after the superior court decided in favor of the writs, Sewall took up his pen in defense of the administration. In 1763, he blasted Otis in newspaper essays defending the governor's appropriation of provincial funds without the assembly's consent. Later, when the Otis faction launched an attack on Hutchinson for holding offices in all three branches of government, Sewall countered by declaring that citizens should not "give implicit credit to the turbulent harangues of every bold, disaffected, popular disclaimer." He could not have predicted how events in coming years would lead increasing numbers of Americans, including his friend John Adams, to do just that.

"JUST GETTING UNDER SAIL"

John Adams was hardly an impetuous rebel but instead, like Sewall, exhibited an inbred conservatism. In fact, the two men may have been drawn to each other because they had so much in common. Both came from families of modest resources, graduated from Harvard, and pursued legal careers after unhappy stints as schoolteachers. Both developed a deep respect for British institutions and a reverence for the law. Both were ambitious and sought the recognition that each felt was his due.

Born in 1735, the son of a respectable Braintree farmer and shoemaker, Adams grew up on the family farm twelve miles south of Boston. His parents decided that their first-born son would receive the best education their middling circumstances could provide. After progressing through two private academies, young Adams enrolled at Harvard. A reluctant student, he instead aspired to be a farmer, preferring hunting, fishing, and exploring the outdoors to the drudgery of study. At Harvard, however, he discovered a love of books. Upon graduation, he became a schoolmaster in Worcester, fifty miles west of Boston. Teaching "a large number of little runtlings" did not agree with him, so he turned to law. Here was a profession of growing importance in the colony's expanding commercial economy, one that could provide him the "Honor or Reputation" he sought. He was taken in by Worcester's leading attorney and two years later returned to Braintree to practice law.

Adams admired such prominent lawyers as James Otis and the up-and-coming Jonathan Sewall. Yet he had no family connections and lived at home to cut expenses. "[I]t is my Destiny to dig Treasures with my own fingers," he lamented. "No Body will lend me or Sell me an axe." Nor would polish or social graces pave the way. A lingering Puritan ethic had a deep impact on Adams, who was content to hole up in his study for hours on end. Reserved and serious, he was far too stiff to backslap his way to success. Instead, he imposed on himself a harsh discipline of study and hard work.

Gradually, his client list grew. In 1761, he was admitted to practice before the Massachusetts Superior Court. At about the same time, his personal life improved. He courted Hannah Quincy at the same time that Jonathan Sewall wooed her sister Esther, and the two lawyers frequently met at the Quincys' Braintree home. Hannah married another man, but Adams soon recovered after he met Abigail Smith, the daughter of a minister from nearby Weymouth. By 1763, John and the "prudent, modest, delicate, soft, [and] sensible" Abigail were inseparable, and the next year they were married. He was twenty-eight; she was nineteen. The couple moved into a cottage next door to the house where John had been born and raised. Although court cases frequently took him away from Abigail, it was a happy time, and the next summer Abigail gave birth to a daughter.

Events far from Adams's fireside, however, were about to disrupt his world. After the French and Indian War (1754–1763), the colonists entered a new relationship with Great Britain when Parliament sought additional revenue from them. In 1764, it passed the Sugar Act, which levied new duties on molasses and placed a heavy burden on New England shippers. The next year, Parliament passed the Stamp Act, which placed duties on various paper products already in the colonies. It was met with loud protests and riots up and down the colonies. In Massachusetts, John Adams's cousin Samuel Adams aroused popular sentiment by arguing that the act was part of a plot to destroy the colonists' liberties. Samuel had close contact with Boston's artisans and laborers, many of whom were facing diminished prospects. His ability to rally them was unsurpassed. Even John noticed that the "lowest ranks" had become "more attentive to their liberties … and more determined to defend them." If so, it was due in large part to the work of his cousin.

Samuel encouraged John to play a more active role in the Stamp Act crisis, but John held back. It "is very unfortunate for me," he wrote, for "[I am] just getting under Sail." Writing newspaper essays under a pen name, he attacked the Stamp Act as misguided. He also wrote the instructions of the town of Braintree to its representative in the legis-lature regarding the crisis. **[See Source 1.]** Yet his participation was limited and reluc-tant. He did not want to be seen as irresponsible, and he was skeptical about the motives of the "designing persons" who were leading the popular protests, including his cousin. John found mob action frightening and distasteful. "That way madness lies," he told James Otis, who had asked Adams to "harangue" colonists in 1765. Even a decade later, he declared that "breaking open Houses by rude and insolent Rabbles, must be discountenanced." For the time being, he stayed home with his family, "thinking, read-ing, searching, concerning Taxation without Consent."

"RENDERED HIMSELF QUITE SUBSERVIENT"

Jonathan Sewall's life was also going well. The same year the colonies entered their new relationship with Britain—and John Adams with Abigail—Sewall married Esther Quincy. According to Adams, Esther was "celebrated for her beauty, her vivacity, and spirit," and when Sewall first set eyes on her, he "viewed her with … unruffled pleasure." Political rewards soon followed, especially after Sewall voiced his views about the growing popular unrest. Like Adams, Sewall opposed the Stamp Act. But whereas Adams believed that royal officials were a "restless grasping turbulent Crew," Sewall feared turbulence from another quarter. To him, the great danger was not the tax, but Samuel Adams and other rabble-rousers who defied the British government's authority. Submission to a bad law was far better than unlawful resistance to it, he argued. In the growing colonial crisis, such arguments would not go unnoticed. When Samuel Adams and James Otis continued to challenge Governor Bernard's authority after the Stamp Act was repealed in 1766, Sewall defended the governor in newspaper essays. Those in power had to be obeyed, he insisted, as long as they "steadily pursue[d] the sole end of their creation, the good of the community." Bernard liked what he read and quickly named Sewall advocate general of the Massachusetts vice-admiralty court,[*] which had been established by Parliament to take smuggling cases out of the hands of sympathetic colonial juries. A short time later, Bernard named him attorney general of the colony. At age forty, Sewall had arrived.

Before long, however, Sewall found himself in the midst of a growing struggle be-tween the Crown and Massachusetts's merchant class. His problems started with the Townshend Acts[*] of 1767, which imposed new import duties and set up an American Board of Customs Commissioners in Boston. As attorney general and advocate general of the vice-admiralty court, Sewall was responsible for enforcing the customs laws and prosecuting violators. He had no problem with the laws, but he often disagreed with their application by customs commissioners, who routinely engaged in racketeering. Nowhere was Sewall's conflict with the commissioners more evident than in their treatment of John Hancock, the colonies' richest merchant. When a customs man

---

[*]*Vice-admiralty court:* A special British court that heard cases involving shipping and mari-time disputes.

[*]*Townshend Acts:* Laws passed by Parliament that placed taxes on certain colonial imports, including glass, paper, paint, and tea.

without a writ of assistance rummaged below deck on Hancock's ship *Lydia* in 1768, Hancock had him forcibly removed. Sewall believed that Hancock had acted within the law and refused to prosecute him. When Hancock's ship *Liberty* docked in Boston later that year, customs officials seized the ship, claiming that it had smuggled in wine. Hancock had already become a symbol of a growing struggle between imperial interests and colonial rights. Now the seizure of the *Liberty* set off a riot in which customs officers were attacked and driven from Boston. Undaunted, the commissioners proceeded with their case against Hancock, which was a reluctant Sewall's responsibility to prosecute. Hancock and five others faced fines of nine thousand pounds each for allegedly avoiding seven hundred pounds in duties. Hancock's lawyer was an equally reluctant John Adams. Concerned about the effect that political activism might have on his career, Adams looked with "disgust" at his duties in defending the imperial authorities' prime target. The commissioners' case was weak, however, and they had Sewall drop the charges the next year.

The case made Hancock a hero and sullied Sewall's reputation. Samuel Adams declared that Sewall was nothing more than a "little creature of the court" who had betrayed the colony's interests. Sewall had just been appointed to the Halifax vice-admiralty court at the considerable salary of six hundred pounds a year. He now held seats on the Massachusetts and Halifax vice-admiralty courts and as Massachusetts attorney general. Sewall, concluded Samuel Adams, had "rendered himself quite subservient" by accepting so many "favors" from the governor. Certainly, he had learned all about the perquisites of power. In response to these accusations, Sewall urged John Adams to succeed him as attorney general. Though still fearful of an association with radicals, Adams felt a growing disdain for royal officials such as Lieutenant Governor Thomas Hutchinson, whose death, he concluded, "would have been a Smile of Providence." Thus, he quickly turned Sewall down.

Sewall's troubles only mounted. In 1770, guards outside the customs house opened fire on an angry mob, killing five civilians. It was Sewall's job to prosecute the soldiers involved in what came to be known as the Boston Massacre. He believed that the troops were innocent. He was also convinced that James Otis and Samuel Adams had orchestrated the mob. Prosecuting the case vigorously would violate Sewall's sense of justice, but a weak prosecution would surely raise charges of conspiracy. Only one reasonable course seemed open to him. Sewall drew up the indictment against the soldiers and then returned to his country home in Middlesex, where he stayed in personal exile for a year.

While Sewall ran, John Adams stepped into the fray by agreeing to defend the soldiers. Adams later claimed that he accepted their defense because he thought they deserved a fair trial. Yet Samuel Adams and other radicals may have pushed him into it, convinced that the propaganda value of a guilty verdict would be greater if one of the province's best lawyers defended the soldiers. The promise of a seat in the Massachusetts legislature may have been another inducement. Whatever his motives, John Adams waged a brilliant defense. He argued that the soldiers were following orders and had the right to shoot in self-defense against a "motley rab[b]le of saucy boys, Negroes and Mulattoes, Irish teagues and outlandish jacktars." The commander and six redcoats were acquitted, while two soldiers were convicted of manslaughter and punished lightly. Remarkably, Adams emerged unscathed from the controversy. In fact, the trial enhanced his reputation as a gifted lawyer, and within months, he won a seat in the legislature. A couple of years later, John and Abigail moved into a handsome brick home in Boston. Adams could have easily concluded that he had followed a wiser course than the timid Sewall, whom he accused of "desertion."

At the same time, Sewall could believe that *he* had made the correct decision. As the hysteria surrounding the incident died down, Sewall looked optimistically to a stable future. Most Americans had no thought of revolution in 1771. Only a few radicals were thinking about independence. Like many colonists, Sewall felt secure in the assumption that the status quo would be preserved and that he would enjoy the rewards of a successful career. About this time, he moved his family into a large house on Cambridge's fashionable Brattle Street. There and at their country retreat outside Boston, the Sewalls enjoyed the perquisites of their position atop Massachusetts society: servants, an elegant coach, fine wine, and the company of others who shared their small and secure world. From that position, Sewall soon took up his pen in defense of the British government. **[See Source 2.]**

"ATLAS OF AMERICAN INDEPENDENCE"

John Adams would not have disagreed with Sewall's assessment of the future. He also had good reason to believe that the colonial crisis was over. After Parliament repealed all but one of the Townshend duties—the tax on tea—in 1770, colonial protests had died down. Resigning his seat in the Massachusetts legislature after one term, Adams declared that he had served his country "at an immense Expense ... of Time, Peace, Health, Money, and Preferment." He was determined to avoid "Politicks, Political Clubs, Town Meetings, [or] General Court," confessing that his "Heart" was "at Home." In fact, Adams had long been reluctant to commit himself fully to the colonial cause. As late as 1772, James Otis accused him of "moaping about the Streets of this Town" and caring about little more than money. Otis's "Rant" obviously stung Adams, who protested that he had sacrificed as much to "the public Cause" as had his accuser.

Soon, however, few would doubt Adams's commitment. In 1773, Parliament required that judges' salaries be paid by the Crown rather than the colony's legislature, a move Adams believed was intended to destroy the independence of the judiciary. In addition, Thomas Hutchinson, who had replaced Bernard as governor, declared that Parliament's power over the colonies was unlimited. The legislature's reply, drafted by John and Samuel Adams, argued that colonial legislatures had sovereign power. When Parliament passed the Tea Act later in 1773, it was clear to John that the colonial crisis was not over. Many colonists saw the measure, which reduced the price of East India Company tea in the colonies, as a plot to make it easier to pay the remaining Townshend tax on it. When fifty men slipped onto the company's ships in Boston Harbor and threw overboard forty-five tons of tea, thousands cheered, including John Adams. The Boston Tea Party, he declared, was the "grandest event" since the beginning of the controversy with Britain.

Parliament quickly cracked down on Massachusetts with the Intolerable Acts. These drastic measures closed Boston's port, limited town meetings, strengthened the power of the royally appointed governor at the expense of the popularly elected legislature, and replaced Hutchinson with a military governor, General Thomas Gage. When the colonists responded to the growing crisis by calling the First Continental Congress,[*] the Massachusetts legislature selected four delegates. One of them was John Adams. Like

---

[*]*First Continental Congress:* A meeting of delegates from twelve colonies in Philadelphia held in the fall of 1774.

other Whigs (opponents of Britain's policies) and Tories (supporters of the policies), Adams and Sewall were now divided as never before. Like many colonists, Adams believed that British actions reflected more than a desire to raise revenue from the colonies. Rather, he thought, Britain's government was engaged in a plot to rob colonists of their cherished liberties. If it succeeded, they would be reduced to abject slavery. Sewall, an appointee of the royal governor, saw no such danger, and he continued to defend the British government and its right to tax the colonies. By the summer of 1774, friends could no longer set aside their political differences. When Sewall and Adams met in Falmouth, Maine, in July to conduct business before the court, the two men bade each other farewell.

After Sewall returned home from Maine, his circumstances quickly deteriorated. A mob surrounded the Sewalls' Cambridge home, smashed the windows, and threatened the family. Jonathan was in Boston at the time, and a terrified Esther finally dispersed the attackers by offering up the contents of the wine cellar. When Sewall returned to Cambridge the next day, he and his family decided to join the growing number of Tories seeking refuge in Boston. Conditions in the besieged city were abysmal. Prices skyrocketed, food was scarce, and people died daily as a result of dysentery. Sewall continued as attorney general and also served as Gage's personal secretary and adviser. Although he found time to record his ideas on the rebellion **[see Source 3],** mostly he despaired. "Everything I see is laughable, cursable, and damnable," he wrote. "My pew in church is converted into a pork tub; my house into a den of rebels, thieves, & lice; [and] my farm in possession of the very worst of all god's creations." By the summer of 1775, in the face of "musketry, bombs, great guns, … battles, sieges, murder, plague, pestilence, famine, rebellion, and the Devil," he was ready to leave. Before the end of the summer, Sewall and his family boarded a ship bound for England. He would never see Boston again.

Adams, too, was quickly caught up in the rush of events. After attending the Philadelphia convention, he returned home to a loud counteroffensive launched by Tories in provincial newspapers. He responded in twelve essays in which he laid out the nature of the threat posed by the British government. **[See Source 4.]** He finished his last essay shortly before Gage dispatched troops to Concord in April 1775 to seize the colonists' weapons. Bloodshed at Lexington and Concord was on Adams's mind as he left for the Second Continental Congress the next month, still hopeful that peace could be restored. For the next two years, Adams sat in Congress, his influence growing as he gradually impressed the other delegates with his intellect and his immense capacity for work.

By early 1776, a swift series of events made Adams realize that independence was inevitable. First, the crisis had descended into open warfare. The previous year, when Congress had expressed its hope for reconciliation with its Olive Branch Petition, King George III had rejected it outright. Then Thomas Paine's *Common Sense*, a devastating attack on monarchy, had radicalized many colonists. When the delegates named Adams to a committee to draft a declaration of independence, he declined the task, leaving the job to Thomas Jefferson instead. It was Adams, though, who took to the floor in early July to defend the move for independence. His speech was so masterful that Jefferson called him "our Colossus on the Floor." Another awed delegate commented that "the man to whom the country is most indebted for the great measure of independency is Mr. John Adams of Boston. I call him the Atlas of American Independence."

"UNGRATEFUL SONS OF BITCHES"

By July 1776, Jonathan Sewall had been in London for a year and had found much to encourage him. He was greeted by Thomas Hutchinson and other prominent Loyalists from Massachusetts who had already established a refugee colony in the British capital, and he looked for an appointment to high office. And then there was London itself. Everything in the city was on such a grand scale that Sewall was "lost and confounded." Surely, the colonies would not be able to withstand Britain's greatness.

As the war dragged on, however, his mood changed. Only a few refugees secured offices, and he was not among them. Although Sewall found Britain's wealth "truly astonishing," he discovered that his six-hundred-pound vice-admiralty court salary was now "as a Drop in the Ocean." "Everything I have seen in my own Country," he wrote, "is all Miniature, yankee puppet-show." Britain's inability to crush the rebellious colonists made matters worse. Sewall yearned for Massachusetts, and his homesickness only increased his hatred of the rebels. He longed for "one peep at my house," but the "damned, fanatical, republican, New England, rebellious, ungenerous, ungrateful sons of bitches" had confiscated and sold his property and banned him from the state. News of the stunning British defeat at Saratoga in 1777 dashed Sewall's hopes for a speedy return home, and the following spring, he left London for less expensive Bristol.

Even when Americans won their independence, Sewall consoled himself with the belief that they still faced certain ruin. "Poor Beasts," he wrote, "I pity them from my soul." In fact, Sewall himself was defeated. Suffering from debt and depression, he moved into a room detached from his family's main house, where his only company was a cat and two goldfinches. Blaming Esther for his circumstances, he told a friend that he wished she was out of his life forever. Meanwhile, his financial difficulties mounted. The Royal Commission on Losses and Services of American Loyalists, established to settle Loyalists' claims for service and loss of property in the Revolution, awarded only a portion of his six-thousand-pound claim. He was forced to move again to more economical accommodations. Complaining of headaches, stomachaches, and dizziness, he retreated to his bedroom for eighteen months. "I was mad as the Devil the whole time," he later observed. Only the desire to be reunited with his son in Canada finally drew him out of his isolation. In 1787, Jonathan, Esther, and their other son departed Britain.

They settled in St. John, New Brunswick. Shortly after their arrival, the royal treasury abolished the Halifax vice-admiralty court, depriving Sewall of his remaining official position. He was left with a pension of only two hundred pounds. "I have sacrificed to my Duty, my property in America," he protested in a letter to treasury officials. It did no good, although within a couple of years Sewall did receive a settlement from the Royal Commission on Losses, as well as another pension for his "loss of profession." By the standards of his new home, he was well off, but he never escaped the belief that he had been wronged. Sewall's bitterness found numerous targets, including the freed slaves he saw arriving in St. John after the Revolution. "I believe the Maker of all never intended Indians, Negroes or Monkeys, for Civilization," he told a friend. He never rid himself of his anger or melancholy. In the last six years of his life, he was confined to bed. Esther nursed him even as he complained that she denied him peace and solitude. He died in 1796. John Adams later concluded that the cause of death was a "broken heart."

By that time, Adams had also paid a price for his "unalterable" commitment to his country. Two years before the start of the Revolution, he had written Abigail that he longed for his Braintree farm, where his family again lived. There, he said, a "Hoe and Spade, would do for [his] Remaining Days." He could not know how long it would be before he was able to enjoy his farm and the uninterrupted pleasure of Abigail's company. In the meantime, he found life as a delegate to the Continental Congress "solitary" and "gloomy." He returned home in late 1777, but early the next year, he accepted an assignment as emissary to France. He shared quarters with Benjamin Franklin, who Adams thought got by with guile and charm rather than substance. Adams was shocked by Franklin's extravagant tastes and excessive socializing. Franklin would "come home at all hours," noted a dismayed Adams, who found his own skills lacking for a diplomatic assignment "in highly polished society." He also realized that Abigail, back home in charge of the farm and family, was growing distant. Her letters now contained "a Strain of Unhappiness and Complaint."

Nonetheless, after Adams returned home from Paris in 1779, he soon departed again, this time as a delegate to the state constitutional convention. There, he drafted the document that became the Massachusetts Constitution. Later that fall, Congress appointed him to negotiate an end to the war with Britain. He headed back to Paris with sons John Quincy and Charles. Not long after his arrival, he traveled to Amsterdam, where he spent nearly two years working to secure from the Dutch desperately needed financial support for the American cause. Then he was back in Paris to help negotiate the treaty ending the Revolution. Not until 1784 were John and Abigail reunited in London. For the next three years, he served as American minister to Britain, with Abigail at his side.

When they returned to Massachusetts in 1788, John and Abigail bought a new home in Quincy, near the Adams homestead. They had just gotten settled when he was elected the first vice president of the United States. In 1797, he succeeded George Washington as president. Finally, in 1801, he returned permanently to his farm and family.

As a young man, Adams had feared that he would die in obscurity. Before he died on July 4, 1826—fifty years after the signing of the Declaration of Independence and within hours of Thomas Jefferson's death—he knew that his early fears would not be realized. Yet he was also convinced that Americans would never place him in the same category as Washington, Franklin, or even Jefferson. "I am not, never was, & never shall be a great man," he declared. Still, his long public service, often at tremendous personal sacrifice, had done much to launch the new nation.

"AS ARDENT AN AMERICAN ... AS I"

When the Revolution divided Whigs and Tories, both sides were quick to assign petty motives to the other. Although John Adams asserted that his old friend Jonathan Sewall was "as ardent an American … as I ever had been," Adams saw in Sewall a personal flaw. He believed that when James Otis had not supported Sewall's petition in the legislature regarding his deceased uncle's estate "with as much zeal as he wished," Sewall became bitter and resentful. "Hutchinson, Trowbridge, and Bernard soon perceived his ill humor, and immediately held out to him prospects of honor, promotion, and wealth," Adams concluded.

Sewall was unquestionably interested in "honor, promotion, and wealth," but Adams's explanation for his friend's loyalism was unfair. Sewall was not manipulated by powerful royal officials such as Bernard and Hutchinson. Rather, his sympathies sprang from a long pattern of experience. Sewall's life was a testament to the importance of paternalistic relationships. Older, well-connected patrons repeatedly took an interest in his education and career and helped him achieve a measure of wealth. He learned that status and comfort were to be found in loyalty to men who served established institutions. His desire to establish his rightful place through attachment to men in power led Sewall to value authority, deference, and order. Whig fears about the destruction of liberty at the hands of powerful and corrupt rulers never gripped him. Rather, he embraced an ideology that emphasized the fragility of established institutions and the inherent dangers of disobedience and disorder.

Adams was just as interested as Sewall in "honor, promotion, and wealth" and just as concerned about the effect of his political commitments on his career. In addition, he shared Sewall's concerns about social order and the rule of law. Forced to "dig Treasures with [his] own fingers," however, Adams never hitched personal ambition to powerful men who served imperial interests. On the contrary, as the crisis with Britain deepened, service to the colonial cause became Adams's means to achieve recognition and honor. Even so, his patriotism sprang from more than his own ambition. He had grown up in a town of freeholders—independent and upright, if not rich. Government was conducted with their consent. Moreover, in his society, someone like himself could rise above his inherited station through hard work. Finally, as his Puritan forebears could have told him, America was to be a place of virtuous inhabitants ever vigilant against the enervating effects of luxury, corruption, and self-indulgence. As naturally as Sewall embraced royal administrators and loyalism, Adams accepted the Whig argument that Americans' liberties and very way of life were threatened by the policies of a tyrannical government in a corrupt mother country. Although these two sons of Massachusetts had much in common, their personal histories were different, and thus only one would risk his position to oppose the "conduct of Britain toward America."

• PRIMARY SOURCES •

Source 1: "Instructions of the Town of Braintree to the Representative" (1765)

During the Stamp Act crisis in 1765, the town of Braintree turned to John Adams to draft instructions to its representative in the Massachusetts legislature. In this document, what does Adams see as the important issues raised by the British government's actions? What does this document's tone reveal about the fears raised by those actions?

To EBENEZER THAYER, Esq.
SIR,
"In all the Calamities which have ever befallen this Country, we have never felt so great a Concern, or such alarming Apprehensions, as on this Occasion.—Such is our Loyalty to the King, our Veneration for both Houses of Parliament, and our Affection for all our Fellow subjects in Britain, that Measures, which discover any Unkindness in that

SOURCE: From THE ADAMS PAPERS: PAPERS OF JOHN ADAMS, VOLUME I, edited by Robert J. Taylor, Mary-Jo Kline, and Gregg L. Lint, pp. 132–134, Cambridge, Mass.: The Belknap Press of Harvard University Press.

Country towards Us, are the more sensibly and intimately felt. And we can no longer forbear complaining, that many of the Measures of the late Ministry, and some of the late Acts of Parliament, have a Tendency, in our Apprehension, to divest us of our most essential Rights and Liberties.—We shall confine ourselves, however, chiefly to the Act of Parliament, commonly called the Stamp-Act, by which a very burthensome, and in our Opinion, unconstitutional Tax, is to be laid upon us all....

We have called this a burthensome Tax, because the Duties are so numerous and so high, and the Embarrassments to Business in this infant, sparsely-settled Country, so great, that it would be totally impossible for the people to subsist under it, if we had no Controversy at all about the Right and Authority of imposing it. Considering the present Scarcity of Money, we have Reason to think, the Execution of that Act for a short Space of Time would drein the Country of its Cash, strip Multitudes of all their Property, and reduce them to absolute Beggary. And what the Consequence would be to the peace of the Province, from so sudden a Shock and such a convulsive Change, in the whole Course of our Business and Subsistence, we tremble to consider.—We further apprehend this Tax to be unconstitutional: We have always understood it to be a grand and fundamental Principle of the Constitution, that no Freeman should be subjected to any Tax, to which he has not given his own Consent, in Person or by Proxy. And the Maxims of the Law as we have constantly received them, are to the same Effect, that no Freeman can be separated from his Property, but by his own Act or Fault. We take it clearly, therefore, to be inconsistent with the Spirit of the Common Law, and of the essential fundamental Principles of the British Constitution, that we should be subjected to any Tax, imposed by the British Parliament: because we are not represented in that Assembly in any Sense, unless it be by a Fiction of Law, as insensible in Theory as it would be injurious in Practice, if such a Taxation should be grounded on it.

But the most grievous Innovation of all, is the alarming Extension of the Power of Courts of Admiralty. In these Courts, one Judge presides alone! No Juries have any Concern there!—The Law, and the Fact, are both to be decided by the same single Judge, whose Commission is only during Pleasure, and with whom, as we are told, the most mischievous of all Customs has become established, that of taking Commissions on all Condemnations; so that he is under a pecuniary Temptation always against the Subject....

Source 2:   *Jonathan Sewall Offers a Defense of British Authority* (1771)

Sewall defended the British government in a series of newspaper essays published after the Boston Massacre verdict. On what important premises does he base his argument? What does he see as the real danger of recent events?

Man is a social Animal—a Being whose wants, whose natural powers of Reason and whole capacity of improving those powers continually demonstrate to him that he was made for a social life.... Reason and experience soon convince him that the advantages of society cannot be enjoyed without the establishment of certain rules, to which he and all of the

SOURCE: "Jonathan Sewall Offers a Defense of British Authority (1771)" from the BOSTON EVENING POST, January 14, 1771.

community must conform[.] [T]hese rules, so long as he takes Reason for his guide, he will always hold sacred, notwithstanding they abridge him of a part of ... unlimited freedom of action.... [B]ecause he sees the necessity of them, in order to his obtaining and enjoying the more valuable blessings and benefits of society[,] he no longer considers himself as an individual, absolutely unaccountable and uncontrol[l]able, but as one of a community, every member of which is bound to consult and promote the general good.... [H]e sees that ... the publick good and his own are so intimately connected and interwoven together that whatever is inconsistent with the former is equally incompatible with the latter; and therefore, from the most for ceable principle in human nature, will be, at all times, a true Patriot[.] [H]ence 'the publick peace and happiness will be the principal object of his care and attention.... [H]e will hold his right of private judgment as subordinate to that of the public, and of those in whom the society have placed the right of judging; and of consequence he will be very cautious in charging with want of ability or integrity those to whom any of the powers of government are intrusted[.] [H]e will honor the King as supreme, and will upon no pretence, however plausible, presume to revile or speak evil of the Rulers of the people[.] [I]f it happens that from the enacting unpopular laws or from any untoward accident the minds of the multitude are disturbed and inflamed, he will consider their passions as a flood which knows no bounds when once the dikes are broken, and will carefully avoid every thing which may encourage them in breaking thro' that essential subordination upon which the well being and happiness of the whole absolutely depends.... [I]f he should judge that a wrong step has been taken in one department of government, he will by no means take occasion from thence to persuade himself or others that ... all in authority are traiterously combined in plotting the slavery, misery and ruin of the society[.] [H]e will consider human fallibility and integrity of intention as being perfectly consistent and will therefore be disposed to conclude either that he himself is mistaken in his judgment, or that those whose conduct he disapproves will see their error and reform the grievance[.] [H]e will not weaken the pillars of the state by arraigning, accusing and condemning those in the important stations, whose inflexible virtue has been proved and confirmed by long experience....

Slavery I detest, and would be foremost in execrating the sordid unnatural wretch, who, for a kingdom, could stoop to enslave the lowest peasant, in the meanest village of his country—but wide, infinitely wide is the difference between social liberty, and savage licentiousness.... [L]et us consider where is the danger of slavery[.] [T]hro' the favor of an indulgent providence, we have a good King, whom God Almighty bless & long preserve, who is, and who glories in being, the father of a free people[.] [W]e are his children and while George the third sits on the British throne, I never can be made to believe his American subjects can be slaves, unless by their own madness and folly they enslave themselves[.]

Source 3:   *Jonathan Sewall on the Revolutionary Threat (1775)*

Shortly before Sewall departed for Britain, he analyzed the nature of the patriots' challenge to British authority. What threats to society does he see in their actions? What is his view of his fellow Americans? What is his solution to the crisis?

SOURCE: Reprinted in Jack P. Greene, *Colonies to Nation: 1763–1789* (New York: McGraw-Hill Book Company, 1967), pp. 266–267; originally from Dartmouth Papers, William Salt Library, Stafford, England.

It is now become too plain to be any longer doubted, that a Union is formed by a great Majority, almost throughout this whole Continent, for opposing the Supremacy, and even the lowest Degree of legislative Jurisdiction, of the British Parliament, over the British Colonies—that an absolute unlimited Independence, is the Object in View—and that, to obtain this End preparations for War are made, and making, with a Vigor, which the most imminent Dangers from a foreign Enemy, could never inspire. It should seem astonishing, that a Country of Husbandmen, possessed every one, almost, of a sufficient Share of landed property, in one of the finest Climates in the World; living under the mildest Government, enjoying the highest portion of civil and religious Liberty that the Nature of human Society admits, and protected in the Enjoyment of these, and every other desirable Blessing in Life, upon the easiest Terms, by the only Power on Earth capable of affording that protection—that a people so scituated for Happiness, should throw off their rural Simplicity, quit the peaceful Sweets and Labours of Husbandry, bid open Defiance to the gentle Intreaties and the angry Threats of that powerful parent State which nursed their tender Years, and rush to Arms with the Ferocity of Savages, and with the fiery Zeal of Crusaders!—and all this, for the Redress of Chimerical Grievances—to oppose a claim of Parliament, made explicitly, exercised uniformly over, and quietly acquiesced in by, the Colonies from their earliest Origin! It is, I say, so truly astonishing ... that we must search deeper for the grand and more hidden Spring.... [B]y the help of the single Word, *Liberty*, they conjured up the most horrid Phantoms in the Minds of the common people, ever, an easy prey to such specious Betrayers—the Merchants, from a Desire of a free and unrestrained Trade, the sure and easy Means of arriving at a Superiority in Wealth, joined in Bubbling the undiscerning Multitude—the Clergy ... opined, as Leaders of the pack, upon those never failing Topics of Tyranny and Popery—the simple unmeaning Mechanics, peasants and Labourers, who had really no Interest in the Matters of Controversy, hoodwinked, inflamed and goaded on by their Spiritual Drivers, fancied they saw civil and religious Tyranny advancing with hasty Strides....

It is in vain to think any longer of drawing them—to such a pitch is the Frenzy now raised, that the Colonists will never yield Obedience to the Laws of the parent State, till, by Experience, they are taught to fear her power. Such is the Infatuation, that, like madmen, they are totally incapable of attending to the Dictates of reason, and will remain so till the passion of Fear is awakened; this will never be effected by Threats, or by the Appearance of a Force with which they imagine themselves able to contend.... I am so well convinced that my Countrymen, at least a Majority of them, act under the power of mere Delusion, rather than from positive vicious Intentions, that I most ardently wish to see them brought back to a Sense of their Duty, with as little Havock and Bloodshed as may be; to this End, I wish to see Great Britain rise with a power that shall strike Terror through the Continent, and leave it no longer problematical whether she is in earnest or not.

Source 4:   John Adams, *"Novanglus"* (1775)

Writing as "Novanglus" (New England), John Adams responded to the Tory newspaper offensive in 1775. What does he see as the threat posed by Britain? What is his position on independence?

SOURCE: Reprinted in Robert J. Taylor, ed., *The Adams Papers: Papers of John Adams* (Cambridge: Harvard University Press, 1977), Volume 2, pp. 264–265, 307, 336; originally from *Boston Gazette*, February 13, 1775; March 6, 1775; March 13, 1775.

"The whigs were sensible that there was no oppression that could be seen or felt." The tories have so often said and wrote this to one another, that I sometimes suspect they believe it to be true. But it is quite otherwise. The castle of the province was taken out of their hands and garrisoned by regular soldiers; this they could see, and they thought it indicated an hostile intention and disposition towards them. They continually paid their money to collectors of duties, this they could both see and feel. An host of placemen, whose whole business it was to collect a revenue, were continually rolling before them in their chariots. These they saw. Their governor was no longer paid by themselves according to their charter, but out of the new revenue, in order to render their assemblies useless and indeed contemptible. The judges salaries were threat[e]ned every day to be paid in the same unconstitutional manner. The dullest eye-sight could not but see to what all this tended, viz. to prepare the way for greater innovations and oppressions. They knew a minister would never spend his money in this way, if he had not some end to answer by it. Another thing they both saw and felt. Every man, of every character, who by voting, writing, speaking, or otherwise, had favoured the stamp act, the tea act, and every other measure of a minister or governor, who they knew was aiming at the destruction of their form of government, and introducing parliamentary taxation, was uniformly, in some department or other, promoted to some place of honour and profit for ten years together; and on the other hand, every man who favoured the people in their opposition to those innovations, was depressed, degraded and persecuted as far as it was in the power of the government to do it.

This they considered as a systematical means of encouraging every man of abilities to espouse the cause of parliamentary taxation, and the plan of destroying their charter privileges, and to discourage all from exerting themselves, in opposition to them. This they thought a plan to enslave them, for they uniformly think that the destruction of their charter, making the council and judges wholly dependent on the crown, and the people subject to the unlimited power of parliament as their supreme legislative, is slavery. They were certainly rightly told then that the ministry and their governors together had formed a design to enslave them, and that when once this was done, they had the highest reason to expect window taxes, hearth taxes, land taxes and all others. And that these were only paving the way for reducing the country to lordships....

America has all along consented, still consents, and ever will consent, that parliament being the most powerful legislature in the dominions, should regulate the trade of the dominions. This is founding the authority of parliament to regulate our trade, upon *compact* and *consent* of the colonies, not upon any principle of common or statute law, not upon any original principle of the English constitution, not upon the principle that parliament is the supream and sovereign legislature over them in all cases whatsoever...

That there are any who pant after "independence," (meaning by this word a new plan of government over all America, unconnected with the crown of England, or meaning by it an exemption from the power of parliament to regulate trade) is as great a slander upon the province as ever was committed to writing. The patriots of this province desire nothing new—they wish only to keep their old privileges. They were for 150 years allowed to tax themselves, and govern their internal concerns, as they tho't best. Parliament governed their trade as they tho't fit. This plan, they wish may continue forever. But it is honestly confessed, rather than become subject to the absolute authority of parliament, in all cases of taxation and internal polity, they will be driven to throw off that of regulating trade.

QUESTIONS TO CONSIDER

1. How would you compare Jonathan Sewall's defense of British policies and John Adams's argument against them? What threats did Sewall see in the colonial challenge to British authority? What threats did Adams see in that authority? What did each see as the cause of the crisis?

2. One historian has written that Loyalists reveal "the interrelationship of public and private experience" and that the key to understanding their commitment during the American Revolution may be found in their childhood experiences. How do Sewall and Adams, friends whose lives often overlapped, reveal a link between "public and private experience" in the revolutionary crisis? Do you think the key to understanding their loyalties is to be found in their early lives or elsewhere? What do their lives reveal about the Revolution's divisive impact on Americans?

3. Sewall's biographer concluded that he was "a man at odds with his times." Considering Sewall's and Adams's political and social views, do you agree? How were Adams's ideas in step with the times?

4. One exiled Loyalist complained about the "shameless partiality" of late-eighteenth-century historians of the Revolution toward the patriots. From your understanding of Sewall, Adams, and the colonial crisis, what defense can you offer for loyalism?

5. How do Sewall and Adams use images and wording to bolster their arguments? Cite examples in which you think the wording is intended to stir emotions.

FOR FURTHER READING

Thomas B. Allen, *Tories: Fighting for the King in America's First Civil War* (New York: Harper, 2010), sheds light on the variety of Americans who took up arms in support of the crown and the War for Independence as a civil war.

Bernard Bailyn, *Faces of Revolution: Personalities and Themes in the Struggle for American Independence* (New York: Vintage Books, 1992), examines the central themes of the Revolution and the personalities and ideas of Loyalists and Whigs.

Carol Berkin, *Jonathan Sewall: Odyssey of an American Loyalist* (New York: Columbia University Press, 1974), offers the only full-length biography of Sewall.

Joseph J. Ellis, *Passionate Sage: The Character and Legacy of John Adams* (New York: W. W. Norton & Company, 1993), provides a study of Adams in his later years, but the book offers great insight into the way his ideas shaped his actions throughout his life.

David McCullough, *John Adams* (New York: Simon & Schuster, 2001), offers an engaging account of Adams's public and private lives.

William H. Nelson, *The American Tory* (London: Oxford University Press, 1961), provides perhaps the best brief introduction to the Loyalists and their ideas.

5

The Conflict over the Constitution: Patrick Henry and James Madison

In the summer of 1788, Patrick Henry was desperate. Just the previous year, the Federalist enemies of liberty had proposed a new Constitution to replace the Articles of Confederation. Henry was sure that the Federalists' plan for a new central government would concentrate enormous power in the hands of the few. In fact, it would establish the very kind of government that Americans had rebelled against during the Revolution. Under the Constitution, an elite would promote its own interests and rob ordinary citizens of their freedoms. If approved, it would surely bring tyranny once again. Yet Henry also realized that the Federalists were vulnerable. To go into effect, the Constitution had to be ratified by nine states in special conventions. Right here in Virginia, the Constitution could be stopped. After all, Virginia was the most populous state in the nation. If the Federalists did not win here, they stood little chance of success. Buoyed by the thought, Henry rose to speak at the ratifying convention. With unmatched eloquence, he tore into the Constitution, raised the specter of government run roughshod over the people, and reminded the delegates of the Revolution so recently won.

Across the room sat an angry and frustrated James Madison. The principal architect of the Constitution, Madison was just as convinced that a far more powerful central government was necessary for the country to survive. He had heard enough of Henry's demagoguery, however, to think that the situation was hopeless. Henry had roused the convention with his eloquence and presented a formidable attack on the Constitution. He had to be countered. But to whom could the Federalists turn? None of them could hope to match Henry's rhetorical skill. Moreover, the opposition to the Constitution might well have the majority of the convention. Madison had listened long enough as

Patrick Henry

James Madison

Federalists argued back and forth about what to do. The time had come, he decided, for him to lead the fight.

Madison was an unlikely champion for the Federalist cause. To be sure, he was brilliant and possessed a fine education and breadth of knowledge. Perhaps no one in the nation had thought more deeply about government than Madison. Yet he was so shy and timid that most of his public speeches ended in disaster. Usually, no one in the audience could even hear what he said. Only slightly over five feet tall, he was referred to by some as "Little Jemmy Madison." And although he was a member of the Virginia gentry who disdained the common people, he was plagued with doubts about his own abilities. In fact, he often preferred the company of books to people. As one disappointed belle concluded, he was "the most unsociable creature in existence."

Nonetheless, Madison would lead the Federalist counterattack at the Virginia Ratifying Convention. In the debates that raged through the summer of 1788, he and Henry squared off again and again. While Henry moved the convention with his eloquence, Madison responded with calm logic. Quietly, he disputed his opponent's arguments as the audience strained to hear his voice. Hanging in the balance was the fate of the Constitution and the future of the nation.

"I SPEAK THE LANGUAGE OF THOUSANDS"

Patrick Henry was almost a failure. Throughout his early adult years, he tried to find a career, but each attempt fell short. His father was a planter, a member of the "back country gentry," which traced its roots to England's lesser nobility. In the 1600s, this group had established its dominance over the colony. The planters made fortunes growing tobacco and built vast plantations that sometimes stretched for miles along Virginia's rivers.

Those who lived in the more settled eastern low country, or tidewater, became the elite of the colony. In succeeding generations, some of their offspring moved west and continued to assert their social dominance. John Henry, Patrick's father, had migrated to Virginia from his native Scotland in 1727. He married a wealthy widow and through her attached himself to the gentry. "Marrying up" was one route to wealth and status, and widows of good fortune were much sought after. With his marriage, John Henry gained the status of gentleman.

Patrick, born in 1736, and his older brother, William, grew up in comfortable circumstances. Patrick received little more than a common-school education, instead spending much of his time roaming the woods with an uncle, who taught him how to hunt and survive in the wilderness. Unlike the sons of many tidewater aristocrats, he was neither polished nor well read. His eloquent oratory was honed by listening to another uncle, a Presbyterian minister, preach on Sundays. Young Patrick would memorize the sermon and then recite it from memory, complete with appropriate gestures, during the carriage ride home.

John Henry proved to be a poor businessman and planter, and his wife's fortune was tied to her family. John hoped to secure his sons' future by setting them up as shopkeepers. When Patrick was fifteen, his father gave him and William money to invest in a supply of goods and establish a general store. The boys had inherited their father's poor business sense, however, and the store failed. Patrick's fortune seemed to take a turn for the better when he married Sarah Shelton in 1754 and received her dowry, which consisted of a three-hundred-acre farm and six slaves. But he proved to be as poor a planter as he was a storekeeper. His tobacco crop was destroyed by worms, drought, and an early frost. His father-in-law then offered him the opportunity to operate a tavern at Hanover Court House. For the next several years, he eked out a living as a tavern keeper, but it was barely enough to keep the family fed.

Henry then decided to study law. After passing the bar, he served as a circuit-riding lawyer for several years. He earned his reputation in a case involving religious freedom. Under the practice of established religion, the government of Virginia was supported by the Anglican Church[*] and the church by the civil authorities. The question in this case was whether a clergyman had to be paid by the local officials. Henry's eloquence carried the day, and the jury decided against payment. From that day forward, Henry was associated with the cause of religious liberty.

During the decade leading up to the Revolution, few colonists were more radical or outspoken for the American cause than Henry. His oratory during the Stamp Act crisis of 1765 electrified the colonies. His "Give Me Liberty or Give Me Death" speech in 1775 helped unite and mobilize Britain's opponents. During the Revolution, he served as governor of Virginia, compiling a mediocre record. When he left office, he returned to his law practice, but he remained an important political figure—a man who could be counted on to have an opinion on nearly every issue. Even before the end of the war, he was elected to the Virginia legislature.

Late in the Revolution, Henry moved his family to a newly settled area of Virginia near the North Carolina border. He established a ten-thousand-acre plantation, Leatherwood, and eventually acquired seventy-five slaves to work the land. Despite his newfound wealth, Henry was not a full-fledged member of Virginia's planter aristocracy, and he did not share its social and political outlook. Removed from the tidewater, he

---

[*]*Anglican Church:* Also known as the Church of England, it was the official, or established, church in England and in several of the colonies, including Virginia.

was surrounded by yeomen farmers with whom he could easily identify. He did not believe in a natural order that made some superior and others inferior. His own roots were too humble for that.

Ironically, Henry claimed to be a "democrat" and self-appointed watchdog of the people's rights, even though he held many slaves. In his world, only property-holding white males could vote and participate in politics, and his fears regarding tyranny extended only to these citizens, not black slaves. He believed that unchecked government power was a great threat to ordinary people, whose rights as property holders and freemen were always in jeopardy. The recent colonial past had taught Henry and many other Americans about the dangers of a powerful central government too far removed from the people. In fact, those concerns were reflected in the central government Americans created during the Revolution. The one-house Congress under the Articles of Confederation had no power to tax, regulate domestic or foreign commerce, or compel citizens to obey its laws. The states, not the central government, were clearly sovereign.

After the Revolution, however, the serious problems facing the nation left some Americans wondering whether the central government had too little power. Many of those problems were economic. Before the war, the colonists had been dependent on manufactured goods imported from Britain. During the war, British imports had been cut off, and Americans had done without. In fact, wearing homespun was a patriotic act. After the war, Americans rushed to import long-denied goods, often on credit. What little gold and other hard money they possessed quickly slipped out of their hands and into the pockets of British merchants. Yet there was little the government could do to stem the flow. When Congress attempted to pass a 5 percent tax on imports, it was voted down.

Unable to tax, the central government attempted to pay for the Revolutionary War effort by borrowing and issuing paper money. It printed so much paper currency and Americans had so little faith in the government, however, that the money had little value. Many Americans refused to accept it as payment. The states only added to the problem by issuing their own currency. Meanwhile, Americans' postwar spending spree created another problem. Drowning in a sea of worthless currency, they quickly found themselves without any money of real value to buy goods. Before long, the country slid into a severe and prolonged depression.

Hard times in turn raised the threat of class conflict. Once again, debt was the catalyst. State governments had borrowed money to finance the Revolution. With little money to pay their debts, they were often forced to raise taxes. At the same time, poor farmers often owed money to rich creditors. With little money to pay *their* debts, small farmers now faced the prospect of higher taxes and the foreclosure of their farms. Many were literally up in arms. In 1786 and 1787, no less than six states experienced rebellions against legal authority.

The most shocking was Shays's Rebellion in Massachusetts. Captain Daniel Shays served with distinction in the Revolutionary War but returned home to his farm in western Massachusetts without receiving the land or money promised him for his service. During the economic crisis following the Revolution, the Massachusetts legislature took steps to support the merchants and bankers. They owed money to England but were creditors within the state. To help bail out these wealthy men, the legislature raised taxes but provided no relief for the poor artisans and farmers in debt to the merchants. Underrepresented in the legislature, farmers in the western areas of the state began to protest. Shays stepped up to lead them. They tarred and feathered tax collectors, shouted "no taxation without representation," and stockpiled arms and ammunition. Finally, in early 1787, the governor sent out the state militia to crush the rebellion.

To many Americans, Shays's Rebellion demonstrated the central government's weakness. The government was not even able to ensure domestic tranquillity. In the words of George Washington, the country seemed to be moving toward "anarchy and confusion." There were other problems, too. After the Revolution, Britain had maintained a string of forts from upstate New York through the Great Lakes region. Americans knew that these forts were on their soil, but their weak central government could do nothing about them. Meanwhile, Spain closed the Mississippi River to Americans, preventing farmers on the western side of the Appalachians from shipping their products to market. As if that were not enough, the Spaniards signed an agreement with the Creek Indians in the Southeast to supply the Indians with guns and powder.

Henry was well aware of these problems, but he believed that they were solvable under the existing government. In fact, he had quietly supported Shays's Rebellion and the other uprisings. He knew that the small backcountry farmers often involved in these disturbances were underrepresented in their state legislatures. He also knew firsthand the crisis that farmers faced as markets dried up and agricultural prices slumped. Their only hope, he believed, was debt relief. That, not the use of armed force against them, would solve the problem. Likewise, Henry was worried about securing the country's western boundaries. He saw the frontier as a land of opportunity for common people. In an agricultural society, ownership of land was the primary form of property holding. It was the principal means by which individuals attained economic independence—and the right as property holders to participate in the political life of their society. Land was the key to creating independent republican citizens. These were the people for whom Henry spoke when he said, "I speak the language of thousands."

"TO CONTROL THE GOVERNED"

James Madison assumed that he spoke for everyone. By the time of the Revolution, his father and uncle had accumulated more than ten thousand acres of land and owned more than one hundred slaves. Already wealthy when James was born in 1751, they continued to add more land and more slaves to their holdings. From his early childhood, James was taught that he was to be master of his universe, to have control over himself, his family, and his neighbors. It was his birthright.

Naturally, he had a first-rate education, attending the College of New Jersey. An excellent student, he quickly mastered philosophy, science, languages, and history. He studied Greek and Roman politics and political philosophy and learned about the short histories of the ancient republics. Returning to Virginia after graduation, he began to study law, although he was unsure what he wanted to do with his life. He was still pondering his future when the American Revolution began, presenting him with the prospect of a career in politics.

Excited by the tumultuous events of the Revolution, Madison ran for office and won election to the Virginia legislature in 1776. He allied himself with Patrick Henry, a distant relative, on the issue of religious toleration, defeating those who wanted to continue an established church. Nonetheless, Madison lost his bid for reelection in 1777. His opponent was a man named Charles Porter, a tavern keeper. Madison refused to campaign in the acceptable manner—stumping and treating voters to whiskey during the campaign. He deplored this practice, and his shyness made him reluctant to engage in debates or public speaking. Instead, he hoped to win on his merits. After all, the people had a clear choice: Madison, the born statesman, or Porter, a rude tavern keeper. So he stayed home. On Election Day, Madison was appalled to learn that he had lost.

From that day forward, Madison began to doubt the ability of the people to govern themselves. He was committed to a republican form of government—that is, one in which the people govern through elected representatives. Yet he worried that too much democracy was dangerous. He had read John Locke, the English political philosopher who argued that government was a social contract. Madison accepted Locke's view that in society, people agreed to limit their rights and freedoms for security. Yet he disagreed with Locke's belief that human beings were basically good. Instead, he sympathized with Thomas Hobbes's view of human nature. In his classic *Leviathan* (1651), the English social philosopher defended absolute monarchy and argued that humans would be overcome by their grasping self-interest if left to themselves. Madison did not agree with Hobbes's preference for monarchy, however. Instead, he preferred a republic with the power divided among and shared by different governing bodies. This made the concentration and abuse of power more difficult. A republic, though, was not a democracy. Certain rights and powers, Madison believed, should not be subject to majority rule. A republic was the best form of government because it allowed the citizens to express their concerns through representatives and set up checks and balances against the accumulation of power. Furthermore, Madison agreed with David Hume, the eighteenth-century Scottish philosopher who believed that people were naturally governed by their passions. Far from being rational beings, the masses were a mob of unthinking creatures. In a democracy, passions ruled because the mob voted emotionally and without regard to the long-term welfare of the nation. In a republic, government helped people control their passions to achieve the good of the country.

With these lessons driven home by his election defeat, Madison returned to his family's plantation and took up the duties of a planter. Unlucky in love, he did not take a wife until 1794, when he married a wealthy young widow named Dolley Payne Todd. Until then, politics was his mistress. He returned to the assembly in 1778 and two years later was elected to the Continental Congress, where he emerged as a national leader. Other representatives recognized the power of the young Virginian's mind and turned to him for advice on matters ranging from diplomacy to finance. He also strengthened his relationship with Thomas Jefferson, a fellow Virginian, with whom he had already forged a friendship.

While in Congress, Madison concluded that the Articles of Confederation were fatally flawed. This was especially true during the dark days of the war. He feared that the new national government, unable even to raise adequate supplies, was not up to the task of winning the war. His fears were heightened after the Revolution, especially as the country slipped into a depression and many Americans clamored for debt relief. Although Madison himself was not a major creditor, he believed that debts had to be repaid in order to strengthen the economy. Hard work and money saved were the bases of a sound financial future. Loans received with real money should not be paid back with worthless currency. Madison thus insisted that the money system had to be based on specie—gold or silver money. This stance placed him in opposition to the poor and indebted, and he was naturally opposed to the poor farmers who joined in such armed uprisings as Shays's Rebellion. He always claimed, however, that he was not insensitive to the poor. He simply wanted a sound currency to prevent economic chaos, stabilize the economy, and promote domestic and foreign trade.

Like Patrick Henry, Madison was concerned about securing the country's western boundaries. Unlike Henry, he believed that only a stronger government could protect the territory of the United States. Negotiations with Great Britain, Spain, and France were critical to keep the frontier open. If the national government lacked the military power to back up its will, those foreign powers might simply take what they wanted.

A strong government would not only secure what already belonged to the nation but also add new territory to it.

Others, such as the young nationalist Alexander Hamilton from New York, felt the same way. In 1786, they had already moved to reform the Articles of Confederation with a meeting at Annapolis, Maryland. Delegates from only six states showed up, and Hamilton had insisted that another meeting take place. The next year, fifty-five men from twelve states arrived in Philadelphia to revise the Articles. The existing Congress had given its blessing to the meeting. The Federalists dominated the gathering, and early on, they voted to scrap the Articles and start over. When they did, Madison was ready. Through fellow Virginian Edmund Randolph, he presented his Virginia Plan to the convention, which quickly adopted it as the basis for debate. Working behind locked doors throughout the sweltering summer, the delegates debated and revised Madison's plan. When they were finished, it remained the foundation of the new Constitution.

The Constitution created a central government with vast powers, including the power to tax, regulate domestic and foreign commerce, and compel citizens to obey its laws. Yet as it increased power, it also divided the power among three branches of government and devised a system of checks and balances to prevent one branch from tyrannizing the others. And although the people would be directly represented in the House of Representatives, those sitting in every other part of the new government—the Senate, the presidency, and the Supreme Court—would be chosen only indirectly by more qualified people sitting in state legislatures, the Electoral College, or the new federal government itself. Madison noted, "You must enable the government to control the governed; and in the next place oblige it to control itself." His plan, he believed, had done that by removing the people from too much direct say in the government, separating the government's powers, and establishing checks and balances. Madison was confident that the new framework would alleviate the country's problems while preserving the republic.

"OVERPOWERED IN A GOOD CAUSE"

Submitted to the states in the fall of 1787, the Constitution sparked a fierce debate as voters elected delegates to state ratifying conventions. The Antifederalists (as those who opposed the Constitution came to be called) attacked the document immediately. They were no radical fringe. Indeed, their fears about government were widely shared. The loyalty of most Americans was to their states, not the new nation. Most, too, were farmers, rooted in a particular place and fearful of concentrated power too far removed from them. As they examined the Constitution, the Antifederalists feared that a national government would replace a confederation of sovereign states. They also believed that it did not adequately protect the people's rights. **[See Source 1.]**

In response, the Federalists fired back. Many of their arguments were contained in newspaper essays, collectively known as *The Federalist Papers,* written by James Madison, Alexander Hamilton, and John Jay. Perhaps Madison's most important essay was "The Federalist No. 10," in which he countered the Antifederalists' fear that a large republic would inevitably place power in the hands of better-represented factions and thus lead to oppression by a minority. In fact, he turned this argument on its head. Rather than deny that factions would exist in the national government, Madison argued that the very size and diversity of the country would prevent the influence of special interests over the government. Moreover, fewer representatives speaking for more people would actually "refine and enlarge the public views." **[See Source 2.]**

For Patrick Henry, such arguments were proof that the new Constitution was dangerous. It was the work of a small group of men who wanted to gain power for themselves at the expense of the people. The Federalists, he argued, were the rich and the elite. They wanted to keep the people down and ensure that their own power and wealth were protected and extended. Only a few men had attended the convention, and most of them were wealthy and powerful members of society. Leaving the comforts of Leatherwood, he returned to the Virginia legislature and, in 1788, took his place as a delegate to the Virginia Ratifying Convention that June. By then, eight states had already voted to ratify, and Henry was alarmed. He was sure that the Federalists' desire for order and strong government threatened the liberties only recently won in the Revolution. Thus, from the opening moments, he went on the attack. Reading the Preamble to the Constitution, Henry found the opening phrase objectionable. "What right had they to say, *We, the People?*" he asked. "My political curiosity ... leads me to ask: Who authorized them to speak the language of, *We, the People,* instead of, *We, the states?*" He argued that the "states are the ... soul of a confederation." **[See Source 3.]**

Here were two of his major arguments against the Constitution. First, the Philadelphia convention had overstepped its bounds by doing more than revising the Articles. Second, the republic was a confederacy of sovereign states. The Constitution established what he called a "consolidated government"—a centralized, national government that had all the power. This would jeopardize state sovereignty and, along with it, the rights and liberty of the people. When the planter-aristocrat George Mason argued that he could not support the new Constitution because it did not contain a Bill of Rights specifically protecting the liberties of the people, Henry became even more convinced that the Constitution would lead to tyranny. He attacked the Constitution on other points as well. He opposed the power to levy taxes and feared a standing army. He argued that the power of Congress would eventually destroy the right of suffrage to the point that elections would not really matter. And he objected that "there is no true responsibility," since the Congress would not make laws to govern itself. Those in power would not have to obey the laws they forced the people to obey. **[See Source 4.]**

Each time the Antifederalists attacked the Constitution, the Federalists looked to Madison to lead the defense. Each time he followed his set plan of action: He rose very calmly, took his notes from his hat, and responded point by point. Despite his anger and frustration, he did not interrupt Henry and the other Antifederalists during their long orations. Instead, he sat and took careful notes. When he rose to respond, he did so with quiet grace. Doing so, he hoped, would defuse Henry's oratory and restore a sense of civility, rationality, and levelheaded discourse to the convention.

Often Madison's remarks could barely be heard. Yet his frustration with Henry gradually warmed him to his topic, and his voice grew stronger as he responded to each challenge. He urged the convention to consider the Constitution "on its own merits solely." Then he turned to the specifics of Henry's arguments. Far from being held by a tiny minority, the Federalist position was widely popular, since all the states had acknowledged their problems and wanted change. As for standing armies, they would preserve, not threaten, liberty. He outlined the "various means whereby nations lost their liberties" and concluded that an army was necessary to make the nation respected and secure. He chided Henry for his objections to taxation, since the right to tax was not for direct taxation on citizens, but for tariffs and other indirect taxes. These taxes were necessary to address the problems confronting the republic, such as the Indian wars on the frontier and the instability of the currency system. The notion that the national government would destroy all other levels of government was absurd, because the national body derived its power from the state and local governments and the people. Furthermore, the checks and balances of the new system would prevent any single branch or individual from taking complete control and abusing the power of the Constitution. Refuting Henry's charges about the creation of a "consolidated" government, he pointed out that the new system was a federal one, with the states maintaining powers and rights. **[See Source 5.]**

Madison threw all his energies into the defense. In fact, he wore himself out physically and emotionally. When he became so ill that he could not speak, his friends and allies rallied to carry on the debate. They knew by late June that the Constitution had been ratified when the ninth state—New Hampshire—approved the document. Yet they also realized that the new government had little chance of success without the support of large states such as Virginia and New York. And in Virginia, the Antifederalists had a majority. The Federalists grew desperate. They went to George Mason and asked him what changes he required to support the Constitution. He told them a Bill of Rights needed to be attached to the Constitution. When they promised to do that, he agreed to ratify, bringing some of his allies with him. Henry and his supporters, however, still had enough votes to reject the Constitution. Finally, the Federalists played their trump card. They called on George Washington to publicly support the Constitution. Washington had been president of the Philadelphia convention and supported the new framework, but he wanted to stay out of the controversy. He believed that he might be the first president under the new government and wanted to be able to heal the wounds inflicted by the battles over ratification. Now realizing how desperate the situation was, Washington announced his position, swinging more votes. In the end, Virginia ratified the Constitution by ten votes, eighty-nine to seventy-nine. Backcountry delegates interested in a more powerful government able to stop Indian attacks ultimately tipped the balance for the Federalists.

The battle over ratification was close in other states as well. In New York, an Antifederalist majority was led by the promising young attorney Aaron Burr. Only the deft political maneuvering of Alexander Hamilton saved the day. Hamilton wisely delayed the vote until it was clear that the Constitution would be adopted by other states like Virginia. By a slim margin of three votes, New York then ratified. Resistance to the new government was strong in other areas, especially in more isolated counties. Once the largest and most influential states voted to support it, though, the Federalists had their victory.

Henry left the battlefield gracefully. Although he retained "a conviction of being overpowered in a good cause," he pledged his allegiance to the new government. Soon thereafter, he retired from politics and returned to his career as a lawyer.

The Federalist victory came at a price. After the Constitution was ratified in 1788 and national elections were held the following year, the Federalists carried out their promise to enact a Bill of Rights. Yet bitter divisions remained between them and their Antifederalist opponents. The Federalists' exercise of power in the new national government only made matters worse (see Chapter 6). President Washington tried to cool partisan passions, but he was not successful. In 1799, he even urged Henry to run for the Virginia legislature in an effort to lessen partisan bickering. Henry agreed to help Washington for the good of the country and easily won the election. The old Antifederalist's health, however, had been growing steadily worse, and shortly after making his dramatic return to the legislature, he died.

By then, the rift between the Federalists and their opponents, led by Thomas Jefferson, was complete. Ironically, Henry's old adversary had joined the Jeffersonian opposition long before. Earlier in the 1790s, Madison had become convinced that the Federalist administrations of Washington and his successor, John Adams, were going too far in consolidating and centralizing power in the national government. When the Jeffersonian Republicans swept the Federalists from power in 1800, Madison served under Jefferson as secretary of state. Then in 1808, he was elected to the first of two consecutive terms as president. After retiring from politics in 1817, Madison came to be known as the "Last of the Fathers." As the last of the revolutionary generation's dominant figures, he frequently offered advice to younger politicians. He continued to emphasize the dangers of democracy and the necessity of protecting the rights of those in the minority. And even though he had left the Federalist Party, he made clear his continued faith in the new government that he had helped create. Two years before he died in 1836, Madison drafted a brief essay titled "Advice to My Country." In it, he urged that "the union of states be cherished and perpetuated" by his fellow Americans.

•PRIMARY SOURCES•

Source 1:   Mercy Otis Warren, *"Observations on the New Constitution"* (1788)

As a woman, Mercy Otis Warren was unable to participate directly in politics or the debates over the Constitution. Nonetheless, in a pamphlet written under the pseudonym "Columbian Patriot," this daughter of a prominent Massachusetts family expressed the fears of many Antifederalists about the Constitution. What are her objections to the proposed government? How do you think Madison would have responded to her?

I will first observe … the best political writers have supported the principles of annual elections with a precision; that cannot be confuted….

2. There is no security in the profered [*sic*] system, either for the rights of conscience or the liberty of the Press….

3. There are no well defined limits of the Judiciary Powers, they seem to be left as a boundless ocean….

4. The Executive and the Legislative are so dangerously blended as to give just cause of alarm….

5. The abolition of trial by jury in civil causes.—This mode of trial the learned Judge Blackstone observes, "has been coeval with the first rudiments of civil government, that property, liberty and life, depend on maintaining in its legal force the constitutional trial by jury." …

6. Though it has been said by Mr. Wilson and many others, that a Standing-Army is necessary for the dignity and safety of America, yet freedom revolts at the idea…. Standing armies have been the nursery of vice and the bane of liberty from the Roman legions to the … planting of the British cohorts in the capitals of America….

7. Notwithstanding the delusory promise to guarantee a Republican form of government to every State in the Union—… there are no resources left for the support of

SOURCE: Mercy Otis Warren, OBSERVATIONS ON THE NEW CONSTITUTION AND ON THE FEDERAL AND STATE CONVENTIONS (Boston, 1788), pp. 9, 10, 11, 12, 13.

internal government, or the liquidation of the debts of the State. Every source of revenue is in the monopoly of Congress....

8. As the new Congress are empowered to determine their own salaries, the requisitions for this purpose may not be very moderate, and the drain for public moneys will probably rise past all calculation....

9. There is no provision for a rotation, nor anything to prevent the perpetuity of office in the same hands for life; which by a little well timed bribery, will probably be done, to the exclusion of men of the best abilities from their share in the offices of government...

14. There is no provision by a bill of rights to guard against the dangerous encroachments of power in too many instances to be named: ... The rights of individuals ought to be the primary object of all government, and cannot be too securely guarded by the most explicit declarations in their favor....

15. The difficulty, if not impracticability, of exercising the equal and equitable powers of government by a single legislature over an extent of territory that reaches from the Mississippi to the Western lakes, and from them to the Atlantic Ocean, is an insuperable objection to the adoption of the new system.

Source 2:   James Madison, *"The Federalist No. 10"* (1788)

James Madison defends the Constitution in this essay. How does he attempt to allay the concerns raised by Mercy Otis Warren, Patrick Henry, and other Antifederalists about the proposed government?

By a faction I understand a number of citizens, whether amounting to a majority or minority of the whole, who are united and actuated by some common impulse of passion, or of interest, adverse to the rights of other citizens, or to the permanent and aggregate interests of the community....

[T]he most common and durable source of factions has ever been the unequal distribution of property. Those who hold as opposed to those who are without property have ever formed distinct interests in society. Those who are creditors, and those who are debtors, likewise share different concerns. A landed interest, a manufacturing interest, a mercantile interest, a moneyed interest, with many lesser interests, grow up of necessity in civilized nations, and divide them into different classes, actuated by different sentiments and views. The regulation of these various and interfering interests forms the principal task of modern legislation, and involves the spirit of party and faction in the necessary and ordinary operations of government....

A common passion or interest will, in almost every case, be felt by a majority of the whole; and there is nothing to check the inducements to sacrifice the weaker party or individual. Hence it is that such pure democracies have ever been spectacles of turbulence and contention; have ever been found incompatible with personal security or the rights of property; and have in general been as short in their lives as they have been violent in their deaths....

SOURCE: James Madison, "The Federalist No. 10" (1788).

A republic, on the other hand, by which I mean a government in which a scheme of representation takes place, opens a different prospect and promises the cure for which we are seeking. Let us examine the points in which it varies from pure democracy, and we shall comprehend both the nature of the cure and the efficacy it must derive from the Union.

The two great points of difference between a pure democracy and a republic are: first, the delegation of the government in a republic to a smaller number of citizens elected by the rest; secondly, the greater number of citizens and greater sphere of country over which the republic may be thus extended.

The effect of the first difference is, on the one hand, to refine and enlarge the public views by passing them through the medium of a chosen body of citizens, whose wisdom may best discern the true interest of their country and whose patriotism and love of justice will be least likely to sacrifice it to temporary or partial considerations. Under such conditions it may well happen that the public voice, pronounced by the representatives of the people, will be more consonant to the public good than if pronounced by the people themselves. It is possible, of course, that the effect may unhappily be inverted. Men of factious tempers, of local prejudices or of sinister designs, may, by intrigue, by corruption, or by other means, first obtain the votes and then betray the interests of the people. The question resulting is, then, whether small or extensive republics are most favorable to the election of proper guardians of the public weal; and it is clearly decided in favor of the larger.

Source 3:   Patrick Henry, *Speech to the Virginia Convention* (June 4, 1788)

In his opening speech to the Virginia Ratifying Convention, Patrick Henry charged that the Federalists had no authority to create the Constitution. What does this speech reveal about Henry's fears?

Make the best of this new government—say it is composed of any thing but inspiration—you ought to be extremely cautious, watchful, jealous of your liberty; for, instead of securing your rights, you may lose them forever. If a wrong step be now made, the republic may be lost forever. If this new government will not come up to the expectation of the people, and they shall be disappointed, their liberty will be lost, and tyranny must and will arise. I repeat it again, and I beg gentlemen to consider, that a wrong step, made now, will plunge us into misery, and our republic will be lost. It will be necessary for this [Virginia Ratifying] Convention to have a faithful historical detail of the facts that preceded the session of the federal Convention, and the reasons that actuated its members in proposing an entire alteration of government, and to demonstrate the dangers that awaited us. If they were of such awful magnitude as to warrant a proposal so extremely perilous as this, I must assert, that this Convention has an absolute right to a thorough discovery of every circumstance relative to this great event. And here I would make this inquiry of those worthy characters who composed a part of the late federal Convention. I am sure they were fully impressed with the necessity of forming a great consolidated government, instead of a

SOURCE: Patrick Henry, *Speech to the Virginia Convention* (June 4, 1788).

confederation. That this is a consolidated government is demonstrably clear; and the danger of such a government is, to my mind, very striking, I have the highest veneration for those gentlemen; but, sir, give me leave to demand: What right had they to say, *We, the people?* My political curiosity, exclusive of my anxious solicitude for the public welfare, leads me to ask: Who authorized them to speak the language of, *We, the people,* instead of, *We, the states?* States are the characteristics and the soul of a confederation. If the states be not the agents of this compact, it must be one great, consolidated, national government, of the people of all the states. I have the highest respect for those gentlemen who formed the Convention, and, were some of them not here, I would express some testimonial of esteem for them. America had, on a former occasion, put the utmost confidence in them— a confidence which was well placed; and I am sure, sir, I would give up any thing to them; I would cheerfully confide in them as my representatives. But, sir, on this great occasion, I would demand the cause of their conduct. Even from that illustrious man who saved us by his valor [George Washington], I would have a reason for his conduct.... That they exceeded their power is perfectly clear.... The federal Convention ought to have amended the old system; for this purpose they were solely delegated; the object of their mission extended to no other consideration. You must, therefore, forgive the solicitation of one un-worthy member to know what danger could have arisen under the present Confederation, and what are the causes of this proposal to change our government.

Source 4: Patrick Henry, *Speech to the Virginia Convention* (June 5, 1788)

In another speech before the Virginia Ratifying Convention, Henry raised numerous objections to the Constitution. What are they? Are they reasonable?

Having premised these things, I shall, with the aid of my judgment and information, which, I confess, are not extensive, go into the discussion of this system more minutely....

Let me here call your attention to that part which gives the Congress power "to provide for organizing, arming, and disciplining the militia, and for governing such part of them as may be employed in the service of the United States—reserving to the states, respectively, the appointment of the officers, and the authority of training the militia according to the discipline prescribed by Congress." By this, sir, you see that their control over our last and best defence is unlimited. If they neglect or refuse to discipline or arm our militia, they will be useless: the states can do neither—this power being exclusively given to Congress....

If you make the citizens of this country agree to become the subjects of one great consolidated empire of America, your government will not have sufficient energy to keep them together. Such a government is incompatible with the genius of republicanism. There will be no checks, no real balances, in this government. What can avail your specious, imaginary balances, your rope-dancing, chain-rattling, ridiculous ideal checks and contrivances? ...

SOURCE: Patrick Henry, *Speech to the Virginia Convention* (June 5, 1788).

Consider our situation, sir: go to the poor man, and ask him what he does. He will inform you that he enjoys the fruits of his labor, under his own fig-tree, with his wife and children around him, in peace and security. Go to every other member of society,— you will find the same tranquil ease and content; you will find no alarms or disturbances. Why, then, tell us of danger, to terrify us into an adoption of this new form of government? And yet who knows the dangers that this new system may produce? They are out of the sight of the common people: they cannot foresee latent consequences. I dread the operation of it on the middling and lower classes of people: it is for them I fear the adoption of this system....

In this scheme of energetic government, the people will find two sets of tax-gatherers—the state and the federal sheriffs. This, it seems to me, will produce such dreadful oppression as the people cannot possibly bear. The federal sheriff may commit what oppression, make what distresses, he pleases, and ruin you with impunity; for how are you to tie his hands? Have you any sufficiently decided means of preventing him from sucking your blood by speculations, commissions, and fees? Thus thousands of your people will be most shamefully robbed....

What can be more defective than the clause concerning the elections? The control given to Congress over the time, place, and manner of holding elections, will totally destroy the end of suffrage. The elections may be held at one place, and the most inconvenient in the state; or they may be at remote distances from those who have a right of suffrage: hence nine out of ten must either not vote at all, or vote for strangers; for the most influential characters will be applied to, to know who are the most proper to be chosen. I repeat, that the control of Congress over the *manner,* &c., of electing, well warrants this idea. The natural consequence will be, that this democratic branch will possess none of the public confidence; the people will be prejudiced against representatives chosen in such an injudicious manner. The proceedings in the northern conclave will be hidden from the yeomanry of this country....

Where is the responsibility—that leading principle in the British government? In that government, a punishment certain and inevitable is provided; but in this, there is no real, actual punishment for the grossest mal-administration. They may go without punishment, though they commit the most outrageous violation on our immunities. That paper may tell me they will be punished. I ask, By what law? They must make the law, for there is no existing law to do it. What! will they make a law to punish themselves?

This, sir, is my great objection to the Constitution, that there is no true responsibility and that the preservation of our liberty depends on the single chance of men being virtuous enough to make laws to punish themselves.

Source 5: James Madison, *"The Federalist No. 39"* (1788)

In this selection from The Federalist Papers, *James Madison discusses the structure of the new government and its relationship to the people. How does he answer the concerns raised by Patrick Henry in Sources 3 and 4? How does he use the nature of the ratification process to bolster the Federalist case?*

Source: James Madison, "The Federalist No. 39" (1788).

What, then, are the distinctive characters of the republican form? ... [W]e may define a republic to be, or at least may bestow that name on, a government which derives all its powers directly or indirectly from the great body of the people, and is administered by persons holding their offices during pleasure, for a limited period, or during good behavior. It is *essential* to such a government that it be derived from the great body of the society, not from an inconsiderable proportion, or a favored class of it; otherwise a handful of tyrannical nobles, exercising their oppressions by a delegation of their powers, might aspire to the rank of republicans, and claim for their government the honorable title of republic. It is *sufficient* for such a government that the persons administering it be appointed, either directly or indirectly, by the people....

On comparing the Constitution planned by the convention with the standard here fixed, we perceive at once that it is, in the most rigid sense, conformable to it. The House of Representatives, like that of one branch at least of all the State legislatures, is elected immediately by the great body of the people. The Senate, like the present Congress, and the Senate of Maryland, derives its appointment indirectly from the people. The President is indirectly derived from the choice of the people, according to the example in most of the States. Even the judges with all other officers of the Union, will, as in the several States, be the choice, though a remote choice, of the people themselves....

Could any further proof be required of the republican complexion of this system, the most decisive one might be found in its absolute prohibition of titles of nobility, both under the federal and the State governments; and in its express guaranty of the republican form to each of the latter.

But it was not sufficient, say the adversaries of the proposed Constitution, for the convention to adhere to the republican form. They ought, with equal care, to have preserved the federal form, which regards the Union as a Confederacy of sovereign states; instead of which, they have framed a national government, which regards the Union as a consolidation of the States. And it is asked by what authority this bold and radical innovation was undertaken? The handle which has been made of this objection requires that it should be examined with some precision....

[I]t appears, on the one hand, that the Constitution is to be founded on the assent and ratification of the people of America, given by deputies elected for the special purpose; but, on the other, that this assent and ratification is to be given by the people, not as individuals composing one entire nation, but as composing the distinct and independent States to which they respectively belong. It is to be the assent and ratification of the several States, derived from the supreme authority in each State,—the authority of the people themselves. The act, therefore, establishing the Constitution, will not be a *national*, but a *federal* act....

... The House of Representatives will derive its powers from the people of America; and the people will be represented in the same proportion, and on the same principle, as they are in the legislature of a particular State. So far the government is *national*, not *federal*. The Senate, on the other hand, will derive its powers from the States, as political and coequal societies; and these will be represented on the principle of equality in the Senate, as they now are in the existing Congress. So far the government is *federal*, not *national*. The executive power will be derived from a very compound source. The immediate election of the President is to be made by the States in their political characters. The votes allotted to them are in a compound ratio, which considers them partly as distinct and coequal societies, partly as unequal members of the same society. The eventual election, again, is to be made by that branch of the legislature which consists of the national representatives; but in this particular act they are to be thrown into the form of individual delegations, from so many distinct and coequal bodies politic. From this aspect of the government, it appears to be of a mixed character, presenting at least as many *federal* as *national* features....

The proposed Constitution, therefore, is, in strictness, neither a national nor a federal Constitution, but a composition of both. In its foundation it is federal, not national; in the sources from which the ordinary powers of the government are drawn, it is partly federal and partly national; in the operation of these powers, it is national, not federal; in the extent of them, again, it is federal, not national.

QUESTIONS TO CONSIDER

1. Both Patrick Henry and James Madison were part of the Virginia planter class, but they disagreed on the Constitution. How do you account for that? What important ideas or experiences influenced them to take opposite sides?

2. What were Madison's principal arguments for the Constitution? What were Henry's principal arguments against it? Whose do you find more compelling? Why?

3. How did the recent past, specifically the colonial struggle against Britain and the experience of Americans under the Articles of Confederation, support Henry's fears regarding the Constitution? How did it support Madison's analysis of the government proposed by the Constitution?

4. In the United States today, do you think government matches Madison's vision and fulfills his hopes? Have any of Henry's fears been realized? Explain.

FOR FURTHER READING

Lance Banning, *The Sacred Fire of Liberty: James Madison and the Founding of the Federal Republic* (Ithaca: Cornell University Press, 1995), provides a revisionist view arguing that Madison was not a pragmatic politician but a consistent ideologue committed to democracy and only reluctantly supported the Federalists.

Saul Cornell, *The Other Founders: Anti-Federalism and the Dissenting Tradition in America, 1788–1828* (Chapel Hill: University of North Carolina Press, 1999), offers a sophisticated study of Antifederalist thought.

Christopher Duncan, *The Anti-Federalists and Early American Political Thought* (DeKalb: Northern Illinois University Press, 1993), submits a recent study of the Antifederalists and their contributions to political philosophy.

Henry Mayer, *A Son of Thunder: Patrick Henry and the American Republic* (New York: Franklin Watts, 1986), provides an accessible biography of Henry.

Jack Rakove, *James Madison and the Creation of the American Republic* (New York: Harper Collins, 1990), gives a short, readable biography of Madison.

6

Political Conflict in the Early Republic: Benjamin Franklin Bache and Alexander Hamilton

As Benjamin Franklin emerged from the Constitutional Convention in 1787, according to one oft-told story, a bystander asked him what sort of government the nation was to have. "A republic," replied the Convention's elder statesman, "if you can keep it." Less than a decade later, Franklin's grandson and namesake was convinced that the men who had taken control of the national government under the new Constitution were out to destroy America's infant experiment in representative government. Like his famous grandfather, Benjamin Franklin Bache was a Philadelphia printer and publisher. Like Franklin, Bache believed in the power of the press to enlighten and instruct. By the early 1790s, he was convinced that the need for this power had never been greater. In Bache's mind, the Federalists in George Washington's administration plotted nothing less than rule by an aristocracy, even a return to monarchy. Ambitious and unscrupulous, they used their power in the national government to benefit moneyed interests rather than the people, limit the influence of common people in the government, and put the United States under Great Britain's thumb. Of all these designing men, he believed, none was more dangerous than Alexander Hamilton: a man at the heart of that government and, in Bache's mind, the very head of the Federalist Party.

If Hamilton was not the formal head of the Federalists, few had been more active in defining and promoting a Federalist agenda. Fewer still were more successful in implementing it. Powered by an agile mind and intense drive, Hamilton had made a remarkable rise in life. Named by Washington the nation's first Treasury secretary at the tender age of thirty-two, Hamilton came to this job with firm ideas about government, power, and the people. His assumptions about all these matters could not have been more different than Bache's. An unabashed elitist, Hamilton believed that the people were a beast to

An eighteenth-century printing press—Bache trusted in the power of the printed word to "do good."

North Wind Picture Archives/Alamy

Alexander Hamilton

Library of Congress Prints and Photographs Division Washington, D.C. [LC-US262-48272]

be restrained by the firm hand of government. As in Britain, only when gentlemen ruled and people knew their place could order and stability prevail. And only when the interests of the government and the investing class were aligned would progress prevail.

Bache and Hamilton faced off at nearly every turn in the 1790s. Their lives and careers highlight many of the ideas and events that divided Republicans from their Federalist opponents. Hamilton, born to humble circumstances, embraced elite rule. Armed with detailed plans and the power to implement them, he came to serve as a potent symbol of Federalist domination. Bache, a fortunate grandson with the right pedigree, put his faith in common people. With the printed word as his only weapon, he pressed tirelessly for the Republican opposition. Bitter opponents guided by opposing visions for the nation, these men did much to create what Bache's grandfather and other founders little expected: a nation divided into political parties.

"I RISE TO BE USEFUL"

Benjamin Franklin Bache inherited more than a name and profession from his well-known grandfather. Born in 1769 to Benjamin Franklin's only daughter and a perpetually foundering Philadelphia merchant, young Benny was taken under wing at age seven by his grandfather when it was clear that the financially struggling Richard Bache was unable to provide properly for his family. Franklin would become the most important influence in Benjamin Bache's life. After walking alone into colonial Philadelphia as a lad with little more than a curious mind and a burning desire for self-improvement, the self-educated Franklin had risen to wealth and fame as a printer, journalist, inventor, legislator, and diplomat. In fact, by 1776 when he took the seven-year-old Benny with him on a nine-year diplomatic mission to France, he was arguably the most famous American on either side of the Atlantic.

Without question, he had become a living symbol of the Enlightenment in America. Based on the spread of the printed word, rising levels of material comfort, and scientific advances that seemed to unlock the natural laws of the universe, the eighteenth-century Enlightenment represented an intellectual revolution that unleashed a rising tide of revolutionary optimism in European civilization. Just as the English scientist Isaac Newton explained how the universe operated according to the law of gravity, so Enlightenment thinkers posited that rational laws operated in all spheres of life. With the application of reason, these natural laws could be discovered and applied, bringing social, material, and political progress. In a proper environment, free individuals could finally break the bonds of poverty, ignorance, and superstition. Self-governing and equal citizens, informed and aware of their "natural" rights, could also overthrow political tyranny. Whether preaching self-improvement through his journalistic alter-ego Poor Richard, inventing useful devices to increase life's conveniences and comforts, or warning fellow citizens about threats to their rights, Franklin acted on Enlightenment faith in reason, science, progress, and equality. Sporting a coonskin cap amid royals and aristocrats, he reflected the heights that common but enlightened citizens of the New World could scale.

As he set sail for France with his grandson in tow, there was little question what Franklin had in mind for him. Though he had little opportunity himself for formal learning, Franklin never doubted that knowledge, broadly diffused, was essential to insure widespread opportunities for success or that the preservation of republican government rested on the early inculcation of virtue and morality. Instilling "general virtue," he realized, was more likely to occur by educating young people than "exhorting" adults. As he put it, "bad habits and vices" were "more easily prevented than cured." Ideally, Franklin believed, students should receive an education both "ornamental" and "useful," one that fitted them "to serve the Publick with Honour to themselves, and to their Country."

Broad and "enlightened," Bache's education reflected these views. Franklin enrolled him at a boarding school in Paris, where he learned French, Latin, music, dancing, and drawing. He attended to the boy's education in other ways, too. He arranged a meeting for him with Voltaire, the great French Enlightenment philosopher, critic of France's monarchy, and champion of individual rights. Benny met dignitaries from both sides of the Atlantic who called on his grandfather: the Prussian Prince Henry, the French hero of the American Revolution Lafayette, as well as American diplomats Thomas Jefferson and John Adams. Concerned about his grandson's aristocratic education and his neglect of English in favor of French, he sent the boy for four more years of study to a school founded by John Calvin in Geneva. There, those around him noticed traits that Franklin himself would have appreciated: his calm temperament, careful observations, and simple dress. When Bache returned from Switzerland in 1783, Franklin also made sure that the boy learned a "useful" trade so that he was not "oblig'd to ask Favours or Offices of anybody." Franklin introduced him to type founding—the process of creating type—and to printing. He then saw to it that Bache could learn these crafts at the hands of French master type casters and printers. When Franklin and Bache returned to Philadelphia in 1785, Bache capped his formal education at the University of Pennsylvania, a school his grandfather had founded several decades earlier.

Barely eighteen when he graduated in 1787, Bache was ready to make his way in the world. Once again, he had his grandfather's assistance. Determined that his grandson would not be a mere tradesman, Franklin started him at the top. Together, they opened a type-founding and printing business, which gave Bache valuable experience in managing an enterprise. Before the partnership failed several years later, he had also ventured into book publishing, including children's books that were based on "enlightened" educational theories. Well educated, well connected, and now well placed, young Bache led an active social life, including much time in the company of Margaret Markoe, the daughter of a West Indian sugar planter and stepdaughter of a leading Philadelphia physician. Benjamin and Margaret married in 1791, a year after Franklin's death.

With printing and type-founding equipment inherited from his grandfather, Bache altered course. He decided to publish a newspaper, a choice that some in his social circle found beneath his rank. It would lead to partisanship, they warned, and only tarnish his reputation. Within six months of his grandfather's death, however, Bache's presses rattled off the first issue of the *General Advertiser*. Following Franklin's earlier advice to printers to remain impartial, Bache filled it with foreign and commercial news and advertising. By 1792, though, his paper had begun to associate with the critics of the Washington administration who would come to call themselves Republicans.

The Federalists' opponents were fueled by events in Bache's beloved France, where the bloody French Revolution had toppled the old regime. As Republican government replaced monarchy and aristocracy and French revolutionaries proclaimed the "rights of man," Federalists were appalled. Valuing order and stability, they saw in France mob rule and republicanism run wild. Franklin's acquaintances there had included several leaders in the French Revolution. Like his grandfather, Bache believed that ordinary citizens had a duty to be politically engaged. Guided by an Enlightenment faith in people and their ability to remake society, he never doubted their ability to create a new republican order of liberty, equality, and virtue. He was disappointed that his own country now seemed to be falling behind France in carrying on the ideals of the American Revolution. And he detected a growing anti-republican spirit in the Federalists' "praise of monarchical and aristocratic institutions."

Other developments at home and abroad soon moved Bache and his paper to outright partisanship. In Federalist financial policies and their efforts to enforce them, he perceived a desire to enrich the moneyed elite and suppress popular dissent. In their relations with England and France, he saw only more threats to republican principles. And in Federalist actions at home and abroad, he came to detect the influence of one man: Treasury Secretary and arch-Federalist Alexander Hamilton. Within two years, the *General Advertiser* had a new name, the *Aurora,* to reflect its new purpose. And it sported a new motto on the masthead: "*Surgo Ut Prosim*" or "I rise to be useful." In the spirit of his grandfather, Bache believed that he had found a way to "do good." He would work tirelessly to educate his fellow citizens to the dangers posed by Hamilton and the Federalists who, like the British in 1776, intended to rob Americans of their cherished rights, muzzle the people, and destroy their republican government.

"BASTARD BRAT"

If Benjamin Bache's birth as Franklin's grandson determined his course in life, so too did the circumstances of Alexander Hamilton's birth in 1757. As John Adams so bluntly expressed it, Hamilton was a "bastard brat of a Scottish pedlar." Throughout his life, Hamilton suffered from an inferiority complex. Plagued by self-doubts, he was convinced that others held his illegitimate birth against him. Hamilton's mother, Rachel, was married to a planter named John Lavien and started a family with him on the island of St. Croix in the West Indies. They had a tumultuous relationship, however, and Rachel was jailed for refusing to live with her husband. Upon her release, she moved to the neighboring island of Nevis, where she lived as the wife of James Hamilton and bore him two sons, including Alexander, without getting a divorce from Lavien.

Although Lavien finally divorced her in 1759, when the Hamilton family moved to St. Croix and James learned the truth about Rachel, he left her and his children, never to return.

During his childhood, Alexander learned that to overcome his illegitimacy, he had to work hard and cultivate friendships with powerful men. The islands were the center of a thriving merchant trade, and he grew up in the midst of it. When he moved to the mainland colonies, Hamilton was an outsider, unattached to any particular region or state. This allowed him to view the country as a whole—to love the nation rather than some locality. Thus he approached politics and economics from a national perspective.

Hamilton was exposed early to the world of commerce. At age nine, he went to work as a clerk in a merchant house in Christiansted on St. Croix. Ships from all over the world passed through the bustling port. Most of his employer's transactions were with businessmen from New York, and Alexander grew curious about that British colony. After his mother died in 1768, Alexander attached himself to two important men in Christiansted—his employer and a Presbyterian minister. Both were impressed with his intellect and abilities as a clerk, and they decided that he should pursue an education. They urged him to attend the College of New Jersey. After a year in a preparatory school, he passed the strenuous entrance exams and went off to New Jersey with his benefactors' help. When the faculty at the College of New Jersey refused to let him study at his own pace, he transferred to King's College (now Columbia University) in New York City. Thus, when the American Revolution began, he was in one of the colonies' biggest cities and a hotbed of patriot agitation.

Hamilton was right in the thick of it. He made speeches, passed out pamphlets, and published numerous letters in support of the American cause. He also studied artillery, preparing himself for military service. When the war broke out in 1775, he organized an artillery company and was commissioned as a captain in the Continental Army. He lusted for military glory, believing that heroism on the battlefield would help him overcome his lowly roots. Seeing action repeatedly in the early months of the conflict, he performed boldly. His accomplishments as a soldier, however, were not as impressive as his abilities as an administrator. Before long, he received numerous offers to serve as a staff officer. He refused them all, until General George Washington approached him. Hamilton jumped at the opportunity, hoping that attaching himself to the head of the Continental Army would bring more rewards when independence was won. As Washington's aide, he became indispensable to the general, who relied more and more on his advice and abilities as the war wore on.

The Revolution also brought Hamilton military glory. In 1781, Washington gave his young aide a field command. As a lieutenant colonel, Hamilton led a heroic attack at Yorktown, contributing to Washington's greatest battlefield victory. His thirst for military glory satisfied, he was now convinced that his lasting fame would be ensured by serving his country in politics. In 1782, he turned to the study of law, passed the bar, and became an attorney. About the same time, he married Elizabeth Schuyler, the daughter of an old and very wealthy New York family. Through marriage, Hamilton continued his habit of attaching himself to others as a means to obtain power. Given his political aspirations, the Schuylers' political connections would prove invaluable to a man with no roots in New York and no birthright of his own. Although Hamilton's money came mostly from his own ambition and hard work, his marriage placed him near the highest ranks of American society. With the zeal of a convert, he would have little difficulty embracing the view that the rich were, as he later put it, "generally speaking, enlightened men" and that the common people should not have too much say in government. Such assumptions would guide Hamilton's thinking about politics and economics—and put him squarely opposite Benjamin Bache.

The Revolution, meanwhile, provided Hamilton with ample opportunities to expand his thoughts about politics and economics. Very much unlike Bache, Hamilton came to the view that people were motivated by appeals to self-interest more than public spiritedness. Citizens could be encouraged to do the right thing by aiming at their pocketbooks, not their hearts. Throughout the war, he had to balance the needs of the army with a shortage of funds. Furthermore, the army had to contend with disputes between Congress and the states. This experience convinced him that the country's future depended on a sound economy. Only prosperity could guarantee that future wars would not end in defeat. And prosperity required a powerful national government. With the impatience of youth, Hamilton became involved in a plot to bring it about. It was hatched after the war by former military officers who planned to raise an army that would force Congress to revise the Articles of Confederation. Among their demands was a plan for national taxation that would provide revenue so that war veterans could be paid. Washington put a quick end to this plot, and Hamilton returned to the legal profession.

Within a few years, however, Hamilton would have a chance to shape the nation's future. Convinced that the Articles of Confederation were far too weak, he played a key role in persuading Congress to sanction a meeting to strengthen them. Later, he attended the Constitutional Convention as a delegate from New York. At the convention, he was one of the most vocal supporters of the new framework for a national government, even though he believed that the Constitution did not give the new government enough power. He also played a key role in the ratification process as one of the most outspoken Federalists, contributing dozens of letters and pamphlets in defense of the Constitution. When elections in early 1789 swept the Federalists into power, President George Washington turned to Hamilton as a trusted and dependable adviser. When Hamilton became the nation's first secretary of the Treasury, he took up the problems of the nation's finance with an almost religious zeal. The result was a bold plan designed to assert the new government's power and dramatically transform the country. The details were contained in three reports to Congress in which he proposed a national banking system and developed ways to pay the nation's Revolutionary War debt.

In his *First Report on Public Credit,* issued in 1790, Hamilton insisted that all of the national debt more than fifty million dollars be paid back. Hamilton realized that the government would need to borrow more than fifty million dollars in the future. Repaying all of the national government's debt would make it easier and cheaper to do so. Furthermore, rich investors, who held much of the debt, would be tied through their pocketbooks to the new government. They would be quick to support a government that paid them back their money and all the interest due. The certificates issued to the government's creditors would provide a sound medium of exchange, thereby expanding the nation's supply of badly needed sound money. For the same reasons, Hamilton also called for the national government to assume all the Revolutionary War debts of the state governments. This would further tie the investing class to the national regime and help establish its sovereignty over the states.

In the *Second Report on Public Credit,* also issued in 1790, Hamilton proposed that Congress establish a national bank to be headquartered in Philadelphia. The Bank of the United States, he argued, would perform a number of useful services. It would be able to issue payments for the public debt, serve as a repository for government funds, and print bank notes that would stabilize the nation's currency. In addition, it could also make loans to businesses. To fund the bank, the national government would purchase one-fifth of its stock. The remainder would be sold to citizens. Because private citizens would be able to purchase stock in the bank, their interests would be further tied to the government. Here was another marriage of the investing classes and the government.

Finally, Hamilton's *Report on Manufactures* in 1791 called for a diverse economy based on agriculture, commerce, and manufacturing. The American economy continued to rely on the export of agricultural surpluses, just as in the colonial period. The role of the colonies in the empire had been to produce low-value farm products. The British realized that the real wealth was in making high-value finished products. Now Hamilton wanted the United States to emulate Britain, a wealthy nation with a powerful central government that promoted manufacturing and commerce. Wealth, Hamilton realized, was in making goods, not growing them. While making the economy stronger, industry would also encourage hard work among the populace.

In Congress, Hamilton got most of what he wanted, but his programs sparked a bitter fight. The opposition was led by Antifederalists such as George Mason and Richard Henry Lee, who had opposed a stronger government all along. Especially odious to many was the assumption of the state debts because Virginia and several other states had already retired their debts. Now they would have to share the burden of paying those of the states that had not. Congress narrowly passed Hamilton's proposal to fund, or pay back, the national debt. To pass assumption, however, Hamilton and his Federalist supporters had to strike a deal with Southern opponents to locate the new national capital along the Potomac River.

Meanwhile, Hamilton's proposal to create the Bank of the United States received more support in Congress. Most politicians thought that the bank would quickly prove profitable and the government's credit would become all the more sound. But some leaders were skeptical. They argued that chartering a private corporation was beyond the constitutional scope of the national government. Congress approved the bank, but opposition to it remained fierce. To quell the concerns about its constitutionality, Hamilton argued that chartering a bank was covered under the implied powers given to Congress in the Constitution, specifically the closing clause of Article I, Section 8. That clause empowers Congress to "make all laws which shall be necessary and proper for carrying into execution the foregoing powers." Hamilton argued that this clause applied to the bank, which was both "necessary and proper" for executing Congress's power to regulate commerce.

Only the *Report on Manufactures* failed. Madison and other southern planters rallied to defeat this report in Congress. The Tariff of 1792 provided more protection to agricultural interests than to the few American factories in existence. The bulk of Hamilton's other programs were ignored. Hamilton was disappointed, but the facts were against him. According to the 1790 Census, 95 percent of Americans lived in rural areas. Even in the cities, merchants and artisans outnumbered manufacturers and factory workers. Hamilton had gone too far in attempting to move America away from its agricultural roots.

He was not finished, though. In his *Report on Public Credit* in 1791, Hamilton had proposed a tax on domestically produced whiskey. His intent was to raise revenue and uplift Americans' morals. Backcountry farmers often distilled grain into alcohol either to drink or as a convenient means to transport their crops to market. Passed by Congress in 1791, the tax threatened to eliminate their profits on whiskey. When resistance to the tax escalated into attacks on federal excise officers by 1794, Hamilton was eager for a showdown. He promptly drew up a report alleging that the rule of law had broken down in western Pennsylvania—the center of the so-called Whiskey Rebellion—and called for use of federal force to compel obedience to the law. When Washington called out a militia of nearly thirteen thousand men, Hamilton rode to Pennsylvania with the commander in chief, arrested some of the insurgents, and told Washington that he hoped some "characters fit for examples" might be found. In Hamilton's mind, nothing less than the legitimacy of the new government itself was at stake. **[See Source 1.]**

The Whiskey Rebellion fizzled in the face of Washington's show of force, but Hamilton and the Federalists had betrayed a dangerous weakness. In a nation of small farmers, the Federalists' heavy hand was sure to alienate many Americans. Hamilton had reached into the pocketbooks of poor backcountry farmers to raise revenue to pay back wealthy creditors. Then he conspicuously led troops to smash the tax protesters. The chorus of protests was virtually inevitable. In it, one especially powerful voice would begin to stand out.

"SHAMELESS FALSE HOODS"

In the early 1790s, newspapers played a key role in stoking the animosity between Federalists and a nascent Republican opposition. In fact, Hamilton, whose policies would help stir Republican opposition in the first place, encouraged Federalist editor John Fenno to establish the *Gazette of the United States* in 1789 to convey Federalist thinking to citizens. Thomas Jefferson, around whom Republican opposition coalesced, then encouraged Philip Freneau to establish the *National Gazette* in Philadelphia in 1791 to counter Fenno's paper. By the mid-1790s, though, no newspaper launched more salvos at Hamilton and the Washington administration than Bache's.

Initially, Bache's paper had few criticisms of the Federalists and was even generally supportive of Hamilton's financial plan. Restoring the public credit, Bache argued, was wise, while the Bank of the United States would "facilitate business in every line and profession." Soon, though, Bache began to have second thoughts, and his paper began to take on a partisan tone. In 1792, he decried the speculation in government bonds unleashed by Hamilton's plans to repay the public debt. Such speculation, he declared, replaced industry and frugality with "idleness, dissipation and fraud." Like his grandfather and many future Republican leaders such as Thomas Jefferson, Bache believed that most Americans should remain farmers—independent, hardworking, and thrifty. Hamilton's support for the investing class and his promotion of manufacturing undermined virtue and fostered aristocracy and privilege.

The Federalists' response to the Whiskey Rebellion gave Bache more ammunition. Initially, Bache backed the Washington administration's forceful hand against the rebellion. The western rebels who defied the government only provided evidence to the enemies of Republican government who said that democracy would naturally descend to licentiousness. They "do an injury not only to themselves," he declared, "but to all mankind." Yet Bache still found ample reason to attack the Federalists. Their attempts to collect the tax had been heavy-handed. Worse, the whiskey tax was part of Hamilton's funding plan. Bache now concluded that, like British taxation, it placed too much executive power in the hands of the Treasury, tied the rich to the administration, and burdened the poor with high taxes. Bache saved most of his scorn, though, for Hamilton himself. The Treasury secretary, he charged, was guilty of "usurping the station of the god of war and directing the avenging thunder of the nation" against the rebels. Worse, Hamilton was a potential despot who conspired through a "deep laid scheme" to place himself atop the government. **[See Source 2.]**

The French Revolution stoked Bache's partisanship even further. Hamilton and other Federalists were shocked by revolutionary unrest and bloodshed in France.

Hamilton concluded that attachment to France was "womanish" and French "liberty and equality" were nothing more than a seedbed for anarchy and tyranny. **[See Source 3.]** Bache, on the other hand, shared Jefferson's belief that the further spread of liberty and republicanism depended on the fate of revolutionary France. Even in the face of the execution of Louis XVI and a bloody "Reign of Terror" that carried thousands of people to the guillotine, Bache stood his ground. French revolutionaries demonstrated that people could liberate themselves from the oppressive vestiges of the past. If the French republic were to fail, reactionary forces of aristocracy and monarchy would reassert themselves everywhere. Even in the United States, "advocates of hereditary government" might "come forward with their pernicious doctrines." The United States was duty-bound to support republican France.

Bache's support for the French Revolution reflected the feelings of many Americans. So did his rising partisanship. By the early 1790s, growing opposition to Federalist policies led to the emergence of Democratic societies throughout the states. Modeled on the Revolutionary era Sons of Liberty, these political clubs offered the Federalists' opponents a means to express their views, campaign for opposition candidates, and correspond with like-minded citizens in other states. The Democratic Society of Pennsylvania, where Bache served as a correspondent, was typical in its calls for support of revolutionary France. **[See Source 4.]** Taken aback by the sudden rise in partisanship, Federalists rightly saw these societies as adjuncts of a nascent Republican Party. In a speech to Congress, Washington called them a "diabolical attempt to destroy the best fabric of human government."

Such criticism, though, did little good. Americans continued to divide over foreign policy, especially when the British began to attack neutral American shipping after Britain and revolutionary France went to war in 1793. After British seizures of several hundred American ships stoked rising American anger, Hamilton acted to avoid war with Britain. Like other Federalists, he shuddered at the thought that the contagion of French mob rule would spread through Europe. He also knew that the profits of American merchants still mostly depended on trade with Britain. After arranging negotiations with the British, he picked Federalist John Jay to conduct them and then wrote the tenets of the treaty and Jay's instructions. Although the British agreed to evacuate forts they had held on American soil since the end of the Revolution, Jay's Treaty extracted no assurances from the British that their harassment of American shipping would stop. Hamilton knew the treaty would be unpopular with many Americans, but believed it would help prevent war with Britain. Blaming opposition to the treaty on "enthusiasm" for the French Revolution, Hamilton declared that "it makes no improper concessions to Great-Britain." **[See Source 5.]**

A firestorm, however, erupted soon after the treaty landed in the Senate for ratification in 1795 and no one played a more important role in creating it than Benjamin Bache. Anticipating a hostile public reaction, the Federalists had planned to keep the treaty's provisions a secret until the Senate had ratified it. A Virginia senator, however, secretly sent a copy to Bache—the first leak of a government secret since the Republic's founding. Bache, in turn, quickly published the treaty in pamphlet form. Then he set out to New York and Boston armed with a large number of copies to sell along the way. His hope was that public outrage would force Washington not to sign the treaty after it was approved in the Senate. Bache *did* stir an outcry. As one congressman reported to Hamilton after Bache had passed through Connecticut, "the greatest industry" was made "to disturb the public Tranquility." Indeed, Hamilton experienced public wrath firsthand when a crowd in New York City threw stones at him as he attempted to defend the treaty. Meanwhile, the *Aurora* proclaimed that nine-tenths of the people were opposed to the treaty and after Washington signed it, reported that news to readers, but quickly added that "we ... cannot yet believe it." Even after its ratification, Bache continued to attack the treaty on the grounds that it favored the merchant class. **[See Source 6.]**

After the fight over Jay's Treaty, which was approved in 1795, Bache lifted any restraints in his criticism of Federalists. Over the next three years, he launched scathing attacks on Washington and his successor John Adams, who had to deal with stepped-up assaults on American shipping by the French, themselves angry about Jay's Treaty. Nor did Bache often let Hamilton out of his sights, even after his resignation as Treasury secretary. In one fusillade, Bache characterized him as "artful, well informed, [and] intriguing" and charged that he "has dexterously seized the reins" of the government. After reports surfaced of an affair between Hamilton and a married woman, Bache declared that he "might be proved ... a seducer." Such attacks would have their effect. The Federalists had created the new government under the Constitution and then took control of it. It was easy for them to assume that they *were* the government and that attacks on them represented attacks on the government itself. Moreover, many Federalists, much like Bache and other Republicans, never understood that their political opponents had their own principles. Indeed, Hamilton was so convinced of the correctness of his position that he believed he could win over the worst enemies through logical argument. When that failed, he was sure that they had stooped to the lowest personal and political attacks. That attitude did not serve him or the Federalists well. As attacks on the Adams administration mounted, Federalists in Congress took a drastic step to muzzle the increasingly vocal Republican opposition. In 1798, they passed the Sedition Act, which provided jail time for critics of Adams and other high government officials.

Even Hamilton, who feared that it might lead to civil war, had concerns about the Sedition Act. Nonetheless, he called for its firm enforcement once passed. Meanwhile, Benjamin Bache was one of its first and most prominent victims. In fact, Federalists in Congress targeted him while debating the bill. As one Connecticut congressman declared, the purpose of Bache's newspaper was "to overturn and ruin the Government by publishing the most shameless falsehoods." Bache was arrested before the Sedition Act had even passed in Congress and Adams signed it into law. Released after posting bail, he promptly returned to his printing press to attack the supporters of the Sedition Act and fight for the cause of "truth and republicanism." Like Hamilton and many other Federalists, Bache attributed Federalist actions to the basest of motives. Ironically, he had been arrested because frightened Federalists saw Republicans' motives exactly the same way. His enemies, though, never had the opportunity to bring him to trial. In August 1798, a yellow fever epidemic swept through Philadelphia. Bache refused to take refuge outside the city, declaring that it was "heartrending that the laboring poor should almost exclusively be the victims" while the merchants fled to their rural estates. Two days after the birth of his son in September 1798, Bache fell ill. Eight days later he died. His wife Margaret edited the *Aurora* briefly before turning it over to Republican journalist William Duane, who carried on until 1822.

As for Hamilton, his inability to see political conflict in other than personal terms may have contributed to his own demise a few years later. After resigning as Treasury secretary in 1795, he returned to his law practice in New York. There he resumed a feud with longtime political foe Aaron Burr. Hamilton played a key role in denying Burr the presidency in 1800, while Burr opposed Hamilton's election as governor of New York. In 1804, their political and personal animosity led the two men to a dueling field in New Jersey. There the vice president of the United States shot and killed the former secretary of the Treasury.

By then, Jefferson and the Republicans had swept the Federalists from power. Yet not only did they leave in place Hamilton's Bank of the United States, but during the War of 1812, many of them had even reconsidered their opposition to manufacturing. As Britain brought its enormous power to bear against the United States, Jefferson declared, "We must now place the manufacturer by the side of the agriculturalist." Jefferson was alarmed by the extent to which Americans were dependent on British goods. That dependence was clear during the economic embargoes against Britain that Jefferson and his Republican successor, James Madison, instituted. The shortage of manufactured goods during the war drove the point home further. Only by encouraging domestic industry could the nation be truly independent of foreign nations. Those who opposed manufacturing, Jefferson said, would condemn Americans "to be clothed in skins, and to live like wild beasts in dens and caverns."

After the war, Republicans embraced Hamilton's philosophy with a vengeance, advocating a strong, interventionist government that promoted commerce and industry. In 1816, they created the Second Bank of the United States—a bigger and more powerful version of Hamilton's bank—passed higher tariffs than any Federalist Congress ever had, and even supported the use of federal money for major transportation projects.

Although the Federalist Party would virtually disappear after the War of 1812, the deep partisan divisions that Bache and Hamilton had done so much to create in the 1790s would remain part of American political life. So would the tension between the competing views that separated these two men. Their disagreement about foreign policy would not be Americans' last. They would also continue to argue about the proper role of the people in the government and of the government in the society, and how to balance the principle of equality and the protection of property. Often, too, those arguments have continued to reflect the same basic assumptions that set Bache and Hamilton so deeply at odds: Bache's optimism about people and their ability to engage in government and Hamilton's pessimism about the people and their ability to govern themselves without powerful restraints. In other words, like Bache and Hamilton, Americans continue to disagree about the best way, as Benjamin Franklin put it, to "keep" a republic.

• PRIMARY SOURCES •

Source 1: Alexander Hamilton, "To the People of the United States" (1794)

Writing under the pseudonym Tully, Hamilton in this source warns Americans about the threat to them from the Whiskey Rebellion and alerts them to the deceptive arguments made by some of the its critics. What does Hamilton see as the primary issue raised by the rebellion? What does he see as the real intent of some critics of the rebels?

The adversaries of good order would unite with good citizens, and perhaps be among the loudest in condemning the disorderly conduct of the insurgents. They would agree that

SOURCE: Alexander Hamilton, "To the People of the United States" (1794). Originally from AMERICAN DAILY ADVISOR (Philadelphia), August 23, 1794.

it is utterly unjustifiable, contrary to the vital principle of republican government, and of the most dangerous tendency—But they would, at the same time, slily add, that excise laws are pernicious things, very hostile to liberty (or perhaps they might more smoothly lament that the government had been imprudent enough to pass laws so contrary to the genius of a free people). They would be apt to intimate further, that there is reason to believe that the Executive has been to blame, sometimes by too much forbearance, encouraging the hope that the laws would not be enforced, at other times in provoking violence by severe and irritating measures; and they would generally remark, with an affectation of moderation and prudence, that the case is to be lamented, but difficult to be remedied; that a trial of force would be delicate and dangerous; that there is no foreseeing how or where it would end; that it is perhaps better to temporize, and by mild means to allay the ferment, and afterward to remove the cause by repealing the exceptionable laws.

By these means, artfully calculated to divert YOUR attention from the true question to be decided; to combat, by prejudices against a particular system, a just sense of the criminality and danger of violent resistance to the laws; to oppose the suggestion of misconduct on the part of government to the fact of misconduct on the part of the insurgents; to foster the spirit of indolence and procrastination natural to the human mind, as an obstacle to the vigor and exertion which so alarming an attack upon the fundamental principles of public and private security demands; to distract YOUR opinion on the course proper to be pursued, and consequently on the propriety of the measures which may be pursued. They would expect (I say) by these and similar means equally insidious and pernicious, to abate YOUR just indignation at the daring affront which has been offered to YOUR authority and your zeal for the maintenance and support of the laws; to prevent a competent force, if force is finally called forth, from complying with the call—and thus to leave the government of the Union in the prostrate condition of seeing the laws trampled underfoot by an unprincipled combination of a small portion of the community; habitually disobedient to laws, and itself destitute of the necessary aid for vindicating their authority.

Virtuous and enlightened citizens of a new and happy country! Ye could not be the dupes of artifices so detestable, of a scheme so fatal; ye cannot be insensible to the destructive consequences with which it would be pregnant; ye cannot but remember that the government is YOUR own work—that those who administer it are but your temporary agents; that you are called upon not to support their power, BUT YOUR OWN POWER. And you will not fail to do what your rights, your best interests, your character as a people, your security as members of society, conspire to demand of you.

Source 2:   *Benjamin Bache on Hamilton and the Whiskey Rebellion (1794)*

In November 1794, Benjamin Bache printed numerous commentaries on Hamilton's role in putting down the Whiskey Rebellion. Note Bache's reference in one of them to the circumstances of Hamilton's birth. On what grounds does he attack the Federalist response to the rebellion?

SOURCE: Benjamin Bache on Hamilton and the Whiskey Rebellion (1794). Originally from General Advertiser (Philadelphia).

... [W]e find the Secretary of the Treasury usurping the station of the god of war and directing the avenging thunder of the nation. Yet what is his station in the army? He has no ostensible character there, as far as the public have learnt, and it would be insulting the patriotism and talents of the commander in chief to suppose he needs a director. At any rate the Secretary is there surely out of his element, and as he is paid to attend the financial concerns of this country his absence from the seat of government is a dereliction [*sic*] of his duty. But perhaps, this absence may have the good effect of convincing those not already convinced that his labours in the financial career can be dispensed with, and that money bills can be originated without his *instrumentality*.

......

These who consult the secret springs of the human mind will readily account for the Secretary of the Treasury's presence with the army. The excise as the child of his own heart, tho' a bastard in the soil that give it birth, has called forth the feelings of the father, when the avenging sword was to be drawn for the punishment of its opposers. The Secretary by his presence with the army will, thro' the means of his talents and influence, to forward the views of his faction, assist in placing the principle which led to the almost unanimous exertions against the opposers of the law, in a false light, a favorite end with the faction at the present moment. It is their wish to make the friends of the constitutional law to be considered as friends to the introduction into our soil of all the poisonous exotics of the old world. But the discriminating sense of the people of this country will baffle the attempt and while they hold up their hand against all illegal opposition to measures of the government will also ever raise their voice against all the *instrumentality* systems of the Secretary.

......

The public appear to have some curiosity to learn of the object of the Treasury Secretary's presence with the army, and his meddling interference in the department totally irrelative to his official duties. It is truly inconceivable how the Secretary's presence at the seat of the government can be spared, especially at the opening of an important session of Congress. By some it is whispered that he is with the army without invitation, and by many it is shrewdly suspected his conduct is a first step towards a deep laid scheme—not for the promotion of his country's prosperity—but the advancement of his private interests and the gratification of an ambition, laudable in itself, if pursued by proper means.

......

It is certainly better that the western expedition should cost a million or two more to the United States, than that blood should have been spilt for want of a respectable force being at first sent against the rioters;—yet a correspondent cannot help being of opinion, that in the late crisis, no circumstances, of public notoriety at least, existed, that made it necessary to call into the field 12, or 15,000 men. At the time these troops were ordered out, no insurgents were embodied, and they were without leaders,—nothing portended a systematic opposition to government; their proceedings were confined to a few unwarrantable acts of riot, which no doubt called for repression, but which did not need the exertion of so large a force as was called out.—In the Massachusetts insurrection; at a time when 8000 insurgents were embodied in arms and officered and had already raised contributions in some of the small towns it was thought sufficient to call out 2000 militia, and before the main body of these reached the field of action a handful of them had already quelled the disturbance.

Source 3:   Alexander Hamilton, *"The French Revolution"* (1794)

In this critique of the French Revolution, Hamilton assesses its consequences for French society. What danger does he see in the revolutionary fervor in France? What points in Hamilton's assessment do you think Bache would have disputed?

In the early periods of the French Revolution, a warm zeal for its success was in this Country a *sentiment truly universal.* The love of Liberty is here the ruling passion of the *Citizens of the UStates* pervading every class animating every bosom. As long therefore as the Revolution of France bore the marks of being the cause of liberty it united all hearts concentered all opinions. But this unanimity of approbation has been for a considerable time decreasing. The excesses which have constantly multiplied, with greater and greater aggravations have successively though slowly detached reflecting men from their partiality for an object which has appeared less and less to merit their regard. Their reluctance to abandon it has however been proportioned to the ardor and fondness with which they embraced it. They were willing to overlook many faults—to apologise for some enormities—to hope that better justifications existed than were seen—to look forward to more calm and greater moderation, after the first shocks of the political earthquake had subsided. But instead of this, they have been witnesses to one volcano succeeding another, the last still more dreadful than the former, spreading ruin and devastation far and wide—subverting the foundations of right security and property, of order, morality and religion—sparing neither sex nor age, confounding innocence with guilt, involving the old and the young, the sage and the madman, the long tried friend of virtue and his country and the upstart pretender to purity and patriotism—the bold projector of new treasons with the obscure in indiscriminate and profuse destruction. They have found themselves driven to the painful alternative of renouncing an object dear to their wishes or of becoming by the continuance of their affection for it accomplices with Vice Anarchy Depotism and Impiety....

It is not among the least perplexing phœnomia of the present times, that a people like that of the UStates—exemplary for humanity and moderation surpassed by no other in the love of order and a knowledge of the true principles of liberty, distinguished for purity of morals and a just reverence for Religion should so long perservere in partiality for a state of things the most cruel sanguinary and violent that ever stained the annuals of mankind, a state of things which annihilates the foundations of social order and true liberty, confounds all moral distinctions and *substitutes* to the mild & beneficent religion of the Gospel a gloomy persecuting and desolating atheism. To the eye of a wise man, this partiality is the most inauspicious circumstance, that has appeared in the affairs of this country. It leads involuntarily and irresistibly to apprehensions concerning the soundness of our principles and the stability of our welfare. It is natural to fear that the transition may not be difficult from the approbation of bad things to the imitation of them; a fear which can only be mitigated by a careful estimate of the extraneous causes that have served to mislead the public judgment....

If there be any thing solid in virtue—the time must come when it will have been a disgrace to have advocated the Revolution of France in its late stages.

SOURCE: Alexander Hamilton, "The French Revolution" (1794).

This is a language to which the ears of the people of this country have not been accustommed. Everything has hitherto conspired to confirm the pernicious fascination by which they are enchained.

Hence the voice of reason has been stifled and the Nation has been left unadmonished to travel on in one of the most degrading delusions that ever disparaged the understandings of an enlightened people.

To recal them from this dangerous error—to engage them to dismiss their prejudices & consult dispassionately their own good sense—to lead them to an appeal from their own enthusiasm to their reason and humanity would be the most important service that could be rendered to the UStates at the present juncture. The error entertained is not on a mere speculative question. The French Revolution is a political convulsion that in a great or less degree shakes the whole civilized world and it is of real consequence to the principles and of course to the happiness of a Nation to estimate it rightly.

Source 4:   *Resolutions of the Pennsylvania Democratic Society* (1794)

In these resolutions of a Democratic Society in Philadelphia, Benjamin Bache and other members protest Federalist attacks on the societies and declare their support for revolutionary France. How does the society portray France's cause against its enemies? How does the view of France's cause expressed here differ from Hamilton's in Source 3?

1st. Resolved, that it is one of the unalienable rights of freemen at all times to meet together in a peaceable manner, to discuss with temper, but with freedom and firmness all subjects of public concern, and to declare and publish their Sentiments to their fellow citizens, whenever they think they can thereby promote the general good. That as a consequence of this principle and from a Sense of the advantages which result to a community from such discussion, popular societies have been cherished—and incouraged in every free country, and never have been dreaded but by men, whose conduct or principles could not bear the test of public investigation.

2d. Resolved, that the democratic society, founded on the purest principles of civil liberty, and of respect and attachment to the constitution and laws of their country; unbiased by any party views, and actuated solely by patriotic motives, at a time when the most momentious concerns agitate the public mind, and call forth thro' every channel the expressions of the public sentiments, have thought it their duty to take these important subjects into their serious consideration, and declare their sense of them by the following resolutions:

3d. Resolved, that we view with inexpressible horror the cruel and unjust war carried on by the combined powers of Europe against the French republic—that attached to the French nation (our only true and natural ally) by sentiments of the liveliest gratitude for the great and generous services she has rendered us, while we were struggling for our liberties and by that strong connection which arises from a similarity of government and of political principles, we cannot sit passive and forbear expressing our anxious concern, while she is greatly contending against a World, for the same rights which she assisted us to establish—that exclusive of the sentiments, so natural to every true american, the

SOURCE: "Resolutions of the Pennsylvania Democratic Society" (1794).

powerfull motive of self interest combines to connect us still closer to france; for when we see so many sovereigns, having different interests, and some of whom are natural enemies to each other. Confederate against a single Nation with no other avowed object than that of changing her internal government, we cannot believe that they are making war against that Nation solely, but against liberty itself. Impressed with this idea, we cannot help concluding, that if those lawless despots succeed in destroying an enemy in france so formidable to their tyranical usurpations, they will not rest satisfied until they have exterminated it from the earth; it therefore behoves us, as we value our dear bought rights to give to a cause so just in itself, and which we may so properly call our own, every countenance and support in our power, consistently with the laws of our Country.

4th. Resolved, that we ought to resist to the utmost of our power all attempts to alienate our affections from france and detach us from her alliance, and to connect us more intimately with great britain; that all persons who, directly or indirectly, promote this unnatural succession ought to be considered by every free american as enemies to republicanism and their country.

5thly Resolved, that our interest as well as our national dignity requires that the sentiments of the people of america should be manifested at the present important period, and that it should be known…; that we are determined to abide by our national engagements, and preserve our national friendships; that a firm and manly conduct, is the best calculated to secure to us the blessings of peace, while timid and wavering measures will expose us to numberless insults and outrages, and after a painful career of humiliation, finally draw us ingloriously into a war, which firmness and decision might have prevented.

Source 5:   *Hamilton Defends Jay's Treaty* (1795)

Writing under the pseudonym Camillus, Hamilton analyzes opposition to Jay's Treaty and makes reference to Benjamin Bache's early publication of the treaty through "a medium noted for hostility to the administration." What is his view of the motives of Bache and other treaty opponents? How does he relate Jay's Treaty to events in France?

IT was to have been foreseen, that the treaty which Mr. Jay was charged to negociate with Great Britain, whenever it should appear, would have to contend with many perverse dispositions and some honest prejudices. That there was no measure in which the government could engage so little likely to be viewed according to its intrinsic merits— so very likely to encountre misconception, jealousy, and unreasonable dislike. For this many reasons may be assigned.

It is only to know the vanity and vindictiveness of human nature, to be convinced, that while this generation lasts, there will always exist among us, men irreconciliable to our present national constitution–embittered in their animosity, in proportion to the success of its operation, and the disappointment of their inauspicious predictions.…

SOURCE: Alexander Hamilton, "Hamilton Defends Jay's Treaty" (1795).

It was not to be mistaken that an enthusiasm for France and her revolution through-out all its wonderful vicissitudes has continued to possess the minds of the great body of the people of this country, and it was to be inferred, that this sentiment would predispose to a jealousy of any agreement or treaty with her most persevering competitor—a jeal-ousy so excessive as would give the fullest hope to insidious arts to perplex and mislead the public opinion. It was well understood, that a numerous party among us … have been steadily endeavouring to make the United States a party in the present European war, by advocating all those measures which would widen the breach between us and Great Britain, and by resisting all those which could tend to close it; and it was morally certain, that this party would eagerly improve every circumstance which could serve to render the treaty odious, and to frustrate it, as the most effectual road to their favorite goal.…

Before the treaty was known, attempts were made to prepossess the public mind against it. It was absurdly asserted, that it was not expected by the people, that Mr. Jay was to make any treaty; as if he had been sent, not to accommodate differences by ne-gociation and agreement, but to dictate to Great Britain the terms of an unconditional submission.

Before it was published at large, a sketch, calculated to produce false impressions, was handed out to the public through a medium noted for hostility, to the administration of the government. Emissaries flew through the country, spreading alarm and discontent: the leaders of clubs were everywhere active to seize the passions of the citizens and pre-occupy their judgments against the treaty.

At Boston it was published one day, and the next a town meeting was convened to condemn it, without ever being read; without any serious discussion, sentence was pro-nounced against it.

The intelligence of this event had no sooner reached New York, than the leaders of the clubs were seen haranguing in every corner of the city to stir up our citizens into an imitation of the example of the meeting at Boston. An invitation to meet at the City Hall quickly followed, not to consider or discuss the merits of the treaty, but to unite with the meeting at Boston to address the president against its ratification.

This was immediately succeeded by a hand bill, full of invectives against the treaty as absurd as they were inflammatory, and manifestly designed to induce the citizens to sur-render their reason to the empire of their passions.

In vain did a respectable meeting of the merchants endeavour, by their advice, to moderate the violence of these views, and to promote a spirit favourable to a fair discus-sion of the treaty; in vain did a respectable body of citizens of every description, attend for that purpose. The leaders of the clubs resisted all discussion, and their followers, by their clamours and vociferations, rendered it impracticable, notwithstanding the wish of a manifest majority of the citizens convened upon the occasion.

Can we believe, that the leaders were really sincere, in the objections they made to a decision, or that the great and mixed mass of citizens then assembled had so thoroughly mastered the merits of the treaty, as that they might not have been enlightened by such a discussion.

It cannot be doubted that the real motive to the opposition, was the fear of a discus-sion; the desire of excluding light; the adherence to a plan of surprise and deception. Nor need we desire any fuller proof of that spirit of party which has stimulated the opposition to the treaty, than is to be found in the circumstances of that opposition.

To every man who is not an enemy to the national government, who is not a pre-judiced partisan, who is capable of comprehending the argument, and passionate enough to attend to it with impartiality, I flatter myself I shall be able to demonstrate satisfactorily in the course of some succeeding papers—

1. That the treaty adjusts in a reasonable manner the points in controversy between the United States and Great-Britain, as well those depending on the inexecution of the treaty of peace, as those growing out of the present European war.
2. That it makes no improper concessions to Great-Britain, no sacrifices on the part of the United States.
3. That it secures to the United States equivalents for what they grant.
4. That it lays upon them no restrictions which are incompatible with their honour or their interest.
5. That in the articles which respect war, it conforms to the laws of nations.
6. That it violates no treaty with, nor duty toward any foreign power.
7. That compared with our other commercial treaties, it is upon the whole, entitled to a preference.
8. That it contains concessions of advantages by Great-Britain to the United States, which no other nation has obtained from the same power.
9. That it gives to her no superiority of advantages over other nations with whom we have treaties.
10. That interests of primary importance to our general welfare, are promoted by it.
11. That the too probable result of a refusal to ratify is war, or what would be still worse, a disgraceful pas[s]iveness under violations of our rights, unredressed and unadjusted; and consequently, that it is the true interest of the United States, that the treaty should go into effect.

It will be understood, that I speak of the treaty as advised to be ratified by the Senate—for this is the true question before the public.

CAMLLUS.

Source 6: *Benjamin Bache Assaults Jay's Treaty* (1795)

Jay's Treaty made it possible for British creditors to seek payment on American debts owed to them before 1776 and provided for some compensation to northern merchants for British seizures, but made no mention of payment for loss of slaves to the British during the Revolutionary War. What provisions of the treaty does Bache focus on in this commentary? Why was it important for him to emphasize the claim that the treaty was pro-British?

The indemnification for British robberies, which Mr. Jay was sent to demand, has been completely metamorphosed by the treaty into an indemnification to British merchants, trading to America, for debts incurred previous to the war. The amount of the sum to be paid by virtue of this ingenious bargain, is supposed in the aggregate to amount to about ten millions of dollars. The part of which sum will necessarily fall to the share of this state [Pennsylvania], is somewhere, upon a rough calculation, nearly one million five hundred thousand dollars. But as it is to be paid by an indirect tax, and not a direct assessment, it seems to some as if it was not to be paid at all. The sum we may receive for all our losses, and at the highest computation, deducting the legal costs of the collection, in a country [Great Britain] where the 'laws's delay' is a proverb, may rise possibly and at a strained calculation to one million dollars on the whole. Upon the first debt, interest and damage is to be paid. Upon the debt due for their piracies in time of profound

SOURCE: Benjamin Bache, "Benjamin Bache Assaults Jay's Treaty" (1795). Originally from AUROROA Philadelphia), July 25, 1795.

peace, there is not a word of interest. The Massachusetts creditors may receive, perhaps, two hundred thousand dollars.

... The best of the bargain is, that no other man ever "whispered" an idea that the Americans would have had anything to pay, although we all expected something to be received. For the fact is, the British never thought of demanding this debt, until Mr. Jay thought proper to remind them of it, lest we might have too good a bargain with our good old friends. But after all if this debt was fairly due, why not the individuals pay it, and not the public? This question no doubt will be fully explained by the friends of Mr. Jay at his next election;* although for reasons good and wholsome [sic], it is now a "secret."

QUESTIONS TO CONSIDER

1. What issues in the early 1790s divided Alexander Hamilton and Benjamin Bache? What assumptions about the people, government, and society influenced each man's position on these issues? How do divisions between politicians and political parties on important issues today also reflect these assumptions?

2. Hamilton, born in obscurity, became a champion of the "rich and well-born." Bache, born into favorable circumstances, denounced the influence of a selfish elite within the government and celebrated the political influence of common people. How do you account for this contrast? How did each man's background and experiences influence his political views?

3. How do you account for the view of both Hamilton and Bache that the other was out to destroy Republican government? Citing examples from the primary sources, how were these views reflected in arguments regarding specific issues?

4. In his Farewell Address in 1796, George Washington warned the nation about the "baneful effects of the spirit of party" and "excessive partiality for one foreign nation and excessive dislike of another." What does the conflict between Alexander Hamilton and Benjamin Bache reveal about the role that this "partiality" played in the partisan conflict between Federalists and Republicans in the 1790s? How do you account for that "partiality" in the case of each man?

FOR FURTHER READING

Ron Chernow, *Alexander Hamilton* (New York: Penguin Press, 2004), offers a recent biography of the nation's first Treasury secretary that details his contributions to the nation's financial system.

John C. Miller, *The Federalist Era, 1789–1801* (New York: Harper & Row, 1960), remains a highly accessible overview of the Federalists in power and the political conflict of the 1790s.

---

*John Jay was chief justice of the U.S. Supreme Court from 1789 to 1795, when he resigned to become the governor of New York.

William Nester, *The Hamiltonian Vision, 1789–1800: The Art of American Power during the Early Republic* (Washington, D.C.: Potomac Books, 2012), highlights the influence of foreign affairs on American political conflict in the 1790s.

Jeffery A. Smith, *Franklin and Bache: Envisioning the Enlightened Republic* (New York: Oxford University Press, 1990), emphasizes the impact of Franklin and Enlightenment ideas on Bache.

Thomas P. Slaughter, *The Whiskey Rebellion: Frontier Epilogue to the American Revolution* (New York: Oxford University Press, 1988), provides a history of the Whiskey Rebellion and its political dimensions.

James Tagg, *Benjamin Franklin Bache and the Philadelphia Aurora* (Philadelphia: University of Pennsylvania Press, 1991) details Bache's career as a journalist and the role played by his newspaper in the partisan conflict of the 1790s.

7

Resistance and Western Expansion: Tecumseh and William Henry Harrison

The negotiations had gone nowhere. Tempers had flared, and now William Henry Harrison drew his sword to kill Tecumseh. The governor of Indiana Territory viewed the Shawnee chief as a dangerous enemy. His movement to unify Native Americans in armed resistance to whites was a frightening obstacle in the path of American progress. The United States had bought this land from other tribes. Now settlers were pouring into the territory to carve farms, homes, and towns out of the wilderness. No Indian leader was going to stand in the way of that. Harrison would eliminate Tecumseh's threat to the country in hand-to-hand combat. This was politics on the frontier in 1810: nation versus nation, Native American versus European American, man versus man. It was political, and it was personal.

Harrison and Tecumseh had two very different visions of the future. For Harrison, the area west of the Appalachian Mountains, east of the Mississippi River, and north of the Ohio River represented an unrivaled opportunity for the expansion of the nation. The Ohio Country, or Northwest Territory as it was often called, could support millions of Americans in future generations. Settlers would build a vast commercial empire there. At the same time, they would prevent European powers such as Great Britain and Spain from blocking the westward growth of the United States. Whoever ensured that American civilization advanced into this area would be a hero.

For Tecumseh, the land along the Spaylaywitheepi (Ohio River) was sacred. The Shawnees were one of the most warlike Indian nations in North America. For generations, they had battled their traditional enemies, the Cherokees and Iroquois. The Shawnees had lived in what is now Pennsylvania, Tennessee, and other areas before

Tecumseh

William Henry Harrison

finally coming to the Ohio Country. In about 1725, another powerful tribe, the Miamis, had invited the Shawnees to live on the lands to their east. The Shawnees would serve as a buffer between the Miamis and the Iroquois. For the first time in tribal history, the Shawnees had a defined homeland. They thanked Waashaa Monetoo (the Great Spirit, who had created the world) for this land. Here they could live in peace, grow crops and hunt game, and follow the ways of their ancestors.

To the east, though, the Long Knives[*] had begun to push westward into the Ohio country. The end of the Revolutionary War had brought a small stream of them. But now it flowed continuously, bringing thousands across the Appalachians. Watching the white settlers tramp into the Ohio country, Tecumseh had done his best to avoid warfare. Yet he longed for the day when the Shawnees would drive the Americans out and restore their former power and glory. In 1810, Harrison and Tecumseh met at Vincennes, on the Wabash River north of the Ohio River. In a long tirade, Tecumseh taunted the governor. He shouted so angrily that one of the officers standing nearby ordered his men to seize the Indians in front of them. As the soldiers started forward, the Indians produced their tomahawks. Harrison pulled his sword, convinced that the time had come to kill the Indian leader, but cooler heads prevailed. Tecumseh spun on his heels and stalked away. Both leaders now knew that only bloodshed would resolve their differences.

---

[*]*Long Knives:* A term for Americans used by the Shawnee and other Indians of the Ohio country in the early years of the nineteenth century, apparently derived from the swords often worn by military officers.

"PANTHER PASSING ACROSS"

Tecumseh (Panther Passing Across, or Shooting Star) was born in 1768 as a huge meteor streaked across the sky. His father, Pukeshinwau (Something That Falls), named his son after Panther, a spirit who traveled like a powerful meteor. From the first, Tecumseh's family thought that he had the blessing of the spirit world. His father was a great warrior who had become one of the most important chiefs in the tribe. He had married an attractive woman named Methoataaskee (Turtle Laying Her Eggs in the Sand), and they had begun to raise a family. Tecumseh was their fourth child. He far surpassed the other boys in the tribe and showed an uncommon skill with weapons. Attentive and intelligent, he spent hours listening to the elders of the village as they passed on the tribe's history and customs. By the time he was ten, Tecumseh was a successful hunter and a tribal historian. When he brought home a deer, he shared it with the elderly members of the village, earning their respect. Such generosity was expected of a great hunter and warrior.

The young man also learned the religious rites that governed Shawnee life. The Shawnees organized every aspect of day-to-day living around rituals. Social relations, war, trade, hunting, and planting crops all required rituals that summoned or appeased the spirits. Tecumseh had great respect for these rites, but he learned that many young people did not. Some older members of the tribe feared that the spirits would someday punish the Shawnees for this. They blamed the loss of interest in old ways on the whites who were encroaching on Shawnee land. The whites' trade goods, they said, created among the Indians a growing dependency on the Long Knives. They also blamed the Christian missionaries, who brought new ideas and a new religion to challenge the old. And they blamed the whites' "firewater" (usually rum and brandy), to which so many young warriors were addicted.

Even before the American Revolution, many Shawnee leaders were ready to take up arms. Hokolesqua (Cornstalk), the principal chief of the tribe, opposed war. He argued that fighting the Long Knives would do far more harm than good. Eventually, however, the push to fight was too strong, and he reluctantly agreed to lead the Shawnees on the warpath. When an army of Virginia militia threatened to invade Shawnee territory in 1774, Cornstalk struck first. The result was the Battle of Point Pleasant. Both sides claimed victory, but the Indians had inflicted many more casualties than the whites. One of the Indians who died was Tecumseh's father. The family was adopted by Chiungalla (Black Fish), a respected chief and longtime family friend, who became Tecumseh's foster father.

The war with the Long Knives raged on after the Revolution. It also split the Shawnee tribe. More than half had chosen not to fight in a war they believed they could not win. They did not want to risk their lives and the children's futures and had instead moved farther west, beyond the Mississippi. The rest of the tribe had stayed behind, fighting desperately for their land as allies of the British. Tecumseh and his family were among those who stayed. Accompanied by his older brother Chiksika, Tecumseh led raids on the Americans and in time became an accomplished warrior.

The Indian style of warfare was personal. Face-to-face relations in peace became hand-to-hand combat in war. Adversaries often knew and had great respect for each other. The Shawnees and their allies won many great victories. The Miami chief, Mishikiniqua (Little Turtle), joined Chiungalla and other great chiefs in leading the warriors. They ambushed entire armies and humiliated the young United States with devastating defeats. But in the end, it was a losing effort. In 1794, twenty years of warfare came to an end when General "Mad Anthony" Wayne defeated the allied tribes at the Battle of Fallen Timbers. The following year, Wayne forced the chiefs to sign the Treaty of Greenville, which turned over half of what is now the state of Ohio to the United States. Included in the treaty was most of the land the Shawnees had called home for two generations. Wayne also forced the Indians to accept the conditions of previous treaties. Some of those treaties involved fraudulent land sales, including the sale to whites of Shawnee land by the Iroquois. Some Shawnee chiefs refused to sign Wayne's treaty and argued that those who did sign lacked the authority to do so. Many warriors, including Tecumseh, followed the lead of these chiefs.

"A MOST DESIRABLE OBJECT"

William Henry Harrison was not born under a celestial sign. He did enter the world in 1773, however, under very favorable circumstances. Harrison's father was a prominent planter and politician, a member of the Virginia gentry, a delegate to the Continental Congress, and a signer of the Declaration of Independence. His mother also hailed from the gentry. The Harrisons lived on a sprawling plantation along the James River called Berkeley. William was well educated and attended Hampden-Sydney College, although he did not graduate. Instead, he went off to Philadelphia, where he studied medicine under the renowned Dr. Benjamin Rush, a leading man of medicine and hero of the American Revolution. Yet Harrison was not cut out for a career in medicine. Military glory was what he sought. When his father died, he expressed his displeasure with the medical field, left his studies, and was commissioned as an officer in the U.S. Army.

Harrison served as a lieutenant in the infantry and was posted to the Northwest Territory. By the time he arrived there in 1792, the area was aflame with the Indian wars. He served as General Wayne's aide and distinguished himself in the campaign that ended the long conflict with the allied tribes in 1795. Military service suited Harrison. Although he did not like the long periods of inactivity and boredom between battles, his thirst for combat allowed him to endure the slow times, and he flourished under military discipline. He came to admire Wayne, whose decisiveness led to victory on the battlefield. A bold fighter, Wayne once told Harrison that his standing battle order was "Charge the damned rascals with the bayonets!" Emulating his commanding officer, Harrison never shied away from a fight. Still, the boredom of military life wore on him. During the long hours in camp, he began to study theology, thinking that he might pursue a career as a minister. He soon gave that up and turned instead to the art of distilling spirits, thinking he might open his own distillery. Then he began studying the law, but he gave that up as well.

Following Wayne's successful campaign in 1794–1795, Harrison went to Lexington, Kentucky, where he met Anna Symmes. Lovely, graceful, and well educated, she was the daughter of Judge John Cleves Symmes, who had large claims in Ohio. Symmes headed up a grand real estate scheme called the Symmes Purchase. Along with other investors, Symmes proposed to buy a vast tract in Ohio and then sell it off to settlers. Harrison cut a dashing figure as he courted Anna. He rode well, looked handsome in uniform, and projected ruggedness as a result of his long military service.

Judge Symmes, however, was unimpressed. When he asked young Harrison how he expected to support his daughter, the soldier replied with a flourish, "By my sword and my own right arm." The answer impressed Symmes, but he found the match distasteful nonetheless. Referring to Harrison's inability to decide on a profession, Symmes wrote to a friend that his daughter's suitor "can neither bleed, plead, nor preach." Eventually, though, he came to accept Harrison's military career. "His best prospect is in the army," Symmes said, "he has talents, and if [he] can dodge [bullets] a few years, it is probable he may become conspicuous."

After marrying Anna in secret in 1795, Harrison settled near what is today Cincinnati. He was promoted to captain, but the boredom of garrison duty proved too much, and he resigned his commission in 1798. Then, using his family connections, he obtained a position as territorial secretary of the Northwest Territory. The following year, the territorial legislature elected him its delegate to Congress. As territorial representative, Harrison served on a committee to oversee the sale of public lands. The position enabled him to solidify friendships and political connections. In 1800, President John Adams appointed him governor of Indiana Territory, one of two territories carved out of the original Northwest Territory.

Convinced that the residents of Indiana wanted slavery, Harrison attempted to introduce the institution there, even though it was prohibited under the Northwest Ordinance.* His family had owned slaves in Virginia, and he faced a labor shortage on his own farm near Vincennes. He managed to push a bill through Congress that allowed slavery under another name, but when this was later repealed, he did not object. Still, Harrison tried several temporary slavery experiments on his farm and continued privately to support the "peculiar institution." As governor and superintendent for Indian affairs, he efficiently carried out President Thomas Jefferson's Indian policy. Jefferson urged him to acquire all Indian land within the territory for the United States and even suggested loaning the tribes money so that their land could later be taken away by way of collection. Harrison agreed that doing away with Indian titles to the land was "a most desirable object." **[See Sources 1 and 2.]**

All the while, Harrison saw himself as a moderate when it came to dealing with the Indians. He sincerely believed that friendly relations should be developed with the tribes. He claimed to respect the Native Americans and acknowledged that many of their arguments about the land were correct. He also believed that he understood their culture. In fact, he arrogantly claimed to have a better understanding of the Indians than did some of their own chiefs. After all, he had traded with them, practiced some of their rituals, and negotiated and fought with them many times. And he certainly felt qualified to expound on them in print. Later, he would write a book about the tribes titled *A Discourse on the Aborigines of the Ohio Valley*. In this short tract, Harrison argued that the tribes who had sold their territory to the United States had never owned the land and had no right to do so. Of course, this was long after Harrison had already carried out the policies that took the Indians' land away from them. **[See Source 3.]**

In fact, Harrison had few qualms about enforcing Indian land sales. As an officer of the U.S. government, his duty was to implement the policies that its leaders devised. Yet there was more to his actions than that. He also had personal ambitions and knew that opening up Indian land for white settlement could win him fame and fortune. Furthermore, he knew that the land in question rightfully belonged to the United States by the laws of nature, politics, and conquest. And he suspected that the British were behind recent Indian attacks on the frontier. The British had fought alongside the Indians in the American Revolution and had maintained a string of forts on American soil in the Great Lakes region after the war. Now operating from Canada, they were deeply

---

Northwest Ordinance: This 1787 law organized the Northwest Territory and established the process by which territories could become states. It also prohibited slavery, a measure that Harrison and other proponents of slavery opposed.

involved in the fur trade around the Great Lakes. Harrison believed that they had designs on the entire Northwest, and he was determined to keep it from them.

"THE OPEN DOOR"

Sometime in the fall of 1803, Tecumseh's younger brother Lalawethika (Loud Mouth) underwent a religious transformation. Lalawethika was generally regarded as a failure among the Shawnees. Unlike Tecumseh, he had not become a successful hunter and warrior. In fact, he had lost an eye in a hunting accident and in other ways had fallen short of the expectations of Shawnee manhood. Instead of hunting with the men, he preferred to sit around camp and converse with the women. In addition, he was surly, arrogant, and disliked by nearly everyone. Only Tecumseh showed him any respect. Lalawethika had become an alcoholic in his early teens and depended on Tecumseh to keep him supplied with whiskey bought or stolen from the whites. He had married a woman with a strong personality, and she constantly nagged him and humiliated him in front of the other men of the tribe. He spent most of his days and nights in a drunken stupor.

In 1803, Lalawethika fell into a drunken coma, and his family thought that he had died. While they were making preparations for his funeral, he suddenly awoke and announced that he had been in a religious trance. He had been transported to the spirit world, had had a vision of the future, and had been given a new name. He insisted that he now be called Tenskwatawa—"The Open Door." He called for the Shawnee people to avoid the whites, to give up their trade goods and be independent of them. He predicted that the dwindling game would return in great numbers, that long-dead ancestors would come back to life, and that the whites would eventually be driven out of the Indians' land forever. He claimed that the Great Spirit had ordered him to destroy those Indians who practiced witchcraft or prayed to the Christian God. Such individuals, he declared, should be burned at the stake.

Many suspected that it was Tecumseh who had had this vision. Perhaps he had simply asked his younger brother to convey the vision for him. Whatever the case, Tenskwatawa, aided by Tecumseh, attracted a following of young warriors from the Shawnees and other tribes. This Indian religious revival spread quickly. In fact, it resembled the series of Christian revivals known as the Second Great Awakening[*] that were sweeping the country at the time. Before long, hundreds of Indians were moving to live near Tenskwatawa, who came to be called "the Prophet." The movement was a cultural revitalization, a return to traditional values, and a promise that the Indians' lost greatness would be restored.

When word of Tenskwatawa reached Governor Harrison, he suspected that this was all part of a plan devised by Tecumseh to stir up trouble with the whites. He challenged Tenskwatawa to prove himself. The Prophet agreed to do so, saying that he would blot out the sun. Hundreds of skeptical Indians joined his devoted followers to see what would happen. On the appointed day, the Prophet chanted and prayed to the spirits. As high noon approached, he spread out his hands, and the sun was darkened by a full solar eclipse. The onlookers were amazed, and the religious awakening became even more widespread.

---

[*]*Second Great Awakening:* The Protestant religious revival in the first decades of the nineteenth century. Often characterized by tremendous emotional outpourings, this revival spread from the frontier to urban areas and resulted in thousands of conversions.

In 1808, Tecumseh and Tenskwatawa moved their followers from the area around Greenville, Ohio, and established a new Indian town in central Indiana. Called Prophet's Town, it was soon home to several thousand Indians. To keep their followers fed, the leaders of the movement depended on the annual food supplies and trade goods that the U.S. government gave the conquered tribes. These annuities had been part of the hated Treaty of Greenville. Harrison used these supplies to his advantage and tried to bargain with Tecumseh by threatening to withhold them if he did not contain his movement. Realizing the advantage the trade goods gave the whites, Tecumseh now refused to accept the supplies on principle.

The two men met on several occasions. There were heated arguments and threats from both sides. As mentioned earlier, during one meeting in 1810, Harrison nearly physically attacked Tecumseh. **[See Source 4.]** At another meeting, Tecumseh told Harrison that there was nothing he could do to stop the Indians. He also told the governor that he was going south to bring the southern tribes into the movement. He would build a pan-Indian movement, uniting all the tribes between the Appalachian Mountains and the Mississippi River. He would persuade them to set aside their differences and accept the leadership of those the Great Spirit had appointed to restore them to greatness. Once united, the Indians would be in a position of strength and would set the terms for future treaties with the whites. If the Americans refused to negotiate and accept the Indians' position, then the great alliance would attack all across the frontier, from the Great Lakes to the Gulf of Mexico. It would drive the whites east of the Appalachians.

In the 1670s, the Wampanoag leader Metacom (also called Philip) had forged an alliance that had killed thousands of whites in New England in King Philip's War. At the conclusion of the French and Indian War,[*] the Ottawa leader Pontiac had tried to unite all of the Great Lakes tribes against the British. Pontiac's confederation had nearly destroyed all of the British posts on the frontier, but in the end his plans had failed. Now, as Tecumseh and Tenskwatawa hatched a similar plan, Harrison was alarmed. He had great respect for Tecumseh, and he feared the young leader's influence. He heard reports that the Prophet's followers accused Christian Indians of witchcraft and burned them at the stake. His spies brought news of large numbers of warriors coming to Prophet's Town, supposedly to hear Tenskwatawa's religious message. He viewed the religious awakening among the Indians as a serious threat to the United States and was convinced that he had to act.

In 1811, Tecumseh toured the camps of the southern tribes. He spoke before the gathered councils of the Cherokee, Creek, Chickasaw, and Choctaw Nations. He implored them to set aside their differences and join his pan-Indian confederation. He asked them to give up their tribal identities and become brothers with all other children of the Great Spirit. He called for them to give up white culture and return to their own traditional ways. He pleaded for them to take up the hatchet and join the northern tribes in an all-out war against the Americans the following year. **[See Source 5.]**

Although war appealed to many young warriors, Tecumseh was unable to rally all the tribes. He failed to overcome the Cherokees' traditional hatred of the Shawnees. The Choctaws also refused to join the confederacy, although for a time it seemed that they were inclined to do so. In the end, an influential chief, Pushmataha, single-handedly opposed Tecumseh in debate and convinced his people to remain at peace with the whites. Tecumseh was more successful among the Creeks, persuading nearly half of

---

[*]*French and Indian War:* The war fought in North America from 1754 to 1763. It pitted Britain and its colonial allies against France and its Indian allies.

them to join the northern tribes on the warpath the following summer. A small number of warriors from the other southern tribes also agreed to fight. Some even started north to join the movement at Prophet's Town. Tecumseh left the southern tribes, telling those who would listen to him to look for a great sign—a trembling of the earth—that would demonstrate his power and signal the beginning of the war against the whites.

While Tecumseh was in the South pleading his case, Harrison decided to strike. In November 1811, he mustered his troops and led them toward Prophet's Town. Before leaving, Tecumseh had instructed Tenskwatawa to avoid conflict. The time for battle, he said, had not yet come. The Indians were not quite ready. When reports of Harrison's march reached Tenskwatawa, however, he insisted that he had had a vision. The spirits, he said, were telling him that the time for war was at hand. The Indians would attack in the predawn darkness, and Tenskwatawa predicted that the spirits would enable the warriors to see in the dark as if it were the middle of the day. The whites, he declared, would be blinded. And so Tenskwatawa ordered the attack that started the Battle of Tippecanoe. The result was a devastating defeat for the Indians. Harrison and his army killed nearly two hundred warriors, burned Prophet's Town, and in one fell swoop destroyed the Prophet's power.

Tecumseh returned after the defeat. He saved his disgraced brother from execution at the hands of his disillusioned followers. Then, as Tecumseh had predicted, came a great earthquake that shook the entire Midwest and much of the South. He became the Indians' religious leader, but they could not overcome the military defeat at Tippecanoe. Many of the warriors who had dedicated themselves to the cause went home disgusted. Only Tecumseh's forceful leadership and suddenly evident prophetic abilities managed to keep the movement alive.

By the following year, the rising Indian unrest on the frontier symbolized by Tecumseh and Prophet's Town helped foment anti-British sentiment in many Americans. Like Harrison, they were convinced that the British had instigated Tecumseh's movement. Unable to see that their troubles with Native Americans were of their own making, they were looking for a scapegoat. British agents operating from Canada did have relations with the Indians, and the British navy, locked in a war with France, had been harassing neutral American commercial vessels for years. In the minds of many Americans, the United States was under assault on land and sea. The result was a rising chorus for war, and in 1812, President James Madison succumbed. When the War of 1812 began, Tecumseh's followers joined with the British to fight the Americans.

Tecumseh fought bravely, even recklessly, during the war, especially in battles against his old foe Harrison. His ferocious attacks thwarted American plans to conquer Canada at the Battle of the Raisin River, and Canadians would later praise Tecumseh for saving their country. The final battle with Harrison was the last of Tecumseh's life. They met in October 1813 at the Battle of the Thames along Canada's Thames River north of Lake Erie. The day before the conflict, Tecumseh had another vision. This time, it was a premonition of his death. When he told his fellow warriors, they protested. Surely, he must be mistaken, for he had never suffered even a slight wound in battle. They all believed that he enjoyed the special blessing of the spirits and could not be hurt in battle. Tecumseh insisted that his vision was accurate and told them that when they saw him fall, they should strike his body four times with a ramrod. Then, he said, he would rise from the dead and lead them to victory. After that, Tecumseh prophesied, all that Tenskwatawa had preached would come true: The game would return, their long-dead ancestors would join them, and the whites would be driven out forever. The following day, the Indians went into battle against Harrison and his troops. In the heat of the fray, Tecumseh was killed. A warrior, ramrod in hand, rushed forward to carry out his instructions. He struck his fallen leader's body once, twice, three times—then was shot and killed himself. Tecumseh did not rise from the dead. The Indians did not win a great victory.

By the time the British and Americans signed the treaty ending the War of 1812, Tecumseh's Indian confederation was smashed. In the coming years, Andrew Jackson would carry out mopping-up actions against the Creeks and other hostile tribes. Even the Choctaws, Cherokees, and other Indians who had fought with the United States in the war were removed to the trans-Mississippi West. The door was now wide open to a flood of white settlers. Within five years, two more new states—Indiana and Illinois—would enter the union from the Northwest Territory. By 1820, the surge of settlers would cross the Mississippi into territory acquired in the Louisiana Purchase. By 1830, more Americans lived west of the Appalachians than had lived in the original thirteen states in 1790. Many of them had settled on land taken from Indians in treaties negotiated after the War of 1812.

Harrison's vision for the Northwest Territory became a reality as thousands, and eventually millions, of whites settled on old tribal lands. His role in defeating the Indians in the War of 1812 made him a hero. His career in politics carried him to the House of Representatives, the U.S. Senate, and eventually the White House. When he ran for the presidency with John Tyler in 1840, it was as a military hero and Indian fighter. Their slogan "Tippecanoe and Tyler Too" was a powerful reminder of Harrison's military feats. Harrison served as president for only one month, however, before dying of pneumonia.

His death, of course, did the Indians little good. By 1841, the Indians between the Appalachians and the Mississippi had been defeated. Their game had been depleted, and the old traditions and rituals had fallen by the wayside. They had lost the battle, the war, their land, and their culture. In Tecumseh, they had also lost a great leader. In helping to kill Tecumseh, Harrison had extended the domain of the United States.

• PRIMARY SOURCES •

Source 1:   Thomas Jefferson, *Letter to William Henry Harrison* (1803)

Thomas Jefferson wrote this letter to William Henry Harrison when Harrison was governor of Indiana Territory. What changes does Jefferson propose in the Indians' way of life? What means does he suggest for bringing these changes about? What conclusions do you think Tecumseh would have drawn from this document?

[T]his letter being unofficial and private, I may with safety give you a more extensive view of our policy respecting the Indians.... Our system is to live in perpetual peace with the Indians, to cultivate an affectionate attachment from them, by everything just and liberal which we can do for them within the bounds of reason, and by giving them effectual protection against wrongs from our own people. The decrease of game

SOURCE: Thomas Jefferson, "Letter to William Henry Harrison" (1803).

rendering their subsistence by hunting insufficient, we wish to draw them to agriculture, to spinning and weaving. The latter branches they take up with great readiness, because they fall to the women, who gain by quitting the labors of the field for those which are exercised within doors. When they withdraw themselves to the culture of a small piece of land, they will perceive how useless to them are their extensive forests, and will be willing to pare them off from time to time in exchange for necessaries for their farms and families. To promote this disposition to exchange lands, which they have to spare and we want, for necessaries, which we have to spare and they want, we shall push our trading uses, and be glad to see the good and influential individuals among them run in debt, because we observe that when these debts get beyond what the individuals can pay, they become willing to lop them off by a cession of lands. At our trading houses, too, we mean to sell so low as merely to repay us cost and charges, so as neither to lessen or enlarge our capital. This is what private traders cannot do, for they must gain; they will consequently retire from the competition, and we shall thus get clear of this pest without giving offence or umbrage to the Indians. In this way our settlements will gradually circumscribe and approach the Indians, and they will in time either incorporate with us as citizens of the United States, or remove beyond the Mississippi. The former is certainly the termination of their history most happy for themselves; but, in the whole course of this, it is essential to cultivate their love. As to their fear, we presume that our strength and their weakness is now so visible that they must see we have only to shut our hand to crush them, and that all our liberalities to them proceed from motives of pure humanity only. Should any tribe be fool-hardy enough to take up the hatchet at any time, the seizing the whole country of that tribe, and driving them across the Mississippi, as the only condition of peace, would be an example to others, and a furtherance of our final consolidation.

Source 2:   William Henry Harrison, *Letter to William Eustis, Secretary of War* (1809)

William Henry Harrison negotiated a number of treaties with the Indian tribes of the Ohio country while serving as governor of Indiana Territory. In this letter, Harrison reports on the actions of the Prophet and discusses his own plans for buying more land in Indiana. At the time, he believed that the Prophet had been unable to unify the tribes and hoped to use that failure as an opportunity to purchase more land. Why did Harrison think that he had to acquire more territory in yet another treaty?

I have great pleasure in being enabled to inform you that there no longer exists the least probability of a rupture with any of the Indian tribes of this frontier. The party which the Prophet had assembled have dispersed with manifest indications of terror and alarm. Whether this is to be attributed to the military preparations which were made here, [t]o the want of provisions, disappointment upon the part of the Prophet as to the force he expected to raise, or to the combination of all these causes, or whether indeed he had ever any design of attacking us I cannot at present determine. Whatever I shall be able to discover on this subject shall form the matter of another

SOURCE: William Henry Harrison, "Letter to William Eustis, Secretary of War" (1809).

communication. I have engaged a confidential Frenchman who speaks the Indian languages to reside at the Prophet's Town for a few weeks to watch his movements and discover his politics.

I have for several years considered a further extinguishment of Indian title to the North East of this and extending from the Wabash to the purchase made at the Treaty of Grouseland as a most desirable object. And it appears to me that the time has arrived when the purchase may be attempted with a considerable prospect of success. Our settlements here are much cramped by the vicinity of the Indian lands, which in the direction above mentioned is not more than twenty-one miles. The country on the Wabash below this is sunken and wet, that to the north and west almost entirely Prairie and not of such a quality to be settled for many years. These circumstances must necessarily render the settlements here feeble for a considerable time unless a further extinguishment of title is effected in the direction I have mentioned.

The effecting of this purchase will come within the scope of the Instructions hitherto received, but I shall conclude no bargain until I am honored with the President's further direction.

Source 3: William Henry Harrison, *A Discourse on the Aborigines of the Ohio Valley* (1839)

In the following excerpt from his pamphlet, Harrison describes several Indian leaders, including Tecumseh (Tecumthey). What does Harrison think of these Indians? In his view, what kind of men are they? How do you think Tecumseh would have responded to him?

As it regards their moral and intellectual qualities, the difference between the tribes was still greater. The Shawanees, Delawares, and Miamis, were much superior to the other members of the confederacy. I have known individuals among them of very high order of talents, but these were not generally to be relied upon for sincerity. The Little Turtle, of the Miami tribe, was one of this description, as was the Blue Jacket, a Shawanee chief. I think it probable that Tecumthey possessed more integrity than any other of the chiefs, who attained to much distinction; but he violated a solemn engagement, which he had freely contracted,—and there are strong suspicions of his having formed a treacherous design, which an accident only prevented him from accomplishing. Sinister instances are, however, to be found in the conduct of great men, in the history of almost all civilized nations. But these instances are more than counterbalanced by the number of individuals of high moral character, which were to be found amongst the principal, and secondary chiefs, of the … tribes above mentioned. This was particularly the case with Tarhe, or the Crane, the grand sachem of the Wyandots, and Black Hoof, the chief of the Shawanees. Many instances might be adduced, to show the possession on the part of these men, of an uncommon degree of disinterestedness and magnanimity, and strict performance of their engagements, under circumstances—which would be considered by many as justifying evasion. But one of the brightest parts of the character of those Indians, is

SOURCE: William Henry Harrison, "A Discourse on the Aborigines of the Ohio Valley" from A DISCOURSE ON THE ABORIGINES OF THE OHIO VALLEY (1839; reprint, Chicago: Fergus Printing Company, 1883), pp. 39–40, 92.

their sound regard to the obligations of friendship. A pledge of this kind, once given by an Indian of any character, becomes the ruling passion of his soul, to which every other was made to yield—He regards it as superior to every other obligation. And the life of his friend would be required at the hands of him, (or his tribe,) who had taken it, even if it had occurred in a fair field of battle, and in the performance of his duty as a warrior....

I once asked a very distinguished chief what he supposed was necessary to constitute a good and a great man. He replied, that a good father, a good husband, a good neighbor, a good warrior, and a lover of his nation, was all in his opinion that was necessary for a man to possess, to fulfill the expectations of the Great Spirit, who placed us on this earth; though, the Indians generally appear to care but little about a future state. They are only anxious to live to an old age in this world.

Source 4:   Tecumseh, *Speech to Harrison at Vincennes* (1810)

In 1810, William Henry Harrison and Tecumseh met, and their negotiations nearly culminated in violence. In the following excerpt, Tecumseh argues that the Treaty of Greenville was not legitimate and speaks of Indian relations with the British. At the close of this speech, Harrison stood and drew his sword, preparing to attack Tecumseh. Why do you think Harrison was so upset by this speech?

Brother. This land that was sold and the goods that was given for it was only done by a few. The treaty was afterwards brought here and the Weas [a subtribe of the Miamis] were induced to give their consent because of their small numbers. The treaty at Fort Wayne was made through the threats of Winamac but in future we are prepared to punish those chiefs who may come forward to propose to sell their land. If you continue to purchase of them it will produce war among the different tribes and at last I do not know what will be the consequence to the white people.

Brother. I was glad to hear your speech you said if we could show that the land was sold by persons that had no right to sell you would restore it.... These tribes set up a claim but the tribes with me will not agree to their claim, if the land is not restored to us you will soon see when we return to our homes how it will be settled. We shall have a great council at which all the tribes shall be present when we will show to those who sold that they had no right to sell the claim they set up and we will know what will be done with those Chiefs that did sell the land to you. I am not alone in this determination it is the determination of all the warriors and red people that listen to me.

I now wish you to listen to me. If you do not it will appear as if you wished me to kill all the chiefs that sold you this land. I tell you so because I am authorised by all the tribes to do so. I am at the head of them all. I am a Warrior and all the Warriors will meet together in two or three moons from this. Then I will call for those chiefs that sold you the land and shall know what to do with them. If you do not restore the land you will have a hand in killing them.

Do not believe that I came here to get presents from you[.] [I]f you offer us anything we will not take it. By taking goods from you you will hereafter say that with them you purchased another piece of land from us. If we want anything we are able to

SOURCE: Tecumseh, "Speech to Harrison at Vincennes" (1810).

buy it, from your traders. Since the land was sold to you no traders come among us. I now wish you would clear all the roads and let the traders come among us. Then perhaps some of our young men will occasionally call upon you to get their guns repaired. This is all the assistance we ask of you....

If you think proper to give us any presents and we can be convinced that they are given through friendship alone we will accept them. As we intend to hold our council at the Huron village that is near the British we may probably make them a visit. Should they offer us any presents of goods we will not take them but should they offer us powder and the tom[a]hawk we will take the powder and refuse the Tom[a]hawk.

I wish you *Brother* to consider everything I have said is true and that it is the sentiment of all the red people who listen to me.

By your giving goods to the Kickapoos you killed many they were seized with the smallpox by which many died.

Source 5:   Tecumseh, "Sleep Not Longer, O Choctaws and Chickasaws" (1811)

In 1811, Tecumseh went to the southern tribes and tried to convince them to join his confederacy against the whites. How does he appeal to the Choctaws and Chickasaws? What reasons does he give them for uniting with the northern tribes? What does this passage reveal about the sources of Tecumseh's appeal as a leader?

[H]ave we not courage enough remaining to defend our country and maintain our ancient independence? Will we calmly suffer the white intruders and tyrants to enslave us? Shall it be said of our race that we knew not how to extricate ourselves from the three most dreadful calamities—folly, inactivity and cowardice? But what need is there to speak of the past? It speaks for itself and asks, Where today is the Pequod? Where the Narragansetts, the Mohawks, Pocanokets, and many other once powerful tribes of our race? They have vanished before the avarice and oppression of the white men, as snow before a summer sun. In the vain hope of alone defending their ancient possessions, they have fallen in the wars with the white men. Look abroad over their once beautiful country, and what see you now? Naught but the ravages of the pale face destroyers meet our eyes. So it will be with you Choctaws and Chickasaws! Soon your mighty forest trees, under the shade of whose wide spreading branches you have played in infancy, sported in boyhood, and now rest your wearied limbs after the fatigue of the chase, will be cut down to fence in the land which the white intruders dare to call their own. Soon their broad roads will pass over the grave of your fathers, and the place of their rest will be blotted out forever. The annihilation of our race is at hand unless we unite in one common cause against the common foe. Think not, brave Choctaws and Chickasaws, that you can remain passive and indifferent to the common danger, and thus escape the common fate. Your people, too, will soon be as falling leaves and scattering clouds before their blighting breath. You, too, will be driven away from your native land and ancient domains as leaves are driven before the wintry storms.

SOURCE: Tecumseh, "Sleep Not Longer, O Choctaws and Chickasaws" (1811).

Sleep not longer, O Choctaws and Chickasaws, in false security and delusive hopes. Our broad domains are fast escaping from our grasp. Every year our white intruders become more greedy, exacting, oppressive and overbearing. Every year contentions spring up between them and our people and when blood is shed we have to make atonement whether right or wrong, at the cost of the lives of our greatest chiefs, and the yielding up of large tracts of our lands. Before the palefaces came among us, we enjoyed the happiness of unbounded freedom, and were acquainted with neither riches, wants nor oppression. How is it now? Wants and oppression are our lot; for are we not controlled in everything, and dare we move without asking, by your leave? Are we not being stripped day by day of the little that remains of our ancient liberty? Do they not even kick and strike us as they do their black-faces? How long will it be before they will tie us to a post and whip us, and make us work for them in their corn fields as they do them? Shall we wait for that moment or shall we die fighting before submitting to such ignominy?

… Shall we give up our homes, our country, bequeathed to us by the Great Spirit, the graves of our dead, and everything that is dear and sacred to us, without a struggle? I know you will cry with me: Never! Never! Then let us by unity of action destroy them all, which we now can do, or drive them back whence they came. War or extermination is now our only choice. Which do you choose? I know your answer. Therefore, I now call on you, brave Choctaws and Chickasaws, to assist in the just cause of liberating our race from the grasp of our faithless invaders and heartless oppressors.

QUESTIONS TO CONSIDER

1. How would you compare the visions of the Northwest Territory held by Tecumseh and William Henry Harrison? How did their personal histories influence those visions?

2. Harrison and Tecumseh met many times to negotiate. They ultimately failed to reach a compromise. Was there any way their competing visions for the territory could have been reconciled and allowed to coexist? Why or why not?

3. What does the conflict between Harrison and Tecumseh show you about the westward expansion of the United States in the early nineteenth century? Were individual personalities, government policy, or conflicting values most important in explaining the conflict between these two men?

4. If Tecumseh had survived and the Indians had won at the Thames or Tippecanoe, do you think his vision for the future would have become reality? Why or why not?

FOR FURTHER READING

Colin G. Calloway, *The Shawnees and the War for America* (New York: Viking, 2007), discusses the Shawnee resistance to white encroachment that culminated with Tecumseh's campaign.

Gregory Evans Dowd, *A Spirited Resistance: The North American Indian Struggle for Unity* (Baltimore: Johns Hopkins University Press, 1992), offers an intriguing study that concentrates on Tenskwatawa, the Prophet.

James A. Green, *William Henry Harrison: His Life and Times* (Richmond: Garrett and Massie, 1941), provides a reliable, if dated, biography of Harrison.

Francis Paul Prucha, *American Indian Policy in the Formative Years: The Indian Trade and Intercourse Acts, 1780–1834* (Cambridge: Harvard University Press, 1970), provides an overview of early American Indian policy.

John Sugden, *Tecumseh: A Life* (New York: Henry Holt and Company, 1997), provides the most reliable biography of the Shawnee leader.

8

The Fruits of the Factory System: Sarah Bagley and Nathan Appleton

Nathan Appleton had every reason to be happy. The father of the Massachusetts mill town of Lowell had just traveled with thirteen other cotton mill owners from Boston to New Hampshire's Lake Winnipesaukee. There they had scouted out a site for another textile mill complex. Confident that it would eventually rival the Massachusetts mill town, the men decided to celebrate with a dinner at Lowell's plush Merrimack Hotel. Appleton and the other mill owners had built the Merrimack to accommodate them on their periodic trips from Boston. Now, on this late March evening in 1845, they could bask in their good fortune over a fine dinner prepared by the hotel's cooks.

It was a perfect occasion for Appleton to reflect on his own success. At age sixty-five, he was the central figure among the Boston Associates, the group of merchants-turned-manufacturers who controlled dozens of New England textile mills. His stake in those properties at Lowell and elsewhere had made him a rich man. In the past fifteen years, his income from five textile companies alone had amounted to $336,000—enough to provide a fine home in Boston, servants, trips to Europe, and expensive schooling for his seven children. No wonder this "lord of the loom" had become one of the nation's leading spokesmen for an emerging industrial order.

As he dined with his companions, Appleton could also take satisfaction in knowing that he had done well by doing good. He and his associates had not enriched themselves at the expense of their employees. Rather, they had built Lowell as a model factory town where workers would be uplifted, not degraded as in England's wretched mills. And although his profits had been great, Appleton had a reputation as a scrupulously honest man and one of the nation's leading philanthropists. In fact, what he called an "enlightened public spirit" had guided all of his activities.

Yet not everyone in Lowell was happy. Only a few weeks earlier, Appleton could have joined another social gathering in a reading room just a few blocks from the Merrimack Hotel. This one featured various comic performances, including one by a "Reformed Drunkard Player." Appleton might have been amused by the entertainment, but he would not have appreciated its purpose. Sponsored by the Lowell Female Labor Reform Association (LFLRA), the gathering was intended to raise funds for this organization of female mill workers. Appleton would have learned that the LFLRA, founded only three months before, already claimed nearly three hundred members. And he could have met its president, a thirty-nine-year-old worker named Sarah Bagley.

If Appleton was a leading spokesman for the emerging industrial system, Bagley was quickly becoming one of its most outspoken critics. Brought face to face with the mill owner, she would have given him an earful regarding the conditions at Lowell. At a time when women were supposed to remain silent on controversial subjects, Bagley founded the LFLRA to fight for a ten-hour workday and to show the "*driveling* cotton lords" that "our rights cannot be trampled upon with impunity." She would go on to serve as an officer in a male-dominated labor organization and as an editor of the *Voice of Industry*, a newspaper that printed articles critical of conditions in the mills. She even took her case for shorter hours of labor to the Massachusetts legislature. Although Bagley never faced off against Appleton, by the time her brief career as a labor leader was over, she had called into question the beneficence of the new industrial system and left Americans with a competing image of it that survives to this day.

"LIKE THE SETTING AT AN OPERA"

Born in 1779 to a prosperous New Hampshire farmer, Nathan Appleton was fifteen when he arrived in Boston to begin his career in business. He had just turned down a chance to attend Dartmouth College for the opportunity to join his brother's trading firm. Working as a clerk for Samuel Appleton, a retailer of goods, Nathan applied himself

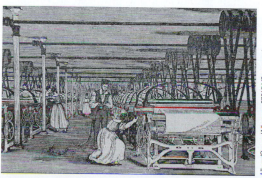

Women tending power looms: Sarah Bagley's first job at Lowell

Nathan Appleton

Album/Oronoz/Alburn crz07814/Superstock

National Park Service>Longfellow National Historic

diligently. In his spare hours, he studied French and taught himself double-entry book-keeping. Soon Samuel expanded into imports and gave Nathan the job of managing them. When Nathan turned twenty-one, his brother made him a partner in the firm. They were no longer just shopkeepers but merchants—that is, importers and wholesalers as well as retailers. They were also well connected. Related to several prominent Boston merchants, including the Cabots, Jacksons, and Lowells, the Appletons were able to secure space on Boston ships. With Samuel based in England to supervise purchases, Nathan was left in charge of S. & N. Appleton's Boston countinghouse. There he over-saw the sale of various dry goods, cutlery, notions, and luxury items.

It was a profitable business, and the Appletons gradually established contacts in French and Dutch ports and even as far away as Calcutta (now Kolkata). Often handling shipments of ten thousand dollars or more, they soon began to buy and sell southern cotton and rice and West Indian sugar and coffee. Nathan often supervised those pur-chases and proved to be an astute trader. On one trip to the South, he recorded markups of up to 120 percent over his purchase price for goods. No wonder he could write to Samuel that if the shipments arrived safely in England, they would bring "handsome profits."

By 1807, however, safe passage of the Appletons' goods was a problem. Britain and France were at war, and both sides struck hard at American neutral shipping. Before Thomas Jefferson responded to these attacks in 1807 with an embargo on all American exports, the Appletons had already severely curtailed their business. It was a sound decision. Jefferson's embargo resulted in a drastic decline in American commerce that sparked a se-vere nationwide depression. The Appletons found other goods to sell in the American market, including Turkish opium. Nonetheless, the Republicans' attempt to coerce Britain and France to respect American neutral shipping proved ruinous to many merchants. Although Congress replaced the embargo in 1809 with a prohibition on trade only with Britain and France, the Appletons decided "by mutual consent" to dissolve their partner-ship in the face of continued disruption of their trade.

Yet Nathan Appleton had no intention of leaving the trading business. With a for-tune standing at $200,000, he quickly formed his own wholesale import firm to take advantage of new trading opportunities after the United States lifted the embargo on Britain and France in 1810. Still, turning a profit was not easy. New England markets were slow to recover from the embargoes, forcing Appleton to expand to New York City, Philadelphia, and even the South. Then, in 1811, Madison reimposed the embargo on Britain after France promised to respect American neutral rights. Normally restrained, Appleton was furious. These trade restrictions, he fumed, fell "on the most meritorious part of society." When growing anti-British sentiment finally provoked an American declaration of war on Britain the next year, Appleton declared it the work of "madmen." During the War of 1812, he refused to support some fellow New England Federalists' calls for secession. By importing stockpiled goods from Canada and using ves-sels of foreign registry, however, he aggressively took advantage of loopholes in the law. Nonetheless, by 1814, his business was at a standstill. Conditions did not improve much after the war either. Resuming trade as an importer of British goods in 1815, he battled high American tariffs[*] and a glutted domestic market. By then, however, he was inter-ested in another business.

---

[*]*Tariffs*: Taxes placed on foreign imports to protect domestic producers of competing items.

Five years earlier, in 1810, Appleton and his wife, Maria, had left Boston for a year of travel in Britain. Maria suffered from tuberculosis, and Nathan hoped the trip would improve her health. While there, Appleton met his distant cousin Francis Cabot Lowell. In Britain ostensibly for *his* health, Lowell had visited numerous textile mills, where he saw new power looms—machinery using waterpower to convert thread into finished cloth—in operation. The two men spoke repeatedly, and for the remainder of Appleton's trip, textile factories captured his attention. As a merchant, he could surely sense that conditions were favorable for textile manufacturing in America. Ever since Samuel Slater had opened his Pawtucket, Rhode Island, yarn mill in 1793, the number of spindles operating in New England had grown steadily. By cutting British imports, the embargoes and the War of 1812 had increased domestic yarn production further. Dozens of spinning mills had sprung up in New England to meet the demand for thread. But nobody had yet combined spinning and weaving under one roof.

After meeting with Appleton, Lowell returned home and began work on a loom to produce finished cloth. The British guarded their textile technology closely, and Lowell was forced to steal the design for the loom by making mental notes while in their mills. Like looms in Britain, his would harness waterpower to weave cloth. But Lowell also had something else in mind. He planned to build a mill to spin thread and weave cloth, a far more efficient arrangement than the "putting-out" system in which thread was distributed to weavers tending hand-powered looms at home. In 1813, Lowell and Boston merchant Patrick T. Jackson formed the Boston Manufacturing Company (BMC). The firm's capital was set at $100,000. To raise money, Lowell and Jackson asked ten other relatives and friends to invest. One of them was Appleton, who was reluctant at first to support such a speculative venture. "To see the experiment fairly tried," however, he agreed to purchase five shares at $1,000 each and to serve on the board of directors. The BMC purchased a mill site on the Charles River in Waltham, Massachusetts, and by 1814, Lowell's loom was ready for demonstration. "I well recollect the state of admiration and satisfaction with which we sat by the hour," Appleton later wrote, "watching the beautiful movement of this new and wonderful machine." The BMC's mill, the world's first vertically integrated* textile factory, was up and running by early 1815. Under the roof of the four-story, ninety-by-forty-foot building, cotton was cleaned, corded, spun into thread, and woven into cloth.

Meanwhile, the company's directors had devoted considerable thought to securing workers. A mere village in 1814, Waltham suffered from a lack of housing and a shortage of labor. Lowell and Appleton also realized that manufacturing itself posed a unique and potentially disastrous problem. Both men were concerned about manufacturing's possible effects on the character of workers. In that regard, neither Lowell nor Appleton had been reassured by Britain's textile mills. Appleton was especially appalled by the conditions in the textile center of Manchester, England, where a scarcity of labor had resulted in higher wages, which Appleton considered "a serious evil." Workers could get by on only four days' labor and spent the rest of their time "drinking & spending what they [had] earned." To Appleton, such behavior proved that workers were unwilling to improve themselves even "where they [had] the means."

Lowell and Appleton believed that employing farmers' daughters from the New England countryside would solve the labor shortage in Waltham and avoid these problems. Female workers would command much lower wages than their male

---

Vertically integrated: A vertically integrated factory is one that performs all the steps needed to transform raw materials into finished products.

counterparts, and as products of patriarchal households, they could be expected to respect male authority. In addition, they would never form a permanent laboring class because the young women would work in the mills for only a few years before marrying. Getting them to Waltham, however, required special measures. Early nineteenth-century women were confined to domestic roles, and young single women did not generally leave home until marriage. To attract these workers to Waltham, the company had to build boarding houses and staff them with matrons to protect the girls' morals. Schools, churches, libraries, and a bank where workers could deposit their savings soon followed. Such company paternalism would reassure nervous parents about their daughters' safety outside the domestic sphere. At the same time, it would make it possible to have factories without debasing workers and disrupting the social order. **[See Source 1.]**

The BMC's success made such benevolence easier. By 1817, profits were high enough for the company to pay its first dividend of 17 percent, and for the next nine years, dividends averaged 18.75 percent. Appleton's share in 1817 alone totaled $5,540, at a time when many of his mill hands made less than a dollar a day. Such returns no doubt accounted for his flagging interest in imports and his growing role in the BMC's affairs, especially after Lowell's death in 1817. Increasingly, the company came to bear Appleton's imprint. A frequent witness to commercial bankruptcies, Appleton knew that inadequate funding often spelled doom for a business. As Waltham expanded to three mills by 1821, he insisted that the BMC not tie up all its capital in buildings and other fixed assets. As he had in his own firm, he also established careful accounting procedures. Appleton's trading ventures had led him into domestic markets far removed from New England. Thus he was perfectly suited to handle the sales of textiles, which had to be distributed over a broad market as well. The BMC's exclusive sales agent, Appleton's own firm, garnered a 1 percent commission on the sale of goods. When sales ran into the millions of dollars, even such a low commission made for "a desirable and profitable business."

Soon an optimistic Appleton was ready to apply the Waltham method on a larger scale. With Patrick Jackson, he found a site on the Merrimack River where the water power could accommodate many more mills. In 1821, Jackson and Appleton created the Merrimack Manufacturing Company (MMC). They envisioned a town of fifty mills that would be laid out according to plans developed by Francis Cabot Lowell and named after him. The first mill opened in less than three years. To speed the construction of others, Appleton and his associates established a separate company to own Lowell's mill sites and to build canals, sell land, and lease waterpower to new firms. In this way, other wealthy Boston merchants who had not invested in the BMC or MMC could participate in Lowell's growth and help make sure that the mills were sufficiently capitalized. As a principal owner of the new firms, Appleton would naturally reap the benefits of that growth.

The soundness of this plan was soon apparent. Within another decade, the growing group of Boston Associates had $6 million invested in nineteen mills operating eighty-four thousand spindles and three thousand looms. By 1833, Lowell's population topped twelve thousand, and five thousand workers, called operatives, labored in the mills, including three thousand women. Yet Lowell was more than a sound investment. It was also a showcase. Following Waltham's paternalistic model, Appleton and the other mill owners provided boarding houses and matrons for the female operatives. By 1833, Lowell claimed ten churches, schools, a savings bank, a library, and a lyceum,[*] which offered lectures for fifty cents. It had also attracted numerous visitors who could not help comparing this

---

[*]*Lyceum:* A hall where public lectures or concerts are held; also an organization that presents such activities.

industrial paradise to the dismal cities of Europe. Setting his eyes for the first time on Lowell's tree-lined streets, red-brick mills, trim dormitories, and "little wooden houses, painted white," one awestruck European visitor could hardly believe it was real. "It was new and fresh," he exclaimed, "like the setting at an opera."

More than the massive mills and tidy houses, however, it was Lowell's "acres of girlhood," as New England poet John Greenleaf Whittier put it that attracted the notice of admiring observers. Especially impressive was Lowell's success in safeguarding the morals of its female operatives. Only three cases of illicit relations had occurred, one company director informed a visitor in 1834. In "all three cases," he quickly added, "the parties were married immediately." The mill girls seemed not only virtuous but also industrious and content. Thrifty depositors at the Lowell Savings Bank, they could return home after several years with enough money to marry. They were so different from European workers "clamoring for work, starving unless employed, and hence ready for a riot," another admirer noted. It was no accident that President Andrew Jackson was greeted by a procession of twenty-five hundred mill girls, each wearing a white muslin dress and carrying a parasol, when he visited in 1833. After filing past the president, the girls marched to their respective mills, where Jackson later observed them tending their machines. As Appleton and his associates realized, what "Old Hickory" called the "very pretty women" of Lowell had become its biggest selling point.

"DOOMED TO ETERNAL SLAVERY"

Four years after Andrew Jackson visited Lowell, a middle-aged woman from the village of Meredith Bridge (now Laconia), New Hampshire, arrived there. We do not know much about Sarah Bagley's youth, except that she was born in 1806, probably the third of five children, and was likely educated in common schools. Her father farmed in Candia and then Gilford, New Hampshire. At thirty-one, Sarah was older than most of the mill girls, whose ranks had swollen even since Jackson's visit. (About sixty-four hundred women, typically between seventeen and twenty-four years old, worked in Lowell by 1840.) Perhaps she was drawn by Lowell's glowing reputation, or maybe she had been recruited by an agent hired by one of the mills to scour the countryside for workers. Or perhaps she just needed the work.

By the 1830s, the region's farm families faced declining futures as the rich farmland of the Old Northwest was put to the plow. In addition, farmers' daughters had previously spent much of their time assisting their mothers with spinning and weaving, but cheap cloth from Waltham, Lowell, and elsewhere now made their work unnecessary. For these or other reasons, the Bagleys' fortunes, like those of so many other rural New England families, seem to have been declining. Thus Sarah decided that it made sense to seek a job in the mills.

When Bagley arrived in Lowell in the fall of 1837, she went to work tending the power looms in the weaving room of a mill owned by the Hamilton Manufacturing Company, one of the new firms founded by Appleton. She found accommodations in a boarding house run by a widow. Board came to $1.25 a week, and like the fifty or so other women living there, she was expected to follow strict regulations set by Appleton. [See Source 2.] In the summer, she would be awakened by the bells at 4:30 a.m. and work until 7:00 p.m., with only a half-hour for meals. In the winter, the hours were shorter, but work was often performed by the light of whale-oil lamps. Only on Sundays and four annual holidays did the noisy mills fall silent.

Like other newcomers, Bagley earned about fifty cents a day, although by her second year, her wages had doubled. In 1840, she moved to the dressing room, which required intricate handwork to prepare the warps for weaving. The pay was lower, but the pace of work was slower. The slower pace may have appealed to Bagley, whose health had begun to deteriorate, possibly because of the poor ventilation in the mills. In the coming years, Bagley missed work for long periods of time, during which she returned to her family in New Hampshire. Already, though, she had achieved some financial success. On a trip home in 1840, she purchased a piece of property that became the family's residence. She put down $371 of the $1,071 purchase price, no doubt savings from her work in the mills. Although many observers believed that mill work provided female operatives with money only for wedding dresses and dowries, in Bagley's case, it represented essential support for her family.

Still, to a remarkable degree, Bagley fit the image of the Lowell girls that Appleton and his associates wished to project. They pointed proudly to the $100,000 deposited by female operatives in the Lowell Savings Bank by the 1840s. In only a few years, Bagley had put her name on a deed, proving it was possible for thrifty, hardworking employees to accumulate property. They believed that Lowell morally uplifted its female workers by enforcing discipline and order and offering numerous opportunities for education and refinement. Like many other female operatives, Bagley eagerly pursued self-improvement on Sundays and at the end of the long workdays. In the evenings, she helped other boarders compose letters. She attended the lyceum, where the philosopher and poet Ralph Waldo Emerson, John Greenleaf Whittier, and other visiting luminaries delivered lectures. She was active in temperance work and joined one of Lowell's many "Improvement Circles," where operatives read and corrected their own literary compositions.

Bagley even saw her essays published in the *Lowell Offering*, a literary magazine founded in 1840 by a minister to give a voice to the women who toiled in the mills. Soon funded by the mill owners, the *Lowell Offering* further enhanced Lowell's image by demonstrating that factory workers could take up literary pursuits in their spare time. In fact, in "The Pleasures of Factory Life," Bagley offered an account of life as a female operative that Nathan Appleton himself would have endorsed. **[See Source 3.]** Yet Bagley's views were already changing. In 1840, she also wrote an article, rejected by the *Lowell Offering* that referred to the mill owners as a "mushroom aristocracy." By then, she had been in the mills long enough for the novelty to have worn off and to see that Lowell itself was changing.

By the 1830s, expanding textile production had led to falling prices and lower dividends for a growing number of stockholders. The mill owners countered by lowering wages and lengthening the workday. In response to wage cuts in 1834, a fledgling Lowell Factory Girls Association led about eight hundred operatives in a walkout. Their protest lasted for only a few days, but two years later, twice as many female workers took to the streets to protest an increase in their board. The mill owners fired the strike leaders and blacklisted them from other mills. Evicted from their boarding houses and without funds, the strikers straggled back into the mills as the Lowell Factory Girls Association collapsed. Hard times quickly put a damper on further mill girl militance. By the time Bagley arrived in Lowell, the Panic of 1837[*] had ushered in a severe depression that lasted through the early 1840s. With one-third of the nation's labor force out of work, operatives were less likely to voice their grievances. Not until the economy recovered fully in

---

[*]*Panic of 1837*: A financial panic, caused by a contraction in bank lending and in the money supply, that led to a collapse of the national economy.

the mid-1840s did widespread labor unrest erupt once again at Lowell. When it did, Bagley was at its center.

In late 1844, Bagley and four other female operatives met in a dimly lit room after work to form the first trade union of industrial women in the United States. The LFLRA intended to fight for a ten-hour workday. At that time, mill girls worked on average seventy-five hours a week. Even British mill workers worked fewer hours. Lowell operatives were also required to tend three or four machines instead of one or two and, as time went on, twice as many spindles. As mechanics and laborers associations in the Northeast revived with the return of prosperity, Lowell's female operatives joined with them in demanding a ten-hour day. In 1843 and 1844, several thousand Lowell operatives had signed petitions calling on the state legislature to pass a ten-hour law. By early 1845, the LFLRA was busy collecting several thousand signatures on yet another petition. Signed first by Bagley, it declared, "We the undersigned peaceable, industrious and hard working men and women of Lowell, ... [work] from 13 to 14 hours per day, confined to unhealthy apartments, exposed to the poisonous contagion of air."

A legislative committee met in early 1845 to investigate the complaint. It was headed by William Schouler, a representative from Lowell and a financial benefactor of the *Lowell Offering*. Bagley, one of the eight operatives invited to testify, told the legislators that her health had begun to fail, forcing her to return home for frequent rests. The short meal breaks and long days, she said, offered little time to cultivate the mind. When one committee member demanded that she provide evidence that "these girls want to improve their mental capacities," Bagley explained that after working all day, she instructed many of them "in simple branches of education." When the committee released its report several months later, it declared that the mills were "neat and clean" and the girls "healthy and robust." It recommended that the legislature take no action to limit the hours of labor. The report also distorted the operatives' testimony. It said, for instance, that Bagley "had kept school during the winter months, for four years and thought that this extra labor must have injured her health." Bagley was livid. "If they gave the operatives the same protection as they gave animals," she said, "our condition would be greatly improved."

Despite the legislature's inaction, the LFLRA's ranks and Bagley's stature in the labor movement continued to grow. Bagley and other LFLRA officers helped form the New England Workingmen's Association (NEWA), which united numerous local labor organizations and admitted male and female groups on an equal basis. When the NEWA met in Boston for its first convention, Bagley represented the LFLRA and addressed the delegates. "For the last half century, it has been deemed a violation of woman's sphere to appear before the public as a speaker," she said, "but when our rights are trampled upon what shall we do but appeal to the people?" Several months later, Bagley, now an NEWA vice president, addressed the members at a picnic in Woburn, Massachusetts, where some two thousand male and female workers gathered to celebrate the Fourth of July. According to one witness, when she spoke, the crowd was so quiet that you could hear the rustling of the leaves as she paused to catch her breath. The mill proprietors, she proclaimed, were trying to lengthen the hours of work, ending all hope that workers could improve their condition. They were, she went on, "doomed to eternal slavery." Bagley saved her harshest words for the *Lowell Offering*, charging that it was "controlled by the manufacturing interest to give a glow to their inhumanity."

Bagley's attacks had an impact. By the end of 1845, declining subscriptions forced the *Lowell Offering* to shut down. By then, Bagley had lent her support to a labor newspaper called the *Voice of Industry*, which the NEWA made its official organ. As president of the LFLRA, Bagley joined the *Voice*'s publishing committee and on occasion even served as its editor. She also contributed articles condemning the conditions in the mills. **[See Source 4.]** While LFLRA members recruited subscribers in the mills, the *Voice* publicized the activities of the association. By 1846, it had more than two thousand subscribers, and the LFLRA claimed six hundred members. Together, they used their influence to defeat William Schouler when he ran for reelection to the state legislature in 1846. Meanwhile, Bagley had not given up the fight for a ten-hour day. In 1846, the LFLRA presented the legislature with another petition, with Bagley's name heading up 4,500 signatures on a scroll 130 feet long. Ten thousand more signatures on petitions from other towns were not enough, however, to budge the legislature, which declared that a ten-hour law would only harm business and "deprive the citizen of his freedom of contract."

By that time, Bagley had quit the mills to open a dress shop and devote more time to the *Voice* and labor organizing. As female operatives elsewhere requested the LFLRA's assistance, Bagley took her campaign to other towns with mills owned by the Lowell corporations. She presided over a meeting at the Manchester, New Hampshire, Town Hall that was attended by a thousand workers, most of them women. Within months, three hundred operatives had joined the Manchester branch of the FLRA, and soon branches also were established in Dover, Nashua, and other New Hampshire towns. As Bagley traveled throughout New England, she visited several prisons, ostensibly to report to the *Voice*'s readers about prison reform. In one article, she noted that the inmates had a good library and "time to read" because they worked four hours less a day than workers in Lowell. In another article, she observed that a man incarcerated for forgery should have been more careful in his choice of crime. He could have robbed, she observed, without committing forgery. Then he could have "passed as an Appleton."

"HIGH PRICED, ... INTELLIGENT LABOR"

The object of Bagley's attack was little concerned with the living and working conditions of his operatives in the 1840s. Long removed from active management of the mills, Nathan Appleton spent more time on family matters after the death of his first wife in 1833 and his remarriage six years later. Increasingly active in politics, he was elected repeatedly to the Massachusetts legislature and once to the U.S. House of Representatives. Meanwhile, his investments in banking, insurance, and railroads required more time, as did his numerous philanthropic endeavors. Appleton supported institutions such as the Massachusetts General Hospital, the Massachusetts Historical Society, the Boston Atheneum,* and the Boston Public Library. Committed to self-improvement, he also pursued various intellectual interests, traveled widely, and wrote on a variety of topics.

Thus Appleton only occasionally dropped by Lowell to show off the factories to a visiting dignitary or to dine with his partners at the Merrimack Hotel. And then he did not see a labor problem. The Boston Associates had erected Lowell with built-in safeguards to protect their operatives. Of course, workers had suffered wage cuts, especially in the difficult years following the Panic of 1837. Appleton himself had approved one such cut in 1840. Still, wages had risen 33 percent between 1842 and 1845 as the textile industry gradually recovered with the rest of the economy. If workers shared in the

---

Atheneum: A literary or scientific club named after the temple of Athena, where ancient Greek writers and scholars met.

prosperity of the enterprise, then should they not also share in its losses? When sales and dividends fell, should wages not fall, too?

Guided by such assumptions, Appleton's companies threatened to fire workers who supported a ten-hour law. Such legislation would only bring harmful state interference in business enterprise and impede material progress. The protests of the LFLRA and other troublemakers, Appleton believed, were the result of incompetence or lack of ambition. Clinging to an ideology forged in the small shops and farmsteads of the eighteenth century, he saw no obstacles to the advancement of virtuous individuals. In America, he declared after visiting Britain's bleak industrial towns as a young man, even the "poorest [of] sons *knows* that by industry and economy he can acquire property & respectability." Appleton never abandoned this faith in individual mobility. Much later in life, he recalled how he had arrived in Boston to start work at his brother's firm carrying his clothes with "a pocket-handkerchief in ... hand." The point of his reminiscence was clear: Industrious boys from humble backgrounds could rise dramatically in life through hard work and perseverance.

In fact, only when it came to the federal tariff did Appleton see a need for state intervention to protect labor. As a merchant, he had opposed the tariff because it made imported items more expensive. Even after he invested in textiles, Appleton did not embrace protectionism.* He was "perfectly satisfied," he declared in 1827, that American textile manufacturers could compete with the British because female labor in American mills kept wages down. By 1830, however, when Appleton, a Whig,* defeated a staunch free-trade Democrat for a seat in the House of Representatives, he was a vocal advocate of protection for American industry. (Massachusetts Whig Daniel Webster also became a defender of the tariff in the Senate after the Boston Associates gave him shares in the MMC and other financial assistance.) Even as the tariff became an explosive issue during the administration of Andrew Jackson, Appleton continued to denounce free trade. He supported the Tariff of 1832, which provoked opponents of the tax in South Carolina to nullify the law. When the standoff between Jackson and South Carolina, known as the nullification crisis, was over, Appleton railed against the Compromise Tariff of 1833, which lowered duties to appease the earlier tariff's opponents. In widely circulated articles, he defended protectionism in the name of higher wages, not higher profits. The choice, he argued, was between "high priced, well fed, intelligent labor" protected by tariffs and "cheap, starving" labor mercilessly exposed to free trade. Protectionism was the answer to attacks on the factory system by labor leaders such as Sarah Bagley. Unlike Europe, where an aristocracy exploited its workers, America honored labor and provided the opportunity for wage earners to become capitalists. By promoting higher wages, tariffs guaranteed ambitious individuals the opportunity to advance themselves. **[See Source 5.]**

Appleton trumpeted tariffs as a means of preserving upward mobility in the emerging factory system. Bagley, however, was far less certain how to respond to that system. In 1846, when one of the Lowell companies cut wages while requiring weavers to tend more looms, female operatives walked out. It was the only strike begun by members of the LFLRA, but the union was not responsible for it. In fact, the LFLRA declared itself opposed to "all hostile measures, strikes and turn-outs until all pacific measures prove

---

Protectionism: The policy of protecting American products by placing high tariffs on competing foreign imports; the opposite of a free-trade policy.
Whigs: The political party organized in 1834 in opposition to Andrew Jackson's *Democratic Party.* The Whigs favored a strong government committed to aiding business enterprise.

abortive." Unlike modern unions, it was not able to negotiate wages and contracts and was thus more interested in petitions and conventions than in direct action. In fact, by 1847, the LFLRA was renamed the Female Labor Reform and Mutual Aid Society, reflecting its new goal of offering sick pay and other benefits to its members.

The turn away from militant action was hastened by the involvement of numerous social reformers in the labor movement. Bagley used the *Voice of Industry* and the LFLRA to promote a variety of reform causes. She frequently provided a forum for speakers such as abolitionist William Lloyd Garrison, journalist Horace Greeley, and transcendentalist[*] George Ripley. In time, causes such as abolition, land reform, and utopian socialism drew many operatives away from the labor movement. In 1846, Bagley became a vice president of the Lowell Union of Associationists, a group influenced by the utopian social theorist Charles Fourier, who proposed reorganizing society into communal living groups. Indeed, one of her last contributions to the *Voice of Industry* was a letter written as a delegate to the convention of the American Union of Associationists.

The Massachusetts legislature did not pass a ten-hour law until 1874. By that time, the LFLRA was long gone, as was the *Voice of Industry*. By the 1850s, most of the native-born mill girls had been replaced by Irish operatives, victims of English oppression and the Irish potato famine. In Lowell, they found a city of rundown tenements and little evidence of Appleton's paternalistic impulses. An abundance of cheap labor had made the Boston Associates' earlier efforts to attract and safeguard female workers unnecessary.

"FOR THE HAPPINESS OF OUR COUNTRY"

Late in life, Nathan Appleton hoped to be remembered for more than making a lot of money. He need not have worried. When he died in 1861, he was widely lauded for his benevolence. Practically forgotten was his role in the founding of Lowell. Sarah Bagley, however, was not remembered at all. After serving in Lowell as America's first female telegraph operator, she returned home in 1847 to care for her dying father. She quickly slipped into obscurity, and today, even the date of her death remains a mystery.

Although their fates were different, Appleton and Bagley were more alike than either of them would have been willing to admit. Both came from rural New England stock and demonstrated a lifelong Yankee commitment to self-improvement. More important, both were transitional figures as a new industrial society emerged out of an older agrarian one. Neither of them, it seems, could quite come to terms with that new society.

As a businessman, Appleton epitomized the shift from an economy dominated by merchants to one ruled by industrialists. He also represented the transfer of control from owners to managers. Among the first industrialists to relinquish the responsibilities of factory management, Appleton eventually had no more to do with making cloth than J. P. Morgan[*] would have to do with managing blast furnaces. He also ushered in a factory system that closed off opportunity for most workers to become independent. In doing so, he helped make his own social philosophy obsolete. Appleton looked fondly to

---

[*]*Transcendentalist:* A member of a nineteenth-century literary and philosophical movement associated with Ralph Waldo Emerson, Margaret Fuller, and others.

[*]*J. P. Morgan:* The New York financier who created the U.S. Steel Corporation in 1901. Morgan was the symbol of late-nineteenth-century finance capitalism, in which bankers seized control of companies from the industrialists who had founded and run them.

the past, but he pointed to a future in which those receiving the dividends were far removed from the means of production and few workers became "capitalists." He held up an ideal of individual mobility formed in a commercial economy in which capital and labor were often indistinguishable. At the same time, he was unable to see the rise of a permanent factory labor force right before his eyes.

Bagley's career also pointed to things to come. Later in the nineteenth century, millions of workers would find strength in unions. By then, they confronted a fully developed industrial system dominated by powerful corporations that had long since shed any concern for the moral uplift of their workers. Yet Bagley, like Appleton, failed to grasp the factory's full impact on society. Also holding dear the ideal of individual advancement, she championed the ten-hour day and other reforms so that women could have more time for their own improvement. Bagley simply could not see that many workers faced the prospect of permanent factory work. Like Appleton, therefore, she was incapable of preventing Lowell from becoming the kind of English factory town that he had hoped, "for the happiness of our country," would never come to America.

•PRIMARY SOURCES•

Source 1: Nathan Appleton, "The Introduction of the Power Loom, and Origin of Lowell" (1858)

In 1858, Nathan Appleton wrote a history of the power loom and the beginnings of textile manufacturing in Waltham and Lowell. What does Appleton reveal here about the motivation behind the Boston Associates' paternalistic approach to factory labor?

The introduction of the cotton manufacture in this country, on a large scale, was a new idea. What would be its effect on the character of our population was a matter of deep interest. The operatives in the manufacturing cities of Europe were notoriously of the lowest character for intelligence and morals. The question therefore arose, and was deeply considered, whether this degradation was the result of the peculiar occupation, or of other and distinct causes. We could not perceive why this peculiar description of labor should vary in its effects upon character from all other occupations.

There was little demand for female labor, as household manufacture was superseded by the improvements in machinery. Here was in New England a fund of labor, well educated and virtuous. It was not perceived how a profitable employment has any tendency to deteriorate the character. The most efficient guards were adopted in establishing boarding houses, at the cost of the Company, under the charge of respectable women, with every provision for religious worship. Under these circumstances, the daughters of respectable farmers were readily induced to come into these mills for a temporary period.

The contrast in the character of our manufacturing population compared with that of Europe has been the admiration of the most intelligent strangers who have visited us.

SOURCE: Nathan Appleton, "The Introduction of the Power Loom, and Origin of Lowell" (1858). Originally from Nathan Appleton, "The Introduction of the Power Loom, and Origin of Lowell" (Lowell, Mass.: B. H. Penhallow, 1858).

The effect has been to more than double the wages of that description of labor from what they were before the introduction of this manufacture. This had been, in some measure, counteracted for the last few years, by the free trade policy of the government; a policy which fully carried out, will reduce the value of labor with us, to an equality with that of Europe.

Source 2:   *Regulations of the Appleton Company* (1833)

The Appleton Company posted strict rules for its employees. What do these regulations reveal about life and work in the Lowell mills? Do you think these rules were intended to ensure the virtue of Appleton's workers or reflect other motives?

REGULATIONS

TO BE OBSERVED BY ALL PERSONS EMPLOYED IN THE FACTORIES OF THE

APPLETON COMPANY.

THE Overseers are to be punctually in their rooms at the starting of the mill, and not to be absent unnecessarily during working hours. They are to see that all those employed in their rooms are in their places in due season. They may grant leave of absence to those employed under them, when there are spare hands in the room to supply their places; otherwise they are not to grant leave of absence, except in cases of absolute necessity.

ALL persons in the employ of the APPLETON COMPANY are required to observe the regulations of the overseer of the room where they are employed. They are not to be absent from their work, without his consent, except in case of sickness, and then they are to send him word of the cause of their absence.

THEY are to board in one of the boarding houses belonging to the Company, and conform to the regulations of the house where they board.

A regular attendance on public worship on the Sabbath is necessary for the preservation of good order. The Company will not employ any person who is habitually absent.

ALL persons entering into the employment of the Company are considered as engaging to work twelve months, and those who leave sooner will not receive a discharge unless they had sufficient experience when they commenced, to enable them to do full work.

ALL persons intending to leave the employment of the Company, are to give two weeks' notice of their intention to their overseer; and their engagement with the Company is not considered as fulfilled, unless they comply with this regulation.

PAYMENTS will be made monthly, including board and wages, which will be made up to the last Saturday in every month, and paid in the course of the following week.

THESE regulations are considered part of the contract with all persons entering into the employment of the APPLETON COMPANY.

G. W. LYMAN, *Agent.*

Tompe & Press, Gorham-Street.

SOURCE: Reprinted in Benita Eisler, ed., *The Lowell Offering: Writings by New England Mill Women* (1840–1845) (New York: W. W. Norton & Company, 1998), p. 25; originally from Merrimack Valley Textile Museum, Lowell, Mass/American Textile History Museum, Lowell, MA

Source 3: Sarah Bagley, *"The Pleasures of Factory Life"* (1840)

Sarah Bagley wrote several articles for the Lowell Offering. In this article, what does she see as the "pleasures" of factory life? What does she reveal about her values?

Pleasures there are, even in factory life; and we have many, known only to those of like employment. To be sure it is not so convenient to converse in the mills with those un-accustomed to them; yet we suffer no inconvenience among ourselves. But, aside from the talking, where can you find a more pleasant place for contemplation? There all the powers of the mind are made active by our animating exercise; and having but one kind of labor to perform, we need not give all our thoughts to that, but leave them measur-ably free for reflection on other matters.

The subjects for pleasurable contemplation, while attending to our work, are nu-merous and various. Many of them are immediately around us. For example: In the mill we see displays of the wonderful power of the mind. Who can closely examine all the movements of the complicated, curious machinery, and not be led to the reflection, that the mind is boundless, and is destined to rise higher and still higher; and that it can accomplish almost anything on which it fixes its attention!

In the mills, we are not so far from God and nature, as many persons might suppose. We cultivate, and enjoy much pleasure in cultivating flowers and plants. A large and beautiful variety of plants is placed around the walls of the rooms, giving them more the appearance of a flower garden than a workshop. It is there we inhale the sweet per-fume of the rose, the lily, and geranium; and, with them, send the sweet incense of sin-cere gratitude to the bountiful Giver of these rich blessings. And who can live with such a rich and pleasant source of instruction opened to him, and not be wiser and better, and consequently more happy.

Another great source of pleasure is, that by becoming operatives, we are often en-abled to assist aged parents who have become too infirm to provide for themselves; or perhaps to educate some orphan brother or sister, and fit them for future usefulness....

Let no one suppose that the "factory girls" are without guardian. We are placed in the care of overseers who feel under moral obligations to look after our interests; and, if we are sick, to acquaint themselves with our situation and wants; and, if need be, to re-move us to the Hospital, where we are sure to have the best attendance, provided by the benevolence of our Agents and Superintendents.

In Lowell, we enjoy abundant means of information, especially in the way of public lectures. The time of lecturing is appointed to suit the convenience of the operatives; and sad indeed would be the picture of our Lyceums, Institutes, and scientific Lecture rooms, if all the operatives should absent themselves.

And last, though not least, is the pleasure of being associated with the institutions of religion, and thereby availing ourselves of the Library, Bible Class, Sabbath School, and all other means of religious instruction. Most of us, when at home, live in the country, and therefore cannot enjoy these privileges to the same extent; and many of us not at all. And surely we ought to regard these as sources of pleasure.

S.G.B.

SOURCE: Sarah Bagley, "The Pleasures of Factory Life" (1840). Originally from the LOWELL OFFERING, December 1840.

Source 4: Sarah Bagley, *"Voluntary?"* (1845)

In this essay from the Voice of Industry, Sarah Bagley discusses the condition of Lowell's female operatives. What are her chief complaints? How have her views changed since she wrote "The Pleasures of Factory Life" in 1840 (see Source 3)?

Whenever I raise the point that it is immoral to shut us up in a close room twelve hours a day in the most monotonous and tedious of employment, I am told that we have come to the mills voluntarily and we can leave when we will. Voluntary! Let us look a little at this remarkable form of human freedom. Do we from mere choice leave our fathers' dwellings, the firesides where all of our friends, where too our earliest and fondest recollections cluster, for the factory and the Corporations boarding house? By what charm do these great companies immure human creatures in the bloom of youth and first glow of life within their mills, away from their homes and kindred? A slave too goes voluntarily to his task, but his will is in some manner quickened by the whip of the overseer. The whip which brings us to Lowell is necessity. We must have money; a father's debts are to be paid, an aged mother to be supported, a brother's ambition to be aided, and so the factories are supplied. Is this to act from free will? When a man is starving he is compelled to pay his neighbor, who happens to have bread, the most exorbitant price for it, and his neighbor may appease his conscience, if conscience he chance to have, by the reflection that it is altogether a voluntary bargain. Is anyone such a fool as to suppose that out of six thousand factory girls of Lowell, sixty would be there if they could help it? Everybody knows that it is necessity alone, in some form or other, that takes us to Lowell and keeps us there. Is this freedom? To my mind it is slavery quite as really as any in Turkey or Carolina. It matters little as to the fact of slavery, whether the slave be compelled to his task by the whip of the overseer or the wages of the Lowell Corporation. In either case it is not free will, leading the laborer to work, but an outward necessity that puts free will out of the question.

S.G.B.

Source 5: Nathan Appleton, *"Labor, Its Relations, in Europe and the United States, Compared"* (1844)

In this defense of tariffs, Nathan Appleton discusses their impact on labor. What does he argue about the relationship between labor and capital? Was he consistent about the desirability of government interference in business enterprise?

The founders of the American colonies, brought with them, neither wealth nor titles of nobility. They had no accumulated stores of either wealth or honors, on which to subsist.

SOURCE 4: Sarah Bagley, "Voluntary?" (1845). Originally from VOICE OF INDUSTRY, September 18, 1845.

SOURCE 5: Nathan Appleton, "Labor, Its Relations, in Europe and the United States, Compared" (1844). Originally from HUNT'S MERCHANTS' MAGAZINE AND COMMERCIAL REVIEW, September 1844, pp. 217, 218–219, 220–222.

Nature offered them this fertile domain, on the sole condition of appropriation by labor. Their earliest political institutions, establishing perfect equality, left no avenue open to wealth or power, but labor. Under these circumstances, it followed, of course, that active industry should be in the highest esteem. Industry was the only road to wealth, and wealth is power, in every part of the world. There are instances of fortunes accumulated in large masses, during the life of an individual, but, subject to our laws of equal distribution, they are sure to be absorbed or dissipated, in the course of one or two generations.

In this state of things, it is not surprising that the acquisition of property, by one's own labor and skill, should be held in equal, or even higher estimation, than the inheritance by the accident of birth. It is true, that the sons of the rich usually receive a better education than their fathers; and we award higher honors to the successful efforts of intellect, than to those of mere industry in the accumulation of wealth. Such an estimation, is, however, wholly founded on personal character.

Manual labor has a position with us, which it has never possessed in any period of the world.

Agricultural labor is, in a very great measure, performed by the owners of the soil and their sons. The universal diffusion of education, places our mechanics higher in the scale of intelligence, than the same class has ever stood in any country. They have the elements of character, which enable them to rise to any position in society.

The high reward of labor, in all its branches, is the great, the important distinction, which diffuses comfort, intelligence, self-respect, through the whole mass of the community, in a degree unknown in the previous history of civilization....

With us, labor is, in fact, the great accumulator. It goes to work, without difficulty, on its own account. It is, therefore, perfectly clear, that that legislation which calls most labor into action, which gives it its fullest scope, is, with us, most productive of wealth.... The protective system rests as its basis, on the principle of an enlarged field for labor, resulting from that legislation which restricts or shuts out the competition of the cheaper and more degraded labor of Europe.... [W]ith us, labor and capital are so mixed together, that, in the general prosperity resulting from an active, well-paid industry, capital is sure to get its share. All writers on political economy, recognise the high reward of labor as indicating the highest measure of general prosperity. It elevates the industrial classes in the scale of society, by giving them a power and a taste, in the enjoyments of civilized life, and in the cultivation of their minds. With us, it does more. In addition to all this, it enables them to lay by a surplus as capital.

QUESTIONS TO CONSIDER

1. One historian has argued that to portray Nathan Appleton "as a bloated capitalist grinding his heel into the necks of downtrodden workers would be the grossest caricature." Do you agree? How would you characterize him?

2. Sarah Bagley's activities as an antebellum labor leader have only recently begun to be fully appreciated, prompting one historian to predict that eventually she "will be seen as one of the true heroines of her time." Do you agree? Should she be studied for that reason or others?

3. How do you account for the transformation of Lowell from a "model" factory town to one that resembled those that Appleton had seen in Britain? In explaining this change, how important were the attitudes of mill owners like Appleton and labor

reformers like Bagley, as opposed to other factors? Which sources are most revealing of those attitudes?

4. Do you agree with the conclusion of this chapter's essay that neither Appleton nor Bagley was capable of preventing the transformation of Lowell? What would have made Lowell turn out differently in the end?

5. Given the increasing globalization of business and the controversy surrounding American trade with other nations today, do you think Appleton was correct in arguing that a tariff on imported goods was the key to "high priced" and "intelligent" labor in the United States?

FOR FURTHER READING

Thomas Dublin, *Women at Work: The Transformation of Work and Community in Lowell, Massachusetts, 1826–1860* (New York: Columbia University Press, 1979), provides a thorough discussion of the lives and work of Lowell's female workers and how both changed.

Frances W. Gregory, *Nathan Appleton: Merchant and Entrepreneur, 1779–1861* (Charlottesville: University Press of Virginia, 1975), provides the only full-length biography of Appleton, focusing on his career as a merchant and manufacturer.

Hannah Josephson, *The Golden Threads: New England's Mill Girls and Magnates* (New York: Russell & Russell, 1967), offers a highly readable account of Appleton's life and the activities of Sarah Bagley and other female operatives in Lowell.

Bruce Laurie, *Artisans into Workers: Labor in Nineteenth-Century America* (New York: Hill and Wang, 1989), offers a broad study of changes in labor in pre–Civil War America.

Bernice Selden, *The Mill Girls: Lucy Larcom, Harriet Hanson Robinson, Sarah Bagley* (New York: Atheneum, 1983), provides brief biographical sketches of three female operatives in Lowell.

Politics, Morality, and Race in the Abolitionist Crusade: William Lloyd Garrison and Frederick Douglass

Frederick Douglass felt his heart pound as he glanced nervously at the crowd. A runaway slave just three years out of bondage, Douglass had learned to observe people carefully. As his eyes darted around the packed meeting hall, he saw a multitude of curious white and black onlookers. He knew he was in a friendly crowd, but he felt his stomach tighten nevertheless. Here in Nantucket at the meeting of the Massachusetts Anti-Slavery Society in the summer of 1841, under the watchful gaze of William Lloyd Garrison and other prominent abolitionists, he was about to deliver his first major public address. When Douglass finally rose to speak, he trembled. The first words out of his mouth seemed confused. He stammered, and people strained to hear him. Then he began to tell his story, and the throng was mesmerized.

When a dazed Douglass sat down, he had no memory of what he said and little idea of his impact. But then it was William Lloyd Garrison's turn to speak. The editor of the abolitionist newspaper the *Liberator*, a founder of the American Anti-Slavery Society, and a powerful antislavery speaker, Garrison was perhaps the most famous abolitionist of the day. With characteristic evangelical fervor, Garrison quickly demonstrated his skill at rousing antislavery crowds. First, he asked the assembly if it had been listening to a "thing" or "a man." "A man! A man!" it responded. Then, raising his voice, he asked if "such a man [should] be held a slave in a Christian land?" "No! No!" the crowd cried. Then raising his voice to a shout, he asked if "such a man [should] ever be sent back to bondage." Jumping to its feet, the crowd yelled back, "No! No! No!"

Hulton Archive/Getty Images

William Lloyd Garrison

A. H. Ritchie/Hulton Archive/Getty Images

Frederick Douglass

As he listened to the roaring multitude, Douglass knew he had triumphed. He had spoken and people—white people—had listened. William Lloyd Garrison—the man Douglass most admired—was using him "as a text" for *his* speech. And in so doing, Douglass later recalled, Garrison had summoned words "of unequaled power." When the famous abolitionist finished, people rushed forward to shake *Douglass's* hand. And before the runaway left the meeting, he had been invited to become an agent of the Massachusetts Anti-Slavery Society. The world would soon hear much more from Frederick Douglass. In time, he would become as well known as Garrison himself. As he later put it, "a new life" had "opened up" for him that day.

Douglass had every reason to be grateful to Garrison in this new life. This man would be at his side as friend and mentor in coming years as Douglass spread his anti-slavery message far and wide. In fact, their collaboration would be as effective as their speechmaking at Nantucket. Within a half dozen years, though, the friendship was over and the two men had become bitter enemies. Very different men, Garrison and Douglass were engaged as both friends and foes in a common cause. Together, they reveal much about the sources and impact of that cause—and the factors that divided and limited it.

"I *WILL* BE HEARD"

William Lloyd Garrison was no runaway slave, but he knew all about privation and instability. He was born in 1805 in Newburyport, Massachusetts, to an alcoholic father who made an uncertain living as a sailor and abandoned his family when Garrison was only three. With three small children, his mother found only unsteady work as a domestic. Pail in hand, William was forced to collect table scraps from the tables of Newburyport's prosperous residents, while his devout Baptist mother received assistance from local church members. When William's mother sought work in nearby Lynn and, later, in Baltimore, he was sent to live with the family of Ezekiel Bartlett, a Baptist deacon, who apprenticed him to a cabinetmaker and, after William ran away from that after six weeks, to the owner of a newspaper.

When Garrison entered the office of the Newburyport *Herald*, he had unknowingly stumbled into his life's work. He picked up typesetting quickly, and from the *Herald*'s pages, he absorbed information about a larger world. He learned, too, how words were used. In his spare time, he read literature. And he joined a self-improvement club devoted to reading and debate. Eventually, he saw his own essays printed in the paper. When his seven-year apprenticeship ended in 1825, young Garrison was an experienced printer and a forceful writer.

He soon put his talents to work on a broader field—and just as quickly demonstrated firm views and a willingness to express them. The next year, Garrison headed to Boston and soon found work as editor of a temperance journal put out by a Baptist missionary. It proved an appropriate vehicle for Garrison, who had imbibed his mother's and Deacon Bartlett's rock-ribbed Baptist beliefs. He also subjected himself to the fire-and-brimstone preaching of Boston's Baptist ministers. And he listened to the powerful sermons of Lyman Beecher, one of the most prominent preachers to emerge during the period of intense religious fervor in the early nineteenth century known as the Second Great Awakening. He was drawn immediately to Beecher's call for the moral regeneration of society. At age twenty-two, Garrison was enlisted in the cause of evangelical uplift. He would never waver from it, and, endowed by his religious faith with enormous moral certitude and scant patience for compromise, he would never endorse halfway measures.

As Garrison set out to "raise the moral tone of the country," he soon found a cause more compelling than temperance. In 1828, he was introduced to Benjamin Lundy, a Quaker antislavery reformer who published a Baltimore-based abolitionist paper called *The Genius of Universal Emancipation*. Lundy advocated gradual emancipation and colonization of freed slaves outside the country, positions shared by most abolitionists in the early nineteenth century. The emancipation of slaves, they believed, would be achieved when slaveholders were gradually persuaded of the immorality of human bondage and assured that former slaves would be removed from American society. Garrison's talks with Lundy convinced him of the righteousness of the gentle Quaker's cause. Lundy invited him to edit the *Genius*, and in 1829, he joined the man to whom he later confessed that he "owe[d] everything." He had found the cause that would consume nearly the rest of his life.

Thanks to Lundy, Garrison had come to see slavery as an evil, in fact, the greatest evil of all. He was also convinced that it could be eradicated only in a moral crusade designed to transform people's hearts. But by the time he joined Lundy, he had changed his mind about gradual emancipation and colonization. Abolitionists in Britain had already taken up the call for immediate emancipation in their battle to eliminate slavery from their country's West Indian colonies. The doctrine appealed naturally to Garrison. Colonization, he believed, was impractical. More important, if slavery was immoral—an abomination—then it must be ended immediately. There could be no compromise with evil!

On the pages of the *Genius*, Garrison espoused what he called his "new and alarming doctrine." He was not gentle. With a slashing, acerbic style, he lashed out at the "monster" of slavery. Incensed by what he saw of this evil in Baltimore, he also launched bitter attacks on individuals. Intending to provoke people, he did. After he called two slave traders "highway robbers and murderers," one of them responded with a libel suit against the paper. Even after the jury slapped Garrison with a $50 fine, he remained defiant. "My pen cannot remain idle," he declared, "nor my voice be suppressed." Unable to pay the $50 fine levied by the jury, he sat in jail for forty-nine days.

Even before Garrison's cell door slammed shut, the moderate Lundy and his vociferous partner had wisely parted ways. Upon his release, Garrison determined that he would establish his own abolitionist newspaper. Unlike Lundy, who targeted Southern slaveholders for conversion, Garrison wanted to persuade the entire nation of the sinfulness of slavery. Convinced that such a "revolution in public sentiment" was more likely to be achieved first in New England rather than in the South, he returned to Boston. There he published the first issue of his new paper in January 1831. In a front-page editorial, he explained that the *Liberator* stood not for the "pernicious doctrine of gradual abolition," but for immediate emancipation. "On this subject," he boldly declared, "I do not wish to think, or speak, or write with moderation.... I will not equivocate— I will not excuse—I will not retreat a single inch—AND I *WILL* BE HEARD." Garrison had launched his moral crusade. **[See Source 1.]**

His timing could not have been better. When he returned to the North, the spirit of reform suffused the air. Thousands of Americans had already been swept up in the massive temperance crusade. By the early 1830s, temperance enthusiasts were being joined by reformers convinced that nearly every facet of society could be revamped. In the next two decades, they worked to reform prisons, poor houses, schools, and even families. Hoping to plant seeds of a new society, other reformers retreated to utopian communities, which sprouted by the score from Massachusetts to the Mississippi River. Whatever their commitment, these individuals shared a belief in the ability of people to improve themselves and their society.

Such optimism sprang from several sources. One was the lingering influence of eighteenth-century Enlightenment* thought, which stressed the power of the environment to shape individuals and taught that institutions, laws, and practices should be changed if they undermined equality or natural rights. Another was early nineteenth-century romanticism,* which emphasized the individual's power to perceive truth and, by cultivating one's own divinity, to achieve a state of perfection. Optimism was also reflected in—and fed by—the early nineteenth-century religious revivals of the Second Great Awakening. Unlike earlier Calvinist theologians who preached that God alone determined who was saved, thunderous revival preachers now claimed that all people could achieve salvation through their own efforts. Often, these same preachers also taught that the saved had a moral obligation to battle evil in all its forms. Souls aflame, thousands of converts streamed out of early nineteenth-century revivals and rushed straight into the era's numerous reform causes.

Abolition was a beneficiary of this reform enthusiasm. In the years before the *Liberator*'s founding, however, organized antislavery had few signs of life. It had actually been a more powerful force in the Revolutionary era. In the afterglow of a struggle waged in the name of natural rights and equality, Northern states began to pass laws doing away with slavery, and thousands of slaves were freed by Southern slaveholders. Southerners and Northerners calling for gradual emancipation and colonization had joined together to form the nation's first abolitionist movement. Shortly after the establishment of the

---

Enlightenment: A philosophical movement in the seventeenth and eighteenth centuries that assumed a universe governed by certain knowable laws. Enlightenment thinkers believed that human reason could understand those laws and that people could mold their own society and behavior to conform to these laws.

Romanticism: A philosophical and artistic movement in the late eighteenth and early nineteenth centuries that drew on emotions, rather than reason, as the source of truth. It also emphasized that creative work should not adhere to some classical standard, but reveal an individual's own soul.

American Colonization Society in 1817, however, the movement began to languish. As cotton production expanded after the War of 1812, fewer Southerners were interested in freeing their own slaves. Despite the continued agitation of Lundy and some others, an end to slavery through the conversion of slaveholders now seemed ever more distant. In the 1820s, Southern abolitionists fell away, voluntary emancipations dried up, and few in the North seemed to care. As interest in reform rose in the next decade, however, so gradually did enthusiasm for abolition.

At first, however, only a few people seemed to care about Garrison's radical message. And he seemed bent on merely riling up the few who did. When the *Liberator's* slashing attacks on colonization—a "blasphemous" doctrine that called for the "gradual abolition of wickedness"—occasionally elicited a protest from colonizationists, Garrison countered with even harsher language. When one sympathetic minister cautioned him about his incendiary editorials, he replied that many readers would be unhappy with his words, but "to displease them is my intention." In fact, after eight months, most of the names on the debt-ridden paper's short subscription list belonged to free blacks in Boston, New York, or Philadelphia.

Many more people, however, soon began to pay attention to Garrison and his paper. In August 1831, Nat Turner led a slave revolt of fellow slaves in Virginia that left nearly sixty whites dead. The biggest slave revolt in American history, Turner's rebellion sent shock waves through the South. Convinced that abolitionists had fomented Turner's uprising, many Southern newspaper editors began to point fingers at the one who seemed to be the most fanatical of them all. Garrison was a pacificist who opposed all violence, but he was vilified in the Southern press. He quickly became the very symbol of abolitionist fanaticism and the target of numerous death threats. Subscriptions to the *Liberator* rose, and Garrison's reputation as a radical agitator was sealed.

Garrison seized on the opportunity created by his new notoriety. Early the next year, he founded the New England Anti-Slavery Society (renamed the Massachusetts Anti-Slavery Society in 1836) with a small group of Boston abolitionists. The *Liberator* soon became the official organ of the new organization, which called for immediate emancipation. Later that year, Garrison published *Thoughts on African Colonization*, a searing indictment of colonization as a "corroding," racist "evil" that left no place for free blacks in American society and only worked to reinforce slavery. Then, in 1833, he joined with New York businessmen and evangelicals Arthur and Lewis Tappan, Philadelphia Quaker Lucretia Mott, free black Robert Purvis, and other abolitionists to help found the American Anti-Slavery Society. Set up to agitate for immediate emancipation and to encourage the formation of local abolitionist societies across the North, the American Anti-Slavery Society sought the peaceful conversion of Americans to abolitionism through "moral suasion." Its goal, as Garrison put it, was "to bring the whole nation to speedy repentance."

Garrison and a growing cadre of abolitionists met intense opposition as they evangelized the North in coming years. Never more than a minority of white Northerners before the Civil War, abolitionists stirred up fears that they would drive the slave states out of the Union. They also raised the frightening prospect of a hoard of free blacks rushing north to compete with white workers. By 1840, abolitionists had incited scores of riots. During one of them, an angry mob stormed a gathering of abolitionists in Boston, forcing Garrison to crawl out a rear window. Others were not so lucky. Ohio abolitionist Theodore Dwight Weld suffered a concussion after he was hit by a brick in one melee. And in 1837, abolitionist editor Elijah Lovejoy was killed when a mob stormed the offices of his paper in Alton, Illinois.

The violence surrounding the abolitionist crusade evoked growing sympathy in some observers. In Garrison, it unleashed a militant, uncompromising perfectionism. Convinced that American society was utterly corrupt, he announced to surprised readers in 1836 that he had decided to "reject all allegiance to the nation." Its government and even its churches, most of which remained hostile to abolitionism, were hopelessly polluted and must be "dashed to pieces." About the same time, disputes over the proper role of women in abolitionist societies led Garrison to take up the cause of women's rights (see Chapter 10). In 1838, Garrison declared that the *Liberator* would also agitate for women's rights, peace, and the "universal emancipation of all humanity from all bondage to human government." **[See Source 2.]**

In an age of unbridled optimism about social improvement, Garrison continued to attract devoted followers. Though bespectacled and balding, he was charismatic. His argument that the struggles for the liberation of slaves and women were inseparable especially attracted many female abolitionists. By the late 1830s, however, he was under mounting criticism from abolitionists themselves. Some were alarmed by his strident language. Others were repulsed by what they saw as his sense of moral superiority and his unwillingness to tolerate opposition. As one member of the Massachusetts Anti-Slavery Society put it, Garrison's "overgrown conceit" had deluded him into "the belief that his mighty self was abolition incarnate."

Most important, many abolitionists disagreed with Garrison about the best way to end slavery. Garrison insisted that the only way to end slavery was through "moral suasion"—convincing Americans of the immorality of slavery. Thus, Garrison spurned political action, insisting that abolitionists who took their struggle into a corrupt political arena would be forced to make compromises with evil. Many abolitionists, however, had come to believe that moral appeals were not enough, and that politics was the only practical way to end slavery. To politically minded abolitionists, Garrison's attacks on churches, clergy, and the government—and, in particular, his call for female equality—undermined abolitionism's appeal to voters. Such views led the Tappans and many other abolitionists to storm out of the Garrison-controlled American Anti-Slavery Society and create the politically focused American and Foreign Anti-Slavery Society in 1840. The same year, Gerrit Smith of New York, former slaveholder James Birney of Kentucky, and others established the abolitionist Liberty Party.

By the time Frederick Douglass rose to speak at the Nantucket meeting of the Massachusetts Anti-Slavery Society in 1841, a deep wedge divided Garrison and his abolitionist opponents. On one side, the "Garrisonians" defined the abolitionist cause in moral rather than political terms and linked it to a wholesale revamping of American society. On the other, the "anti-Garrisonians" sought to focus only on slavery—and take the fight against it to the voters. Douglass could not foresee that he would end up in the enemy camp.

"I BECAME MY OWN MASTER"

Frederick Douglass traveled a long journey to Nantucket. Born in 1818 near the Chesapeake shore in Maryland, he was the son of a slave named Harriet Bailey and a white man whose identity he never learned. Harriet worked for her owner Aaron Anthony, who owned some thirty slaves. Harriet's work for Anthony made it impossible for her to care for her son. So she took the small boy to live with her parents, Betsy Bailey, a slave also owned by Anthony, and Isaac Bailey, a black freeman, who lived in a cabin twelve miles away. Frederick's mother died a few years later, leaving Betsy to raise the boy. At age six, however, Frederick made the long walk with his grandmother to the Anthony plantation. One by one, Betsy's other grandchildren—Frederick's brothers, sisters, and cousins—had been summoned around the same age from their grandmother's cabin to live at the plantation. Although the boy did not realize it, his turn had come. When he discovered his grandmother was gone, he threw himself in the dirt and wailed. He would not see her again until he was an adult.

On the Anthony plantation, young Bailey discovered the violent reality of slavery. He witnessed the brutal flogging of slaves. He was there when one of his aunts arrived after walking more than ten miles to show Anthony wounds she had suffered in a beating by an overseer. Anthony sent her back to the overseer and told her that she would be beaten again if she did not obey. Bailey also saw a rebellious cousin sold and taken away forever to Alabama.

Fortunately, Bailey's new circumstances proved temporary because his master's daughter took a liking to him. Lucretia Anthony Auld and her husband Thomas used their influence with Anthony to have the eight-year-old Frederick sent to Baltimore. There, he would work in the household of Thomas's brother and his wife, Hugh and Sophia Auld. In 1825, the eight-year-old boy was sent away from home again.

In his new surroundings, Frederick Bailey would move a step closer to freedom. Sophia Auld taught him to read the Bible until her husband found out and flew into a rage. "Learning," Auld scolded his wife, "would spoil the best nigger in the world." After learning to read, he would want to learn to write. And after that, Auld declared, "he'll be running away with himself." In time, young Bailey would prove Auld correct. For now, his words made Bailey even more determined to learn. He persuaded white boys in the neighborhood to share their school lessons with him. He read everything he could get his hands on, including litter in the streets. Hearing his companions talk about what they would do when they grew up drove home the reality that he was a slave for life—and that his status had nothing to do with innate abilities. On the city's streets and at its docks, the ever-curious Bailey also saw free blacks and the condition of other slaves, including those on the docks waiting for shipment to markets further south. He learned what the word "abolition" meant. In the city's free black churches, he listened to lay preachers and embraced religion. And there, too, he heard talk about slavery and aiding runaways.

Abruptly, however, the freedom offered by the city came to an end. In 1836, after the deaths of Aaron Anthony and his daughter Lucretia, Bailey became the property of Lucretia's husband. Thomas Auld demanded that the boy return to him to live on his Maryland plantation. When he discovered that Bailey was teaching other slaves to read, Auld hired Bailey out to a nearby farmer who tried to break the sixteen-year-old boy by whipping him nearly every day. After a year, Bailey was sent to work on another farm, where he organized a secret school to teach fellow slaves to read and began plotting with several to escape. Bailey's plan was uncovered at the last minute, and he and five others were thrown in jail. But Thomas Auld decided to send Bailey back to his brother in Baltimore. Auld promised that if Bailey stayed out of trouble and learned a trade, he would free the slave when he turned twenty-five.

When he arrived back in Baltimore, Frederick went to work in the shipyards where he became a skilled caulker. Tired of watching his wages go to Hugh Auld, he eventually cut a deal to give Auld three dollars a week. Anything he earned over that amount was his to keep. Taking advantage of his greater freedom, he joined self-help and other groups where he met free blacks and other slaves. At one such gathering, he met a free black housekeeper named Anna Murray. The two became close friends and made plans to marry.

With Anna's encouragement, Frederick also plotted his escape. First, he borrowed from a black sailor his seaman's papers, which free black sailors were required to carry. Dressed as a sailor, he then jumped on a Philadelphia-bound train. As the train chugged northward, he sat terrified that a sharp-eyed conductor would determine that he did not resemble the description of the man on his papers. "Minutes were hours," he recalled, "and hours were days."

But Bailey was not caught. He made his way to New York and the house of David Ruggles, a well-known black abolitionist. Bailey quickly wrote Anna, who soon joined him. Shortly after her arrival, the two were married by a black minister who had fled slavery in Maryland a decade before. The couple then set off for the Massachusetts port of New Bedford, where Frederick hoped to find work at his trade. And because he still legally belonged to someone else, he changed his name to make it more difficult for slave catchers to trace him. Frederick Bailey became Frederick Douglass.

In the fall of 1838, Douglass started a new life in a new town with a new bride and name. It was not easy. Competing with white workers in New Bedford's shipyards and frozen out of his trade as a skilled ship caulker, Douglass became a common laborer, while Anna—pregnant with their first child—took in laundry. The couple joined a black Methodist church and moved into a small house. Douglass attended abolitionist meetings. He also began to read the *Liberator* and, as he later put it, "was brought into contact with the mind of William Lloyd Garrison." After speaking briefly about his bondage at a New Bedford antislavery meeting at his church in 1841, Douglass was approached by an associate of Garrison who believed that more people should hear the former slave's story. Later that summer, Douglass boarded a steamer for Nantucket, where he moved the abolitionist crowd gathered there. That fall, he began touring as an agent of the Massachusetts Anti-Slavery Society and then of the American Anti-Slavery Society.

In coming years, Douglass would deliver hundreds of speeches, often in the company of his good friend Garrison. He continued to mesmerize Northern audiences as he spoke about his own experiences—and risked his own exposure and capture. Before long, an increasingly self-confident Douglass also began to lash out at racial discrimination in the North. He had plenty of evidence. Most Northern states denied blacks the vote, and many prohibited them from testifying in court against whites. Until 1860, blacks could serve on juries only in Massachusetts. Often states also barred blacks from certain occupations and restricted their movements. In many states, including Douglass's own Massachusetts, white and black children attended separate schools. Douglass, of course, had encountered plenty of discrimination since his escape, and now as he traveled he experienced more, including segregated railroad cars and other public facilities. Abolitionists were often greeted by hostile crowds and frequently pelted with eggs, but Douglass took more than his fair share of abuse. While attempting to speak to one Indiana crowd in 1843, for instance, he was beaten by a mob screaming "kill the damn nigger."

Douglass discovered that he also had to put up with white abolitionists' patronizing attitudes. Many of them wanted him to stick to his own story and not sound too eloquent. Better, advised one, to "have a *little* of the plantation" in his speeches. Even his friend and mentor Garrison declared that if he sounded too "learned," people would not believe that he had ever been a slave. Douglass rejected all this advice. And indeed, skeptical audiences insisted that a black man who was this eloquent and intelligent could never have been a slave! Under mounting pressure, he finally decided to write his story, including places and names he had previously refused to reveal. The result was *Narrative of the Life of Frederick Douglass, an American Slave*. Published in 1845, the thin book was Douglass's story of how, as he put it, "*I became my own master*." At the same time, it offered a powerful indictment of the slave system. **[See Source 3.]**

Douglass's *Narrative* created new opportunities for him to agitate against slavery. The details of his account and the fame it generated, of course, put him in even greater danger of being tracked down. Partly for that reason and partly to bring his message to an even-wider audience, Garrison and other friends encouraged him to travel to Great Britain to speak to antislavery sympathizers there. Forced to find accommodations in steerage after being refused a cabin on the trans-Atlantic steamer, Douglass arrived in Ireland in late 1845 and then traveled on to Scotland and England. Everywhere, he delivered scores of ringing condemnations of slavery to enthusiastic gatherings. By the time Garrison joined him for three more months of speechmaking, he was a celebrity.

When Douglass returned home in early 1847, he was literally a free man. British friends, concerned for his safety in the United States, had purchased his freedom from the Aulds. The price was roughly $700. Even now, though, some abolitionists criticized Douglass. They argued that allowing himself to be bought implied that he could be legitimately sold. "[B]uying men *into slavery*," he responded, "was not the same as "buying men out of it."

If Douglass was now legally free, he still sought more independence. While traveling in Britain, he had been subjected to slights from American abolitionists, who refused to trust him with money and constantly watched over him, especially as he broke the American taboo of conversing freely with white women. As he told one American abolitionist, "If you wish to drive me from the Anti-Slavery society, put me under overseership and the work is done." He had also grown weary of the way he had been put on stage as a specimen. In Britain, he had won enormous respect and gained more confidence. Slowly, he began to realize that Garrison and his supporters, no less than Aaron Anthony or the Aulds, "owned" him. Craving an independent role and voice in the movement, he realized that he had to set his own course.

"AN AGREEMENT WITH HELL"

Arriving home, Douglass set off on one more speaking tour with Garrison. It would be their last together. Douglass, of course, had long been Garrison's protégé. But the pupil had become a powerful voice in the abolition movement, and Garrison watched now as Douglass often upstaged him. When Garrison introduced his friend at one American Anti-Slavery Society annual meeting, the impatient crowd interrupted him with chants of "Douglass, Douglass!" When Garrison fell gravely ill while speaking in Ohio, he emerged from a long convalescence complaining that he had heard nothing from his friend who had departed. Douglass's "inconsiderate" conduct, Garrison declared, "grieves me to the heart." More important, Garrison fumed over Douglass's decision to start his own abolitionist newspaper. Struck by the contrast between his treatment in Britain and the United States, Douglass planned to use the paper to fight against racism as well as slavery. Garrison strenuously argued against it. A husband and the father of five children, he was understandably fearful that a rival paper might drain subscriptions and funds from the financially insecure *Liberator*. With moral and financial support from British abolitionists, Douglass rejected Garrison's advice. After moving with his family to Rochester, New York, Douglass published the first issue of the *North Star* in December 1847. Declaring his allegiance to "no party," he announced his paper's goals: "to attack slavery in all its forms and aspects" and to "promote the moral and intellectual improvement of the colored people."

Before long, Douglass would reject Garrisonian abolition's main tenet: the superiority of "moral suasion" over political agitation. Since 1842, the main pillar supporting that position was Garrison's belief that the Constitution was polluted with the evil of slavery and should be swept away. That year, Garrison had publicly proclaimed that the Constitution protected and legalized slavery—the same argument, ironically, that slavery's defenders made. Appealing to "higher law," Garrison now called on Americans to dissolve their allegiance to a union based on "a covenant with death and an agreement with hell." The Northern states must secede! As the *Liberator* now proclaimed, there could be "NO UNION WITH SLAVEHOLDERS!" **[See Source 4.]**

Douglass had been naturally drawn to Garrison's call for moral regeneration and rejection of political action. Outraged at the treatment of blacks in American society, he placed no trust in the political system to attack racial injustice. For the same reason, he cut ties to any Christian church, convinced that they all upheld slavery. From behind the podium, Douglass's anger led him to denounce repeatedly the moral rottenness of American institutions. After moving to Rochester, however, Douglass began to question Garrison's uncompromising moralism and his rejection of political action. His doubts were partly driven by his desire for independence from Garrison and partly by larger events.

When Douglass returned from Britain in 1847, the nation was divided by war. In 1845, the United States had annexed Texas as a slave state, leading to a boundary dispute with Mexico and then to war in the spring of 1846 (see Chapter 11). Like other abolitionists, Garrison charged that the Mexican War was part of a slaveholders' plot to enlarge the nation's territory for the spread of slavery. That charge struck a chord with many Northerners. To Garrison and his followers, this "slaveholders' war" was further evidence that slavery was an implacable evil with which there could be no compromise. The free states, he declared, must immediately withdraw from "the compact of bloody and deceitful men."

That argument gained Garrison new supporters in the late 1840s. But it also created a far larger number of antislavery people that Garrison could never reach with his radical message of disunion. By the end of the 1840s, most white Northerners were still antiblack and opposed to *abolition*. But many of them had become *antislavery* in the sense that they opposed slavery's expansion into the territories, fearful that slavery's spread would close off opportunities for free white labor to find economic opportunity in the West. Anti-Garrisonians who sought an end to slavery through political action could argue that their approach now made even more sense. Politically minded abolitionists could point to increasing numbers of *antislavery* politicians and the formation of the antislavery-expansion Free Soil Party[*] in 1848. Garrison, however, continued to insist that political abolitionists compromised with evil. They were "hypocrites," he charged, bedfellows with those who tolerated slavery in the South, but wished to prevent its expansion into the West. If these abolitionists got their way, he predicted *abolition* would be swallowed whole by *antislavery*, leaving slavery in the South untouched. This uncompromising stance placed Garrison squarely against more and more fellow abolitionists. As Garrison's fellow American Anti-Slavery Society founder Joshua Leavitt put it, abolition was "no longer a moral crusade."

After moving to Rochester and founding the *North Star*, Douglass could see the change in Northern antislavery opinion. He also came into contact with Liberty Party

---

[*]*Free Soil Party*: A political party founded in 1848 to oppose the extension of slavery in territory taken by the United States in the Mexican War.

founder Gerrit Smith, who argued that the Constitution was not proslavery. The principles in its Preamble, insisted Smith, actually made it an antislavery document. Douglass, who had defended Garrison's view of the Constitution for years, soon agreed. He concluded that while disunion with the South would assuage the consciences of abolitionists like Garrison, the slaves would be freed only by changing the law of the land through political action. When Douglass announced his new position at the American Anti-Slavery Society's annual convention in 1851, a livid Garrison was convinced that "there was roguery somewhere." He now considered Douglass an "enemy" and soon the one-time friends were trading barbs in their respective newspapers. The *Liberator* subjected Douglass to repeated attacks as an unprincipled opportunist. Douglass countered that Garrison could neither tolerate differences of opinion nor treat blacks in the abolitionist movement as equals. **[See Source 5.]**

"THIS FOURTH [OF] JULY IS *YOURS*, NOT *MINE*"

As events pushed slavery to the forefront of political debate in the 1850s, abolitionism became more respectable in the North. With more Northerners becoming alarmed at the prospect of slavery's expansion, more of them were willing to give abolitionists a hearing. More newspapers, too, began to print abolitionist pieces, even Garrison's own. But the very events that stoked antislavery sentiment in the North—the Fugitive Slave Law,* Kansas–Nebraska Act,* and Dred Scott Decision*—only reinforced Garrison's conviction that political means would never bring an end to slavery. Indeed, to Garrison, they proved the power possessed by slaveholders under a proslavery government and a proslavery Constitution. The *Liberator*'s masthead continued to boldly proclaim "NO UNION WITH SLAVEHOLDERS!" Garrison's actions at an abolitionist rally on the Fourth of July in 1854, however, offered the most dramatic reminder of his unyielding position. Holding up a copy of the Fugitive Slave Law and other proslavery legal documents, he set them on fire with a match. Then, declaring that the Constitution was the "source and parent of [these] other atrocities," he set a copy of it on fire as well. "So perish all compromises with tyranny," he proclaimed as it went up in smoke.

But Garrison's moral absolutism and continuing insistence that abolition must be linked to other reforms prevented him from ever becoming antislavery's leading voice. By the mid-1850s, he watched as "voting abolitionists" flocked to the new Republican Party, which called for an end to slavery's expansion, and as Republican senators Charles Sumner of Massachusetts and Benjamin Wade of Ohio and other political abolitionists stepped to the forefront of the abolitionist movement (see Chapter 14). His rigid stance also put him in an awkward position once the sectional crisis finally led to secession and war. He had preached disunion and pacifism for decades. But once the South fired on

---

Fugitive Slave Law: A federal law passed in 1850, which provided harsh penalties for those who did not assist in the capture of alleged fugitive slaves.

Kansas–Nebraska Act: A federal law passed in 1854 that provided for the organization of the Kansas and Nebraska territories. Because this law provided for the question of slavery to be decided by a vote of the settlers in each territory, it overturned the Missouri Compromise of 1820, which had barred slavery from this area. (See Chapter 13.)

Dred Scott Decision: A Supreme Court decision in 1857 finding that the prohibition of slavery north of the 36° 30′ parallel line in the Missouri Compromise of 1820 violated the Constitution, in effect declaring that Congress had no power to bar slavery from any federal territories.

Fort Sumter in 1861, he threw his support to the Union, even though Abraham Lincoln's stated goal was to save the Union without necessarily moving against slavery. Garrison realized now, as Frederick Douglass had years before, that secession would only ensure the continuation of slavery.

Meanwhile, the growing sectional conflict of the 1850s confirmed for Frederick Douglass that "moral suasion" and nonviolence were inadequate to destroy slavery. And he, too, dramatically used an Independence Day celebration to advance that view. On July 5, 1852, Douglass told an abolitionist gathering that the Constitution needed to be changed to reflect its antislavery ideals. Until it was, he declared, "This Fourth [of] July is yours, not mine." **[See Source 6.]** Embracing political action, Douglass was able to come to terms with men whose views were far from his own. In the early 1850s, he supported the Free Soil Party, even though it took a stand only against slavery in the territories. Later, he took the same stance toward the new Republican Party after it replaced the Free Soil Party. He had no illusions about Republicans. Few of them were abolitionists. But, unlike his old mentor, Douglass refused to believe that antislavery would swallow up abolition and leave slavery in place. "We can turn Republicans," he declared, "into abolitionists." And when the Civil War came, he was willing to work with Lincoln, even though frustrated by the president's slow pace on the issue of emancipation. At the same time, he fought to make sure that abolition was one of the war's results. Fearful that whites in the North and South might make peace and leave the slavery in place, he demanded that the Union allow blacks to join the ranks. If blacks were allowed to fight, he believed, slavery could never be preserved once the Union was restored.

The Emancipation Proclamation made black enlistment possible and, with the Thirteenth Amendment in 1865, made abolition a reality. By the time he died in 1879, Garrison had not only seen the cause he had committed his life to finally bear fruit. The man who had attracted relatively few followers but much animosity also lived long enough to see himself become the preeminent symbol of abolitionism's victory over slavery. Taking his last breath in 1895, Frederick Douglass lived long enough to see his suspicions about Garrison's commitment to black equality proved correct when his old mentor opposed black voting after the Civil War until the freedmen proved their moral "worth." Garrison would not be alone in such views, and after the Civil War, Douglass would watch as blacks won and then lost their political rights (see Chapter 15). By then, Douglass had been proven correct about something else: the struggle for black freedom was not the same as the fight for black equality.

• PRIMARY SOURCES •

Source 1:   *Detail of* Liberator *Masthead* (1831)

Like the rest of William Lloyd Garrison's Liberator, *the newspaper's masthead reflected Garrison's message and his technique for spreading the abolitionist message. What does this image reveal about Garrison's approach to abolition? How does it attempt to gain sympathy for this cause?*

THE LIBERATOR.

Our Country is the World, our Countrymen are all Mankind.

BOSTON, FRIDAY, JANUARY 21, 1859.

Source 2: *Garrison Announces His New Reform Policy (1837)*

In 1837, William Lloyd Garrison advanced a sweeping critique of American society and announced his intention to combine abolition with other reforms. How does Garrison link abolition with them? What is the basis for his radical, "perfectionist" stance?

The termination of the present year will complete the seventh volume of the *Liberator*: we have served, therefore, a regular apprenticeship in the cause of LIBERTY, and are now prepared to advocate it upon a more extended scale.

In commencing this publication, we had but a single object in view—the total abolition of American slavery, and as a just consequence, the complete enfranchisement of our colored countrymen. As the first step towards this sublime result, we found the overthrow of the American Colonization Society to be indispensable—containing, as it did, in its organization, all the elements of prejudice, caste, and slavery.

In entering upon our eighth volume, the abolition of slavery will still be the grand object of our labors, though not, perhaps, so exclusively as heretofore. There are other to-pics which, in our opinion, are intimately connected with the great doctrine of inalienable human rights; and which, while they conflict with no religious sect, or political party, as such, are pregnant with momentus consequences to the freedom, equality, and happiness of mankind. These we shall discuss as time and opportunity may permit.

The motto upon our banner has been, from the commencement of our moral warfare, "OUR COUNTRY IS THE WORLD—OUR COUNTRYMEN ARE ALL MANKIND." We trust that it will be our only epitaph. Another motto we have chosen is, UNIVERSAL EMANCIPATION. Up to this time we have limited its application to those who are held in this country, by Southern taskmasters, as marketable commodities, goods and chattels, and implements of husbandry. Henceforth we shall use it in its widest latitude: the emancipation of our whole race from the dominion of man, from the

SOURCE: William Lloyd Garrison, "Garrison Announces His New Reform Policy (1837)." Originally from THE LIBERATOR (Boston), December 15, 1837.

thraldom of self, from the government of brute force, from the bondage of sin—and bringing them under the dominion of God, the control of an inward spirit, the government of the law of love, and into the obedience and liberty of Christ, who is *"the same, yesterday, to-day, and forever."* ...

Next to the overthrow of slavery, the cause of PEACE will command our attention. The doctrine of non-resistance as commonly received and practised by Friends[1] and certain members of other religious denominations, we conceive to be utterly indefensible in its application to national wars:—not that it "goes too far," but that it does not go far enough. If a nation may not redress its wrongs by physical force—if it may not repel or punish a foreign enemy who comes to plunder, enslave or murder its inhabitants—then it may not resort to arms to quell an insurrection, or send to prison or suspend upon a gibbet any transgressors upon its soil. If the slaves of the South have not an undoubted right to resist their masters in the last resort, then no man, or body of men, may appeal to the law of violence in self-defence—for none have ever suffered, or can suffer, more than they. If, when men are robbed of their earnings, their liberties, their personal ownership, their wives and children, they may not resist, in no case can physical resistance be allowable, either in an individual or collective capacity.

Now the doctrine we shall endeavor to inculcate is, that the kingdoms of this world are to become the kingdoms of our Lord and of his Christ; consequently, that they are all to be supplanted, whether they are called despotic, monarchical, or republican, and he only who is King of kings, and Lord of lords, is to rule in righteousness....

As to the governments of this world, whatever their titles or forms, we shall endeavor to prove that, in their essential elements, and as at present administered, they are all Anti-Christ; that they can never, by human wisdom, be brought into conformity to the will of God; that they cannot be maintained except by naval and military power; that all their penal enactments, being a dead letter without an army to carry them into effect, are virtually written in human blood; and that the followers of Jesus should instinctively shun their stations of honor, power, and emolument—at the same time "submitting to every ordinance of man, for the Lord's sake," and offering no *physical* resistance to any of their mandates, however unjust or tyrannical....

As our object is *universal* emancipation,—to redeem woman as well as man from a servile to an equal condition,—we shall go for the RIGHTS OF WOMAN to their utmost extent.

Source 3:   *Douglass Recounts His Life as a Slave* (1845)

The most widely read of several dozen slave narratives published in the nineteenth century, Frederick Douglass's Narrative *sold some thirty thousand copies within five years and was translated into Dutch, German, and French. It also made its author famous. In this selection, Douglass discusses his experiences at the hands of Edward Covey. Douglass had been sent by his master to Covey's farm to be "broken" after he found out that Douglass was teaching other slaves to read. How does Douglass underscore slavery's effects and its contradictions in this passage?*

SOURCE: Frederick Douglass, "Douglass Recounts His Life as a Slave" (1845).

---

[1]Society of Friends, more commonly known as Quakers.

I left Master Thomas's house, and went to live with Mr. Covey, on the 1st of January, 1833. I was now, for the first time in my life, a field hand. In my new employment, I found myself even more awkward than a country boy appeared to be in a large city. I had been at my new home but one week before Mr. Covey gave me a very severe whipping, cutting my back, causing the blood to run, and raising ridges on my flesh as large as my little finger. The details of this affair are as follows: Mr. Covey sent me, very early in the morning of one of our coldest days in the month of January, to the woods, to get a load of wood. He gave me a team of unbroken oxen.... I had never driven oxen before, and of course I was very awkward. I, however, succeeded in getting to the edge of the woods with little difficulty; but I had got a very few rods into the woods, when the oxen took fright, and started full tilt, carrying the cart against trees, and over stumps, in the most frightful manner. I expected every moment that my brains would be dashed out against the trees. After running thus for a considerable distance, they finally upset the cart, dashing it with great force against a tree, and threw themselves into a dense thicket. How I escaped death, I do not know. There I was, entirely alone, in a thick wood, in a place new to me. My cart was upset and shattered, my oxen were entangled among the young trees, and there was none to help me. After a long spell of effort, I succeeded in getting my cart righted, my oxen disentangled, and again yoked to the cart. I now proceeded with my team to the place where I had, the day before, been chopping wood, and loaded my cart pretty heavily, thinking in this way to tame my oxen. I then proceeded on my way home. I had now consumed one half of the day. I got out of the woods safely, and now felt out of danger. I stopped my oxen to open the woods gate; and just as I did so, before I could get hold of my ox-rope, the oxen again started, rushed through the gate, catching it between the wheel and the body of the cart, tearing it to pieces, and coming within a few inches of crushing me against the gate-post. Thus twice, in one short day, I escaped death by the merest chance. On my return, I told Mr. Covey what had happened, and how it happened. He ordered me to return to the woods again immediately. I did so, and he followed on after me. Just as I got into the woods, he came up and told me to stop my cart, and that he would teach me how to trifle away my time, and break gates. He then went to a large gum-tree, and with his axe cut three large switches, and, after trimming them up neatly with his pocketknife, he ordered me to take off my clothes. I made him no answer, but stood with my clothes on. He repeated his order. I still made him no answer, nor did I move to strip myself. Upon this he rushed at me with the fierceness of a tiger, tore off my clothes, and lashed me till he had worn out his switches, cutting me so savagely as to leave the marks visible for a long time after. This whipping was the first of a number just like it, and for similar offences.

I lived with Mr. Covey one year. During the first six months, of that year, scarce a week passed without his whipping me. I was seldom free from a sore back. My awkwardness was almost always his excuse for whipping me. We were worked fully up to the point of endurance. Long before day we were up, our horses fed, and by the first approach of day we were off to the field with our hoes and ploughing teams. Mr. Covey gave us enough to eat, but scarce time to eat it. We were often less than five minutes taking our meals. We were often in the field from the first approach of day till its last lingering ray had left us....

Mr. Covey's *forte* consisted in his power to deceive. His life was devoted to planning and perpetrating the grossest deceptions. Everything he possessed in the shape of learning or religion, he made conform to his disposition to deceive.... Poor man! such him-self into the solemn belief, that he was a sincere worshipper of the most high God....

If at any one time of my life more than another, I was made to drink the bitterest dregs of slavery, that time was during the first six months of my stay with Mr. Covey. We were worked in all weathers. It was never too hot or too cold; it could never rain, blow, hail, or snow, too hard for us to work in the field. Work, work, work, was scarcely more the order of the day than of the night. The longest days were too short for him, and the shortest nights too long for him. I was somewhat unmanageable when I first went there, but a few months of this discipline tamed me. Mr. Covey succeeded in breaking me. I was broken in body, soul, and spirit. My natural elasticity was crushed, my intellect languished, the disposition to read departed, the cheerful spark that lingered about my eye died; the dark night of slavery closed in upon me; and behold a man transformed into a brute!

Source 4:   *Garrison Announces "No Union with Slaveholders" (1844)*

In 1840 Garrison and his supporters took control of the American Anti-Slavery Society. Four years later, the organization announced in the following statement written by Garrison and reprinted in the Liberator *that it was in favor of the breakup of the Union. What is the basis for Garrison's and the American Anti-Slavery Society's anti-Union position? Is there a connection between the position announced by Garrison in Source 2 and the one expressed here for the secession of the Northern states from the Union?*

At the Tenth Anniversary of the American Anti-Slavery Society, held in the city of New-York, May 7th, 1844,—after grave deliberation, and a long and earnest discussion, —it was decided, by a vote of nearly three to one of the members present, that fidelity to the cause of human freedom, hatred of oppression, sympathy for those who are held in chains and slavery in this republic, and allegiance to God, require that the existing national compact should be instantly dissolved; that secession from the government is a religious and political duty; that the motto inscribed on the banner of Freedom should be, NO UNION WITH SLAVEHOLDERS; that it is impracticable for tyrants and the enemies of tyranny to coalesce and legislate together for the preservation of human rights, or the promotion of the interests of Liberty; and that revolutionary ground should be occupied by all those who abhor the thought of doing evil that good may come, and who do not mean to compromise the principles of Justice and Humanity....

Three millions of the American people are crushed under the American Union! They are held as slaves—trafficked as merchandize—registered as goods and chattels! The government gives them no protection—the government is their enemy—the government keeps them in chains! There they lie bleeding—we are prostrate by their side— in their sorrows and sufferings we participate—their stripes are inflicted on our bodies, their shackles are fastened on our limbs, their cause is ours! The Union which grinds them to the dust rests upon us, and with them we will struggle to overthrow it! The

Source: William Lloyd Garrison, Garrison Announces "No Union with Slaveholders" (1844). Originally from THE LIBERATOR (Boston), May 31, 1844.

Constitution which subjects them to hopeless bondage, is one that we cannot swear to support! Our motto is, "NO UNION WITH SLAVEHOLDERS," either religious or political. They are the fiercest enemies of mankind, and the bitterest foes of God! We separate from them not in anger, not in malice, not for a selfish purpose, not to do them an injury, not to cease warning, exhorting, reproving them for their crimes, not to leave the perishing bondman to his fate—O no! But to clear our skirts of innocent blood—to give the oppressor no countenance—to signify our abhorrence of injustice and cruelty—to testify against an ungodly compact—to cease striking hands with thieves and consenting with adulterers—to make no compromise with tyranny—to walk worthily of our high profession—to increase our moral power over the nation—to obey God and vindicate the gospel of his Son—to hasten the downfall of slavery in America, and throughout the world....

Secede, then, from the government. Submit to its exactions, but pay it no allegiance, and give it no voluntary aid. Fill no offices under it. Send no Senators or Representatives to the national or State Legislature; for what you cannot conscientiously perform yourself, you cannot ask another to perform as your agent. Circulate a declaration of DISUNION FROM SLAVEHOLDERS, throughout the country. Hold mass meetings—assemble in Conventions—nail your banners to the mast!

Source 5: *Frederick Douglass Responds to William Lloyd Garrison* (1853)

Frederick Douglass used his newspaper to respond to the attacks of Garrison and his followers on him. What does the following passage reveal about Douglass's perception of Garrison and at least one of the reasons for his break with him?

"One thing should always be remembered in regard to the Anti-slavery cause. It is not based upon complexion, but upon justice; its principles are world-wide, though the victims whom it seeks to deliver are groaning in the Southern prison-house; concerns man as man, not merely as an African or one of African descent."

Theoretically and abstractly it is easy to admit the truth of this first postulate laid down by Mr. Garrison, as the necessary preliminary to his strictures upon me. Practically, however, and in point of fact, it fails to express the *whole* truth. If Mr. Garrison means here to assert, merely, that the principles of justice and liberty are universal; having neither respect to country, color or condition, I agree with him; but if he means what it seems he really does mean; that white men are as deeply concerned in the success of the Anti-Slavery cause in this country, as are Africans, or persons of African descent he contradicts the plainest truths, and flies directly in the face of facts, with no other apparent motive than to disparage the very people of whose claims to Liberty he is the acknowledged defender and advocate.

As if to leave no doubt of this disparagement, Mr. Garrison says.

"Unswerving fidelity to it, (the cause) in this country, requires high moral attainments, the crucifixion of all personal considerations, a paramount regard for principle, absolute faith in the right. It does not follow, therefore, that because a man is or has

SOURCE: Frederick Douglass, "Frederick Douglass Responds to William Lloyd Garrison" (1853). Originally from NATIONAL ANTI-SLAVERY STANDARD, May 20, 1847.

been a slave, or because he is identified with a class meted out and trodden under foot, he will be the truest to the cause of human freedom. Already, that cause, both religiously and politically, has transcended the ability of the sufferers from American slavery and prejudice, as a class, to keep pace with it, or to perceive what are its demands, or to understand the philosophy of its operation." ...

If it be true (as Mr. Garrison alleges) that the anti-slavery "cause, both religiously and politically, has transcended the ability of the sufferer from American Slavery and prejudice, as a class, to keep pace with it, or to perceive what are its demands, or to understand the philosophy of its operations," it is equally true that it has transcended the ability of white men as well; and it is, therefore, difficult to perceive any good motive in Mr. Garrison for thus branding the *colored* people—the sufferers from slavery and prejudice thus invidiously, with a want of apprehension and moral capacity.

Source 6:   Frederick Douglass, *"The Meaning of July Fourth for the Negro"* (1852)

Speaking in Rochester, New York, Frederick Douglass delivered perhaps his most famous address, which commemorated the signing of the Declaration of Independence seventy-six years earlier. What does this speech reveal about Douglass as an abolitionist orator? What do you think the reaction of non-abolitionist Northerners might have been to his rhetoric?

Fellow citizens, pardon me, allow me to ask, why am I called upon to speak here today? What have I, or those I represent, to do with your national independence? Are the great principles of political freedom and of natural justice, embodied in that Declaration of Independence, extended to us? and am I, therefore, called upon to bring our humble offering to the national altar, and to confess the benefits and express devout gratitude for the blessings resulting from your independence to us?

Would to God, both for your sakes and ours, that an affirmative answer could be truthfully returned to these questions! Then would my task be light, and my burden easy and delightful. For *who* is there so cold, that a nation's sympathy could not thankfully acknowledge such priceless benefits? Who so stolid and selfish, that would not give his voice to swell the halleujahs of a nation's jubilee, when the chains of servitude had been torn from his limbs? I am not that man. In a case like that, the dumb might eloquently speak, and the "lame man leap as an hart."

But such is not the state of the case. I say it with a sad sense of the disparity between us. I am not included within the pale of this glorious anniversary! Your high independence only reveals the immeasurable distance between us. The blessings in which you, this day, rejoice, are not enjoyed in common.—The rich inheritance of justice, liberty, prosperity and independence, bequeathed by your fathers, is shared by you, not by me. The sunlight that brought light and healing to you, has brought stripes and death to me. This Fourth July is *yours*, not *mine*. *You* may rejoice, *I* must mourn. To drag a man in fetters into the grand illuminated temple of liberty, and call upon him to join you in joyous anthems, were inhuman mockery and sacrilegious irony. Do you mean, citizens, to mock me, by asking me to speak to-day? If so, there is a parallel to your conduct. And

SOURCE: Frederick Douglass, "The Meaning of July Fourth for the Negro" (1845)

let me warn you that it is dangerous to copy the example of a nation whose crimes, towering up to heaven, where thrown down by the breath of the Almighty, burying that nation in irrevocable ruin! I can to-day take up the plaintive lament of a peeled and woe smitten people....

What, to the American slave, is your 4th of July? I answer; a day that reveals to him, more than all other days in the year, the gross injustice and cruelty to which he is the constant victim. To him, your celebration is a sham; your boasted liberty, an unholy license; your national greatness, swelling vanity; your sounds of rejoicing are empty and heartless; your denunciation of tyrants, brass fronted impudence; your shouts of liberty and equality, hollow mockery; your prayers and hymns, your sermons and thanksgivings, with all your religious parade and solemnity, are, to Him, mere bombast, fraud, deception, impiety, and hypocrisy—within a thin veil to cover up crimes which would disgrace a nation of savages. There is not a nation on the earth guilty of practices more shocking and bloody than are the people of the United States, at this very hour.

Go where you may, search where you will, roam through all the monarchies and despotisms of the Old World, travel through South America, search out every abuse, and when you have found the last, lay your facts by the side of the everyday practices of this nation, and you will say with me, that, for revolting barbarity and shameless hypocrisy, America reigns without a rival.

QUESTIONS TO CONSIDER

1. How did the backgrounds of William Lloyd Garrison and Frederick Douglass influence each man's views about slavery and the best method for destroying it? Why was each drawn to "moral suasion" as a means to end slavery?

2. Although involved in a common cause, abolitionists were often divided among themselves. What factors helped bring about these divisions? How did personality and issues divide Garrison and Douglass? Were personality or issues more important in explaining their break?

3. Why was the issue of the Constitution so important to Douglass, Garrison, and other abolitionists? How did this issue relate to the split among abolitionists about the wisdom of political action? What does the division created by the issue of politics and the Constitution reveal about the impact of Garrison's ideas on abolitionism?

4. Some critics of William Lloyd Garrison have charged that he actually limited the movement that he helped create. Do you agree? What do you think Frederick Douglass would have said?

5. Garrison and Douglass reflect the division between other abolitionists willing to compromise for small gains and those unwilling to compromise on anything. Discuss the pros and cons of each position in terms of achieving the goal of abolition. Do you see similar divisions in other movements in the past or present?

FOR FURTHER READING

Frederick Douglass, *Narrative of the Life of Frederick Douglass, an American Slave,* (Garden City: Anchor Books, 1969), presents the classic slave narrative of the nineteenth century.

Lawrence J. Friedman, *Gregarious Saints: Self and Community in American Abolitionism, 1830– 1870* (Cambridge: Cambridge University Press, 1982), offers a brief overview of the origins of, and divisions within, abolitionism.

Henry Mayer, *All on Fire: William Lloyd Garrison and the Abolition of Slavery* (New York: St. Martin's Press, 1999), provides a recent and engaging account of Garrison's life and impact.

William S. McFeely, *Frederick Douglass* (New York: W. W. Norton & Company, 1991), provides the most recent, thorough biography of Douglass.

Steven Mintz, *Moralists and Moralizers: America's Pre-Civil War Reformers* (Baltimore: Johns Hopkins University Press, 1995), places abolitionism within the context of broader antebellum reform sentiment.

James Brewer Stewart, *Holy Warriors: The Abolitionists and American Slavery* (New York: Hill and Wang, 1976), offers a brief, approachable overview of abolitionism.

10

The Feminine Sphere in Antebellum Society: Catharine Beecher and Elizabeth Cady Stanton

Elizabeth Cady Stanton could not wait to get to London. Her trip to Britain in the spring of 1840 was her first one abroad. It was also an opportunity to spend time with her new husband. Less than two weeks before departing, the twenty-four-year-old woman had eloped with Henry Stanton. Now they traveled as husband and wife to the English capital, where Henry would attend the first World Anti-Slavery Convention.

In London, however, Stanton got more than she bargained for. American antislavery societies had sent female delegates to the convention, and Stanton watched the convention debate whether to seat them. As a female guest, she was forced to sit apart in a curtained gallery with the women in question. There she listened to pleas by her husband and other men to seat the female delegates, who were not permitted to speak for themselves. She also heard other speakers condemn the whole idea as "promiscuous." And she watched as the convention resoundingly voted down the proposal. Observing this debate, Stanton later recalled, was "refined torture." She left London feeling "humiliated and chagrined"—and determined to fight for female equality. In coming years, Stanton would challenge conventional ideas about women's proper place in society. When American women were virtually without rights, she called for legal equality and the right to vote. In the face of scorn and ridicule, she questioned the assumption that women inhabited a separate sphere in society apart from the "masculine" world of politics and business.

Many women would oppose Stanton's goals, but few more persistently than Catharine Beecher. Like Stanton, Beecher was the daughter of a prominent family. And

Elizabeth Cady Stanton

Catharine Beecher

she also believed that women had to be elevated in American society. Beyond that, however, these two women shared little in common. Beecher insisted that women would have their greatest impact by remaining in their own feminine sphere and performing the important work for which they were uniquely qualified. And that work, she believed, was urgently needed.

Beecher and Stanton were not alone in their desire to change the position of women in American society in the three decades before the Civil War. The Second Great Awakening aroused in many Americans an intense desire not only to save themselves but also to remake society. Many of the reforms being promoted were intended to liberate Americans from old customs and institutions. Often, though, reform could be a means of control. Disturbed by rapid economic and social changes, many reformers feared social disorder and sought new ways to restrain behavior. Perhaps nowhere were the rival impulses behind reform more evident than in the struggle over the position of women in American society. Denied equal rights and excluded from the world of business and the professions, women had little power within the household and no power outside it. In an age of increasing political equality for white men, the status of women posed a glaring contradiction to the ideology of natural rights and equality that underlay the American Revolution. Some reformers responded to this situation by arguing that women needed to be liberated from the home. Others argued that women needed to be elevated within their domestic sphere. Only then would they be able to do the work for which they were uniquely suited: guarding moral virtue. For these reformers, uplifting women and ensuring social order were one and the same.

Few early nineteenth-century women better exemplified these competing ideas than Beecher and Stanton. Beecher wanted to elevate the position of women in the private world. Because women were by their very nature more virtuous, their role was to instruct and uplift. Their greatest influence was in the feminine, household sphere, although they could do more outside the home to civilize the nation and protect its morals. By contrast, Stanton believed that the ideals of the Declaration of Independence applied to women as well as men. Thus women's proper role was in the public sphere, right alongside men.

"THE SUBORDINATE STATION"

Catharine Beecher was a member of one of the most illustrious families in the early American Republic. Her father, Lyman Beecher, was a clergyman who became one of the most famous ministers in the country. Her brothers Edward and Henry Ward followed their father into the ministry. Edward became an important theologian, and Henry Ward became a leading preacher in the second half of the century. Her abolitionist sister, Harriet Beecher Stowe, wrote *Uncle Tom's Cabin* (1852), an abolitionist novel that caused an outcry in both the North and the South prior to the Civil War.

Born in 1800 in East Hampton on the eastern tip of New York's Long Island, Catharine Beecher grew up in isolated but comfortable circumstances. Although her father sprang from humble beginnings, her mother was from a well-to-do and socially secure Connecticut family. By the time Catharine was nine, her father had moved to a pulpit in prosperous and socially conservative Litchfield, Connecticut, where he gained a powerful influence in the community by preaching the need for personal salvation and obedience to established authority. He was also a powerful force in Catharine's life. Lyman instilled in his daughter an abiding desire for moral leadership, and she would share his concerns about social order and morality throughout her life. Indeed, Lyman and Catharine Beecher were living examples of the link between evangelism, which demanded individual regeneration, and reform, which demanded moral regeneration of society.

At the same time, Catharine resisted Lyman's encouragement that she assume a traditionally dependent female role. The Beecher family's circumstances no doubt contributed to her growing sense of independence. After their mother died in 1816, Catharine did not like her father's second wife, nor did she approve of his third choice after his second wife died. These feelings may have made it easier for her to reject her father's urgent message of repentance and salvation. Young people in evangelical Christian families were expected to undergo a conversion experience, something Catharine would not—or could not—do. She further asserted her independence when her fiancé, a young Yale College professor, died in a shipwreck in 1822. After her fiancé's death, Lyman increased his pressure on her to convert and not to "cling to the shipwrecked hopes of earthly good." But Catharine did not have her conversion experience, nor did she ever marry. Freed from the obligations of marriage, she would concentrate instead on doing "earthly good."

For the rest of her life, most of Catharine Beecher's efforts were directed at helping women achieve their proper place in society and the family. Education, she believed, was the key to that. Since the eighteenth century, education for females beyond the primary grades was limited to daughters of well-off families who had the opportunity to attend private academies. There they received an "ornamental" education, designed to prepare them for their roles in the private, domestic sphere with a curriculum emphasizing sewing, music, and art—subjects designed to provide young women with polish. The goal was to make them more acceptable companions for men, not to help them enter the masculine sphere of politics and business.

Beecher rejected education designed only to make women shining ornaments. She believed that girls should receive the same curriculum as boys: mathematics, science, history, literature, rhetoric, and logic. The year after her fiancé's death, she acted on her belief by founding the Hartford Female Seminary. Like a number of other female academies opened in the 1820s, Beecher's seminary went beyond the "ornamental" subjects and soon became one of the most rigorous girls' schools in the country. Seeking to elevate women within their sphere, Beecher argued that an "advanced" education would actually make women better housekeepers and mothers. Thus, at the Hartford Female Seminary, domestic economy replaced "ornamental" subjects as the chief course of study. As Beecher noted in 1827, "A lady should study, not to *shine,* but to *act.*" Educated women, she insisted, could exert a powerful influence "upon the general interest of society."

The belief that women could have an impact on society even in the domestic sphere was not new. In the decades after the American Revolution, many Americans saw a connection between women's activities at home and the "general interests of society." The Republic, they argued, rested on the character of the citizenry. Child rearing took on new importance, as virtuous republican mothers were necessary to raise good republican citizens. Beecher's views about society's "general interests," however, also reflected broad economic and social changes during the early nineteenth century. These changes dramatically affected middle-class families, especially in the North. They also helped transform many Americans' views about women.

By the 1820s, what historians now call a market revolution[*] drew more and more Americans into a commercial capitalist economy characterized by cash transactions, occupational specialization, and economic fluctuations. As commercial capitalism spread, trade and manufacturing expanded, cities grew, and more work was performed outside the home. While women remained within the home, husbands more often left it to "make a living." As more and more families ceased to be productive units, the household became a social rather than an economic unit. Women in urban, middle-class families now had more time to devote to child rearing and housekeeping. As the functions of husbands and wives began to be differentiated in a conscious way as never before, domestic life became an exclusively feminine domain. New publications such as *Godey's Lady's Book* and *Ladies Magazine* held up the home as a feminine retreat isolated from the harsh outside world of politics and business.

Embedded in this view was the assumption that the masculine and feminine spheres reflected distinctive character traits. Men were naturally individualistic, competitive, and materialistic. Women were passive, affectionate, and pure. They were expected to exhibit distinctly "feminine" traits, such as submissiveness, piety, self-sacrifice, and humility, which would naturally counteract the "masculine" traits so important for success in the emerging market economy. **[See Source 1.]** Related to female piety was the idea of purity and moral superiority. Unlike men, women lacked lust. Indeed, their very lack

---

[*]*Market revolution:* An economic transformation revolving around the dominance of a free market—that is, the production and sale of goods for profit. In the early nineteenth century, it was associated with the increasing use of cash, rather than barter, and the growing importance of impersonal, rather than face-to-face, transactions.

of passion gave them influence over their weaker-willed male counterparts. Because these "feminine" traits were also Christian virtues, ministers such as Lyman Beecher played an important role in fostering the idea of female moral superiority. For the same reason, religion was one of the few activities outside the home in which women could safely engage without leaving their sphere.

By the 1820s, Catharine Beecher and some other women began to argue that women's "natural" traits made them better qualified than men for another activity: teaching. In fact, Beecher's seminary was designed to prepare women to become teachers. To that end, its curriculum also emphasized instruction in "moral philosophy"—in a course taught by Beecher herself. Here was a career for women outside the home, but one related to the feminine sphere. Schools, like families, were incubators of character. And women far more than men were suited to the task of character formation, whether in the family or the school. Harriet Beecher Stowe, who taught at her sister's seminary, summarized this view well: Men did not have the "patience, the long-suffering, and gentleness necessary to superintend the formation of character."

In one way, Beecher's timing was perfect. During the 1820s, public schools expanded across the nation, especially in the North. At the same time, men, who had traditionally dominated the teaching profession, began to find new opportunities in factories and offices. As school boards discovered by the 1830s, many women were eager to serve in these positions, already low paying, at half the salaries received by male teachers. By 1860 one-quarter of the nation's teachers were female.

Despite these long-term changes, after operating for eight years, the Hartford Female Seminary failed in 1831 for lack of funds. The school depended on financial assistance from the community, which was not ready to embrace Beecher's curriculum or the idea of women working outside the home—even in a role related to natural feminine traits. As the editor of the *Connecticut Courant* said, "I had rather my daughters would go to school and sit down and do nothing, than to study Philosophy, etc. These branches fill young Misses with *vanity* to a degree that they are above attending to the more useful parts of an education."

Beecher was not about to give up, though. Instead, she decided to accompany her father when he moved to Cincinnati in 1832. Lyman Beecher had accepted the position of president of the Lane Theological Seminary, where he would direct the education of ministerial students, many of whom would go on to serve in the reform movements of the coming decades. For Catharine Beecher, the move west represented an opportunity not only to start over but also to apply her ideas on an even grander scale. In the years after the War of 1812, a flood of settlers had moved into the Old Northwest. Many of them had come from New England. Others, however, were European immigrants, especially Germans, or southerners who had moved north across the Ohio River. Like many New England Protestants, Beecher was convinced that these non-Yankee westerners were in urgent need of civilization and uplift. For one thing, the area lacked churches and schools. Even worse, too many of the newcomers were "uncivilized." Many of them were Roman Catholics, who many Protestants feared did not share their own middle-class values of self-restraint and sobriety. As Beecher put it, "Thousands and thousands of degraded foreigners, and their ignorant families, are pouring into this nation at every avenue." These growing hordes of uneducated, unrestrained, lower-class people represented a crisis for American democracy. The West, she believed, was a battleground between morality and degeneration.

Here, she declared, "it shall be decided whether disenthralled intellect and liberty shall voluntarily submit to the laws of virtue and of Heaven, or run wild to insubordination, anarchy and crime."

The remedy was clear. Beecher estimated that one-third of the children in the West were without schools. Ninety thousand teachers, she believed, were needed immediately in the name of civilization and democracy. And male teachers alone could not address the problem. In short, the nation needed a corps of female teachers. To fill that need, Beecher started another female seminary in Cincinnati in 1832. It was called the Western Female Institute. The school would teach Protestant, middle-class values and, she hoped, serve as a model for the nation, giving women an opportunity to be an "all-pervading" influence in American society.

Championing her new seminary in lectures and essays, Beecher always insisted that female teachers would uphold rather than challenge traditional relations between the sexes. "Heaven has appointed to one sex the superior, and to the other the subordinate station," she declared. In fact, women's method of gaining influence and exercising power had nothing to do with their similarity to men. "Let every woman become so cultivated and refined in intellect, that her taste and judgment will be respected; so benevolent in feeling and action, that her motives will be reverenced," Beecher declared in 1837. Then, she concluded, "the fathers, the husbands, and the sons, will find an influence thrown around them, to which they will yield not only willingly but proudly." **[See Source 2.]**

This was Beecher's primary appeal as she continued to drum up support for her Western Female Institute. She envisioned the school as the first in a national system of female seminaries designed to train teachers who would help create a "virtuous democracy." Like Lyman Beecher and other evangelical preachers, Catharine Beecher called for a moral crusade to battle national corruption and moral decline. Hers, however, would be led by women.

Despite high hopes for her Cincinnati school, Beecher's fundraising activities fell short, and the school closed in 1837. Beecher continued to campaign for a corps of teachers to elevate western society, and she gradually emerged as the nation's leading authority on domestic life. In a stream of articles and books, she called for more power for women within the domestic arena and in related functions outside the home. Her views were fully developed in her best-known work, *A Treatise on Domestic Economy*. First published in 1841 and reprinted annually well into the 1850s, the book was a phenomenal success. With it, Beecher joined a growing number of women writers who quietly entered the masculine world of the marketplace. Meanwhile, by elevating what Beecher called "the importance and dignity of domestic knowledge," *A Treatise on Domestic Economy* helped transform housekeeping into a profession as important to social harmony as any filled by men. **[See Source 3.]**

As Beecher labored to uphold women's traditional place and evangelized for a female assault on ignorance and immorality, a young upper-class belle from upstate New York was about to launch her attack on the very idea of a separate female sphere. It would not take long for Elizabeth Cady Stanton and others like her to catch Beecher's attention. These women's rights activists, Beecher feared, would actually retard the progress of women in society. Stanton countered that only women's continued submission to outmoded traditions did that. And as long as women were denied the right to vote, she insisted, there would be no way to throw them off. Stanton's name became synonymous with women's fight to secure that right.

"ABSOLUTE TYRANNY OVER HER"

Born in 1815, Elizabeth Cady grew up in the wealthy and conservative family of Daniel and Margaret Livingston Cady. The Cadys were the first family of Johnstown, New York, where Daniel practiced law, oversaw significant real estate investments, and entered politics. A staunch Federalist and then Whig,[*] Cady served in the state assembly, the House of Representatives, and later on the New York State Supreme Court. Margaret, a descendant of one of the state's oldest and wealthiest families, kept order in the Cady's elegant mansion with the help of servants, nurses, maids, a cook, and a laundress. The couple raised their children in the conservative fashion befitting their privileged status. The six Cady children who survived childhood were taught self-control and respect for authority. In addition, Margaret trained her five daughters in the domestic arts and manners appropriate for future wives of her class.

In this conventional environment, however, the Cady's middle daughter developed a strong sense of independence. Family tragedies and the Cady's conventional expectations for their children had much to do with that. In the early nineteenth century, an upper-class family's fortune and name were perpetuated by the activities of sons who were encouraged to pursue careers in law, business, or politics. Daughters were expected simply to marry into another family. Like many other parents, the Cadys preferred boys. But before Elizabeth was born, the couple had already lost two sons. After Elizabeth, Margaret gave birth to two more daughters. The Cadys' disappointment was deep. In fact, Elizabeth's first memory was of a neighbor consoling her parents about the arrival of yet another girl. Disappointment turned to grief in 1826 when the Cadys' one surviving son died two weeks after graduating from college. Daniel Cady never fully recovered from the loss. When she climbed on her father's knee as he sat in the family parlor mourning his son's death, Elizabeth recalled, Daniel sighed and confessed: "Oh, my daughter, I wish you were a boy!" Elizabeth vowed then to do all she could to be "manly" and to become "learned and courageous," a desire reinforced by the death of yet another Cady son born a year later. Although not yet in her teens, Elizabeth never forgot these resolutions. As she recalled, they were "destined to mold my character in a new way."

Elizabeth became the son that her father never had. While a neighbor tutored her in Greek and mathematics, subjects thought suitable only for male students, her brother-in-law taught her to ride. She learned how to debate, and she developed an insatiable curiosity. Her father also allowed her to spend hours in his library and law office. He took her to court with him. He also encouraged her to debate the law clerks who shared dinner at the Cady home. In his office and library, Elizabeth began to see evidence of the discrimination women faced. One case left an especially strong impression. After her husband died, one of the Cadys' servants came to Daniel to gain control of a farm purchased with her earnings. Unfortunately, the husband's will left the property to the couple's son. The law in New York and other states declared that husbands had full control over their wives' earnings, as well as their property and children. Considered legal extensions of their spouses, wives were not even able to testify against their husbands in court. Elizabeth listened as her father explained to the woman that he could do nothing for her.

---

[*]*Whigs:* The political party organized in 1834 in opposition to Andrew Jackson's Democratic Party. The Whigs favored a strong government committed to the moral improvement of the nation.

As bright and curious as Elizabeth was, college was out of the question. No college admitted women when she graduated from the Johnstown Academy in 1830 at the top of her class. Unhappy after watching her male classmates go off to college, she enrolled at the nearby Troy Female Seminary, run by the women's education pioneer Emma Willard. In addition to the usual social graces emphasized at finishing schools, Willard taught her students academic subjects usually thought unsuitable for young women. Here Elizabeth also came into contact with an assertive, intelligent woman who hardly fit the submissive feminine ideal. Nonetheless, after graduating in 1833, Elizabeth returned home to lead a life typical of a young, single woman of her class who had virtually no professional or career opportunities. When not helping her mother around the house, she spent time reading, riding, sleeping in late, or visiting.

As was often the case for young upper-class women, social contacts soon led to marriage. In nearby Peterboro, Elizabeth frequently visited the home of cousin Gerrit Smith, whose father was the husband of Margaret Cady's sister and one of the largest landowners in New York. At her cousin's manor, Elizabeth found a lively house filled with a steady stream of visitors and conversation on controversial issues. One of them was abolition, to which Smith, first involved in missionary activities then temperance, ultimately committed. As a founder of the abolitionist Liberty Party in 1840, he became a leader of abolitionists who sought an end to slavery through political means. When Elizabeth began her frequent stays at Smith's house, she learned about the reality of slavery through conversations with fugitive slaves who sometimes stayed there. Here, too, she was introduced in 1839 to Henry Stanton, one of her cousin's abolitionist associates. Ten years older than Elizabeth, Stanton was an officer in the American Anti-Slavery Society and a well-known antislavery speaker. He could tell tales of narrow escapes from antiabolitionist mobs and move listeners with his eloquence. Elizabeth was swept away and within a month the couple was engaged.

Elizabeth's engagement to Stanton was an act of rebellion. Her parents were appalled by her choice. They viewed abolitionists as disreputable fanatics, and Stanton, the son of a bankrupt New England woolen manufacturer, had no family connections, little money, and no prospects. They persuaded Elizabeth to break off the engagement, but she did not accept their decision, and Stanton did not give up. When he told her the next year that he was going to London as a delegate to the World Anti-Slavery Convention and would be gone for eight months, she insisted that they marry before the trip. While she and her new husband shared a romantic trip abroad, she hoped, her parents' anger would cool. Henry and Elizabeth wed in May 1840, in a ceremony that omitted the word "obey" from the vows. Departing for London less than two weeks later, Elizabeth looked forward to the time with Henry—and to a marriage based on independence and equality.

The London antislavery conference was a turning point in Elizabeth Stanton's life. She attended it because her husband was a leading American abolitionist, but she came away from it more concerned about the status of women than of slaves. In London, she made the acquaintance of a well-known Philadelphia Quaker named Lucretia Mott. A Garrisonian abolitionist, Mott believed in immediate emancipation and refused to use any product produced by slave labor, including cotton and sugar. She was twenty-two years older than Elizabeth, soft spoken, and serene. But she was also an outspoken advocate for female equality. Over meals, Elizabeth listened to Mott's arguments in favor of female participation in antislavery societies. She watched as Mott preached in a London church before a mixed audience of men and women. Enthralled by Mott and brimming with questions, she took every opportunity to be at the Quaker's side. Here, she recalled much later, was "an entire new revelation of womanhood."

If Elizabeth Cady Stanton found a mentor in London, she also came away in deep disagreement with her own husband on the issue of women. Initially a protégé of William Lloyd Garrison, Henry Stanton had earlier broken ranks with *his* mentor over the issues of abolitionists' involvement in politics and women's involvement in abolition. In fact, he traveled to London as a representative of the new anti-Garrisonian American and Foreign Anti-Slavery Society. Along with other political abolitionists, Stanton opposed female participation in antislavery activities out of fear that it might alienate voters. In London, however, William Lloyd Garrison and his followers insisted that female delegates be seated as equals. Assured that his fellow anti-Garrisonians had enough votes to reject Garrison's proposal, Stanton spoke eloquently for seating the women. While he remained in his seat after the vote, however, Garrison left his in protest to sit with the women. As he sat down in the female gallery, Henry Stanton's enemy became Elizabeth Stanton's hero.

The impact of Elizabeth's London experience was evident after the Stantons returned home. Elizabeth continued to disagree with Henry about the position of women in antislavery societies. She also refused to attend antislavery meetings with him because she knew that she and other women "would have no voice." The very next year, she wrote to Lucretia Mott that the more she thought about the condition of women, the more she was depressed by the reality of their "degradation." Seeking her own identity, she began to call herself by her full name: Elizabeth Cady Stanton.

At the same time, the reality of marriage set in. While Cady Stanton settled into life as a wife and mother, Henry Stanton's economic circumstances became a pressing issue. Abolitionism did not pay the bills, and so he decided to study the law under Daniel Cady. After Henry's two-year apprenticeship, the Stantons moved to Boston. There Henry could practice law and, he hoped, establish a beachhead for political abolitionism in William Lloyd Garrison's own stronghold. By then, Elizabeth had already given birth to two sons. A third arrived shortly after the move to Boston. As a young mother, Cady Stanton settled down in a house purchased by her father. She later recalled that her circumstances fit perfectly the doctrine of separate spheres for husbands and wives. Henry informed her that business would consume all of his time and that she must "take entire charge of housekeeping."

Charged with running her new home, Cady Stanton loved it. She threw herself into decorating, gardening, cooking, and household management. She studied housekeeping and, she later declared, "enjoyed it all." She also read up on child rearing and decided to reject traditional methods. Ignoring the advice of her husband, parents, and child rearing manuals, she threw out medicines and swaddling clothes—the long band of cloth in which babies were traditionally wrapped. When the children were a little older, she also threw out parental strictness for a more lenient, permissive approach. The children were allowed to sleep late and to make their own decisions about such matters as church attendance. Immersed in domesticity, Cady Stanton put off her commitment to fight for woman's rights. On trips home, she occasionally lobbied on behalf of the Married Women's Property Act, a bill introduced in the New York state legislature in 1836 to guarantee married women greater control over their own property. Yet Cady Stanton did not become active in the reform seedbed of Boston.

The Stantons' move from Boston to the quiet town of Seneca Falls in upstate New York in 1847 sparked in her a renewed commitment to woman's rights. Henry sought a career in politics and believed the area provided more fertile ground than Garrisonian Boston for political abolitionism to take root. For Elizabeth, however, Seneca Falls, with only about four thousand residents, proved barren. Their new home was rural and relatively isolated. With Henry gone on business much of the time, the thirty-one-year-old housewife was left by herself to take care of the house on the outskirts of town. Cady Stanton began to feel isolated and trapped. "The novelty of housekeeping had passed away," she recalled later, "and much that was once attractive in domestic life was now irksome." Feeling "mental hunger," she was lonely and depressed.

Cady Stanton's marriage only heightened her discontent. Elizabeth and Henry, of course, continued to disagree over the role of women in the antislavery movement. Acquaintances, moreover, sometimes noted how overbearing Henry was with Elizabeth. Thirty-five years old when he married, Stanton was set in his ways and often wished not to be disturbed when home. Meanwhile, his legal practice and involvement in antislavery politics, including the founding of the Liberty Party in 1840 and the anti-slavery-expansion Free Soil Party in 1848, took more and more of his time. He was not even home for the birth of two of his children. Increasingly, Henry's freedom to come and go as he pleased annoyed her. He could, as she later put it, "walk at will through the wide world or shut himself up alone."

Personal discontent finally led to action in 1848. That summer, Lucretia Mott and her husband traveled to a Quaker meeting near Seneca Falls. Meeting with Mott and a group of other Quaker women, Cady Stanton poured out her frustrations. It was, as she recalled, with "such vehemence and indignation that I stirred myself, as well as the rest of the party, to do and dare anything." The women decided to hold the woman's rights convention, an idea Cady Stanton and Mott had discussed years earlier.

If Cady Stanton's outburst raised the women's courage, so did the restlessness exhibited by other women by the 1840s. Already in the late 1820s, Scottish-born woman's rights activist Fanny Wright had created a stir by touring the United States and calling for complete equality between the sexes. More important, the women at Seneca Falls were well aware of the discrimination against women in the abolitionist movement. As Cady Stanton well understood, such treatment was a midwife to woman's rights activism. It led many of them to conclude, as the Quaker abolitionist and woman's rights advocate Angelina Grimke put it in 1837, that women could "no longer remain satisfied in the circumscribed limits with which corrupt custom[s] ... have encircled her." The Seneca Falls organizers were also well versed in the writings of other female rights advocates: English writer Mary Wollstonecraft's *Vindication of the Rights of Women*, which had been in circulation since 1792; *Letters on the Equality of the Sexes* (1838), written by Angelina Grimke's sister, Sarah; and Margaret Fuller's *Woman in the Nineteenth Century* (1845), which rejected the doctrine of separate spheres for men and women and called on women to develop their intellectual abilities. In short, the women at Seneca Falls were not operating in a vacuum.

Yet it was Cady Stanton's outburst that moved them to action. They placed an announcement in the Seneca Falls newspaper for a "convention to discuss the social, civil, and religious condition and rights of women" to be held in July. To prepare for the convention, the women decided to write a statement of principles. Then, they scoured various publications for ideas, but as Cady Stanton wrote later, all of them seemed "too tame and pacific for the inauguration of a rebellion." Finally they decided to rewrite the Declaration of Independence, substituting "all men" for King George III, and listing eighteen specific grievances against them. They had a lot to choose from. In 1848, married women had no legal right to their earnings or property and had few rights over their own children. Women earned less than men. They had unequal educational opportunities. Indeed, only Oberlin College in Ohio even admitted them. With the exception of school teaching, the professions were virtually closed to them. They faced a double standard regarding sexual morality. And, of course, they could not vote. After assembling the grievances, it fell to Cady Stanton to draft the document. Titled "A Declaration of Rights and Sentiments," it began with this bold recasting of Thomas Jefferson's words: "The history of mankind is a history of repeated usurpations on the part of man toward woman, having in direct object the establishment of an absolute tyranny over her."

When the Seneca Falls Convention was called to order, more than three hundred men and women crowded into the meeting hall. Many were residents of the Seneca Falls area. Some were committed to woman's rights, others just curious. Among those in attendance was Frederick Douglass, who had recently moved to upstate New York and had taken up the cause of women's rights in his newspaper, *The North Star*. On the first day, Cady Stanton addressed the convention. Although she was so nervous that she felt like "running away," she declared that it was "grossly insulting" to know that "drunkards, idiots, horseracing[,] rum-selling rowdies, ignorant foreigners, and silly boys" could vote, while women could not. **[See Source 4.]** The next day, Cady Stanton read the "Declaration" and the convention adopted it unanimously. Then, it debated several resolutions to be attached to it. One of them was a call for "the right to the elective franchise." Mott and the other organizers feared that demanding the right to vote would make them look foolish. But Cady Stanton insisted on the suffrage proposal's inclusion. The debate was lively. Opponents pointed out that the suffrage resolution would undermine efforts to secure other rights for women. Frederick Douglass countered that "the power to choose rulers and make laws was the right by which all others could be secured." Douglass's eloquent plea probably saved the proposal, which barely passed.

When the Seneca Falls Convention adjourned after two days, Cady Stanton and the other convention organizers had launched a bold assault on gender relations in American society. Although the grievances and many proposals expressed at Seneca Falls were not new, no women had ever dared to hold such a meeting before. And the Seneca Falls meeting had placed the demand for the vote at the center of the woman's rights movement. Increasingly, woman suffrage would be seen as Cady Stanton viewed it—as the key to securing all other rights. Finally, Seneca Falls had underscored *one* rationale for women's equality. It was worth fighting for not so that women could uplift society or help others achieve freedom, but simply because women were entitled to it.

As word of the Seneca Falls meeting spread, many people pointed to the alarming prospect of women abandoning home, marriage, and family. As one Philadelphia paper declared, "A woman is nobody. A wife is everything." If enacted, declared a New York paper, the proposals would "demoralize and degrade [women] from their high sphere and noble destiny." A Massachusetts paper was harsher, labeling the participants "*Amazons*" and concluding that they had leapt from their sphere "with a vengeance." In response to this public outburst, Cady Stanton took up her pen. In a letter to a Rochester paper, she responded to the convention's numerous critics by taking aim at their most basic assumption. "There is, she declared, "no such thing as a sphere for a sex." **[See Source 5.]**

"YOU *CAN* DO *EVERY ONE* OF YOUR DUTIES"

Catharine Beecher, of course, could not have disagreed more with Cady Stanton's conclusion about sexual spheres. Whether Beecher realized it or not, though, Cady Stanton's argument for full equality for women made Beecher's call for elevating women within the domestic sphere seem sensible and moderate in comparison. Beecher continued to acknowledge that there were some areas in which women should not to be involved, such as politics. Women, she insisted, should protect and extend morality. Entering the political world would only stain their virtue and prevent them from fulfilling their own unique duties. Unlike Cady Stanton, who wanted women to have power in the public sphere, Beecher wanted them to have influence. She was satisfied in knowing that behind every good citizen was a woman's domestic power. In contrast to the breakdown of longstanding customs endorsed by Cady Stanton, Beecher held out the comforting image of familiar gender roles and the promise that maintaining them would uplift the nation's morals.

If Cady Stanton and other suffrage advocates drew inspiration from the Declaration of Independence, moreover, Beecher's argument echoed familiar refrains repeated by the defenders of "republican womanhood" in the late eighteenth century. "The success of democratic institutions," she maintained, depended on the "intellectual and moral character of … the people." The formation of that character, she went on, "is committed mainly to the female hand." As the guardians of moral virtue and the bearers of culture, women were responsible for instilling values and ethics in their children. Mothers and teachers should appeal to each child's heart with emotional reactions. They should teach valuable lessons with Bible reading and proper correction. In similar ways, women would have influence over men. Women could encourage their husbands to work and behave properly. They could give their husbands valuable advice and moral perspective. Thus, she advised, women should have more power over finances, work, and child rearing. Men should acknowledge the important role women played in domestic life. Marriage, in short, should be based not on male authority, but on mutual love and respect.

While Beecher preached this domestic ideal in a stream of advice books, Cady Stanton struggled within the confines of her own domestic sphere. The Seneca Falls Convention changed very little about her life as a homemaker. The birth of four more children during the coming decade only heightened her domestic duties. As the enthusiasm generated by the convention waned, she grew frustrated by her renewed isolation. With Henry away from home for up to ten months a year, she came to consider herself a "household drudge" and longed to be free of housekeeping for time to read and write. Numerous women's rights conventions convened after 1848, but she attended only two in upstate New York.

Nonetheless, Cady Stanton remained committed to various women's causes. By the early 1850s, she was active in the temperance movement. Drunkenness was a male problem, but women were frequently its victims. Temperance, she realized, was a way for women to battle the "protracted outrages" committed against wives by drunken husbands. She also took up the cause of dress reform. In 1850, Gerrit Smith's daughter, Elizabeth, visited the Stantons while wearing a short dress covering baggy trousers. She maintained that it was much easier to do housework and other chores in this outfit than in traditional dress, including a skirt, layers of petticoats, and a tightly laced corset designed to shrink the waist. When a temperance journal published by Amelia Bloomer publicized the new fashion, it became known as the "bloomer." Cady Stanton took it up enthusiastically. Like the ideology of separate spheres, she believed, women's traditional dress confined women. But the bloomer engendered even more outrage than the Seneca Falls Convention. Women, many critics charged, were dressing like men! The reaction convinced Cady Stanton that the bloomer undermined the effort to achieve woman's rights and within two years she stopped wearing it in public.

Tired of the ridicule heaped on woman's rights advocates and discouraged by her isolation, Cady Stanton was often tempted to give up reform for domesticity. Three years after the Seneca Falls Convention, however, she met Susan B. Anthony. Until she came to Seneca Falls in 1851 for an antislavery rally and met Cady Stanton, Anthony was more interested in abolition and temperance than woman's rights. The two women became fast friends. Unmarried and free to travel and attend meetings, Anthony provided Cady Stanton with a link to the outside world and encouragement to continue the struggle. From now on, Cady Stanton would have an effective partner.

The collaboration proved long and fruitful. Often confined to home, Cady Stanton wrote resolutions and speeches on temperance, workers' rights, divorce reform, and suffrage, while Anthony delivered them. "I forged the thunderbolts," Cady Stanton said later, "and she fired them." They struck with some effect. Through Anthony, she helped campaign for rights for married women. The New York legislature responded in 1860 by giving married women equal custody rights over their children and a right to their earnings.

Such victories were few, however. By the end of the 1850s the woman's rights movement was submerged by a growing sectional crisis between the North and South. During the Civil War, many woman's rights organizations disbanded, and the few legal gains won earlier were sometimes overturned. In 1862, for instance, the New York legislature repealed most of the woman's property law it had passed just two years earlier. Meanwhile, many women's suffrage advocates abandoned that cause to champion suffrage for black men. After the war, Cady Stanton and Anthony launched a vigorous campaign to extend the vote to women as well as blacks, only to see Republican Party politicians sacrifice support for woman's suffrage out of fear that it would undermine support for black suffrage.

Yet Cady Stanton and Anthony persisted. In 1869, Cady Stanton formed the National Woman Suffrage Association to carry on the fight for a change in the national law to allow women to vote. When she finally stepped down as the association's president in 1892, a woman's suffrage amendment had yet to be passed. Nor would it be part of the Constitution when she died ten years later. Anthony continued the battle, however, and in 1920—nearly three quarters of a century after the Seneca Falls Convention—women finally won the vote nationwide with the ratification of the Nineteenth Amendment.

Meanwhile, Catharine Beecher would never have a home of her own. As Cady Stanton struggled within her domestic sphere, the woman most responsible for broadcasting the domestic ideal remained single her entire life. As was often the case with "respectable" unmarried women in the nineteenth century, she lived with her siblings' families. Beecher went on to found several more schools for women. She also continued to argue against the vote for women, which she believed would only undermine women's moral influence—an argument that continued to have a large and sympathetic audience of men *and* women. And she never stopped promoting the domestic ideal in her writings. With advice that could have been directed to Cady Stanton, she encouraged women overwhelmed with domestic duties to carry on. As she said in 1863, "You *can* do *every one* of your duties, and do them well."

Ironically, Beecher's participation in the public world of education and publishing gave credence to Cady Stanton's argument that women should not be confined to a domestic sphere. Until Beecher died in 1878, however, she could rest assured that the ideal of the domestic sphere was secure. And she could also take satisfaction in knowing that, thanks in part to her own work, Americans' consciousness about women and families had been transformed. By the middle of the nineteenth century, middle-class women had broader powers within the home. Most men now idealized families. They accepted the nurturing hand of the mother and the role of education and religious faith in the development of good citizens. They embraced the idea that mothers were responsible for imparting morality in the form of a conscience. In the end, Beecher's persistent claim to female moral virtue helped promote some of the most important changes affecting women in nineteenth-century America.

• PRIMARY SOURCES •

Source 1:   *"Differences Between the Sexes"* (1835)

Thomas R. Dew, the president of William and Mary College in Virginia, was one of the many writers in the North and South who upheld an antebellum feminine ideal. What does he see as women's unique characteristics? Why, according to Dew, do they fit women uniquely for a domestic sphere? How do you think Stanton and Beecher would have responded to Dew's assertions?

The relative position of the sexes in the social and political world, may certainly be looked upon as the result of organization. The greater physical strength of man, enables him to occupy the foreground in the picture. He leaves the domestic scenes; he plunges into the turmoil and bustle of an active, selfish world; in his journey through life, he has to encounter innumerable difficulties, hardships and labors which constantly beset him. His mind must be nerved against them. Hence courage and boldness are his attributes. It is his province, undismayed, to stand against the rude shocks of the world to meet with a lion's heart, the dangers which threaten him. He is the shield of woman, destined by nature to guard and protect her. Her inferior strength and sedentary habits confine her within the domestic circle; she is kept aloof from the bustle and storm of active life; she is not familiarized to the out of door dangers and hardships of a cold and scuffing world: timidity and modesty are her attributes. In the great strife which is constantly going forward around her, there are powers engaged which her inferior physical strength prevents her from encountering. She must rely upon the strength of others; man must be engaged in her cause. How is he to be drawn over to her side? Not by menace—not by force, for weakness cannot, by such means, be expected to triumph over might. No! it must be by conformity to that character which circumstances demand for the sphere in which she moves; by the exhibition of those qualities which delight and fascinate—which are calculated to win over to her side the proud lord of creation, and to make him an humble suppliant at her shrine. Grace, modesty and loveliness are the charms which constitute her power. By these, she creates the magic spell that subdues to her will the more mighty physical powers by which she is surrounded. Her attributes are rather of a passive than active character. Her power is more emblematical of that of divinity: it subdues without an effort, and almost creates by mere volition;—whilst man must wind his way through the difficult and intricate mazes of philosophy; with pain and toil, tracing effects to their causes, and unravelling the deep mysteries of nature—storing his mind with useful knowledge, and exercising, training and perfecting his intellectual powers, whilst he cultivates his strength and hardens and matures his courage; all with a view of enabling him to assert his rights, and exercise a greater away over those around him. Woman we behold dependant and weak; but out of that very weakness and dependence springs an

SOURCE: Catharine Beecher, "Differences Between the Sexes" (1835). Thomas Roderick Dew, "Dissertation on the Characteristic Differences Between the Sexes, and on the Position and Influence of Women in Society, No. III," SOUTHERN LITERARY MESSENGER (August 1835).

irresistible power. She may pursue her studies too—not however with a view of triumphing in the senate chamber—not with a view to forensic display—not with a view of leading armies to combat, or of enabling her to bring into more formidable action the physical power which nature has conferred on her. No! It is but the better to perfect all those feminine graces, all those fascinating attributes, which render her the centre of attraction and which delight and charm all those who breathe the atmosphere in which she moves....

Source 2:   *Catharine Beecher on Women's Proper Place (1837)*

In this essay from 1837, Catharine Beecher explains her views about women's "subordinate" place in society. How does she define and justify that position? How does she justify the call for female teachers? Does the predominance of female teachers even today reflect the continuing hold of assumptions about gender expressed here?

It is Christianity that has given to woman her true place in society. And it is the peculiar trait of Christianity alone that can sustain her therein. "Peace on earth and good will to men" is the character of all the rights and privileges, the influence, and the power of woman. A man may act on society by the collision of intellect, in public debate; he may urge his measures by a sense of shame, by fear and by personal interest; he may coerce by the combination of public sentiment; he may drive by physical force, and he does not outstep the boundaries of his sphere. But all the power, and all the conquests that are lawful to woman, are those only which appeal to the kindly, generous, peaceful and benevolent principles.

Woman is to win everything by peace and love; by making herself so much respected, esteemed and loved, that to yield to her opinions and to gratify her wishes, will be the free-will offering of the heart. But this is to be all accomplished in the domestic and social circle. There let every woman become so cultivated and refined in intellect, that her taste and judgment will be respected; so benevolent in feeling and action, that her motives will be reverenced;—so unassuming and unambitious, that collision and competition will be banished;—so "gentle and easy to be entreated," as that every heart will repose in her presence; then, the fathers, the husbands, and the sons, will find an influence thrown around them, to which they will yield not only willingly but proudly. A man is never ashamed to own such influences, but feels dignified and ennobled in acknowledging them. But the moment woman begins to feel the promptings of ambition, or the thirst for power, her ægis of defence is gone. All the sacred protection of religion, all the generous promptings of chivalry, all the poetry of romantic gallantry, depend upon woman's retaining her place as dependent and defenceless, and making no claims, and maintaining no right but what are the gifts of honour, rectitude and love....

It is allowed by all reflecting minds, that the safety and happiness of this nation depends upon having the children educated, and not only intellectually, but morally and religiously. There are now nearly two millions of children and adults in this country who cannot read, and who have no schools of any kind. To give only a small supply of teachers to these

SOURCE: Catharine Beecher on Women's Proper Place (1837). From AN ESSAY ON SLAVERY AND ABOLITIONISM, WITH REFERENCES TO THE DUTY OF AMERICAN FEMALES by Catharine Beecher. (Philadelphia: Henry Perkins, 1837), pp. 100–102, 105–106, 107–108.

destitute children, who are generally where the population is sparse, will demand *thirty thousand teachers;* and *six thousand* more will be needed every year, barely to meet the increase of juvenile population. But if we allow that we need not reach this point, in order to save ourselves from that destruction which awaits a people, when governed by an ignorant and unprincipled democracy; if we can weather the storms of democratic liberty with only one-third of our ignorant children properly educated, still we need *ten thousand* teachers at this moment, and an addition of *two thousand every year.* Where is this army of teachers to be found? ... Men will be educators in the college, in the high school, in some of the most honourable and lucrative common schools, but the *children,* the *little children* of this nation must, to a wide extent, be taught by females, or remain untaught. The drudgery of education, as it is now too generally regarded, in this country, will be given to the female hand. And as the value of education rises in the public mind, and the importance of a teacher's office is more highly estimated, women will more and more be furnished with those intellectual advantages which they need to fit them for such duties.

The result will be, that America will be distinguished above all other nations, for well-educated females, and for the influence they will exert on the general interests of society. But if females, as they approach the other sex, in intellectual elevation, begin to claim, or to exercise in any manner, the peculiar prerogatives of that sex, education will prove a doubtful and dangerous blessing. But this will never be the result. For the more intelligent a woman becomes, the more she can appreciate the wisdom of that ordinance that appointed her subordinate station, and the more her taste will conform to the graceful and dignified retirement and submission it involves.

Source 3:   Catharine Beecher, *A Treatise on Domestic Economy* (1841)

Catharine Beecher's most famous book, A Treatise on Domestic Economy, *became the standard text for teaching the domestic arts. In these excerpts, Beecher argues for the study of domestic economy as an essential part of the curriculum for women. What reasons does she offer for its study? Which points expressed here would Elizabeth Cady have agreed and disagreed with?*

The success of democratic institutions, as is conceded by all, depends upon the intellectual and moral character of the mass of the people. If they are intelligent and virtuous, democracy is a blessing; but if they are ignorant and wicked, it is only a curse, and as much more dreadful than any other form of civil government, as a thousand tyrants are more to be dreaded than one. It is equally conceded, that the formation of the moral and intellectual character of the young is committed mainly to the female hand. The mother writes the character of the future man; the sister bends the fibres that hereafter are the forest tree; the wife sways the heart, whose energies may turn for good or for evil the destinies of a nation. Let the women of a country be made virtuous and intelligent, and the men will certainly be the same. The proper education of a man decides the welfare of an individual; but educate a woman, and the interests of a whole family are secured....

Another reason for introducing [the study of Domestic Economy], as a distinct branch of school education, is, that, as a general fact, young ladies *will not* be taught these

SOURCE: Catharine Beecher, A TREATISE ON DOMESTIC ECONOMY (Philadelphia: Henry Perkins, 1837), pp. 100–102, 105–106, 107–108.

things in any other way. In reply to the thousand-time-repeated remark, that girls must be taught their domestic duties by their mothers, at home, it may be inquired, in the first place, What proportion of mothers are qualified to teach a *proper* and *complete* system of Domestic Economy? When this is answered, it may be asked, What proportion of those who are qualified, have that sense of the importance of such instructions, and that energy and perseverance which would enable them actually to teach their daughters, in all the branches of Domestic Economy presented in this work?

When this is answered, it may be asked, How many mothers *actually do* give their daughters instruction in the various branches of Domestic Economy? Is it not the case, that, owing to ill health, deficiency of domestics, and multiplied cares and perplexities, a large portion of the most intelligent mothers, and those, too, who most realize the importance of this instruction, actually cannot find the time, and have not the energy, necessary to properly perform the duty? They are taxed to the full amount of both their mental and physical energies, and cannot attempt anything more. Almost every woman knows, that it is easier to do the work, herself, than it is to teach an awkward and careless novice; and the great majority of women, in this Country, are obliged to do almost everything in the shortest and easiest way. This is one reason why the daughters of very energetic and accomplished housekeepers often are the most deficient in these respects; while the daughters of ignorant or inefficient mothers, driven to the exercise of their own energies, often become the most systematic and expert.

It may be objected, that such things cannot be taught by books. This position may fairly be questioned. Do not young ladies learn, from books, how to make hydrogen and oxygen? Do they not have pictures of furnaces, alembics, and the various utensils employed in *cooking* the chemical agents? Do they not study the various processes of mechanics, and learn to understand and to do many as difficult operations as any that belong to housekeeping? All these things are studied, explained, and recited in classes, when everyone knows that little practical use can ever be made of this knowledge. Why, then, should not that science and art, which a woman is to practise during her whole life, be studied and recited? ...

Another reason, for introducing such a branch of study into female schools, is, the influence it would exert, in leading young ladies more correctly to estimate the importance and dignity of domestic knowledge. It is now often the case, that young ladies rather pride themselves on their ignorance of such subjects; and seem to imagine that it is vulgar and ungenteel to know how to work. This is one of the relics of an aristocratic state of society, which is fast passing away. Here the tendency of everything is to the equalisation of labor, so that all classes are feeling, more and more, that indolence is disreputable.

Source 4:   *Elizabeth Cady Stanton Addresses the Seneca Falls Convention* (1848)

When Elizabeth Cady Stanton rose at the Seneca Falls Convention to deliver her first public address, it was to defend the call for woman's rights. How does she justify the demand for the vote? What points in this address do you think Catharine Beecher would have agreed and disagreed with?

SOURCE: "Elizabeth Cady Stanton Addresses the Seneca Falls Convention" (1848). Originally from ADDRESS DELIVERED AT SENECA FALLS AND ROCHESTER, NEW YORK (New York: Robert J. Johnson Printers, 1870).

Among the many important questions which have been brought before the public, there is none that more vitally affects the whole human family than that which is technically called Woman's Rights. Every allusion to the degraded and inferior position occupied by women all over the world has been met by scorn and abuse. From the man of highest mental cultivation to the most degraded wretch who staggers in the streets do we meet ridicule, and coarse jests, freely bestowed upon those who dare assert that woman stands by the side of man, his equal, placed here by her God, to enjoy with him the beautiful earth, which is her home as it is his, having the same sense of right and wrong, and looking to the same Being for guidance and support. So long has man exercised tyranny over her, injurious to himself and benumbing to her faculties, that few can nerve themselves to meet the storm; and so long has the chain been about her that she knows not there is a remedy....

We have met here to-day to discuss our rights and wrongs, civil and political, and not, as some have supposed, to go into the detail of social life alone. We do not propose to petition the legislature to make our husbands just, generous and courteous, to seat every man at the head of a cradle, and to clothe every woman in male attire. None of these points, however important they may be considered by leading men, will be touched in this Convention....

We are assembled to protest against a form of government, existing without the consent of the governed—to declare our right to be free as man is free, to be represented in the government which we are taxed to support, to have such disgraceful laws as give man the power to chastise and imprison his wife, to take the wages which she earns, the property which she inherits, and, in case of separation, the children of her love; laws which make her the mere dependent on his bounty. It is to protest against such unjust laws as these that we are assembled today, and to have them, if possible, forever erased from our statute-books, deeming them a shame and a disgrace to a Christian republic in the nineteenth century....

And, strange as it may seem to many, we now demand our right to vote according to the declaration of the government under which we live.... We have no objection to discuss the question of equality, for we feel that the weight of argument lies wholly with us, but we wish the question of equality kept distinct from the question of rights, for the proof of the one does not determine the truth of the other. All white men in this country have the same rights, however they may differ in mind, body or estate. The right is ours. The question now is, how shall we get possession of what rightfully belongs to us. We should not feel so sorely grieved if no man who had not attained the full stature of a Webster, Clay, Van Buren, or Gerrit Smith could claim the right of the elective franchise. But to have drunkards, idiots, horse-racing, rumselling rowdies, ignorant foreigners, and silly boys full recognized, while we ourselves are thrust out from all the rights that belong to citizens, it is too grossly insulting to the dignity of woman to be longer quietly submitted to. The right is ours. Have it we must. Use it we will. The pens, the tongues, the fortunes, the indomitable wills of many women are already pledged to secure this right. The great truth, that no just government can be formed without the consent of the governed, we shall echo and reecho in the ears of the unjust judge, until by continual coming we shall weary him....

But what would woman gain by voting? Men must know the advantages of voting, for they all seem very tenacious about the right. Think you, if woman had a vote in this government, that all those laws affecting her interests would so entirely violate every principle of right and justice? Had woman a vote to give, might not the office-holders and seekers propose some change in her condition? Might not Woman's Rights become as great a question as free soil?

"But you are already represented by your fathers, husbands, brothers and sons?" Let your statute books answer the question. We have had enough of such representation. In nothing is woman's true happiness consulted. Men like to call her an angel—to feed her on what they think sweet food—nourishing her vanity; to make her believe that her organization is so much finer than theirs, that she is not fitted to struggle with the tempests of public life, but needs their care and protection!! Care and protection—such as the wolf gives the lamb—such as the eagle the hare he carries to his eyrie!! Most cunningly he entraps her, and then takes from her all those rights which are dearer to him than life itself—rights which have been baptized in blood.

Source 5: *Elizabeth Cady Stanton Answers the Critics of Woman's Rights* (1848)

In the months following the Seneca Falls Convention, the meeting and its demands came under sharp attack, especially in newspapers. In her own newspaper article, Cady Stanton responded to this criticism. How does she answer the critics of woman's rights? How does she attack the idea of separate gender spheres?

There is no danger of this question dying for want of notice. Every paper you take up has something to say about it, and just in proportion to the refinement and intelligence of the editor, has this movement been favorably noticed. But one might suppose from the articles that you find in some papers, that there were editors so ignorant as to believe that the chief object of these recent Conventions was to seat every lord at the head of a cradle, and to clothe every woman in her lord's attire. Now, neither of these points, however important they be considered by humble minds, were touched upon in the Conventions.... For those who do not yet understand the real objects of our recent Conventions at Rochester and Seneca Falls, I would state that we did not meet to discuss fashions, customs, or dress, the rights or duties of man, nor the propriety of the sexes changing positions, but simply our own inalienable rights, our duties, our true sphere. If God has assigned a sphere to man and one to woman, we claim the right to judge ourselves of His design in reference to *us*, and we accord to man the same privilege. We think a man has quite enough in this life to find out his own individual calling, without being taxed to decide where every woman belongs; and the fact that so many men fail in the business they undertake, calls loudly for their concentrating more thought on their own faculties, capabilities, and sphere of action. We have all seen a man making a jackass of himself in the pulpit, at the bar, or in our legislative halls.... Now, is it to be wondered at that woman has some doubts about the present position assigned her being the true one, when her every-day experience shows her that man makes such fatal mistakes in regard to himself?

There is no such thing as a sphere for a sex. Every man has a different sphere, and one in which he may shine, and it is the same with every woman; and the same woman may have a different sphere at different times. The distinguished Angelina Grimké was acknowledged by all the anti-slavery host to be in her sphere, when, years ago, she went through the length and breadth of New England, telling the people of her personal

Source: "Elizabeth Cady Stanton Answers the Critics of Woman's Rights" (1848). Elizabeth Cady Stanton, Susan B. Anthony, Matilda Joslyn Gage, eds., HISTORY OF WOMAN SUFFRAGE (Rochester, N.Y.: Charles Mann, 1889), I, p. 806.

experience of the horrors and abominations of the slave system, and by her eloquence and power as a public speaker, producing an effect unsurpassed by any of the highly gifted men of her day. Who dares to say that in thus using her splendid talents in speaking for the dumb, pleading the cause of the poor friendless slave, that she was out of her sphere? Angelina Grimké is now a wife and the mother of several children. We hear of her no more in public. Her sphere and her duties have changed. She deems it her first and her most sacred duty to devote all her time and talents to her household and to the education of her children. We do not say that she is not *now* in her sphere. The highly gifted Quakeress, Lucretia Mott, married early in life, and brought up a large family of children. All who have seen her at home agree that she was a pattern as a wife, mother, and housekeeper. No one ever fulfilled all the duties of that sphere more perfectly than did she. Her children are now settled in their own homes. Her husband and herself, having a comfortable fortune, pass much of their time in going about and doing good. Lucretia Mott has now no domestic cares. She has a talent for public speaking; her mind is of a high order; her moral perceptions remarkably clear; her religious fervor deep and intense; and who shall tell us that this divinely inspired woman is out of her sphere in her public endeavors to rouse this wicked nation to a sense of its awful guilt, to its great sins of war, slavery, injustice to woman and the laboring poor. As many inquiries are made about Lucretia Mott's husband, allow me, through your columns, to say to those who think he must be a *nonentity* because his wife is so distinguished, that James Mott is head and shoulders above the greater part of *his sex,* intellectually, morally, and physically. As a man of business, his talents are of the highest order.

QUESTIONS TO CONSIDER

1. How would you compare the ideas of Catharine Beecher and Elizabeth Cady Stanton regarding the proper position of women in American society? What were the most important influences in shaping their ideas?

2. What do the lives and careers of Beecher and Cady Stanton reveal about the limits imposed on women in early nineteenth-century America? Why was Cady Stanton considered so radical? Why was Beecher more successful in getting her ideas accepted? What do you think were the motives of those who upheld the limits placed on women?

3. Some historians have argued that early nineteenth-century reformers were motivated by the desire to impose order on society. Others take the opposite view, suggesting that they were interested in liberating individuals from old institutions, ideas, and practices. What do the ideas of Beecher and Cady Stanton reveal about these interpretations?

4. What points and issues do Beecher and Cady Stanton raise that might be relevant to the position of women in American society in the early twenty-first century? Cite examples and explain their relevance.

FOR FURTHER READING

Nancy Cott, *The Bonds of Womanhood: "Women's Sphere" in New England, 1780–1835* (New Haven, CT: Yale University Press, 1977), studies the emergence of domesticity and separate spheres for men and women in the early American republic.

Lori Ginzberg, *Women and the Work of Benevolence: Morality, Politics, and Class in the Nineteenth Century United States* (New Haven, CT: Yale University Press, 1991), explores the social divisions among women involved in various reform movements.

Elizabeth Griffith, *In Her Own Right: The Life of Elizabeth Cady Stanton* (New York: Oxford University Press, 1984), offers a thorough, balanced account of Cady Stanton's life and work.

Sylvia Hoffert, *When Hens Crow: The Women's Rights Movement in Antebellum America* (Bloomington: Indiana University Press, 1995), offers an overview of the early struggle for women's rights.

Nancy Isenberg, *Sex and Citizenship in Antebellum America* (Chapel Hill: University of North Carolina Press, 1998), focuses on various forms of female political activity in the early nineteenth century.

Kathryn Kish Sklar, *Catharine Beecher: A Study in American Domesticity* (New Haven: Yale University Press, 1973), remains a useful introduction to Beecher's life and ideas.

11

Manifest Destiny and Conquest: Thomas Larkin and Juan Bautista Alvarado

It was a fine September evening in 1842 when Thomas Larkin stepped onto his veranda and watched the excited men rush in and out of his neighbor's house. The unusual activity across the street, Larkin knew, could affect him dramatically. Earlier that day, two American warships had sailed into Monterey Bay, and Larkin had escorted a landing party to see Juan Bautista Alvarado, the governor of Mexican California. As an American, Larkin thought it unwise to enter the governor's residence with the military visitors. So he had walked back to his own house, where he kept a close eye on the comings and goings. He was desperate to know what was happening, though. As Monterey's leading merchant, Larkin was well aware of the growing American interest in California. He had heard the periodic talk of war between the United States and Mexico ever since Texas had won its independence from Mexico in 1836. In recent weeks, rumors had been rampant: British and French fleets had left South American ports for unknown destinations; Mexico and the United States were at war; Mexico was prepared to sell California to settle a debt with Britain. Such rumors had sent Commodore Thomas Jones racing to California. Now two of his ships were anchored in Monterey Bay, and one of his officers was inside the governor's house.

Finally, Larkin's curiosity got the best of him, and he walked across the dusty street to Alvarado's door. The governor greeted Larkin as cordially as ever. Born in Monterey, Juan Alvarado was a true Californio. In fact, his loyalty to California exceeded any feelings he had for Mexico. Far removed from Mexico City, Alvarado and many other Californios believed that they were not treated with the respect they deserved. Following the example of Texas, he had led a revolt against Mexico six years before and declared

Thomas Larkin

Juan Bautista Alvarado

California an independent state. Although Alvarado's independence movement was short-lived, he stayed on as governor and developed a close business and personal relationship with Larkin. Now Larkin listened silently as an American naval officer demanded that Alvarado surrender California. Larkin noticed that Alvarado was agitated as he insisted that he had no authority to do so. His curiosity satisfied, Larkin walked back across the street to go to bed. Before he could retire, though, he was summoned aboard the American flagship. There, as he translated, the governor's representatives negotiated the surrender of California.

A few hours later, Larkin was summoned again—this time to Alvarado's house, where the governor was beside himself. "[N]one the better or clearer for wine or brandy," Larkin reported later, "he fairly raved." Alvarado wanted Larkin to obtain Commodore Jones's permission for the governor and his family to leave Monterey unmolested. The next morning, Larkin again boarded the American warship. No sooner had Jones denied Alvarado's request than American forces landed and occupied the town. They were not there long before the commodore realized that he had blundered. Convinced now that war had not been declared, the commodore promptly signed a new treaty that handed authority back to Alvarado.

The bizarre American takeover of California in September 1842, Larkin later said, "appeared at the time a dream." Yet it was Alvarado's worst nightmare. To him, it only confirmed the Americans' desire for his beloved California. In the end, Alvarado knew that Yankee greed was a far bigger threat to California than the disdain and neglect of Mexican authorities.

"VIVA LA LIBERTAD!"

The Spaniards had been settled in Alta California* for forty years when Juan Bautista Alvarado was born in Monterey in 1809. California was then a remote province of New Spain, home to no more than fifteen hundred people of Spanish descent and perhaps two hundred thousand Indians. As elsewhere in the New World, priests and soldiers had spearheaded the Spanish occupation of California. Concerned about English and Russian encroachment on the Pacific coast, Spanish authorities sent Franciscan* friar Junípero Serra and military leader Gaspar de Portolá on a colonizing expedition from Mexico in 1769. The next summer, Serra and Portolá established a mission and presidio (fort) on the broad Monterey Bay, pushing the Spanish frontier four hundred miles to the north. Monterey was quickly designated the capital of Alta California, a vast area eventually dotted with a handful of presidios, pueblos (towns), and ranchos (ranches). Serra found Monterey's climate and magnificent surroundings to his liking and soon made it the headquarters for Spanish California's most powerful institution—the missions that would soon stretch from San Diego to San Francisco Bay. As Serra wrote to a friend after moving his Monterey mission five miles over the hills to Carmel, "I shall be content to live and die in this spot."

A half century later, Juan Alvarado was also drawn to Monterey's extraordinary natural features. Even as a boy, he loved to walk into the pine-covered hills overlooking the cluster of adobe dwellings that housed three hundred or so Montereños. On these walks, he was often joined by Pablo Vicente Solá, the last Spanish governor of California. Solá, a wealthy aristocrat, took an interest in the boy's education and often loaned him books. Even though Alvarado's father was only a sergeant in the army, his mother was a member of the powerful Vallejo family, and this was a society in which status was based on ancestry, not achievement. Thus, along with his uncle Mariano Vallejo and his cousin José Castro, Alvarado attended a special school that Solá established.

Although Franciscan friars and royal officials still reigned supreme in California, new ideas such as republicanism—the right of the people to rule themselves through their own representatives—had begun to penetrate the region. In fact, one year after Alvarado's birth, Mexico had rebelled against Spanish colonial rule. Eleven years later, in 1821, Mexico won its independence. As a boy, Alvarado witnessed the meeting of California's first provincial assembly. His own boyhood hero was the father of the new American republic, George Washington. With Vallejo and Castro, he formed a secret group to study "radical" political ideas. Later, when Vallejo obtained several banned books from a passing ship, a priest demanded that the trio turn them over. When they refused, they were unofficially excommunicated from the church.

The youthful Alvarado may have harbored some dangerous ideas, but as an educated Montereño, he had opportunities unavailable to other Californios. He mixed freely with foreigners and learned some English. He also worked for an American named Nathan Spear, a Yankee merchant who had set up shop in Monterey in the early 1820s. Spear was one of a growing number of New England traders who moved to California, and Alvarado listened eagerly as the American shared his knowledge. Doors opened for Alvarado in the government as well. At eighteen, he was named secretary of the

---

Alta California: Upper California, a province whose southern boundary was located near San Diego. It was settled about seventy-five years after Baja (Lower) California.
Franciscan: A member of the Catholic religious order founded by St. Francis of Assisi in the thirteenth century.

territorial legislature, where he served for six years, keeping a record of the proceedings and debates. Later, he was territorial treasurer, inspector at the customhouse, and a representative in the legislature. Finally, in 1836, he was named president of the legislature.

By then, Alvarado had had ample opportunity to see firsthand California's political instability. Occasionally, Mexico would send governors to the remote province, but most ruled for only a few years, and some for only a few weeks. Often they were victims of Californios' resentment of Mexico City's interference. In 1836 alone, California had six governors. Two of them were supporters of the new centralist constitution of Mexico, which replaced the old federalist constitution in 1836. Most Californios knew little about Mexican politics and cared less, but they understood that centralism meant less autonomy for them.

Many Californios' resentment of outside political interference reflected their ambivalence toward Mexico itself. They had enough contact with foreigners to know about the country's backwardness. In addition, the authorities' periodic attempts to colonize California with *cholos* (scoundrels) from Mexican jails outraged Californians and made them even more determined to preserve their own identity. As a result, they no longer called themselves Españoles or Mexicanos, but Californios. Emboldened by the expulsion of two recent governors, many Californios believed that the time had come for them to choose their own governor.

Thus when Nicolás Gutiérrez was appointed governor in 1836 (for the second time in six months), Californios reacted with force. Their leader was the twenty-seven-year-old Alvarado, who had gained a following as an articulate opponent of centralization. Educated, magnetic, and well connected, he was a natural choice. With José Castro, Alvarado assembled a force of about a hundred men. He also sought the aid of a rough Tennessee trapper named Isaac Graham, who opposed Mexican rule in California and controlled a motley "army" of about fifty *cholos*, Indians, and American backwoodsmen. Apparently, Alvarado told Graham that he sought independence from Mexico and once it was won he would help repeal the law preventing foreigners from owning land. In truth, however, Alvarado and his supporters sought recognition of California as a state *within* Mexico. In any case, the rebels had little trouble deposing Gutiérrez. Marching on Monterey, they seized the presidio and fired one cannonball, which smashed into the roof of the governor's residence. Covered with dust and broken tiles, the terrified Gutiérrez stumbled out and surrendered immediately. "Everybody shouts *vivas,* for California is free," Alvarado wrote to Mariano Vallejo after the coup. Meanwhile, the territorial legislature named Alvarado governor and proclaimed California a "free and sovereign State" until the old federalist constitution was restored. Amid cries of *"Viva la Libertad!* (Long live Liberty!), Californios had halfheartedly declared their independence from Mexico.

Alvarado moved quickly to consolidate his political control. First he confronted the growing rivalry between northern and southern Californios. The southerners were angry that the capital was in Monterey rather than Los Angeles and suspicious that the northerners had relied on Yankees for assistance in overthrowing Gutiérrez. In 1838, determined to govern all of California, Alvarado marched toward Los Angeles with an army of about a hundred men and defeated a force of hostile southerners. When he received word that Mexico City had named him governor, he quickly swore allegiance to Mexico, and California resumed its territorial status. About the same time, he decided that it would be politically expedient to marry. Already the father of three children by mistresses in Monterey and Los Angeles, Alvarado married Martina Castro, whose prominent family traced its roots in California to 1776. He also gave generous grants of mission lands to his friends. Under Mexican law, the missions were to be secularized and their lands distributed to the Indians. In reality, however, few Indians received any land, and those who did quickly lost it. Alvarado also gave a large land grant on the Sacramento River to the Swiss immigrant John Sutter.* Although Alvarado claimed that he had not enriched himself, others were suspicious of his motives. As one California newspaper said in 1848, "The whole period of Alvarado administration was a perpetual struggle to maintain himself in office."

Generous land grants might have won the support of Californios, but they did little to counter the threat posed by the four hundred or so Americans who now lived in California. Like previous governors, Alvarado granted land to Yankees who became naturalized citizens. Many recent newcomers, however, were different from the New England merchants who had arrived earlier by sea. Rough frontiersmen, they had worked their way overland, following in the footsteps of the trapper Jedediah Smith, who had traveled to California in 1826. More numerous every year, these "gringos" demonstrated no intention of becoming Mexican citizens. Like Isaac Graham, who wore buckskin and swilled brandy, they also showed little respect for authority and even less for Governor Alvarado. By 1840, Alvarado was fed up with these unruly foreigners.

"WE MUST HAVE IT, OTHERS MUST NOT"

Long after California fell to the invading Americans, Juan Alvarado concluded that they came from a nation whose "creed" was "time is money." Even his friend Thomas Larkin, who adopted California as his home, gave him no reason to think otherwise. Born in 1802 in Charlestown, Massachusetts, Larkin demonstrated an early interest in money. As a young man, he confessed that he would "stoop to any means & measures to gain it," a predilection he apparently gained from his stepfather. Larkin's father had died when Thomas was six; then his mother married an acquisitive banker named Amariah Childs. A clue to Childs's, and perhaps Larkin's, character is a letter Larkin received from a cousin years later. Childs, it read, "has no charity for those who owe him … & is as eager for money as he ever was." Larkin soon demonstrated a similar passion.

While still a teen, Larkin moved to Boston to take up book publishing. Quickly learning that printing books was "poor business" and selling them not much better, he decided to sail off with a friend in 1821 to seek his fortune. They chose Wilmington, North Carolina, as their destination. There Larkin found a job as a clerk and soon opened a small store. Three years later, he moved to Duplin County, North Carolina, where he opened another store and was appointed postmaster and magistrate. "If I attend to all," he observed, "I shall hardly ever be idle." By 1830, Larkin had achieved some success. In addition to his store, he owned a small plantation and six slaves. Yet the young New Englander was not satisfied in his new home. Southerners, he believed, were "a miserable, dis[si]pated lot." Nor was he content with his modest wealth. "Why … was I not born with a fortune[?]" he lamented. To gain one, he sold his store and invested in a sawmill, only to lose all his money. Larkin was shattered, saying, "My first prospects are blasted.… All I have accumulated has gone to the winds."

Frustrated in business, he had better luck with women. "[I] hear I am a Ladies man," he boasted about the same time. "[A] Lady told me … I could get any one." Yet if

---

John Sutter: The discovery of gold on his land in 1848 would spark the California gold rush.

Larkin found romantic dalliances amusing, he also realized they were no substitute for money. "All love and no capital will never do for me," he said. A decade after arriving in the South, he wanted to return to Massachusetts and marry a rich cousin. When she expressed no interest, Larkin sought a post office appointment in Washington through another cousin. When that failed to materialize, he turned to his third and least desirable alternative. He would join a half brother, John Cooper, who lived in far-off Mexican California. A sea captain and trader, Cooper had settled in Monterey eight years earlier and now needed a clerk. Larkin knew little about California except that, as he confessed to Cooper, moving there would require him to "forget my Mother tongue" and live among "a people that I always d[e]spised and detested." Yet he also knew that Cooper had settled down, converted to Catholicism, and, like many early Yankee traders in California, married a local woman. But he had not married just anyone. His wife was the daughter of the wealthy Vallejo family. Larkin's imagination caught fire. If he went to Monterey, he observed, he would marry a local woman, provided she had "loot enough for me."

In September 1831, the twenty-nine-year-old Larkin sailed out of Boston on the *Newcastle* bound for Oahu and Monterey. Also on board was a young woman from Ipswich, Massachusetts. Rachel Hobson Holmes had married a sea captain only a short time before he left for Monterey. She sailed now to join him, but when the *Newcastle* arrived in Monterey the following April, Holmes discovered that her husband had just departed on a voyage to South America. By then, whatever relationship had developed between Holmes and Larkin on the long voyage from Massachusetts had been consummated. Several months later, she departed for Santa Barbara, where, in early 1833, she gave birth to a baby girl. After Holmes learned of her husband's death at sea, Larkin found himself under growing pressure to marry her. If he did, his dream of coming into wealth by taking the hand of a California woman would be shattered. Six months after the birth of their daughter, he relented, only to watch their baby die one month later.

Land and cattle would not be Larkin's through marriage, but Captain Holmes's estate of at least three thousand dollars was. It proved to be the stake on which Larkin would build his fortune. After a stint as Cooper's clerk, Larkin began trading for himself. His timing could not have been better. In the mid-1830s, the missions' vast lands and cattle herds were undergoing secularization. California's wealth was slipping from the hands of padres into those of rancheros. These men proved more adept than the mission fathers at producing cowhides, and they were far more anxious to secure the manufactured goods that Yankee traders supplied. By the late 1830s, California was experiencing an economic boom, as a growing shoe industry in Massachusetts fueled the demand for hides. Larkin was perfectly positioned to take advantage of the situation. From his store, he sold cloth, clothing, furniture, tools, china, sugar, and other goods brought by the "Boston ships" that regularly called on Monterey. Most of all, he sold liquor, much of which was consumed at a grog shop in his store. He commanded prices at least four times higher than those in Boston, and patrons mostly paid in "California bank notes": hides. Nor was the enterprising Yankee's business confined to his store. He quickly built a flour mill so he could also receive wheat for payment. Soon he added a bakery, and still later, he owned a blacksmith shop and a soap factory.

As his business grew, Larkin sometimes traveled to Mazatlán and Mexico City to purchase goods and regularly sold lumber and other items as far away as Los Angeles and Honolulu. He also became a frontier financier and by 1844 frequently served as a banker to the often cash-strapped California government. He even had a cousin in Boston begin to invest his surplus capital in stocks. The acquisitive Larkin watched his net worth soar from $2,650 in 1835 to more than $66,600 a decade later. It was never enough, though, for the man described by one contemporary as "active, nervous, quick moving, [and] busy." Larkin confessed, "As I am not up high enough, I keep moving, trying to get up."

There was more to Larkin's success than Yankee industry and a favorable location, however. As many business associates discovered, he could also drive a hard bargain. "[Y]ou have decidedly the most convenient memory for your own interest I have heard for some time," one associate told him. Another was blunter, declaring that Larkin was "an infernal ass." Above all, Larkin thrived because he could adapt to Californio culture. Unlike his half brother and many other Yankee immigrants, Larkin did not marry a local woman or convert to Catholicism. Nor did he secure a land grant by becoming a Mexican citizen. Yet he also did not exhibit the deep prejudice that many of his countrymen brought to California. **[See Source 1.]** Despite his earlier expression of disdain for Mexicans, he later explained to his wife that he did not "look on [them] so ill as many foreigners do." Profiting handsomely in Monterey, in part from his association with Governor Alvarado and other officials, Larkin developed a tolerance born of necessity. "I am remarkably well situated with this Government and its people," he explained to a friend in 1842. "I never speak against their laws, modes or religion."

Larkin's ability to adjust to life in Mexican California was reflected in the home he built in Monterey. The Larkins would eventually have five surviving children and a number of Indian servants. To accommodate the growing family and business, Thomas and Rachel wanted to build a traditional New England Colonial house. The local building material, a mixture of straw and clay known as adobe, was unlikely to produce the desired effect. So Larkin improvised. On top of the adobe walls, he placed an American-style roof, which sloped in four directions rather than just two. Then he extended the roof with four-foot eaves to protect the adobe blocks from the winter rains. He added a veranda on two sides, then whitewashed the walls to give it the look of a traditional New England residence. Soon Juan Alvarado and other prominent Californios were building their houses in this so-called Monterey style. Melding New England and Hispanic architectural elements, Larkin's house symbolized the meeting of two distinct cultures on the California coast and was, appropriately, the scene of lavish entertainment of Californios and foreigners alike. It was "continually frequented by the most respectable citizens," observed Juan Alvarado, who was a frequent recipient of Larkin's hospitality and alcohol.

Larkin built with adobe and entertained as extravagantly as any California don. With little use for the likes of Isaac Graham and his companions, he even declared that he "wanted no more foreigners to come into the country." Yet he was still a Yankee. As time went on, he grumbled more about California's weak and unstable government than about the Tennessee trapper and his ilk. Americans and their property had to be protected, and he had little faith in the ability of the local authorities to do that. His confidence was further weakened when Alvarado's successor, Manuel Micheltorena, arrived from Mexico in 1842 with an army of three hundred *cholos*. When Alvarado and his old schoolmate José Castro led angry Californios in a revolt that overthrew Micheltorena, Larkin became even more critical of Mexico's administration of the province. Larkin had loaned Micheltorena a large sum of money. Now he was anxious to see California secured for the United States.

Larkin's hopes were shared by many other Americans by the 1840s. Since the 1830s, land fever had driven thousands of Americans into Texas and Oregon. By the early 1840s, westward migration stoked a raging desire for national expansion. Many Americans believed that extending the nation to the Pacific Ocean represented nothing less than the fulfillment of its God-given destiny. The assumption that Americans had a divine duty to spread across the continent was neatly encapsulated in the term *manifest destiny,* coined by an eastern newspaperman in the 1840s. By then, of course, manifest destiny was already an old idea. It extended back to the seventeenth-century Puritans, who believed that God had set aside land for them to build their holy commonwealth. Now, however, it was reinforced by eighteenth-century assumptions about the superiority of republican political institutions and by virulent nineteenth-century racism. It also supported far more sweeping conclusions regarding the amount of land set aside for Americans' exclusive use. A boiling stew of political and racial assumptions, ethnocentrism, and land hunger, manifest destiny provided Americans with a powerful justification for getting the Indians, British, or Mexicans out of their way. As they looked longingly toward the Pacific, many Americans would apply it with equal force to the Californios. As one commentator wrote, the Spanish-speaking natives of California were "unfit to control the destinies of that beautiful country."

In the mid-1840s, expansion had become a burning political issue. In 1844, the expansionist-minded Democrat James K. Polk was elected president on a platform calling for America to take the Oregon Territory*and a now-independent Texas. By that time, Larkin had been hard at work for years trying to fulfill manifest destiny in California. Already in 1840, he had headed a group in Monterey to lobby the United States to establish a consulate there. Three years later, he was appointed the first American consul to Mexican California. In his new post, Larkin took up his pen to inform American newspaper readers of the wonders of California. "Solomon in all his glory," he declared in the *New York Herald* in 1845, "was not more happy than a Californian." Alerting his eastern readers about British and French designs on the province, he left them a clear conclusion. "We must have it," he warned, "others must not." At the same time, he sent the American government a stream of reports on California's political and economic conditions that were also intended to stimulate interest in the Mexican province. **[See Source 2.]**

By 1845, Larkin's detailed reports from Monterey had caught the eye of President Polk, who also cast a covetous eye toward California. The new president quickly appointed Larkin a "Confidential Agent." He was instructed to gather intelligence, warn Californians of the danger of foreign intervention, and "arouse in their bosoms that love of liberty and independence so natural to the American Continent." Larkin's appointment letter arrived in Monterey in April 1846, carried by a marine officer posing as an associate of William Appleton & Company.* Not just a businessman but now a secret agent of America's destiny, Larkin received the letter with "unfeigned satisfaction." He quickly wrote back that Californios would be receptive to an American takeover. He told the American vice consul in San Francisco, "The pear is near ripe for falling."

If the attitudes of Larkin's old friend Alvarado were any indication, though, no fruit was going to fall without some shaking. Like many other Californios, Alvarado was tired of American meddling in the province and ready to take up arms to defend it. When John C. Frémont* entered California with a force of sixty men and a howitzer early in 1846, Alvarado was forced to do just that. Frémont's men were allegedly on a mapping

---

Oregon Territory: The area stretching from California to the Yukon, Oregon had been jointly occupied by Britain and the United States since 1818.

William Appleton & Company: One of four Boston firms that dominated the California cowhide trade before it collapsed in the late 1840s. It was owned by Nathan Appleton's cousin. (See Chapter 8.)

John C. Frémont: A soldier and explorer who traveled through the West and later turned to politics, running as the Republican Party's first presidential candidate in 1856.

expedition. When they began to build a fort northeast of Monterey, however, José Castro and Alvarado met them with an army of two hundred men. Although Frémont was forced to retreat to Oregon, he returned to northern California that summer. There he abetted an armed uprising of disgruntled Yankee settlers in Sonoma who hoisted the Bear Flag and proclaimed California an independent republic. By then, Alvarado was livid about the Yankees' obvious designs on California. "I think I shall be down in my grave without forgiving them for the insults which they gave to the flag and authorities of my country," he declared.

Before Alvarado could even attempt to crush this Bear Flag Revolt, he learned that the United States and Mexico were at war. In May 1846, the Polk administration provoked a border dispute between the two countries over Texas, which had been annexed by the United States the previous year. Two months after the war began, Commodore John Sloat sailed into Monterey Bay and demanded that Mexican authorities turn over the province. The next day, Larkin sent Sloat's request for a meeting "for accomplishing the tranquility of the Country" to José Castro. At the same time, Larkin sent a letter to Alvarado expressing his hope for a peaceful American annexation of California. Such a move, he assured Alvarado, was in the Californios' best interests. Larkin's old friend did not see it that way. He replied by asking Larkin to consider what he would do in Alvarado's place "in circumstances like the present."

"HALCYON DAYS THEY WERE"

During the brief skirmishes between American and Mexican forces in California, Larkin and Alvarado were both captured by the enemy. Retreating from the Monterey Bay area in the face of an overwhelming American force, Castro and Alvarado's army was pursued southward to Los Angeles, where it eventually dissolved. Fleeing back toward Monterey, Alvarado and a small contingent were captured by Frémont. Freed later with a pledge that he would cease resistance, Alvarado returned to Monterey, where he was greeted by a party hosted by Commodore Sloat's replacement, Commodore Robert Stockton. "[T]he Americans tried in this way to show me that they were not indifferent to my welfare," Alvarado concluded. Meanwhile, Larkin, traveling to San Francisco shortly after the war started, had been captured by Californios conducting guerrilla raids against Americans. Transported to Los Angeles, he was not released until early 1847, when American forces arrived in the area. As he was let go, one of his captors told him that he had been held because he was "the most active of enemies against Mexico."

By the time Larkin was set free, the American conquest of California was virtually complete. "I shall require days to be myself again," Larkin wrote the U.S. secretary of state shortly after his release. His belief that business would "increase astonishingly" after the American takeover no doubt sped his recovery. Already he had sold Frémont's force $3,600 in goods and would sell the U.S. Navy even more. Anticipating a rising demand for supplies, he invested all his capital in California-bound goods. Once again, he was perfectly positioned for profit. The discovery of gold in early 1848 sent thousands of fortune seekers streaming into California, providing Larkin with a host of new customers and, just as quickly, phenomenal returns. Convinced that a "Yankefied" California would bring untold economic benefits, Larkin saw a path to even greater wealth in real estate. Soon he began buying and selling lots in San Francisco, where prices rose from $600 to $10,000 or more in two years. "My head swirls with speculation," he declared. Looking farther afield, he purchased farms in Carmel, a huge rancho in Sonoma, and another along the Feather River north of Sacramento. Some properties Larkin bought from fellow Americans. Others, like the large tract near the mouth of the Sacramento River belonging to Mariano Vallejo, he gained due to the uncertainty many Californios now faced in an American California.

Altogether, Larkin and his children owned at one time or another about two hundred fifty thousand acres. He was soon rich enough to return to the East and live in style. In 1849, he put his Monterey home on the market and the next year moved his family to New York City. They were greeted by old California friends who put on a California "Jubilee," the most "elegant, dignified affair that had ever been got up in New York," according to one newspaper. The Larkins lived in New York for only three years. Larkin's homesickness and growing conviction that California held more promise "under go ahead Yankees" drove them back.

Larkin built a mansion in San Francisco, began once again to buy and sell real estate, and became active in California railroad promotion. Even then, his success was not enough. He brooded that he was not really rich and lamented that he was no longer the mover and shaker he had been in the old days in Monterey. He began to miss what had been lost in Yankee California. He bemoaned the influx of Americans even as he grew rich off them. Pining for the old days, he declared to a friend, "Halcyon days they were. *We* shall not enjoy there [*sic*] like again." Larkin lived in California until his death, probably from typhoid fever, in 1858.

As for Larkin's old friend Juan Alvarado, the American conquest proved disastrous. At first the conquerors recognized Alvarado's importance in smoothing the transition to American control, offering to name him interim governor or secretary of state. Although Alvarado declined both posts, the new military government named him to the governor's legislative council along with Larkin and five other prominent Californians. The body never met, however, and it was soon clear that Californios were to have little influence in the new political order. For his part, Alvarado had already grown disillusioned with politics. The only honor he had ever received, he complained, was that his landlord addressed him as "Your Excellency, the Governor" when he came by to collect the rent. Only thirty-seven in 1846, Alvarado had seen his time pass. Paunchy from a fondness for alcohol, he settled down to live the quiet life of a ranchero.

Yet his struggle with the Americans was not over. No sooner had he returned home than Larkin was at his door, demanding that he sell his Mariposa rancho near Yosemite to settle his debts. Alvarado had acquired the huge tract at the end of his administration. Acting as an agent for Frémont, Larkin bought the property for three thousand dollars. After deducting his own commission, he passed the parcel to Frémont, who was delighted to learn a short time later of the discovery of gold there. The loss of the Mariposa rancho was only the beginning of Alvarado's woes. Over the next twenty years, he struggled with American squatters on what remained of his land. The problem arose from the Land Act of 1851, passed by Congress to settle the question of land ownership in California. Claims there frequently went back to Mexican government grants, but under the law, the burden of proving legal title fell to the claimant rather than the squatter. After two decades of legal battles, Alvarado managed to hold on to only a small portion of his land. He spent his last years on the rancho that his wife had inherited. Like Larkin, he also turned nostalgically to the past. His *Historia de California,* published in 1876, six years before his death, revealed Alvarado's ambivalence toward the idea of an American California. **[See Source 3.]**

Alvarado's fate mirrored that of most Californios. In 1848, the Treaty of Guadalupe Hidalgo ended the Mexican War and forced Mexico to cede to the United States land stretching from the Texas border to the Pacific. It also guaranteed that former Mexican citizens now under American rule "shall be maintained and protected in the free enjoy-ment of their liberty and property." That safeguard, however, flew in the face of Amer-icans' land hunger and their assumptions about racial and cultural superiority. Manifest destiny had led the United States to conquer California and seize the northern half of Mexico in the first place. Its fulfillment did not bode well for Californios, who soon be-gan to lose their land, influence, and position. Making matters worse, Anglos made no distinction between Californios of Spanish descent and the Mexicans of mixed Indian and Spanish blood who were targets of frequent violence and widespread discrimination. **[See Source 4.]**

In an effort to separate themselves from the despised Mexicans, Californios began to refer to themselves as "Spanish" and to the period before the conquest as "Spanish California," a term that evoked the romantic image of a lost paradise. In time, this semantic sleight of hand had the desired effect. Even as they continued to despise those of Mexican descent, nostalgic Anglo-Californians eventually embraced the Californios and the myth of Spanish California as a pastoral Eden. David Starr Jordan, president of Stanford University and a champion of Anglo-Saxon supremacy, demonstrated in 1893 how completely the conquerors had adopted this myth by the end of the nineteenth century. Jordan had named several streets on the Stanford campus after prominent Californios, including Juan Alvarado. Speaking about California's Hispanic heritage to a Monterey audience, he ex-plained the allure of those names. "The 'color of romance' ... ," he said, "hangs over ev-erything Spanish."

•PRIMARY SOURCES•

Source 1: Richard Henry Dana Assesses the Californios (1840)

New Englander Richard Henry Dana sailed to California in the 1830s and later wrote about his journey in the classic Two Years Before the Mast, *one of the first books to introduce American readers to California. What does Dana reveal about Yankee prejudices toward Californio society? What do you think Larkin and Alvarado would have said about this account?*

The Californians are an idle, thriftless people, and can make nothing for themselves. The country abounds in grapes, yet they buy bad wine made in Boston and brought round by us, at an immense price, and retail it among themselves at a real (121/2 cents) by the small wineglass. Their hides, too, which they value at two dollars in money, they give for something which costs seventy-five cents in Boston—and buy shoes (as like as not made of their own hides, which have been carried twice round Cape Horn) at three and four dollars, and "chicken-skin" boots at fifteen dollars apiece....

The fondness for dress among the women is excessive and is often the ruin of many of them. A present of a fine mantle, or of a necklace or pair of earrings, gains the favor of the greater part of them. Nothing is more common than to see a woman living in a house of only two rooms, and the ground for a floor, dressed in spangled satin shoes,

SOURCE: "Richard Henry Dana Assesses the Californios" (1840).

silk gown, high comb, and gilt, if not gold, earrings and necklace. If their husbands do not dress them well enough, they will soon receive presents from others. They used to spend whole days on board our vessel examining the fine clothes and ornaments, and frequently made purchases at a rate which would have made a seamstress or waiting maid in Boston open her eyes....

In Monterey there are a number of English and Americans ... who have married Californians, become united to the Catholic Church, and acquired considerable property. Having more industry, frugality, and enterprise than the natives, they soon get nearly all the trade into their hands. They usually keep shops in which they retail the goods purchased in larger quantities from our vessels, and also send a good deal into the interior, taking hides in pay, which they again barter with our vessels. In every town on the coast there are foreigners engaged in this kind of trade, while I recollect but two shops kept by natives....

Monterey is also a great place for cockfighting, gambling of all sorts, fandangos, and every kind of amusement and knavery. Trappers and hunters, who occasionally arrive here from over the Rocky Mountains with their valuable skins and furs, are often entertained with every sort of amusement and dissipation until they have wasted their time and their money, and go back stripped of everything.

Nothing but the character of the people prevents Monterey from becoming a great town. The soil is as rich as man could wish, climate as good as any in the world, water abundant, and situation extremely beautiful.

Source 2: *Thomas Larkin on the Situation in California (1845)*

In this report, which contains numerous spelling errors, Larkin attempts to stimulate interest in California among Americans in the East. What natural features or aspects of life in California does he emphasize? How does he justify an American takeover?

California July 1845

By almost evry newspaper from the united States and many from England we find extracts and surmises respectng the sale of this country. One month England is the purchaser the next month the U. States. In the meantime the prorgress of Califonia is onward, and would still be more so if Mexico would not send eviry few years a band of theivng soldiers and rapacous officers....

There are many owners of large tracts of land in C. who hold them under the idea of the Country chang owners, havng no preset use for thm, as the Indians tame & wildsteal several thousand head of Horses yearly from the Rancho. Most of these horses are stole for food. The Indins cut up the meat in strips and dry it in the sun. While this continue Grazng of Cattle cannot be profitible conducted. There is no expectiation that this Govt. will find a prevntive—nothng but the fear of the Indian for the American Settlers will prevent it. They steal but a few horse from Foreigner as there is to much danger of bng followed. Mexico may fret and treatent as much as she pleases but all her Cal. Gov & Gen. give Cal land to all who apply for thm and from the nature of thigs will

SOURCE: "Thomas Larkin on the Situation in California" (1845).

continue to do so. Foreignrs arring here expect to live & die in the Country, Mexican officers to remain 2 or 3 years & be shipt off by force unless they choose to marry a Native and becone a Californian, Body & Soul. This Ports in C. with the exceptin of Mazalan are the only Mexican Pacific Ports that are flourishng. All othrs are fallig & fallig fast. Here there is much advance in every thng and the Country present each year a bolder front to the world. It must change owners. Its of no use to Mexico. To hir its but a eye sore a shame and bone of Contentin. Here are are many fine Ports, the land produces wheat over 100 fold. Cotten & hemp will grow here and every kind of fruit there is in New Eng—granes in abundance of the furst qualuty. Wine of many kinds are made, yet there is no faciluty of makng. Much of it will pass for Port. The Bays are full of fish, the Woods of game. Bears, and Whales can be seen from one view. The latter are offen in the way of the Boats near the Beach. Finaly there is San Francisco with its rivers. This Bay will hold all the ship in the U. S. The entranc is verry narrow between two mountains easly defended and prehaps the most magnuficnt Harbour in the World and at present of as much use to the civilized world as if it did not exist. Some day or other this will belong to som Naval power. This every Native is prepared for.

Source 3:   *Juan Bautista Alvarado on the Conquest of California* (1876)

Thirty years after the start of the Mexican War, Alvarado offered his justification for many Californios' resistance to the invading Americans. On what grounds does he defend it? Do you think his circum-stances after the Mexican War influenced his explanation?

Commodore Sloat ... whenever he had occasion to speak in public always showed him-self disposed to protect the rights of all the inhabitants of the country, irrespective of which language they spoke, the religion they professed or their place of birth. At the same time, however, that Commodore Sloat expressed his satisfaction with the behavior of the inhabitants of Monterey, he complained very bitterly of the political and judicial authorities who, instead of remaining steadfastly at their posts and trying to preserve or-der, had fled to the hills and were trying to gather men together to rescue the capital from the hands of the enemy. In regard to the conduct of the Monterey authorities, Commodore Sloat used to say,

> ... I came with good intentions; I bring wealth and a brilliant future; and they do not appreciate those gifts. Truly, this procedure is more that of insane people than of persons in their right minds, because if they used common sense they would understand that I am too strong to allow myself to be forced to give up what I have acquired.

It may be that this reasoning was in accord with the way of thinking of a nation whose creed is summed up in the phrase "time is money," but we, who from youth up had been reared in the school of adversity, and who loved our country most dearly because we had only been able by dint of immense sacrifices to maintain it at the level

SOURCE: "Juan Bautista Alvarado on the Conquest of California" (1876). From Juan Bautista Alvarado, HISTORIA DE CALIFORNIA (1876), v, pp. 219–222.

of contemporary civilization, felt very differently from that which characterized the thoughts of the renowned Sloat. Even though we knew that nothing short of a Divine miracle would enable us to force the frigate *Savannah* and her consorts to abandon the port of Monterey, not even for this reason would we desist from making a supreme effort to show the world that although we had strong motives for complaint against Mexico, which had for so many years been the bane of our existence and had robbed us unmercifully, we, ever generous, were not willing to take advantage of an occasion when the Mexican Republic was engaged in a foreign war to settle our family differences; nor were my fellow citizens and I who had read the papers and knew the constitution of the United States, unaware that Alta California stood to gain a great deal by the change in flag, for it was well-known that the enterprising spirit of the North Americans ... would know how to make their influence felt on California soil and make towns grow where there had been only rocks before. Although we knew all of the advantages which would accrue to us from the new alliance which Commodore Sloat was proposing, we preferred the life of privation, uncertainty and snares which we expected to continue until the mother country had come out defeated or victorious in the unequal contest to which she had rashly provoked her powerful neighbor. Our resistance was not motivated by the hatred we had for the North Americans, or their government and institutions, but was dictated by a conscience which aspired to fulfilling as far as possible our duties as Mexican citizens.

Source 4: *Vigilante Justice in Los Angeles* (1857)

This account of Anglo vigilante activity in Los Angeles in response to actions by a gang of thieves appeared in El Clamor Público, *a Spanish-language newspaper. What does it reveal about the status of Hispanics in American California? What lessons do you think Alvarado and Larkin would have drawn from this sort of violence against Californians of Mexican descent?*

For three months a band of thieves has run about the streets and outlying areas of this city by night, abandoning themselves to all kinds of wickedness, including the most refined highway robbery. Various persons have complained to the authorities, but the authorities respond: "Do you have witnesses? Do you want to pay to have them arrested?" And the band continued robbing and killing with all security, by the light of day and in the middle of the city under the chin of the police officials who seem to view this as a comedy. This is not strange; [they say] "the Mexicans are killing each other." ... Four or five Americans have established a Vigilante Committee, made a call to all the population for the public security, and named captains of a company to go in pursuit of the bandits. Here is where the drama begins with all its horrors, and wrapped in a mystery so strange that one is obliged to believe that the bandits were not the persecuted ones. In a few words, a company (all Americans), its captain Sanford, headed toward the Mission of San Gabriel. All the Mexican residents in that place were arrested and treated with unequalled brutality. Two of these unfortunates had been arrested at the entrance of the Mission. They had to submit to an interrogation of the most provocative sort. Intimidated by the threats, and impelled by the instinct of self preservation, they began to run, especially when they saw the captain draw his pistol.

SOURCE: "Vigilante Justice in Los Angeles" (1857). Originally from EL CLAMOR PUBLICO, March 21, 1857.

But, ay! at the first movement that they made, a general volley followed. One fell wounded from various shots. The other was able to reach a lake or marsh. He abandoned his horse and concealed himself in the rushes. Vain efforts. The American band arrived, set fire to the marsh, and very soon, among the general cries of gaiety, they discovered the head of the unfortunate above the flames. A second volley and all was done.—I deceive myself. It was not finished so quickly. The body, loaded over a horse, was transported to the Mission in the midst of cries and shouts of joy and gaiety. Here, overtaken by horror, thought stops because it is impossible to find expressions to describe the scene which took place and was related to me by many witnesses worthy of trust. The body was thrown to the ground in the midst of the mob. One being, with a human face, stepped forward with a knife in his hand.... With one hand he took the head of the dead man by its long hair, separated it from the body, flung it a short distance and stuck his dagger in the heart of the cadaver. Afterward, returning to the head, he made it roll with his foot into the middle of his band and the rabble, amidst the cries and the hurrahs of the greater number.... Is it not horrible? But wait, we have not yet seen all. Another band arrived from another place with two Californios. They had been arrested as suspects, one of them going in search of some oxen, the other to his daily work. They were conducted into the middle of the mob. The cries of "To death! To death!" were heard from all sides. The cutter of heads entered his house, coming out with some ropes, and the two unfortunates were hanged—despite the protests of their countrymen and their families. Once hanged from the tree, the ropes broke and the hapless ones were finished being murdered by shots or knife thrusts. The cutter of heads was fatigued, or his knife did not now cut! Perhaps you will believe that this very cruel person was an Indian from the mountains, one of those barbarians who lives far from all civilization in the Sierra Nevada! Wrong. That barbarian, that mutilator of cadavers, is the Justice of the Peace of San Gabriel! ... He is a citizen of the United States, an American of pure blood....

Afterwards, two Mexicans were found hanging from a tree, and near there another with two bullets in the head.

On the road from Tejon another company had encountered two poor peddlers (always Mexicans) who were arrested and hanged as suspects.

QUESTIONS TO CONSIDER

1. Some historians have argued that Californio culture simply could not endure once California's isolation ended in the early nineteenth century. Based on the sources in this chapter, do you agree? What do they reveal about the important differences in attitudes or values between Anglos and Californios? In other words, what did the contact between their two cultures in the early nineteenth century reveal about the most conspicuous aspects of each culture that may have influenced California's fate in the early nineteenth century?

2. Alvarado's boyhood hero was George Washington. Why do you think Alvarado failed to become the George Washington of California? Did forces or circumstances beyond his control dictate his fate, or was it something about Alvarado himself that prevented him from being the father of a free California?

3. One study of Larkin concluded that he was "exuberantly American." Do you agree? What typically American traits did he possess?

4.   Some historians have argued that the ethnically diverse American West was a fertile field for cultural fusion, while others have viewed it as a place of cultural conflict and conquest. What light do the lives of Larkin and Alvarado shed on this issue?

FOR FURTHER READING

Harlan Hague and David J. Langum, *Thomas O. Larkin: A Life of Patriotism and Profit in Old California* (Norman: University of Oklahoma Press, 1990), provides a thorough account of Larkin's rise in business and his role as an agent of the Americanization of California.

Stephen G. Hyslop, *Contest for California: From Spanish Colonization to the American Conquest* (Norman, OK: Arthur H. Clark Co., 2012), traces the history of early California and the interest of various nations in it.

Robert Ryal Miller, *Juan Alvarado: Governor of California, 1836–1842* (Norman: University of Oklahoma Press, 1998), is the only full-length biography of Alvarado.

Douglas Monroy, *Thrown Among Strangers: The Making of Mexican Culture in Frontier California* (Berkeley: University of California Press, 1990), discusses the cultural conflict that resulted in the degradation of Indians and Hispanics in California.

Leonard Pitt, *The Decline of the Californios: A Social History of the Spanish-Speaking Californians, 1846–1890* (Berkeley: University of California Press, 1970), offers a thorough yet highly readable account of the Californios and their downfall in the nineteenth century.

David J. Weber, *The Mexican Frontier, 1821–1846: The American Southwest Under Mexico* (Albuquerque: University of New Mexico Press, 1982), examines Mexico's northern frontier and its relations with both the United States and Mexico.

12

The South and the Slavery Debate: Hinton Rowan Helper and George Fitzhugh

As far as we know, Hinton Rowan Helper never set eyes on George Fitzhugh's house. If he had, all his worst fears for the South would have been confirmed. The Fitzhugh home was located in Port Royal, Caroline County, Virginia. By the 1850s, it had seen better days. As one neighbor put it, the place was a "rickety old mansion" located on the worst end of a "once noble estate." In fact, the house had actually belonged to Fitzhugh's wife, and he had moved there only after their marriage. Fitzhugh fell in love with his new home and spent most of his time there with his large family, but he was little concerned about keeping it up. More than anything, he wished to spend time in his library. Amid the piles of books and papers, he worked tirelessly to promote the very foundation of the South's economy and the heart of its society: slavery.

A prolific author, Fitzhugh believed that slavery was a positive good. It was good for the master, the slave, and the nonslaveholding white person. It was the basis for an orderly, paternalistic society that honored traditional values and took care of the weak. Northern capitalist society, with its factories and free labor, was a disorderly, individualistic, competitive jungle in which the strong devoured the weak. Free laborers, left to fend for themselves or die, were the true "slaves" in American society. In fact, Fitzhugh suggested, slavery's superiority as a social system was so obvious that many white people ought to be enslaved as well. Other writers made arguments in defense of the "peculiar institution" in the years before the Civil War. None, however, did so as boldly as Fitzhugh.

Hinton Rowan Helper was also a son of the South. The North Carolina native had seen firsthand the effects of slavery on the region. It had dragged the South down, he concluded, economically, socially, and culturally. The very sight of Fitzhugh's broken-down

Hinton Rowan Helper

George Fitzhugh

mansion might have offered him proof of that. Helper would not have wasted too many tears on Fitzhugh, though. And he would have shed none at all for Fitzhugh's few slaves. As a nonslaveholder, Helper was little concerned about slavery's impact on the master class or its black bondsmen. He feared instead its effects on the South's yeomen farmers. He was convinced that slavery mired ordinary whites in poverty and backwardness. Worse, it closed off their opportunities for advancement. Just as Fitzhugh eagerly took up the pen to defend slavery, Helper assailed it. On the eve of the Civil War, Helper launched a printed attack on slavery that caught the attention of North and South alike. Others had blasted slavery before, but never quite like this. In the words of Helper's publisher, his assault came as "heavy artillery of statistics" and "rolling volley and dashing charges of argument and rhetoric." And just as Fitzhugh's defense of slave labor did not go unnoticed in the North, Helper's fusillade provoked a violent reaction in the South. Like the North and South, Fitzhugh and Helper were joined in a bitter war of words. In the late 1850s, those words helped nudge the two sections closer to real war.

"THE FREEST PEOPLE IN THE WORLD"

George Fitzhugh was a child of Virginia. Unfortunately, by the time Fitzhugh was born in Prince William County in 1806, the state's best years were behind it. Generations of tobacco cultivation had taken a toll on the Old Dominion's soil by the beginning of the nineteenth century. Nowhere was that more evident than in Prince William County, located between the Potomac and Rappahannock Rivers. In 1800, nearly seven thousand whites lived in the county, along with about fifty-four hundred slaves. Twenty years later, the white population had declined by more than two thousand and the slave population by more than one thousand. The Fitzhughs were among those who left.

When George was six, his father purchased a plantation in Alexandria near the banks of the Potomac. The move did little to revive the family's fortunes. George's father, a small planter and physician, fell victim to worn-out soil, debt, and mismanagement. Given the family's difficult financial circumstances, George's opportunity for formal education was limited to a few years at a neighborhood school. Most of what he learned came from reading. "We are no regular built scholar," he confessed later. "We have ... picked up our information by the wayside."

George Fitzhugh went on to read law under a local attorney and practice before the bar. With little appetite for the law or legal routine, however, he proved to be a mediocre lawyer. Fitzhugh's rural practice brought him little income, and the problem of making a living became a matter of great urgency. That problem was compounded in 1829 when his father died and the Fitzhugh family lost its estate. Quickly, however, things took a turn for the better. The same year, Fitzhugh married and took control of his wife's inheritance, a small plantation not far from Port Royal on the Rappahannock River. He continued to practice law, but he never prospered. He disliked many of his clients and often tried criminal cases rather than more lucrative civil suits because criminal defendants talked less. Listening too much to clients, he declared, "would make a man idiotic."

As it happened, Port Royal had also been the home of John Taylor of Caroline, a leading defender of slavery and spokesman for the rejuvenation of the soil as the key to the South's prosperity. Taylor, who died just five years before Fitzhugh moved to Port Royal, had failed to revive the area's tobacco economy, and the town's battered wharf stood as a silent reminder of a once-thriving tobacco trade. As a defender of slavery and the South's plantation economy, however, his influence was still widely felt. Taylor's books graced the shelves of Fitzhugh's library, and their impact would be clearly evident in his own work. Fitzhugh was impressed by Taylor's agrarian philosophy, which held up agriculture as the "natural interest" of society. He was equally impressed with Taylor's faded Port Royal and in time came to associate it with the finest aspects of a slaveholding society. Here, he boasted, murder, ignorance, starvation, and unemployment were nonexistent. Instead, the village's four hundred to five hundred residents— about half black and half white—enjoyed peace, order, and plenty. "Come and see Port Royal ...," he rhapsodized, "when the crops are growing, the flowers blooming, the birds singing, and the placid lakelike river just rippling into smiles."

Like many southerners by the 1840s, Fitzhugh was increasingly troubled by the growing attacks of abolitionists. He was intimately familiar with their arguments because he read them all. "We have whole files of infidel and abolition papers," he declared. "[They] are our daily companions." He also had developed close friendships with such defenders of slavery as George Frederick Holmes, a professor of history and literature at the University of Virginia, and James D. B. DeBow, the well-known publisher of *DeBow's Review* and a leading voice for southern rights. He had read with intense interest the works of the Scottish philosopher and historian Thomas Carlyle, a critic of abolitionists and life in Britain's emerging industrial society. Modern society, Carlyle charged, tore the very fabric of the community by turning labor into a commodity to be let go when it was no longer needed. The Scot struck an obvious chord in Fitzhugh. As he encountered Carlyle's idealized vision of premodern society, Port Royal no doubt came easily to mind.

By the late 1840s, Fitzhugh was ready to defend slavery publicly. At the end of the Mexican War, slavery had emerged once again as an explosive political issue dividing the North and South. Before the guns fell silent in 1848, northerners and southerners had already divided over slavery's extension into any territory taken from Mexico. Fitzhugh realized that the South was involved in a war for Americans' hearts and minds. And as a propagandist, he knew that he could not be completely honest. "I assure you Sir," he confessed to George Frederick Holmes, "I see great evils in slavery, but in a controversial work I ought not to admit them." Instead, Fitzhugh went on the offensive. Beginning with two pamphlets published in the early 1850s, he advanced themes he would develop in his later work. Liberty and equality, he argued in *Slavery Justified* (1850), were failed concepts. Because "half of mankind are but grown-up children," liberty "is as fatal to them as it would be to children." Slaves needed the protection of the plantation, for the slave "is never without the master to maintain him." The wage-labor system devoured the weak and created social chaos. The South, by contrast, had "no mobs, no trades unions, no strikes for higher wages, no armed resistance to the law, but little jealousy of the rich by the poor. We have but few in our jails, and fewer in our poor houses." **[See Source 1.]** If Fitzhugh believed that many whites were better off under slavery, he had no doubts about blacks. In *What Shall Be Done with the Free Negroes?* (1851), he declared that the wretched condition of the thousands of free blacks in both the North and South proved that liberty was a failed experiment. Slavery, he concluded, was "the only condition" for which blacks were suited.

With these pamphlets, Fitzhugh announced himself not just as another voice in the growing proslavery chorus but as one of the country's most radical philosophers. In fact, his thought represented a clear departure from any previous defense of slavery. Men such as John Taylor of Caroline and fellow Virginian Edmund Ruffin defended slavery in terms of "natural rights" theory. The philosophical underpinnings of this theory sprang from the Enlightenment thought of the seventeenth and eighteenth centuries. Enlightenment theorists assumed that an orderly universe was governed by certain "natural laws" and that individuals possessed "natural rights." In the seventeenth century, English political philosopher John Locke had identified the most important of these rights as "life, liberty, and property." In the next century, of course, Thomas Jefferson proclaimed that citizens were equal in their possession of such natural rights. Both Locke and Jefferson further believed that citizens and their government had entered into a contract: governments were charged with protecting natural rights, and the people retained the right to replace governments when they did not. Given these assumptions, slavery's earlier defenders saw themselves as heirs of John Locke. In their view, broad ownership of property was essential because it provided citizens with economic and thus political independence. By securing this independence for planters, slavery helped protect the liberty of free citizens against the encroachment of government power. Slavery thus represented the best defense of "natural rights."

Fitzhugh would have none of this. In his first book, *Sociology for the South, or the Failure of Free Society* (1854), he offered a radical alternative to the American belief that "all men" were created equal—even if they *were* white. Here he rejected outright a defense of slavery based on natural rights theory. And he spurned the idea that government's duty was to protect liberty, especially the rights associated with the ownership of private property. Humanity, Fitzhugh insisted, was part of an organic—or interconnected and mutually dependent—universe created by God. Society, too, was organically connected. Each part depended on every other part. He argued that individualism, equality, and liberty threatened this organic society. Especially dangerous was the individual's unrestrained liberty to acquire property in a capitalist economic system. Left unchecked, this principle would lead to the collapse of the natural order that God had designed.

Capitalism as practiced in the northern states unleashed selfishness and allowed the rich to exploit the poor.

Fitzhugh also rejected the ideas of the eighteenth-century Scottish economist Adam Smith. According to Smith, the public good was achieved when individuals pursued their own self-interest. Thus he called for the government to curtail its regulation of the economy and allow the profit motive and the laws of supply and demand to work. The result, Fitzhugh countered, was human misery and social chaos. Instead, the best alternative was a society based on slavery and inequality. In Fitzhugh's paternalistic society, the aristocrats had the power and the right to rule and protect society. The majority of the population needed the protection offered by these masters because inequality, not equality, was the natural state of humankind. It was self-evident that men were not born equal. Rather, he declared, "It would be far nearer the truth to say, 'that some were born with saddles on their backs, and others booted and spurred to ride them,'—and the riding does them good."

Three years later, Fitzhugh extended his argument in what would be his best known attack on equality, natural rights, and liberty. In *Cannibals All! or Slaves Without Masters* (1857), he challenged Americans' faith in progress, their assumptions about the goodness of human nature, and their belief in individualism. In short, to defend race-based slavery, he turned their intellectual world upside down. Northern material "progress" was actually a descent into social chaos. What northerners thought was slavery was actually freedom. Their freedom was nothing more than slavery. And what they thought was good was actually evil. All "good and respectable people," he declared, "are 'Cannibals all.' " They do nothing but live off others' labor. By contrast, the "low, bad, and disreputable people" were forced to labor for themselves and support others besides. Thus free labor was more profitable than slavery, because masters took care of their slaves, while capitalist employers exploited their workers. The capitalist was "a slave owner—a master, without the obligations of a master," Fitzhugh wrote. "They who work for you, who create your income, are slaves, without the rights of slaves. Slaves without a master!" The slaves of the South, however, "are the happiest, and, in some sense, the freest people in the world." **[See Source 2.]**

"SUNK ... IN GALLING POVERTY AND IGNORANCE"

On one point, Hinton Rowan Helper would not disagree with George Fitzhugh: Blacks were inferior to whites. In all other ways, though, the two men's views—and visions for American society—could not have been more different. Fitzhugh and Helper stand as reminders that white southerners were not united on the question of slavery. They also remind us that there was more than one South before the Civil War.

Helper was not just a son of North Carolina but a son of *western* North Carolina. Born in 1829 in Rowan (now Davie) County, he was the child of a small farmer who owned about two hundred acres along the Yadkin River. The area may have influenced Helper's views about slavery in two ways. First, the Yadkin Valley was a land of nonslaveholding yeomen farmers. Remote from the area of large plantations farther east, the county boasted more than fourteen thousand residents in 1860, but among them were only three dozen or so planters with twenty or more slaves. Second, it was an area settled by many German pioneers. In fact, Hinton's father, Jacob Helfer (as the family name was originally spelled), had emigrated from Germany in the middle of the previous century.

Although Helper later claimed that his father owned several slaves, Germans in North Carolina and elsewhere in the South demonstrated a marked preference for free labor. Practicing the sort of self-sufficiency and diversified agriculture they had often known in the old country, many German settlers had little inclination to embrace slavery.

Whatever views regarding slavery Helper imbibed in the Yadkin Valley, he was introduced at an early age to the hard life of a yeoman farmer. When he was only nine months old, his father died. Hinton, the fifth son and seventh child, grew up in poverty. As a boy, he spent plenty of time walking behind a plow. He also attended a local school and passed the time on winter nights by reading. It was his escape, he later said, from "those loathsome dungeons of illiteracy in which it has been the constant policy of the oligarchy to keep the masses." After graduation, he was apprenticed as a clerk to a nearby storekeeper. After stealing three hundred dollars from his employer, which he later claimed to have repaid, he headed to New York City, hoping to make his fortune. Unable to find a good job there, Helper soon came down with "goldfever" and traveled to California. After two and a half years in the goldfields, success still eluded him. By 1854, he was back in North Carolina.

Frustrated in his two attempts to advance himself, Helper decided to capitalize on his horrible experience in California by writing a book revealing the state as a moral cesspool. In *The Land of Gold,* published in 1855, Helper laid out "the truth" about California: "its rottenness and its corruption, its squalor and its misery, its crime and its shame, its gold and its dross." California's most appalling feature, however, was its racial diversity, and Helper spared no nonwhite group from savage criticism. Blacks and Mexicans lived in "filth and degradation," Indians were "filthy and abominable," and the Chinese "semi-barbarians." California's ethnic and racial "ingredients," he concluded, "cannot be compounded into a harmonious, perfect, and complete whole." **[See Source 3.]**

Like George Fitzhugh's early writings, Helper's demonstrated themes that would dominate his later, more famous works. Thus *The Land of Gold* revealed the basis for Helper's later assault on slavery. California's racial and ethnic diversity, he concluded, was holding back the state's development. Here Helper had an explanation for his own failure to succeed in the goldfields: the presence of a motley population of "inferior" races. In a few years, Helper would turn his intense racism—and the same conclusions about social advancement—on slavery.

He knew, of course, that the debate over slavery was heating up. In 1854, the year he returned to North Carolina, Fitzhugh published his *Sociology for the South.* More important, Congress passed the Kansas–Nebraska Act, overturning the prohibition on slavery north of 36°30′ north latitude established by the Missouri Compromise. By opening up the possibility that most of the Louisiana Purchase could become slave territory if the settlers there allowed it, the act inflamed many white northerners. They viewed the Kansas–Nebraska Act as proof that slaveholders were conspiring to take over the government and spread slavery everywhere. These fears in turn fueled the growth of the new Republican Party, which called for a halt to slavery's westward expansion. Helper realized that many northerners, fearful about the prospect of competition with slave labor in the West, were ready to hear what slavery had done to the *white* man. Two years before, Harriet Beecher Stowe had published her antislavery novel *Uncle Tom's Cabin.* Stowe's work made blacks the central characters and focused on slavery's inhumanity. Helper dismissed such abolitionist propaganda as sentimental. It might be appropriate for women, he thought, but not for men. "[I]t is all well enough for women to give the fictions of slavery," he declared. "[M]en should give the facts." What the antislavery cause needed was a factual study of slavery, based on a statistical comparison with the free labor system of the North.

Published in 1857, *The Impending Crisis of the South* was just such a study. Rather than show "friendliness or sympathy for the blacks," Helper's book concentrated on slavery's impact on whites. His main arguments rested on the supposition that the North and South had been roughly equal in economic and cultural terms at the time of the signing of the U.S. Constitution in 1787. Since then, however, the North had dramatically increased its power and was now dominant. He rolled out the numbers in relation to population, agriculture, manufactures, the value of real estate, and literacy. The South, he concluded, had grown dependent on the North in nearly every way. Northern factories produced the goods made from southern resources and sold to southern consumers. The North dominated domestic and foreign trade. It produced most of the country's art, literature, and culture. It invented new technologies and new systems of production. The South offered little or nothing in return. Southerners did not write books, nor did they read them. They did not build factories, nor did they care to. Instead, they depended on the North to provide the necessities, as well as the luxuries, of life. Why was this so? Helper's answer was clear: Slavery had "impeded the progress and prosperity of the South" and had "sunk a large majority of our people in galling poverty and ignorance." **[See Source 4.]**

As abolitionist propaganda, *The Impending Crisis* was not totally honest. In demonstrating slavery's impoverishment of the white nonslaveholding class, Helper presented only those facts that suited his arguments. For instance, he did not consider the vast differences in climate, culture, proximity to transportation, and other aspects that might be responsible for the economic imbalance. He compared North Carolina to Massachusetts, and Pennsylvania to South Carolina, but he ignored the West, which had attracted thousands of people in great migrations out of the eastern states. This especially hurt the South in his comparative analysis. Although areas of eastern migration, such as the Midwest, were prosperous, they still lagged behind New England and the Mid-Atlantic States. By contrast, the most prosperous area of the South was the Deep South, stretching from western Georgia to eastern Texas. There slavery and cotton were thriving, and the population was growing. Only in the eastern slave states had competition and soil exhaustion brought population decline and economic malaise.

Helper's argument was not exactly original. In fact, many northern observers had made much the same point about the South's economic, social, and cultural backwardness. **[See Source 5.]** In addition, he ignored the moral issue of slavery. To this "side of the question," he wrote, "Northern writers have already done full and timely justice." In fact, Helper was totally unmoved by any "humanitarian" considerations regarding slavery. Rather, he was steeped in the new "scientific" racism of the mid-nineteenth century, which declared blacks a separate and inferior species. Following the Swiss-born Harvard natural scientist Louis Agassiz, writers in the American School of Ethnology argued that blacks were not descended from Adam and Eve, but instead were the product of a separate creation. Helper embraced this theory and thus declared in *The Impending Crisis* that he did not believe in the "unity of the races." Unlike many southern writers, however, he did not use this conclusion to justify slavery. Instead, he agreed with many other ethnographers that various climatic regions determined the appropriate habitations for the different "types of mankind." Thus the temperate climate of the United States created an inappropriate home for blacks. Those of African descent belonged in the tropics. In *The Impending Crisis,* he wrote, "It is too cold for negroes [in the United States], and we long to see the day arrive when the latter shall have entirely receded from their uncongenial homes in America."

Although Helper believed that blacks were "an undesirable population," he downplayed the question of race in *The Impending Crisis*. Instead, he focused almost exclusively on slavery's ill effects. As he was directing his argument to northern whites, perhaps he thought it wise to submerge his own racial views. If so, he seriously misjudged his audience. Racism, a fear of slavery, and hopes for economic advancement were as intimately connected in many northerners' minds as they were in Helper's. That was especially true by 1857, when the Supreme Court declared in the *Dred Scott* decision[*] that Congress could not pass a law barring slavery from the territories. The Court's ruling further aroused the fears of northern whites about competing with slave labor. At the same time, Helper gave them a powerful demonstration of slavery's impact on free labor. By pushing race into the background, *The Impending Crisis* confirmed northerners' worst fears about slavery and their own economic opportunity without forcing them to confront their racism.

"PURPOSELY KEPT ... IN IGNORANCE"

Published amid the growing controversy over the extension of slavery into the territories, Fitzhugh's and Helper's books only heightened the tensions between North and South in the late 1850s. They fed common misunderstandings and raised fears on both sides, thus increasing the resistance to compromise.

The proslavery views of Fitzhugh enjoyed widespread acclaim in the South. Reviewers praised *Sociology for the South* for its "bold assertion of universal principles" and its "profound views on the comparison of slavery with what is miscalled 'free society.'" Southern editors and readers likewise praised *Cannibals All!* and adopted its arguments and rhetoric as their own. Northern reviewers denounced Fitzhugh's books in the strongest terms. New York newspaper editor and abolitionist Horace Greeley wrote that Fitzhugh was an example of the barren wasteland of southern literature. Abolitionist William Lloyd Garrison called *Sociology for the South* "a shallow, impudent, and thoroughly satanic work." Indeed, in the minds of many northerners, Fitzhugh became the symbol of proslavery thought, especially after he traveled north to debate leading abolitionists. By the late 1850s, many northerners viewed him as representative of all southerners. His ideas, they incorrectly believed, were typical southern ideas. In 1860, abolitionist senator Charles Sumner used Fitzhugh's work as his main target in a speech titled "The Barbarism of Slavery." Abraham Lincoln read *Sociology for the South* and used Fitzhugh's statements as proof of southern extremism. He also borrowed ideas from Fitzhugh, such as in his famous "House divided" speech. It was the Virginian's rhetorical assertion, after all, that "domestic slavery and (attempted) universal liberty cannot long co-exist in the Great Republic of Christendom."

Helper's book, meanwhile, raised friends and foes in exactly opposite quarters. Nonslaveholders—about three-quarters of the white South—were often illiterate and thus never heard his argument at all. The slaveholding class, however, found his arguments troubling. It did not help that Helper had drawn his statistics from the Census of 1850. Ironically, that census had been compiled under the direction of James D. B. DeBow, the well-known newspaper editor who was an ardent defender of slavery and a close friend of George Fitzhugh. Outraged southerners often denounced Helper as a renegade

---

[*]*Dred Scott decision:* The Supreme Court ruling based on the case of a slave named Dred Scott, who argued that living for four years in free territory made him free. The Court denied this and went on to rule that the Missouri Compromise of 1820 was unconstitutional because Congress had no power to bar slavery from federal territories.

scoundrel and a traitor. One North Carolina newspaper even urged the author of *The Impending Crisis* to throw himself into the arms of the famous black abolitionist Frederick Douglass and "mix with that dark, infidel, and traitorous crew upon whose purses all your highest hopes now depend." The accusation that Helper was in favor of interracial relations—sexual or otherwise—was nonsense, of course. Yet it demonstrates how he had touched a sensitive nerve in the white South. Helper may have exaggerated the case, but few southerners could deny that they were "compelled to go to the North for almost every article of utility and adornment, from matches, shoepegs, and paintings up to cotton-mills, steamships and statuary."

Even worse, Helper had called for "an exterminating war" against slavery. Non-slaveholders, he suggested, should join together and rise up against slaveholders. They "have hoodwinked you, trifled with you, and used you," he declared. "They have purposely kept you in ignorance, and have, by moulding your passions and prejudices to suit themselves, induced you to act in direct opposition to your dearest rights and interests." Helper's plan for abolishing slavery called for banning slaveholders from politics. The actual abolition of slavery would be accomplished through legislation making slaveholding a crime and by taxes on slaveholders who did not immediately comply. The money raised by these taxes would be used to colonize the emancipated slaves in Africa or Central and South America. To bring this about, Helper called for nonslaveholding southerners to change their political allegiance. They had supported the proslavery Democratic Party for far too long. The time had come to join the new Republican Party and vote for its presidential candidate in 1860. The Republicans, he believed, would keep slavery out of the territories and open the door for abolition.

Helper's prescription confirmed slaveholders' fears about the rising Republican menace in the North. If Republicans triumphed at the polls, they believed, slavery was doomed. Northerners liked Helper's work as much as they hated Fitzhugh's. William Lloyd Garrison praised his arguments, claiming that they were irrefutable. Horace Greeley printed an eight-page review of the book in his *New York Tribune* and called it one of the most remarkable antislavery works ever written. *The Impending Crisis* sold more than thirteen thousand copies in its first year. It received even greater exposure when the Republican Party distributed more than one hundred forty thousand copies of the book in the 1860 campaign.

The impact of Helper's publication on Abraham Lincoln's election in 1860 is impossible to determine. But as a result of the election, the southern slaveholding states seceded from the Union, thus triggering the Civil War. During the war, most of Helper's yeomen farmers fought for the Confederacy, motivated no doubt in part by the same racial fears that possessed Helper. Slavery, after all, was more than a labor system. It was also a powerful way to control blacks and assert white superiority. At the same time, however, large pockets of the South remained loyal to the Union. Populated mostly by nonslaveholding whites, these areas demonstrated that many southern whites did not see the slaveholders' interests as their own.

The Civil War, of course, would destroy Fitzhugh's allegedly paternalistic slave system. Yet after the war, he had little difficulty finding friends, even among northern Republicans. Fitzhugh privately lamented postwar Republican policies in the South. At the same time, he became a judge in the Freedmen's Bureau, the federal agency set up by Republicans to aid former slaves in their transition from slavery to freedom. Here he was able to act on his paternalistic views by assisting helpless blacks who could not fend for themselves. Before he died in 1881, Fitzhugh even grew fond of the industrial capitalism he had so vehemently attacked. Monopolistic capitalism, he came to believe, was a social system that reflected the natural inequality of humankind.

Helper also found a position with the triumphant Republicans. They had not forgotten the political value of *The Impending Crisis,* and in 1861, Lincoln rewarded him with an appointment as consul to Argentina. There, despite his virulent anti-Catholicism and racism, he married a local woman. When he resigned in 1866, his accounts were short by six thousand dollars, although the Republicans further rewarded him by ignoring the missing funds. Still convinced that the United States was a white man's country, Helper would go on to publish a trilogy of books designed to "write the negro out of America" and "out of existence." Completed in 1871, they established Helper as one of the era's most fanatical white supremacists. Meanwhile, as before the Civil War, his schemes to get rich never quite paid off. Abandoned by his wife and suffering from depression and loneliness, Helper was filled with despair over his failed business ventures. Unable to cope with his own crisis, he committed suicide in 1909.

In the postwar years, the abiding racism of Fitzhugh and Helper was shared by most Americans. At the same time, however, postwar society would not live up to the hopes of either man. Americans rejected Fitzhugh's views about individualism, competition, liberty, and equality. Although Helper's vision seemed fulfilled with the election of Republicans in the postwar South, Republican rule would not last beyond the 1870s. Moreover, Helper never saw the removal from the United States of the "undesirable" black population. In the end, both men's dreams regarding slavery and society were shattered.

• PRIMARY SOURCES •

Source 1:   George Fitzhugh, *Slavery Justified* (1850)

In Slavery Justified, *George Fitzhugh compares northern and southern society. Why does he believe that life in the South is better? How do you think Helper would have responded to him?*

The bestowing upon men equality of rights, is but giving license to the strong to oppress the weak. It begets the grossest inequalities of condition. Menials and day laborers are and must be as numerous as in a land of slavery. And these menials and laborers are only taken care of while young, strong and healthy. If the laborer gets sick, his wages cease just as his demands are greatest. If two of the poor get married, who being young and healthy, are getting good wages, in a few years they may have four children. Their wants have increased, but the mother has enough to do to nurse the four children, and the wages of the husband must support six. There is no equality, except in theory, in such society, and there is no liberty. The men of property, those who own lands and money, are masters of the poor; masters, with none of the feelings, interests or sympathies of masters; they employ them when they please, and for what they please, and may leave them to die in the highway, for it is the only home to which the poor in free countries are entitled....

SOURCE: George Fitzhugh, SLAVERY JUSTIFIED (1850). Originally from George Fitzhugh, SLAVERY JUSTIFIED, BY A SOUTHERNER (Fredericksburg, Va.: Recorder Printing Office, 1850); later included in SOCIOLOGY FOR THE SOUTH, OR THE FAILURE OF FREE SOCIETY (Richmond, Va.: A. Morris, 1854).

There is no rivalry, no competition to get employment among slaves, as among free laborers. Nor is there a war between master and slave. The master's interest prevents his reducing the slave's allowance or wages in infancy or sickness, for he might lose the slave by so doing. His feeling for his slave never permits him to stint him in old age. The slaves are all well fed, well clad, have plenty of fuel, and are happy. They have no dread of the future—no fear of want. A state of dependence is the only condition in which reciprocal affection can exist among human beings—the only situation in which the war of competition ceases, and peace, amity and good will arise. A state of independence always begets more or less of jealous rivalry and hostility. A man loves his children because they are weak, helpless and dependent. He loves his wife for similar reasons. When his children grow up and assert their independence, he is apt to transfer his affection to his grandchildren. He ceases to love his wife when she becomes masculine or rebellious; but slaves are always dependent, never the rivals of their master. Hence, though men are often found at variance with wife or children, we never saw one who did not like his slaves, and rarely a slave who was not devoted to his master....

At the slaveholding South all is peace, quiet, plenty and contentment. We have no mobs, no trades unions, no strikes for higher wages, no armed resistance to the law, but little jealousy of the rich by the poor. We have but few in our jails, and fewer in our poor houses. We produce enough of the comforts and necessaries of life for a population three or four times as numerous as ours. We are wholly exempt from the torrent of pauperism, crime, agrarianism, and infidelity which Europe is pouring from her jails and alms houses on the already crowded North. Population increases slowly, wealth rapidly.... Wealth is more equally distributed than at the North, where a few millionaires own most of the property of the country. (These millionaires are men of cold hearts and weak minds; they know how to make money, but not how to use it, either for the benefit of themselves or of others.) High intellectual and moral attainments, refinement of head and heart, give standing to a man in the South, however poor he may be. Money is, with few exceptions, the only thing that ennobles at the North. We have poor among us, but none who are over-worked and under-fed. We do not crowd cities because lands are abundant and their owners kind, merciful and hospitable. The poor are as hospitable as the rich, the negro as the white man.

Source 2:   George Fitzhugh, *Cannibals All!* (1857)

George Fitzhugh defends slavery in these passages from Cannibals All! *On what grounds does he do so? How does he use conditions in northern society to justify slavery in the South?*

The respectable way of living is to make other people work for you, and to pay them nothing for so doing—and to have no concern about them after their work is done. Hence, white slave-holding is much more respectable than negro slavery—for the master works nearly as hard for the negro as he for the master. But you, my virtuous, respectable reader, exact three thousand dollars per annum from white labor (for your income is the product of white labor) and make not one cent of return in any form. You retain your capital, and never labor, and yet live in luxury on the labor of others. Capital commands

SOURCE: George Fitzhugh, CANNIBALS ALL! (1857). From George Fitzhugh, CANNIBALS ALL! OR SLAVES WITHOUT MASTERS (1857).

labor, as the master does the slave. Neither pays for labor; but the master permits the slave to retain a larger allowance from the proceeds of his own labor, and hence "free labor is cheaper than slave labor." You, with the command over labor which your capital gives you, are a slave owner—a master, without the obligations of a master. They who work for you, who create your income, are slaves, without the rights of slaves. Slaves without a master! Whilst you were engaged in amassing your capital, in seeking to become independent, you were in the White Slave Trade. To become independent is to be able to make other people support you, without being obliged to labor for *them*. Now, what man in society is not seeking to attain this situation? He who attains it is a slave owner, in the worst sense. He who is in pursuit of it is engaged in the slave trade. You, reader, belong to the one or other class. The men without property, in free society, are theoretically in a worse condition than slaves. Practically, their condition corresponds with this theory, as history and statistics everywhere demonstrate. The capitalists, in free society, live in ten times the luxury and show that Southern masters do, because the slaves to capital work harder and cost less than negro slaves.

The negro slaves of the South are the happiest, and, in some sense, the freest people in the world. The children and the aged and infirm work not at all, and yet have all the comforts and necessaries of life provided for them. They enjoy liberty, because they are oppressed neither by care nor labor. The women do little hard work, and are protected from the despotism of their husbands by their masters. The negro men and stout boys work, on the average, in good weather, not more than nine hours a day. The balance of their time is spent in perfect abandon. Besides, they have their Sabbaths and holidays. White men, with so much of license and liberty, would die of ennui; but negroes luxuriate in corporeal and mental repose. With their faces upturned to the sun, they can sleep at any hour; and quiet sleep is the greatest of human enjoyments. "Blessed be the man who invented sleep." 'Tis happiness in itself—and results from contentment with the present, and confident assurance of the future. We do not know whether free laborers ever sleep. They are fools to do so; for, whilst they sleep, the wily and watchful capitalist is devising means to ensnare and exploitate them. The free laborer must work or starve. He is more of a slave than the negro, because he works longer and harder for less allowance than the slave, and has no holiday, because the cares of life with him begin when its labors end. He has no liberty, and not a single right....

We do not agree with the authors of the Declaration of Independence, that governments "derive their just powers from the consent of the governed." The women, the children, the negroes, and but few of the non-property holders were consulted, or consented to the Revolution, or the governments that ensued from its success. As to these, the new governments were self-elected despotisms, and the governing class self-elected despots. Those governments originated in force, and have been continued by force. All governments must originate in force, and be continued by force. The very term, government, implies that it is carried on against the consent of the governed. Fathers do not derive their authority, as heads of families, from the consent of wife and children, nor do they govern their families by their consent. They never take the vote of the family as to the labors to be performed, the moneys to be expended, or as to anything else. Masters dare not take the vote of slaves as to their government. If they did, constant holiday, dissipation, and extravagance would be the result.... Not even in the most democratic countries are soldiers governed by their consent, nor is their vote taken on the eve of battle. They have somehow lost (or never had) the "inalienable rights of life, liberty, and the pursuit of happiness," and, whether Americans or Russians, are forced into battle without and often against their consent.... The governments of Europe could not exist a week without the positive force of standing armies.

They are all governments of force, not of consent. Even in our North, the women, children, and free negroes, constitute four-fifths of the population; and they are all governed without their consent. But they mean to correct this gross and glaring iniquity at the North. They hold that all men, women, and negroes, and smart children are equals, and entitled to equal rights. The widows and free negroes begin to vote in some of those States, and they will have to let all colors and sexes and ages vote soon, or give up the glorious principles of human equality and universal emancipation.

The experiment which they will make, we fear, is absurd in theory, and the symptoms of approaching anarchy … among them leave no doubt that its practical operation will be no better than its theory.

Source 3:   Hinton Rowan Helper on Chinese Immigrants (1855)

In this excerpt from The Land of Gold, *Hinton Rowan Helper discusses Chinese immigrants in California. Why does he object to them? What do his fears about the Chinese have to do with his concerns for whites? How would you compare Helper's argument regarding the Chinese with Fitzhugh's argument in Source 2?*

The national habits and traits of Chinese character, to which they cling with uncompromising tenacity in this country, are strikingly distinct from those of all other nations. There is a marked identity about their features, person, manners and costume, so unmistakable that it betrays their nationality in a moment. Particular fashions and modes of dress give them no concern whatever. All their garments look as if they were made after the same pattern out of the same material and from the same piece of cloth. In short, one Chinaman looks almost exactly like another, but very unlike anybody else….

The Chinese are more objectionable than other foreigners because they refuse to have dealing or intercourse with us. Consequently there is no chance of making any thing of them either in the way of trade or labor. They are ready to take all they can get from us but are not willing to give anything in return. They did not aid in the acquisition or settlement of California and they do not intend to make it their future home. They will not become permanent citizens nor identify their lives and interests with the country. They neither build nor buy, nor invest capital in any way that conduces to the advantage of anyone but themselves. They have thousands of good-for-nothing gewgaws and worthless articles of *virtu*[*] for sale, and our people are foolish enough to buy them.

Though they hold themselves aloof from us, contemn and disdain us, they have guaranteed to them the same privileges that we enjoy and are allowed to exhaust the mines that should be reserved for us and our posterity—that is if they are worth reserving at all. Their places could and should be filled with worthier immigrants—Europeans who would take the oath of allegiance to the country, work both for themselves and for the commonwealth, fraternize with us, and finally, become a part of us….

SOURCE: "Hinton Rowan Helper on Chinese Immigrants" (1855). Originally from Hinton Helper, THE LAND OF GOLD (Baltimore: H. Taylor, 1855).

[*]*Virtu:* Curios or antiques.

However, they have neither the strength of body nor the power of mind to cope with us in the common affairs of life and our people will not always treat them with undue complaisance. They must work for themselves, or we will make them work for us. No inferior race of men can exist in these United States without becoming subordinate to the will of the Anglo-Americans. It was so with the negroes and the Indians and it will be so with the Chinese in California.

Source 4:   Hinton Rowan Helper, *The Impending Crisis of the South* (1857)

In this passage, Hinton Rowan Helper discusses the South's dependence on the North. How does he explain southern backwardness? Do you think this argument would have been effective at the time? Why?

The North is the Mecca of our merchants, and to it they must and do make two pilgrimages per annum—one in the spring and one in the fall. All our commercial,

TABLE NO. I.   Agricultural Products of the Free States—1850.

States.	Wheat, bushels.	Oats, bushels.	Indian Corn, bushels.
California	17,228	0	12,236
Connecticut	41,762	1,258,738	1,935,043
Illinois	9,414,575	10,087,241	57,646,984
Indiana	6,214,458	5,655,014	52,964,363
Iowa	1,530,581	1,524,345	8,656,799
Maine	296,259	2,181,037	1,750,056
Massachusetts	31,211	1,165,146	2,345,490
Michigan	4,925,889	2,866,056	5,641,420
New Hampshire	185,658	973,381	1,573,670
New Jersey	1,601,190	3,378,063	8,759,704
New York	13,121,498	26,552,814	17,858,400
Ohio	14,487,351	13,472,742	59,078,695
Pennsylvania	15,367,691	21,538,156	19,835,214
Rhode Island	49	215,232	539,201
Vermont	535,955	2,307,734	2,032,396
Wisconsin	4,286,131	3,414,672	1,988,979
	72,157,486	96,590,371	242,618,650

Source: Hinton Rowan Helper, "The Impending Crisis of the South" (1857). From Hinton Rowan Helper, THE IMPENDING CRISIS OF THE SOUTH, 1857.

mechanical, manufactural, and literary supplies come from there. We want Bibles, brooms, buckets and books, and we go to the North; we want pens, ink, paper, wafers and envelopes, and we go to the North; we want shoes, hats, handkerchiefs, umbrellas and pocket knives, and we go to the North; we want furniture, crockery, glassware and pianos, and we go to the North; we want toys, primers, school books, fashionable apparel, machinery, medicines, tombstones, and a thousand other things, and we go to the North for them all. Instead of keeping our money in circulation at home, by patronizing our own mechanics, manufacturers, and laborers, we send it all away to the North, and there it remains; it never falls into our hands again.

In one way or another we are more or less subservient to the North every day of our lives. In infancy we are swaddled in Northern muslin; in childhood we are humored with Northern gewgaws; in youth we are instructed out of Northern books; at the age of maturity we sow our "wild oats" on Northern soil; in middle-life we exhaust our wealth, energies and talents in the dishonorable vocation of entailing our dependence on our children and on our children's children, and, to the neglect of our own interests and the interests of those around us, in giving aid and succor to every department of Northern power; in the decline of life we remedy our eye-sight with Northern spectacles, and support our infirmities with Northern canes; in old age we are drugged with Northern physic; and, finally, when we die, our inanimate bodies, shrouded in Northern cambric, are stretched upon the bier, borne to the grave in a Northern carriage, entombed with a Northern spade, and memor[ial]ized with a Northern slab!

But it can hardly be necessary to say more in illustration of this unmanly and unnational dependence, which is so glaring that it cannot fail to be apparent to even the most careless and superficial observer. All the world sees, or ought to see, that in a commercial, mechanical, manufactural, financial, and literary point of view, we are as helpless as babes; that, in comparison with the Free States, our agricultural resources have been greatly exaggerated, misunderstood and mismanaged; and that, instead of cultivating among ourselves a wise policy of mutual assistance and co-operation with respect to individuals, and of self-reliance with respect to the South at large, instead of giving countenance and encouragement to the industrial enterprises projected in our midst, and instead of building up, aggrandizing and beautifying our own States, cities and towns, we have been spending our substance at the North, and are daily augmenting and strengthening the very power which now has us so completely under its thumb....

And now to the point. In our opinion, an opinion which has been formed from data obtained by assiduous researches, and comparisons, from laborious investigation, logical reasoning, and earnest reflection, the causes which have impeded the progress and prosperity of the South, which have dwindled our commerce, and other similar pursuits, into the most contemptible insignificance; sunk a large majority of our people in galling poverty and ignorance, rendered a small minority conceited and tyrannical, and driven the rest away from their homes; entailed upon us a humiliating dependence on the Free States; disgraced us in the recesses of our own souls, and brought us under reproach in the eyes of all civilized and enlightened nations—may all be traced to one common source, and there find solution in the most hateful and horrible word, that was ever incorporated into the vocabulary of human economy—*Slavery!*...

By taking a sort of inventory of the agricultural products of the free and slave States in 1850, we now propose to correct a most extraordinary and mischievous error into which the people of the South have unconsciously fallen. Agriculture, it is well known, is the sole boast of the South; and, strange to say, many pro-slavery Southerners, who, in

TABLE NO. II.   **Agricultural Products of the Slave States—1850.**

States.	Wheat, bushels.	Oats, bushels.	Indian Corn, bushels.
Alabama	294,044	2,965,696	28,754,048
Arkansas	199,639	656,183	8,893,939
Delaware	482,511	604,518	3,145,542
Florida	1,027	66,586	1,996,809
Georgia	1,088,534	3,820,044	30,080,099
Kentucky	2,142,822	8,201,311	58,672,591
Louisiana	417	89,637	10,266,373
Maryland	4,494,680	2,242,151	10,749,858
Mississippi	137,990	1,503,288	22,446,552
Missouri	2,981,652	5,278,079	36,214,537
North Carolina	2,130,102	4,052,078	27,941,051
South Carolina	1,066,277	2,322,155	16,271,454
Tennessee	1,619,386	7,703,086	52,276,223
Texas	41,729	199,017	6,028,876
Virginia	11,212,616	10,179,144	35,254,319
	27,904,476	49,882,979	348,992,282

our latitude, pass for intelligent men, are so puffed up with the idea of our importance in this respect, that they speak of the North as a sterile region, unfit for cultivation, and quite dependent on the South for the necessaries of life! Such rampant ignorance ought to be knocked in the head! We can prove that the North produces greater quantities of bread-stuffs than the South! Figures shall show the facts. Properly, the South has nothing left to boast of; the North has surpassed her in everything, and is going farther and farther ahead of her every day. We ask the reader's careful attention to the following tables, which we have prepared at no little cost of time and trouble, and which, when duly considered in connection with the foregoing and subsequent portions of our work, will, we believe, carry conviction to the mind that the downward tendency of the South can be arrested only by the abolition of slavery.

Source 5:   Emily Burke, *Reminiscences of Georgia* (1850)

New Englander Emily Burke taught for eight years in Savannah, Georgia, in the 1840s. After returning to the North, she joined a growing list of northerners who published accounts of their experiences in the South—and who often found southerners deficient in numerous ways. What is

SOURCE: Emily Burke, REMINISCENCES OF GEORGIA (1850). Originally from Emily P. Burke, REMINIS-CENCES OF GEORGIA (Oberlin, Ohio: J. M. Fitch, 1850).

Burke's view of the white people of northern Georgia? How does she explain their character? What do you think Helper and Fitzhugh would say about her conclusions?

There are but a few water-mills in the south part of Georgia, owing to a want of falls; but in the upper part of the State it is owing to a want of enterprise in the people. The northern part of Georgia, I have been told, very much resembles New Hampshire, being hilly and rocky. Those who have traveled much in that section of country, say that when compared with New England its inhabitants are all of one hundred years behind the times in education, and in all kinds of improvements. In building their houses, they change little, if any more, from one generation to another, than the robins do, who build their nests now just as the first robin did that gathered her sticks and moss, and hatched her innocent brood in the garden of Eden. As it respects conveniences for cooking, they have none. Ovens built of brick are seldom seen; when they are used, they are built out of doors, separated from any building. Iron kettles with covers, sometimes called Dutch ovens, are used when anything of the kind is needed. Most of the bread is baked before the fire on a piece of wood or earthenware. Cellars, which we consider so indispensable, are never dug, to my knowledge. I never saw one either in the city or country; consequently, we never see good butter there in the warm season; its fluid state always required a deep dish when it came upon the table. Meat is not salted and barreled as here, but smoked and dried, and generally tainted during the process. I never saw any meat preserved in this way that I could eat; and it was more than I wished to do, to sit at the table where it was. I was once passing a corn-house on a plantation with a servant woman, where I observed the smell of putrid flesh; and on making inquiry what it was, the woman informed me that it was beef drying upon the top of the house; for they dry all their meat in the summer, when they can have the benefit of a good hot July or August sun. To those educated in New England, the ignorance that is seen in many portions of the northern part of Georgia is truly astonishing; many cannot read a word, or write their own names. I have heard merchants say, that in transacting business with many men of great wealth, they have found them obliged to use a mark for their signature. This deplorable state of ignorance is owing to the circumstance, that the government has made no provision for common schools, and no children can be educated, unless they are sent from home; and board and tuition in the Southern cities are so expensive, that it requires a large fortune to educate a child; consequently but a few are educated....

This part of the population of Georgia and some of the contiguous States ... have no ambition to do any thing more than just what is necessary to procure food enough of the coarsest kind to supply the wants of the appetite, and a scanty wardrobe of a fabric they manufacture themselves. If they should ever cherish a desire for any other life than such as the brutes might lead, it would be all in vain, for the present institutions and state of society at the South are calculated to paralyze every energy of both body and mind. They are not treated with half the respect by the rich people that the slaves are, and even the slaves themselves look upon them as their inferiors. I have seen the servants when one of these poor women came into a planter's house, dressed in her homespun frock, bonnet and shawl, collect together in an adjoining room or on the piazza and indulge in a fit of laughter and ridicule about her "cracker gown and bonnet," as they would call them.

Slavery renders labor so disreputable, and wages of slave labor so low, that if places could be found where they might hire out to service, there would be but little inducement to do so.

QUESTIONS TO CONSIDER

1. How would you compare George Fitzhugh's and Hinton Rowan Helper's analyses of slavery? Both men assumed that blacks were inferior to whites, but they came to very different conclusions about slavery. How do you account for that?

2. What were the most important influences or factors in the lives or backgrounds of Fitzhugh and Helper in shaping their views about slavery? In what ways were they representative voices in the slavery debate before the Civil War? In what ways were their arguments unique?

3. Fitzhugh defended slavery by pointing to the worst features of northern society, while Helper attacked slavery by pointing to the worst features of southern society. How would you compare the men's treatments of life in the North and South? From your understanding of American society in the mid-nineteenth century, whose views do you think are more accurate?

4. Do you think Fitzhugh's or Helper's argument about slavery is more effective? How would you assess the influence of these two propagandists?

5. Helper argued for the abolition of slavery on different grounds than many other abolitionists. How would you compare his arguments to those of William Lloyd Garrison and Frederick Douglass (see Chapter 9)?

FOR FURTHER READING

David Brown, Southern Outcast: *Hinton Rowan Helper and* The Impending Crisis of the South (Baton Rouge: Louisiana State University Press, 2006), offers a biography of Helper that challenges many traditional views about him.

David F. Ericson, *The Debate over Slavery: Antislavery and Proslavery Liberalism in Antebellum America* (New York: New York University Press, 2000), studies the impact of antislavery and proslavery rhetoric on the sectional crisis.

Eugene D. Genovese, *The World the Slaveholders Made: Two Essays in Interpretation* (Hanover: Wesleyan University Press, 1969), offers an important interpretation of Fitzhugh's anti-capitalist views.

Larry E. Tise, *Proslavery: A History of the Defense of Slavery in America, 1701–1840* (Athens: University of Georgia Press, 1987), explores the development of proslavery thought.

Harvey Wish, ed., *Ante-Bellum Writings of George Fitzhugh and Hinton Rowan Helper on Slavery* (New York: Capricorn Books, 1960), provides a concise selection of the two men's writings, with a valuable introduction by the editor.

13

Yankees and "Border Ruffians" in "Bleeding Kansas": Sara Robinson and David Atchison

Sara Robinson loved springtime in her adopted eastern Kansas. In the spring of 1856, though, her enjoyment was soon replaced by thoughts of death and destruction. In May, proslavery southerners seized her husband and threw him in jail. Because she knew the "evil" men who were responsible, Robinson feared for her husband's life. She also feared that these men were not done with their awful work.

Robinson was correct. Less than two weeks after her husband's arrest, hundreds of armed proslavery men—"hoards" from hell, she called them—descended on antislavery Lawrence, Kansas. By sunset, they had looted and destroyed homes, businesses, and even the post office. They had ruined newspaper presses, and burned books and papers. On the edge of town, the Robinson home was a pile of smoldering ashes. Sara knew who was responsible for this attack. A pack of Missouri "Border Ruffians" may have done the work, but she knew there were others behind them. The real culprits were scoundrels like David Atchison!

In 1856, the Kentucky-born and frontier-bred Missourian feared for the property of *his* neighbors. A hard-drinking bear of a man, fond of profanity and sporting a Bowie knife, Atchison knew his Missouri neighbors well. Like all decent, hardworking white men, they sought only to better their lot in life. To do so they, like many Americans before them, had moved to the frontier, where they expected their property to be protected. But now they feared for one valuable kind of property—slaves. Slaveholders or not, these settlers saw slavery, like the frontier itself, as the key to individual advancement. They knew that it was protected in the states that they had moved from and also by the U.S. Constitution. They feared that Yankee abolitionists now threatened its very existence—and their rights as American citizens.

The Kansas State Historical Society

Library of Congress Prints and Photographs Division [LC-US262-109552]

Sara Robinson   David Atchison

To Atchison, teetotaling, city folk from New England had no business settling so far from their homes. The Kansas territory rightly belonged to Southerners, especially the people right next door in Missouri. He feared that if the Yankees succeeded in keeping them out of this territory, slavery was at risk everywhere. Atchison had sat in the U.S. Senate for more than a dozen years. As one of its highest-ranking members, he had played a major role in making sure that slaveholders could live in Kansas in the first place. And now he was not about to let meddling Yankees take this land away!

David Atchison and Sara Robinson were key players in a civil war between northerners and southerners in the mid-1850s that led Americans to refer to "bleeding Kansas." Though not as well known as some other defenders of slavery expansionism, Atchison's commitment to the cause ran straight from the halls of power to the bloody Kansas prairie. Likewise, petite, Massachusetts-born Robinson was not the most prominent opponent of slavery expansion in the 1850s. But her prolific pen helped publicize the plight of antislavery forces on the plains. As a result, she became one of the best-known Yankees in Kansas. As Kansas bled in the mid-1850s, this unpolished son of the frontier and determined daughter of New England were locked in a conflict that had much to do with bringing on the Civil War. At stake in Kansas, each believed, was the future of the nation.

"COMPELLED TO SHOOT, BURN & HANG"

No slavery expansionist ever exerted influence more effectively in the halls of power *and* on the Kansas sod than David Atchison. Whether from behind a podium or the barrel of a gun, Atchison worked to enforce the right of southerners to take slaves into the Kansas territory in the 1850s. Atchison's early life provided ideal preparation for his dual role.

David Rice Atchison was born in 1807 in a Kentucky only a generation removed from its raw frontier beginnings. In the late eighteenth century, his father's family, of Scots-Irish descent, had moved there from Pennsylvania to "bluegrass country" near present-day Lexington in search of a better life. Although David was born in a modest cottage on the family's farm, his father would find prosperity, and three more sons and a daughter followed. The growing family, however, did not provide all the labor for their roughly 450-acre spread. Shortly after David's birth, his father acquired one slave. Twenty years later, he had added seven more—a sign that the move to the frontier had paid off.

With the family in comfortable circumstances, in the fall of 1821, fourteen-year-old David headed off to Lexington's Transylvania College. There he made friends with classmates who would later help him in politics. Founded in 1788 by Presbyterians, Transylvania was one of the best-known and largest colleges in the country and in the 1820s could boast an impressive roster of graduates. Indeed, five of Atchison's classmates would go on to serve with him in the U.S. Senate, including the future Confederate president Jefferson Davis of Mississippi. By the time he graduated in 1825 at the age of eighteen, young Atchison had already decided on a career. After studying law for two years under a former Kentucky senator and member of Transylvania's faculty, Atchison opened a practice in Carlisle, Kentucky, some thirty-five miles northwest of Lexington.

Soon, however, the ambitious son of a Kentucky frontiersman grew restless. By the late 1820s, the frontier had moved west to the Missouri River. So in 1830 Atchison headed to Clay County in western Missouri, where he hung his lawyer's shingle once again. Fond of horses, hunting, and socializing, the burly six-foot two-inch Atchison fit in well with his new neighbors. He demonstrated what one newspaper would call an "easy and unaffected" manner and quickly established a thriving practice.

Atchison demonstrated his ample legal and political skills when he took on the potentially dangerous work of defending some unpopular newcomers to western Missouri. Soon after his arrival in Clay County, a small group of Mormons moved to nearby Independence. The Mormons were followers of Joseph Smith, who claimed to be a prophet and in 1830 founded the Church of Jesus Christ of Latter-day Saints in upstate New York. Smith moved his church to Ohio in 1831 and later the same year to western Missouri. Here, as elsewhere, the Mormons were harassed and assaulted by suspicious non-Mormons and in 1833 church leaders turned to Atchison for legal assistance. For the next seven years, Atchison devoted much of his time to defending the rights of Mormons against the depredations committed by his own neighbors. While risking the enmity of non-Mormons, Atchison won the support of his grateful clients and in 1834 they helped elect him to the lower house of Missouri's state legislature. There Atchison became a loyal follower of another Scots-Irish son of the frontier, President Andrew Jackson, founder of the Democratic Party and an advocate of westward expansion. Elected to a second two-year term in 1838, Atchison continued to straddle the divide between Mormons and non-Mormons. Although Missouri authorities would drive the Latter-day Saints from the state in 1839, Atchison as a division commander in the state militia defied the anti-Mormon governor's proclamation that Smith's followers "should be exterminated or expelled from the State." His troops, he declared, would not be permitted to "disgrace the State and themselves by acting the part of a mob."

Atchison was defeated in the Whig victory of 1840, but his political career was not over. While serving in the assembly, he played an important role in carving out several new counties in western Missouri, one of which would be named in his honor. In 1841, the new governor recommended Atchison's appointment as the first circuit judge for the area and he was quickly confirmed by the state senate. Riding his five-county circuit, the affable Atchison had numerous opportunities to win people over with frontier charm. Increasingly popular in Democratic Party circles, he was the logical choice to fill the seat of Missouri's junior U.S. senator, who died unexpectedly in 1843. As one Missouri newspaper put it, his "knowledge of the wants and rights of the hardy pioneer … will render him one of the most useful members of the Senate."

At age thirty-six, full of jokes and a good story, Missouri's new junior senator cut a popular figure in the Senate. It did not hurt that he knew several of his colleagues from his college days. Less than three years after he entered the Senate, fellow Democrats chose him as its president pro tempore (to preside over the body in the absence of the vice president) and repeatedly reelected him to the post. In fact, few senators would ever put their ability to get along with people to better use in service of the "hardy pioneer."

It was an opportune time to do so. The year after Atchison entered the Senate in 1843, expansionist fever gripped the country. Before long, Americans would proclaim their nation's "Manifest Destiny" to overspread the continent. Expansionism quickly infected politics and in 1844 helped elect militant expansionist James K. Polk president. Before the end of his term, "Manifest Destiny" had been fulfilled. The United States had annexed Texas, acquired more than half of the Oregon Territory, defeated Mexico in the Mexican War, and seized from it the area between Texas and the Pacific, including California.

Missouri's "frontier" senator wholeheartedly supported an expansionist program. He had played a key role in promoting the settlement of Oregon, jointly occupied until 1846 by Great Britain and the United States. He supported legislation calling for fortifications along the Oregon Trail and land for settlers in the territory. He even supported an American claim to the Oregon Country all the way to the Yukon border. He voted for the annexation of Texas and war with Mexico. And after the Mexican War, when many Americans talked of building a railroad to the Pacific to open the West for further settlement, Atchison worked to prepare the way.

In 1854, Democrat Stephen A. Douglas introduced legislation to promote the construction of a transcontinental railroad line. As a senator from Illinois and land speculator in Chicago, Douglas desperately wanted the transcontinental route to link California to the Midwest. One obstacle, however, was the huge area on the plains that had not yet been organized as territory. Without territorial government to protect people and property, no railroad company would dare lay track over this land. But Douglas knew that getting Congress to agree to organize this area into a territory would be difficult. The Missouri Compromise of 1820 prohibited slavery north of the 36°30′ parallel line, and the area in question lay above that line. No one had to tell Douglas that his Southern colleagues in Congress would not support the organization of more free territory and, ultimately, more free states. Yet Douglas thought he knew how to proceed. His legislation proposed, without mentioning the Missouri Compromise at all, to create a new territory—Nebraska—and allow the settlers there to decide the slavery issue by popular vote. In other words, Douglas's bill refused to confront the legal prohibition on slavery in this area, but opened the possibility that southerners could take their slaves into it.

For Atchison, that was not enough. The Missouri senator had been galvanized by Northern efforts to keep slavery out of the territory won from Mexico. As he told his constituents after the defeat of the Wilmot Proviso, which would have banned slavery from territory taken from Mexico, it was the free states' "fixed design" to prevent southerners from further "participation" in the western territories and to reduce them "to a state of *helpless inferiority*." In other words, he had come to stand squarely with John C. Calhoun and other powerful Southern colleagues in the Senate over the absolute right of slaveholders to take their property into the new territory. **[See Source 1.]**

Atchison now put his talents to work behind the scenes to get the Missouri Compromise repealed *outright*. He had already worked closely with Douglas on other railroad legislation. Democratic president Franklin Pierce was under pressure from northerners in his own party not to reopen—and inflame—the issue of slavery in the territories. Meeting with Douglas and Atchison, however, he agreed to support Atchison's position. Douglas then quickly amended his bill to include an outright repeal of the Missouri Compromise (and a division of the area in question into two territories—Kansas and Nebraska).

When Congress passed the Kansas–Nebraska Act later in 1854, it was only because it garnered sufficient Southern support. Douglas had his Missouri colleague to thank for that. Many northerners, of course, were outraged and would soon stream into the new Republican Party, which would take a stand against the further spread of slavery into the territories. Once word of Atchison's meeting with Pierce and Douglas leaked out, angry northerners also realized Atchison's key role. One New York paper sarcastically reported that Atchison had dined at the White House, where "all talked lovingly about democracy." Some observers whispered that the Missouri Democrat was the actual author of the amendment repealing the Missouri Compromise. Almost overnight Atchison became to many northerners the symbol of the "Slave Power's" influence in the Congress—living proof of the devious slaveholders' conspiracy to take over the government and spread slavery everywhere!

Atchison had little time to relish his victory. The ink from President Pierce's signature on Douglas's bill was hardly dry when disturbing rumors reached western Missouri and Washington. New Englanders, it was said, had already organized an emigrant aid society and armed it with five million dollars to assist the settlement of Yankees in the Kansas Territory. Under the Kansas–Nebraska Act's provision of popular sovereignty, which let the territorial settlers vote on the slavery issue, a meddling horde of abolitionists could soon take away the "right" of southerners to occupy this land.

Atchison was not about to let abolitionist Yankees on the ground in Kansas overturn what he had just helped achieve in the halls of Congress. That summer, he raced home to spread the word about this threat and help his fellow Missourians counter it. Atchison, former commander in the state militia, knew that his fellow southerners—and a lot of them—must be mobilized to meet this Yankee threat in no uncertain terms. In one speech, he urged his western Missouri constituents "to give a horse thief, robber, or homicide a fair trial, but to hang a negro thief or Abolitionist, without judge or jury." That sentiment, as he reported to Secretary of War Jefferson Davis, "met almost universal applause." Atchison went on to assure Davis that "we are organizing to meet their organization." Then he concluded ominously: "We will be compelled to shoot, burn & hang, but the thing will soon be over."

"HOMESTEAD OF THE FREE!"

As David Atchison's buggy raced over the rough western Missouri roads in the summer in 1854, some twelve hundred miles away in Massachusetts Sara Robinson was alarmed too. News of the Kansas–Nebraska Act had shocked antislavery New Englanders. Slavery had earlier been barred "forever" from this area, but now Kansas could eventually become a slave state, opening the door for slavery to spread even further. Thus, while

Atchison rallied his neighbors to prepare for a Yankee invasion of the Kansas Territory, Robinson was busy preparing to keep Kansas free by moving there. Given her background, the life she would find on the Kansas prairie would be new in many ways.

Sara Robinson was born Sara Tappan Doolittle Lawrence in Belchertown, Massachusetts, in 1827 into very favorable circumstances. Her father, an attorney, became a Massachusetts state legislator at twenty-seven, later served in the state senate, and was eventually nominated for governor on a temperance ticket. He was also related to Amos Lawrence, whose father had made a fortune investing in textile mills in Lowell, Massachusetts (see Chapter 8). As a member of a leading New England family, Sara witnessed a steady stream of influential visitors to her father's house, including Senator Daniel Webster and writer Harriet Martineau. Unlike most young women of her day, she also had an opportunity to pursue education beyond the rudiments. She attended the Belchertown Classical School and the nearby New Salem Academy, where the curriculum included more than the "ornamental" arts often associated with female education. Sara learned Latin and was fluent in French and German. Meanwhile, her father would instill in her a love of literature and politics.

One incident marred Sara's privileged life—and changed its course. While a student, she suffered a severe fall on some stone steps. The accident injured her spine, causing temporary blindness. During Sara's long recuperation, her family brought in physician Charles Robinson, who had just recently established a practice in the area. Already balding, Robinson was physically unimposing. And he was surely not the most prominent man to set foot in the well-appointed Lawrence home. To his patient, however, he no doubt cut an impressive figure.

Nine years older than Sara, Robinson already had a lifetime of experiences under his belt—and harrowing tales to prove it. After graduating from Amherst College and then earning a medical degree, Robinson settled down in Belchertown, married, and fathered two children. By 1846, though, his wife and both infants had died, and shortly thereafter he suffered a breakdown. Robinson quit his practice and signed on as a physician with a party of gold seekers traveling to California. After a brief sojourn in the gold fields, he settled in Sacramento, where he practiced medicine and became a newspaper editor. There he also took up the cause of "squatters' rights" in a fight that pitted settlers or "squatters" against land speculators. Robinson was shot during this struggle, but managed to fatally wound his assailant before passing out. Arrested and charged with conspiracy and murder, he was thrown onto a prison ship before being tried and acquitted. Robinson next won a seat in the California legislature, where he stood against the extension of slavery in the West. By 1851, however, Robinson had had enough of frontier life in the Far West. Recovered from his physical *and* psychological wounds, he returned to Massachusetts in 1851 to take up medicine again.

Under Robinson's care, Sara recovered completely from her injury. The patient and her physician soon began a courtship. Sara was slightly built, but Robinson found her "quite pretty" and an "exceedingly agreeable young woman, very unpretending, [and] plainly dressed." The couple married in 1851. While Charles practiced medicine and edited a newspaper, the Robinsons settled down, apparently to live out their lives in a quiet New England town. Douglas's introduction of the Kansas–Nebraska Act in Congress changed their plans.

In the spring of 1854, Charles Robinson attended an antislavery meeting conducted by an enterprising Yankee reformer and state legislator named Eli Thayer. Even before Douglas's bill passed Congress, Thayer founded the New England Emigrant Aid Society, chartered by the Massachusetts state legislature to move Yankees to the Kansas Territory and turn a profit by selling land and operating productive enterprises of its own. With their thriving businesses, churches, schools, and free farmers planted in the Kansas sod, Thayer believed, Yankees would demonstrate the superiority of free over slave labor. The antislavery Robinson saw an opportunity to do well by doing good and a short time later offered his services to Thayer.

Not everyone responded the same way to Thayer's pitch, though. His society, later reorganized as a company, was authorized to issue up to $5 million in stock. But there were few takers—until Sara Robinson's relative Amos Lawrence stepped in. Originally a moderate or "Cotton" Whig, Lawrence did not wish to endanger the Union, jeopardize the textile industry's close relationship with the cotton-producing South, or alienate his own party's southern wing. By 1854, however, he had changed his mind. Along with Patrick Jackson, another "lord of the loom," Lawrence also invested a substantial sum of money in Thayer's organization. In the process, these "men of affairs" took control of what was now known as the Emigrant Aid Company. They made sure that it disassociated itself from abolitionism. Lawrence demanded that no abolitionists—people who wanted to overturn slavery in the Southern states as opposed to those who merely wanted to halt its expansion—be allowed to serve as directors. He preferred to see Kansas fill up with hardworking, upright Yankees, but not at the expense of peace with the South.

Lawrence viewed Charles Robinson as the perfect man to spearhead the company's settlement of Kansas. Robinson had already traveled to Kansas, where "squatter sovereignty" would soon decide the slavery issue. He had earlier risked his life in a similar struggle in California. He was reliable—firmly antislavery, but no hothead. And, of course, he had married a Lawrence. In the summer of 1854, Thayer and Lawrence named Robinson a general agent of the company with a $1,000 salary and a commission on all company sales to settlers. They also sent him on a scouting expedition to find suitable spots for settlement. After returning to Massachusetts, Robinson left for Kansas once again at the end of the summer, taking a party of some seventy men, women, and children. The Quaker antislavery poet John Greenleaf Whittier wrote a poem for the departing settlers:

> We cross the prairie as of old
> The pilgrims crossed sea,
> To make the West, as they did the East,
> The homestead of the free!

Once there, Robinson selected a site along the banks of the Kansas River to serve as the company's headquarters. Then he laid out a town and named it Lawrence in honor of the company's chief benefactor.

Charles returned home in early 1855, and when he left again in March to lead another group of emigrants to Kansas, Sara accompanied him. Leaving Boston in a driving snowstorm, the party of some two hundred settlers traveled west by rail and steamboat and arrived in Kansas City twelve days later. Sara's diary noted the spring wild flowers in bloom. After buying provisions in Kansas City, Sara finally arrived at Lawrence in April.

Sara's new home, a partially built cabin, was a far cry from the one she had known back east. Her first morning there, she woke to find a cow standing in the middle of the unfinished dining room. Later that summer, the couple found a rattlesnake curled up behind the stove. Yet the raw circumstances failed to diminish Sara's enthusiasm. "We have reveled," she would write in her diary, "in flowers under our windows and at our doors." Eastern Kansas, she proclaimed, was the "Eden of America." Located on a hill overlooking Lawrence, her new home commanded a view "unequalled for extent, or variety of loveliness, for miles in all directions." From this perch, Sara would have a unique perspective on developments in Kansas: settlers pouring into the area, the intrusions of David Atchison's "ruffians," and the transformation of popular sovereignty into open warfare.

"WHITE SLAVES"

Sara was not in Lawrence long before she noted the continual "change of faces" as newcomers arrived and others left. The Emigrant Aid Company alone had led six parties and nearly six hundred settlers to Kansas in 1854. Many more, including Sara's group, continued to arrive in 1855. To accommodate them, her husband's company had been busy founding other communities, including Topeka and Manhattan. In time, it would be responsible for sending about three thousand settlers to Kansas. Yet New Englanders were always significantly outnumbered by other northerners. Often they hailed from areas of the Old Northwest that had not been settled by New Englanders. Unlike the Robinsons, these free-state migrants had no desire to battle slavery. They were drawn to Kansas only to advance themselves. Southerners like Atchison never made any distinction among northerners. But many free-state settlers often resented New Englanders. With their schools and churches and opposition to alcohol and slavery, they seemed too anxious to impose their culture on the plains. As one newspaper editor declared, they were "mere Sunday school *children*." Meanwhile, Missourians and other southerners had also moved into Kansas by early 1855. Of the eight thousand five hundred people in Kansas by that spring fewer than two hundred were slaves. Nonetheless, newcomers from the South—mostly Missourians—made up nearly 60 percent of the population, with strongholds at Leavenworth and Atchison, named in honor of Missouri's "frontier" senator.

The situation did not bode well for antislavery Yankees when popular sovereignty was put into effect. As it happened, Sara arrived in Kansas on the eve of elections for the territorial legislature. In fact, before leaving Kansas City for Lawrence she had noticed numerous "desperados" on their way into Kansas armed with whiskey and "death-dealing instruments" and talking loudly about driving out "free-state men." They were the fruits of David Atchison's work.

Atchison was not about to take any chances in this election. After all, whoever controlled the territorial legislature would draft the laws about slavery. "[W]e must meet and conquer [the abolitionists]," he declared, "peaceably if we can[,] forcibly if we must." To that end, Atchison helped organize bands of armed Missourians—"Border Ruffians" as they came to be called in the Northern press—to cross the border by the hundreds to vote. Reportedly with revolver and Bowie knife strapped to his waist, he went with them. Although Atchison later denied that he carried weapons into Kansas or voted there, he did admit later that his presence was "great encouragement to the boys."

Whatever Atchison's role in the Kansas election, the vote in the spring of 1855 for the territorial legislature was decisive. The proslavery total was more than five thousand four hundred of the roughly six thousand ballots cast. "What a glorious thing it was," declared Atchison. Yet the Missouri senator may have done his work too well. The 1855 census found fewer than three thousand voters in the territory. A later congressional investigation concluded that only about one thousand four hundred of the votes were legal. Rather than settle the slavery issue in Kansas, the election only set the stage for violent confrontation.

Among free-state settlers, Sara Robinson's reaction—that Atchison's Missourians had stolen the election—was typical. "Will these frauds be allowed?" she wondered. Proslavery settlers in Kansas probably had enough votes to win without chicanery. Like many northerners, however, Sara concluded that the election was "connived ... to force slavery into Kansas against the desire of the actual settlers." Because the Missourians' "theft" of the election seemed so obvious to many Northern settlers—New Englander and non-New Englander alike—David Atchison had unintentionally given them the grounds to come together to defend *their* rights as voters. Many of these same northerners were outraged by the Kansas–Nebraska Act, which had put popular sovereignty into effect. Now a defense of their liberties as white citizens under popular sovereignty became their rallying cry. When proslavery residents organized a territorial legislature that summer based on the spring election results, the administration of President Franklin Pierce recognized it as legitimate. Free soilers,* however, quickly labeled it "bogus," created "by force and fraud." And they connected the direst consequences to it. As Sara Robinson declared in her diary, "We in Kansas already feel the iron heel of the oppressor, making us truly white slaves."

United in the belief that proslavery forces were attacking their rights, free soilers elected delegates to a convention that fall to write a free-state constitution. Comparing themselves to the revolutionaries of 1776, they declared that the people had the right to "abolish governments." Delegate Charles Robinson, who was opposed to slavery itself, proposed a provision for black suffrage in the Constitution. But he quickly realized that calling for black rights would not unite white northerners in Kansas. Only emphasizing "the invasion of their own civil and political rights" would do that. That insight paid off. In elections held by free soilers early in 1856, Robinson was elected governor. The Kansas Territory now had two constitutions and two governments: the proslavery government at Lecompton, recognized as official by President Franklin Pierce; and the free soil government at Topeka, headed by Charles Robinson and quickly condemned by southerners and Pierce as "treasonable."

Threatened by the "iron heel" of the "slave power," free soilers prepared for armed conflict. Shipments of rifles from the East began to arrive in the spring of 1855, some purchased with funds from the New England Emigrant Aid Company. Others were financed by prominent northerners such as Henry Ward Beecher, Catharine Beecher's brother (see Chapter 10). Some of the weapons arrived in boxes marked as books (and were quickly dubbed "Beecher's Bibles"). After the arms arrived, many Lawrence residents broke them in with target practice using pictures of David Atchison. In Lawrence, they also built a new hotel. With walls two feet thick and portholes at the top that could easily accommodate guns, the Free-State Hotel looked to proslavery men suspiciously like an abolitionist fortress. By the end of 1855, Sara Robinson's diary noted the "forts and entrenchments" thrown up around Lawrence and the companies of armed men who drilled near her home. It also detailed the deaths of two free soilers at the hands of proslavery men.

Early the next year, proslavery forces moved to put down the "treasonous" free-soil government. As it assembled at Topeka and Charles Robinson and other leaders took their oaths, a proslavery sheriff wrote down their names. Then a judge called a grand jury to indict the free-state officials, who had returned to Lawrence. The jury also ordered the destruction of the new Free-State Hotel and free-state newspapers in Lawrence as nuisances. Soon, as Sara Robinson noted, "rumors were afloat" in Lawrence that large companies of men were gathering to attack the town. If the free-soil leaders were not handed over, Lawrence would be sacked. If these rumors were true, she concluded, the "bloody tools of slavery" would "strike the blow at the foot of all republican liberty."

Free soilers: People who sought to keep slavery out of federal territories in the West.

"BLOW THEM TO HELL WITH A CHUNK
OF COLD LEAD"

On May 20, a federal marshal entered the "nasty Abolition town," as one southerner called it, to make several arrests. The next day, a proslavery sheriff accompanied by up to seven hundred men arrived to carry out the rest of the court order. After failing to bring down the Free-State Hotel with cannon shots, the intruders finally gutted it with fire. As the hotel went up in flames, the invaders ransacked the town. The Robinson home, of course, was a prime target, and by the end of the day it had been consumed in flames.

Sara Robinson never saw the burning embers of her home. Nearly two weeks before the attack on Lawrence, Topeka government officials decided that Charles Robinson, a warrant hanging over his head, should travel east to seek assistance for the beleaguered free soilers. Sara accompanied him. Shortly after boarding a Missouri River steamboat, however, the "governor" was arrested. As he was hauled off to jail in Leavenworth, Missourians threatened to kill him. Already one free soiler entrusted to proslavery authorities had not lived to tell about it. Sara was terrified, but continued on. Hidden in her clothing were papers handed to her by a congressional committee investigating conditions in Kansas. Her mission was to deliver them to Republicans in Washington, D.C. After arriving in the East, Sara also worked to secure her husband's release. That summer, she sent a letter to Amos Lawrence's mother, Franklin Pierce's aunt. She, in turn, sent it to the First Lady, who then gave it to the president. Later in 1856, Charles would be released unharmed after nearly four months in captivity. Meanwhile, Sara's role as a publicist for the free-soil cause in Kansas had begun. **[See Source 2.]**

The "sack of Lawrence," as free soilers called it, was the opening engagement in a guerrilla war on the eastern Kansas prairie in the late 1850s. Only a few days later, an abolitionist named John Brown, who had arrived in Kansas just the year before, decided to take action. Brown believed that the free-soil movement in Kansas was ineffectual. Charles Robinson, he concluded, was "a perfect old woman." Convinced that it was time to fight violence with violence, Brown led a band of men on a killing rampage near Pottawatomie Creek in southeastern Kansas. When they were done, five nonslaveholding southerners lay dead, shot and viciously mutilated with swords. By the end of the year, roughly fifty more free soilers and proslavery settlers lay dead in "bleeding Kansas."

Both free soilers and proslavery forces were to blame for the guerrilla war that raged in Kansas until 1861. As ballots gave way to bullets, the Emigrant Aid Company and those who supported it bore some of the blame. So did David Atchison. Responding to Brown's attack in August, Atchison marched a "Grand Army" of roughly 450 Missourians into Kansas and engaged in a battle with Brown and his men that left six more dead. Even before that, however, the actions of his armed "Border Ruffians" led many free soilers to arm themselves. Moreover, many of his speeches were incendiary, calling on southerners to counter the "abolitionist" migration with organized armed efforts of their own. As he declared in one such message, "We want men—armed men."

As open warfare broke out on the Kansas prairie in 1856, it was no accident that Atchison's public pronouncements became fodder in a propaganda war between northerners and southerners. And no one better illustrated how effective that propaganda could be than Sara Robinson. In *Kansas: Its Interior and Exterior Life,* published in Boston in 1856, Robinson recounted her move to Kansas. Based on the diary she had kept, it offered an insider's history of the free soilers' travails. As more news about events in "bleeding Kansas" filled the nation's newspapers, her book found a receptive audience among shocked northerners and racked up impressive sales. No one did more to arouse northerners over the threat of the "slave power" to white liberties in Kansas. **[See Source 3.]** Sara was in the East, of course, when the proslavery posse descended on Lawrence and destroyed much of the town. But that did not stop her from offering her own version of events that day. In her retelling, David Atchison himself stood before the "vile" invaders and exhorted them to do their duty to "your Southern friends." Then he concluded: "If one man or woman dare stand before you, blow them to h——l with a chunk of cold lead." **[See Source 4.]**

Ironically, for all of Atchison's inflamed rhetoric, he did not wish to see proslavery men commit violent acts that might play right into free soilers' hands. Thus, when proslavery forces surrounded Lawrence the year before its "sack," Atchison helped negotiate a peaceful resolution. His role in the sack of 1856 is debatable. Robinson's version of Atchison's speech was one of several that circulated in the Northern press afterward—all of them different. One Missouri newspaper and Atchison himself later denied that he gave any of those speeches, although he admitted that he had made several that day. He went on to claim that he had actually sought to restrain the proslavery sheriff who led the posse into Lawrence. "I spoke," he said, "in the interest of peace—exerting myself to check, not to incite, outrage."

If Atchison's role that day is unclear, his subsequent actions are not. Already in 1855, he had lost his Senate seat in a fight in the Missouri legislature between his backers and Democrats who refused to side with slavery expansionists. Yet Atchison had lost none of his desire to fight the "abolitionist threat." And in doing so, he demonstrated that he had learned something from free soilers. Sara Robinson and other free-soil propagandists had effectively portrayed free soilers as martyrs, oppressed by the "slave power" and its clever leader, David Atchison, who intended to rob whites of their rights and debase them to "slavery." And they had found in a defense of popular sovereignty an effective way to unite free-state whites. As Kansas descended into guerrilla war, Atchison turned to similar appeals. Proslavery forces in Kansas were martyrs. They faced a clever leader (Sara's husband!) who carried out the abolitionists' designs to destroy the South. And whites had to unite to prevent their own degradation at the hands of the wicked enemy. As Atchison declared in 1856, the loss of Kansas imperiled the entire white race. Whites, he asserted, would "sink to the level of the freed African." **[See Source 5.]**

For Atchison, however, it was too late. In another territorial election in 1857, free soilers won. And for all his militant rhetoric, Atchison's efforts to rally the South to support the proslavery cause in Kansas fell short. Southerners outside Missouri failed to move there in numbers matching those assisted by the Emigrant Aid Company alone. Atchison repeatedly condemned complacent fellow southerners for failing to see that the battle there would determine the future of the entire South and for failing to do their part in shaping the outcome. As he lamented in 1857, "our friends in the South are very apathetic."

Meanwhile, the damage caused by "bleeding Kansas" had been done. One obvious casualty was Atchison's reputation. More important blows struck the Union and the proslavery cause, itself. "Bleeding Kansas"—and the free-soil propaganda that emerged from it—enraged many northerners, who in the late 1850s continued to stream into the anti slavery-expansion Republican Party. The new party's platform condemned the fraudulent voting and violence in Kansas—and called for its admission as a free state. Enraged by the "crime against Kansas," Republicans in Congress also blocked its admission under the LeCompton constitution. Southerners, in turn, saw in this party a growing "abolitionist" threat to slavery.

By 1857, David Atchison realized the futility of the struggle in Kansas. By then, he had retired to his 1,500-acre farm in Clinton County, Missouri. There he watched the growing sectional crisis lead to secession and war. As the owner of sixteen slaves, he had a large personal stake in the institution that he had defended so boldly. During the Civil War, he supported a pro-Confederate government in Missouri as well as the Confederate war effort. After the war, he returned to his farm where he lived, a life-long bachelor, until his death in 1886.

Meanwhile, Sara Robinson saw Republicans bring Kansas into the Union as a free state in 1861 and her husband's election that year as the new state's first governor. She also had to witness, however, another "sack" of Lawrence when pro-Confederate guerrillas invaded it in 1863, destroyed much of the town, and left nearly 150 people dead. After the war, Sara and her husband lived on Oakridge, their country estate four miles outside Lawrence. Sara and her husband never had children. But as they surveyed Oakridge, the Robinsons could take satisfaction in something else: they had done very well indeed by doing good. And Sara could take delight every spring in the prairie's brilliant display of flowers. After Charles died in 1894, Sara continued living there until she died in 1911.

Only much later would historians get a reminder of Sara Robinson's and David Atchison's impact in the 1850s. Modern historians calculate that far fewer people actually died in "bleeding Kansas" than previously thought. Fewer than sixty people lay dead by 1861—not two hundred as so long thought. That longstanding overestimate reveals a lot about the impact of this bloodshed on the popular imagination. And that, in turn, is testament to the power of the propaganda war waged over Kansas. Robinson's and Atchison's war of words played a large role in shaping—and distorting—perceptions of northerners and southerners. As those words hardened feelings on each side, the entire nation verged much closer to a real war.

• PRIMARY SOURCES •

Source 1:   John C. Calhoun, *"Address to the People of the Southern States"* (1849)

In response to Northern efforts during the Mexican War to limit the spread of slavery into western territories, South Carolina senator John C. Calhoun drafted an address that was signed by David Atchison and forty-seven other congressmen. On what grounds does it defend the right of slaveholders to move into federal territories? Why do you think Calhoun may have taken this position?

[W]e hold that the Federal Government has no right to extend or restrict slavery, no more than to establish or abolish it; nor has it any right whatever to distinguish between the domestic institutions of one State, or section, and another, in order to favor the one and discourage the other. As the federal representative of each and all the States, it is bound to deal out, within the sphere of its powers, equal and exact justice and favor to

SOURCE: John C. Calhoun, "Address to the People of the Southern States" (1849).

all. To act otherwise, to undertake to discriminate between the domestic institutions of one and another, would be to act in total subversion of the end for which it was established—to be the common protector and guardian of all. Entertaining these opinions, we ask not, as the North alleges we do, for the extension of slavery. That would make a discrimination in our favor, as unjust and unconstitutional as the discrimination they ask against us in their favor. It is not for them, nor for the Federal Government to determine, whether our domestic institution is good or bad; or whether it should be repressed or preserved. It belongs to us, and us only, to decide such questions. What then we do insist on, is, not to extend slavery, but that we shall not be prohibited from immigrating with our property, into the Territories of the United States, because we are slaveholders; or, in other words, that we shall not on that account be disfranchised of a privilege possessed by all others, citizens and foreigners, without discrimination as to character, profession, or color. All, whether savage, barbarian, or civilized, may freely enter and remain, we only being excluded.

We rest our claim, not only on the high grounds above stated, but also on the solid foundation of right, justice, and equality. The territories immediately in controversy— New Mexico and California—were acquired by the common sacrifice and efforts of all the States, towards which the South contributed far more than her full share of men, to say nothing of money, and is, of course, on every principle of right, justice, fairness, and equality, entitled to participate fully in the benefits to be derived from their acquisition. But as impregnable as is this ground, there is another not less so. Ours is a Federal Government—a Government in which not individuals, but States, as distinct sovereign communities, are the constituents. To them, as members of the Federal Union, the territories belong; and they are hence declared to be territories belonging to the United States. The States, then, are the joint owners. Now it is conceded by all writers on the subject, that in all such Governments their members are all equal—equal in rights and equal in dignity. They also concede that this equality constitutes the basis of such Government, and that it cannot be destroyed without changing their nature and character. To deprive, then, the Southern States and their citizens of their full share in territories declared to belong to them, in common with the other States, would be in derogation of the equality belonging to them as members of a Federal Union, and sink them, from being equals, into a subordinate and dependent condition.

Source 2:   *Report of the Committee to Investigate the Troubles in Kansas* (1856)

When Sara Robinson traveled east after the arrest of her husband in Missouri in May 1856, she carried with her documents to alert Republicans to the situation in Kansas regarding territorial elections. The House of Representatives had already formed a committee to investigate what Republicans called the "crime against Kansas," and the documents carried by Robinson were evidence for that investigation. This excerpt from the final report contains some of the committee's conclusions. To what does the report attribute the outcome of the elections in Kansas? How does it reflect a fear that the rights of whites were threatened by proslavery forces in Kansas?

SOURCE: "Report of the Commitee to Investigate the Troubles in Kansas" (1856). From REPORT OF THE SPECIAL COMMITTEE APPOINTED TO INVESTIGATE THE TROUBLES IN KANSAS, WITH THE VIEW OF THE MINORITY OF SAID COMMITTEE (Washington, D.C.: C. Wendell, Printer, 1856), pp. 2–3.

Within a few days after the [Kansas-Nebraska] law passed, and as soon as its passage could be known on the border, leading citizens of Missouri crossed into the Territory, held squatter meetings, and then returned to their homes. Among their resolutions are the following:

"That we will afford protection to no abolitionist as a settler of this Territory."

"That we recognise the institution of slavery as already existing in this Territory, and advise slaveholders to introduce their property as early as possible."

Similar resolutions were passed in various parts of the Territory, and by meetings in several counties of Missouri. Thus the first effect of the repeal of the restriction against slavery was to substitute the resolves of squatter meetings, composed almost exclusively of citizens of a single State, for the deliberate action of Congress acquiesced in for thirty-five years.

This unlawful interference has been continued in every important event in the history of the Territory; *every election* has been controlled, not by the actual settlers, but by citizens of Missouri; and, as a consequence, every officer in the Territory, from constable to legislators, except those appointed by the President, owe their positions to nonresident voters. None have been elected by the settlers; and your committee have been unable to find that any political power whatever, however unimportant, has been exercised by the people of the Territory.

In October, a. d. 1854, Gov. A. H. Reeder, and the other officers appointed by the President, arrived in the Territory. Settlers from all parts of the country were moving in in great numbers, making their claims and building their cabins. About the same time, and before any election was or could be held in the Territory, a secret political society was formed in the State of Missouri. It was known by different names, such as "Social Band," "Friends' Society," "Blue Lodge," "The Sons of the South." Its members were bound together by secret oaths, and they had pass-words, signs, and grips, by which they were known to each other; penalties were imposed for violating the rules and secrets of the order; written minutes were kept of the proceedings of the lodges; and the different lodges were connected together by an effective organization. It embraced great numbers of the citizens of Missouri, and was extended into other slave States and into the Territory. Its avowed purpose was not only to extend slavery into Kansas, but also into other territories of the United States, and to form a union of all the friends of that institution. Its plan of operating was to organize and send men to vote at the elections in the Territory, to collect money to pay their expenses, and, if necessary, to protect them in voting.... While the great body of the actual settlers of the Territory were relying upon the rights secured to them by the [Kansas-Nebraska] law, and had formed no organization or combination whatever, even of a party character, this conspiracy against their rights was gathering strength in a neighboring State, and would have been sufficient at their first election to have overpowered them, even if they had been united to a man.

Source 3:   *Sara Robinson on "Bleeding Kansas"* (1856)

Sara Robinson's diary, published as Kansas: Its Interior and Exterior Life, *reflected the views of many antislavery Kansas settlers. How does this free-soil propaganda tract appeal to a largely Northern female audience?*

SOURCE: Sara Robinson on "Bleeding Kansas" (1856). From Sara Robinson, KANSAS: ITS INTERIOR AND EXTERIOR LIFE (Boston: Crosby, Nichols and Company, 1856), pp. 7–8.

The whole country was moved at the prospect of such an outrage as this bill proposed— the annulling of a sacred compact, the breaking of a plighted faith. How, through all that long season of discussion upon the bill, more than three months, every freedom-loving heart was moved to hope this great wrong might not be committed! How every honest feeling was stirred at the eloquent words of ... all our noble men in Congress, who battled mightily against this evil! We can never forget what indignation fired the veins of all lovers of God and men, as the wires brought news of the indignity offered to New England's three thousand protesting clergymen, and what shame mantled the cheek of many to remember that the Benedict Arnold of the age should have been born of any *woman* in a beautiful, thriving town nestled amid the Green Mountains. Well will the North remember how the womanly element mingled its influence to stay this current of evil; how the protests, with many thousands of names, poured in through all the avenues of communication to the capital. Woman's heart was touched; all the deep sympathies of her nature were stirred; and, while hourly she prayed that no new field of suffering and woe should be opened for her down-trodden and oppressed sister, she acted too, and, through the melting snows of early spring, each woman in many towns was called upon for her signature, by one of her own sex. Could she see this great country—only a little less in extent than Italy, France, and Spain, together—thrown open to the foul inroads of slavery, so that no woman with black blood in her veins could be a welcome inmate of her father's house, feel safe in the protection of a husband's love, or, in caressing the children God gave her, call them her own, and make no effort in their behalf? No. It was not thus, thank God! Men felt, and women felt. Notwithstanding all that was done, and all that was felt, the bill, odious in the sight of God and hateful to man, was passed. Mr. Sumner made his final protest, for himself and the New England clergy, against slavery in Kansas and Nebraska, upon the night of the final passage of the Nebraska and Kansas Bill, May 25, 1854. After a most stormy and contentious debate, on Sunday morning the bill was passed. The slave power was again triumphant. A consolidated despotism was striving to crush out every aspiration for truth, for goodness, for freedom, from every free-born soul. Southern men argued that by this new compromise the agitation in our country would cease, and peace be restored. How has it been? Civil feud, strife, and continual agitation, have been the result in all communities. The "crime against Kansas" consummated in Congress, the infraction of solemn obligations, has been acted over in frauds upon the ballot-box in Kansas, and has been the occasion of robberies, murders, civil war, in her fair borders.

Source 4:   *Sara Robinson on the "Sack" of Lawrence* (1856)

In Kansas: Its Interior and Exterior Life, *Sara Robinson described the proslavery assault on Lawrence in May 1856 that left the Robinson home destroyed. What techniques does she use to arouse sympathy in readers? Can Robinson's account be trusted, given that she was in the East at the time of the attack?*

SOURCE: Sara Robinson on the "Sack" of Lawrence (1856). From Sara Robinson, KANSAS: ITS INTERIOR AND EXTERIOR LIFE (Boston: Crosby, Nichols and Company, 1856), pp. 240–241, 242–243.

Tuesday, the 20th, was a still, calm day. O how calm it was! The hurrying bands of horse-men, brutal in their aspect, and uncouth, that had been for days flying over the prairies, making a blot on creation's fair face, were nowhere to be seen. No more the vile men, in companies of two, three, or more, came spying about the dwelling on Mt. Oread,[1] to ask for water, and saying "The head of the house is not at home?" knowing well by what acts of villany [sic] he was taken prisoner at Lexington, and was yet a prisoner. So perfect was the semblance of quiet and peace, that a little party, who sat in the evening's twilight, in front of the same dwelling, wondered if indeed the threatened evil might not again pass by, as on so many previous occasions. A smaller guard than usual were actually on the watch. But, when the morning sun arose on the 21st of May, 1856, hordes of men, armed with United States muskets, were marshalled upon Mt. Oread. While wronged innocence had slept quietly, they in the darkness had gained the height. The fair summit of Oread never before witnessed such an assemblage of creatures calling themselves men. Humanity stands aghast at the idea of brotherhood with such a ragged, filthy, besotted set. But it is only tools the slave power wants, and these could steal, plunder and kill....

In the mean time, the forces, variously estimated from five hundred to eight hun-dred, had been marched down to the base of the hill and formed into a hollow square. Gen. D. R. Atchinson made the following speech, which was received by the unceasing yells of the crowd:

"Boys, this day I am a Kickapoo Ranger, by G——d. This day we have entered Lawrence with Southern Rights inscribed upon our banner, and not one d——d aboli-tionist dared to fire a gun.

"Now, boys, this is the happiest day of my life. We have entered that d——d town, and taught the d——d abolitionists a Southern lesson that they will remember until the day they die. And now, boys, we will go in again, with our highly honorable Jones,[2] and test the strength of that d——d Free-State Hotel, and teach the Emigrant Aid Company that Kansas shall be ours. Boys, ladies should, and I hope will, be respected by every gen-tleman. But, when a woman takes upon herself the garb of a soldier, by carrying a Sharpe's rifle, then she is no longer worthy of respect. Trample her under your feet as you would a snake!

"Come on, boys! Now do your duty to yourselves and your Southern friends.

"Your duty, I know you will do. If one man or woman dares stand before you, blow them to h——l with a chunk of cold lead."

Source 5: *David Atchison on the "Abolitionist" Threat (1856)*

In an address intended to arouse southerners, Atchison and several other slavery expansionists pub-lished an address that focused on the dire consequences awaiting the South if proslavery forces lost in Kansas. How do they use racial fears to enlist support? How does the image of free soilers presented here compare to the free soilers' image of proslavery forces?

SOURCE: David Atchison on the "Abolitionist" Threat (1856).

---

[1]The hill overlooking Lawrence and the site of the Robinsons' home.
[2]Proslavery sheriff Samuel J. Jones.

"Kansas they [the abolitionists] justly regard as the mere outpost in the war now being waged between the antagonistic civilizations of the North and South, and, winning this great outpost and standpoint, they rightly think their march will be open to an easy conquest of the whole field. Hence the extraordinary means the abolition party has adopted to flood Kansas with the most fanatical and lawless portion of Northern society, and hence the large sums of money … expended to surround … Missourians with obnoxious and dangerous neighbors. On the other hand, the pro-slavery element of the law and order party in Kansas, looking to the Bible finds slavery ordained of God.… Slavery is the African's normal and proper state.… We believe it a trust and guardianship given as of God for the good of both races.… This is … a great social and political question of races, … a question whether we shall sink to the level of the freed African and take him to the embrace of social and political equality and fraternity; for such is the natural end of abolition progress.… That man or state is deceived that fondly trusts these fanatics may stop at Kansas.… The most convincing proof … of this was recently given before the congressional investigating committee. Judge Matthew Walker … testified … that before the abolitionists selected Lawrence as their centre of operations their leader, Governor Robinson, attempted to get a foothold for them in the Wyandotte reserve.… Robinson, finding it necessary to communicate their plans and objects, divulged to Walker (whom he then supposed to be a sympathizer) that the abolitionists were determined on winning Kansas at any cost; that then, having Missouri surrounded on three sides, they would begin their assaults on her, and as fast as one state gave way attack another, until the whole South was abolitionized.… We are confident that … the abolition party was truly represented by Robinson, who has always been their chief man and acknowledged leader in Kansas.… It was proved before the investigating committee that the abolition party had traveling agents in the territory whose duty it was to gather up, exaggerate, and report for publication rumors to the prejudice of the law and order party.… In the present imperiled state of your civilization, if we do not maintain this outpost we cannot long maintain the citadel. Then rally to the rescue."

QUESTIONS TO CONSIDER

1. The 1855 census in Kansas found fewer than two hundred slaves out of a population of roughly eight thousand five hundred. In the minds of free soilers like Sara Robinson and slavery expansionists like David Atchison far more was at stake in Kansas than those small numbers suggest. In fact, each believed that it would be disastrous if the other side won the territory. What did free soilers and slavery expansionists believe was at stake in Kansas? What threat did each side see in the other?

2. Based on the information in this chapter, do you think free soilers and slavery expansionists had an accurate perception of one another? In what ways may their perceptions have been distorted? In what ways were they accurate? Was the threat that each side saw in the other real, or was it overblown?

3. To what extent did this conflict reflect cultural differences that had little to do with slavery? Did Atchison and Robinson reflect those differences?

4. Sara Robinson and David Atchison were engaged in a propaganda war to determine the fate of Kansas. What messages or characteristics did their propaganda have in common? Whose do you think more accurately reflected the situation in Kansas? How did each side use race to rally people to its cause?

5.   From the source selections, whose argument do you find more convincing, Atchison's or Robinson's? Why? Cite specific examples in the sources of passages or statements that help sway you for or against each writer.

FOR FURTHER READING

Richard H. Abbott, *Cotton & Capital: Boston Business and Antislavery Reform, 1854–1868* (Amherst: University of Massachusetts Press, 1991), provides useful background regarding the role of Amos Lawrence and the New England Emigrant Aid Company in "bleeding Kansas."

Nichole Etcheson, *Bleeding Kansas: Contested Liberty in the Civil War Era* (Lawrence: University of Kansas Press, 2004), focuses on the way the struggle over Kansas was interpreted by whites as a battle for their own political liberties.

Michael A. Morrison, *Slavery and the American West: The Eclipse of Manifest Destiny and the Coming of the Civil War* (Chapel Hill: University of North Carolina Press, 1997), provides an overview of conflict over the extension of slavery into the West and its role in the sectional crisis.

William E. Parrish, *David Rice Atchison of Missouri: Border Politician* (Columbia: University of Missouri Press, 1967), offers a sympathetic treatment of its subject and remains the only full-length biography of him. (A biography of Sara Robinson is yet to be written.)

Gunja SenGupta, *For God and Mammon: Evangelicals and Entrepreneurs, Masters and Slaves in Territorial Kansas, 1854–1860* (Athens: University of Georgia Press, 1996), examines the relationship between commercial concerns and ideology in the battle over Kansas.

14

Mr. Lincoln's War: Clement Vallandigham and Benjamin Wade

Clement L. Vallandigham knew that Abraham Lincoln was a tyrant. In the name of fighting a war to save the Union, Lincoln had violated the very principles that formed the basis of that Union. Since taking office in 1861, he had broken the laws of the land and ridden roughshod over the U.S. Constitution. Those who dared to oppose him were smeared with derogatory labels, attacked as sympathizers with the rebellion, and even jailed or exiled. Indeed, Vallandigham had experienced firsthand Lincoln's oppressive power. The Ohio congressman believed that he had no choice but to stand up to Lincoln's villainy.

Benjamin F. Wade disagreed. Lincoln was no tyrant, but he was an incompetent fool. Lincoln refused to seize the opportunity for social, economic, and political reform presented by the Civil War. The United States could be made to live up to its professed principles of liberty and equality for all, if Lincoln would adopt Wade's agenda. But Lincoln would not cooperate. He could not see the possibilities open to him and his party. Instead of vigorously pushing the Ohio senator's program forward, Lincoln was an obstacle to it.

Like the nation itself, the North was divided during the Civil War. Few people better illustrate that division than Vallandigham and Wade. Unlike most northern Democrats, who supported the Union's war efforts, Vallandigham opposed the war entirely. The congressman was the leader of the antiwar Democrats, or Copperheads, as the Republicans called them. Some Copperheads wanted to end the war and let the South have its independence. Vallandigham wanted peace and reconciliation—a return to prewar conditions. He wanted the Republic reunited, even if it meant that slavery would be preserved. Most of all, he wanted the Constitution upheld. Wade believed that Lincoln had not exercised enough power during the Civil War. Like many other Republicans, he

Library of Congress Prints and Photographs Division. [LC-DIG-ppmsca-26734]

Clement Vallandigham

Library of Congress Prints and Photographs Division. [LC-DIG-cwpbh-02080]

Benjamin Wade

wanted to punish the South, free the slaves, and transform southern society. Together, Vallandigham and Wade had Lincoln in a bind. While he led the fight to defeat the Confederacy, the president also had to secure enough unity on the home front to see the Union through to victory. To do that, he had to keep these two men at bay. Only then would the North have a chance to defeat the South.

"VALIANT VAL"

Clement Vallandigham was proud to call himself a Jacksonian Democrat. Like Jacksonians earlier in the nineteenth century, he was a representative of the "common man" fighting the forces of "special privilege" and the encroachments of federal power. Thus he criticized banks, which he believed operated with government support to enrich the few at the expense of the many. He also opposed the nation's budding industrial interests, which demanded favors from government such as high tariffs. Taxes on imports, Vallandigham believed, only made manufactured products more expensive for the people. Like most good Democrats in the early nineteenth century, he was a staunch defender of limited government and states' rights. Following Thomas Jefferson, the Democrats believed that the states were sovereign. The federal government, therefore, had no business interfering with slavery. Because slavery was sanctioned by the Constitution, Vallandigham argued, it was a matter for the states to decide.

At first glance, this son of an Ohio Presbyterian minister was an unlikely Jacksonian. Born in 1820, Vallandigham was only a boy when Andrew Jackson was elected president in 1828. He was far too young for "Old Hickory's" presidency to have an impact on him. More important, Presbyterian ministers' sons did not generally flock to Jackson's Democratic Party. Instead, they favored the Whigs, who believed that government had a positive role to play in promoting the moral welfare of the nation. Worried about the moral degeneration of society, New England Protestants such as Lyman Beecher were naturally drawn to the Whigs (see Chapter 10). Hoping to reform the character and behavior of Americans, the Whigs were especially interested in temperance—the restriction or outright elimination of alcohol consumption. The Democrats, by contrast, believed that religion and politics should be separate.

Perhaps Vallandigham's family background determined his fierce partisan loyalties. His father's family traced its roots back to Jefferson's Virginia. Among their ancestors, the Vallandighams counted Indian fighters, Revolutionary War officers, and participants in the Whiskey Rebellion of 1794 (see Chapter 6). A revolt against a Federalist tax on whiskey, this rebellion was centered in western Pennsylvania among small farmers who distrusted the central government. Like many other "common people," the Vallandighams had moved west with the advancing frontier, from Virginia to Pennsylvania to New Lisbon, Ohio. Here were people who understood Jackson's message that government's role was a negative one: to remove obstacles from the path of the common people. They certainly had no use for the Whig conception of government.

Ethnic ties may also have shaped Vallandigham's views. Whereas the Whig Party's moral appeal attracted primarily Protestants of English descent, the Vallandighams were of Dutch extraction. (A colonial ancestor had changed the name from Van Landegham.) Like many other non-English ethnic groups, Dutch immigrants as far back as the eighteenth century had resented the dominance of English Americans in their colonies or states. In the early nineteenth century, the Democratic Party attracted many of these non-English groups who felt alienated from an Anglo-Saxon establishment. For similar reasons, Vallandigham's Scots-Irish mother may also have played a role in shaping his political outlook. Immigrants to the colonies in the eighteenth century, the Scots-Irish were Protestants from Scotland who had moved to Ireland in the seventeenth century. Although the Vallandighams were devout Presbyterians, many Scots-Irish were hard-drinking, hard-fighting, and fiercely independent people who opposed government regulation of morals. Like Jackson, also of Scots-Irish descent, Vallandigham saw a powerful central government not as a benevolent force for reform, but as a dangerous enemy of personal freedom.

Whatever political impact Vallandigham's parents had on him, they most certainly instilled in him a love of learning. His mother read to him at an early age, and his father operated a school in the family's home. When the eloquent and self-confident Vallandigham entered Pennsylvania's Jefferson College, it was as a member of the junior class. He dropped out after a year to teach school in Maryland, only to return and drop out again. Yet books would be his lifelong companions. Back in New Lisbon, he began to study law. After passing the bar in 1842, he joined his brother's legal practice. Personable and analytical, Vallandigham would use his impressive legal talents to great advantage.

His talents also suited him perfectly for politics. In 1840, he campaigned for the Democratic Party. The following year, he served as a delegate to a county Democratic Party convention. This early entrance into politics whetted his appetite for more, and his legal career helped him get it. As an ambitious lawyer, he frequently defended people against merchants, land speculators, and bankers. Many of his clients were poor Irish Americans and German Americans, who invariably voted Democratic. In 1844, he campaigned for the Democratic presidential candidate, James K. Polk. The following year, he won election to the Ohio assembly. As a Jacksonian watchdog, he attacked bankers and manufacturers. When Polk and the Democrats in Congress took the country to war against Mexico in 1846, he attacked Whig legislators who opposed what they derisively called "Mr. Polk's War." Pouncing on Whig opponents of the war, he declared that "by the blood of its slain ye shall have no part in its glories."

Over the next several years, Vallandigham turned from politics to personal affairs. Married in 1846, he moved to Dayton the next year. He devoted himself to his legal practice, his new wife and child, and the many books he purchased for his library. He was inevitably drawn back to politics, though. Within a couple of years, the controversy surrounding the Compromise of 1850* ignited concern among many northerners about slavery. Vallandigham vocally supported the compromise on behalf of Democrats. Back in the political arena, he ran for office over the next several years but without success. He lost a bid for lieutenant governor in 1851 and two congressional elections in 1852 and 1854. He ran for Congress again in 1856, this time with a different outcome.

By the mid-1850s, the Whig Party was falling victim to the growing sectional conflict over slavery. The passage of the Kansas–Nebraska Act in 1854 had heightened northerners' fears about the spread of slavery. The measure, introduced in Congress by Democrat Stephen A. Douglas, overturned the Missouri Compromise's prohibition on slavery in most of the Louisiana Purchase by allowing voters in the area to decide the issue under the principle of popular sovereignty. After the passage of the Kansas–Nebraska Act, northern antislavery Whigs no longer trusted their southern colleagues and vice versa. As the Whig Party disintegrated, the opponents of the Kansas–Nebraska Act met in 1854 to found the Republican Party, which attracted both abolitionists and those who sought to exclude slavery from the western territories. Unlike the Whigs, this exclusively northern party was open to the potent Democratic charge that it was friendly to blacks.

In 1856, Vallandigham's opponent for Congress was a member of the new Republican Party. Vallandigham lost the election by nineteen votes, but he challenged the results, claiming that the Republican had won because of invalid ballots cast by African Americans. In Ohio, as in many other northern states, blacks were free but did not have the right to vote. When a congressional investigation supported by southern Democrats overturned the election, Vallandigham had his victory. He would be reelected twice more, in 1858 and 1860.

From his seat in Congress, Vallandigham watched in despair the growing sectional crisis between the North and South. For the sake of preserving the Union, he took a moderate position. Although he saw slavery as morally wrong, he believed that the federal government had no right to move against it in the states because it was sanctioned by the Constitution. In this regard, Vallandigham agreed with the Republican Party's rising star, Abraham Lincoln. He disagreed with Lincoln and the Republicans, however, on the issue of the expansion of slavery into the western territories. Lincoln and most Republicans called for the containment of slavery in the states where it already existed. Vallandigham placed his faith in popular sovereignty, the solution championed by Stephen Douglas. Embodied in the Kansas–Nebraska Act, popular sovereignty called for voters in the territories to decide the issue of slavery themselves. Like most other Democrats, Vallandigham believed that if the Republicans won the presidential election in 1860, frightened southerners would secede from the Union. While running for reelection in 1860, he launched an all-out assault on the Republicans by playing on his constituents' racial fears. If the Republicans won, he declared, "stinking niggers" would sit next to them in jury boxes and at workbenches, and their daughters would marry "black boys" and have "black babies."

---

*Compromise of 1850: A congressional deal forged by Whig Henry Clay and Democrat Stephen A. Douglas to resolve sectional conflict between the North and South over the issue of the expansion of slavery into the territories taken in the Mexican War. Its provisions included the admission of California as a free state, the end of the slave trade in the District of Columbia, and a stronger Fugitive Slave Act.

Such tactics worked for Vallandigham but failed to carry the day for Douglas. Shortly after Douglas lost the presidential election to Lincoln, the southern states began to secede. The Republicans were determined to use force to preserve the Union. Vallandigham decried the breakup of the Union but also opposed war as a means for preserving it. He believed that peace could be achieved and the Union restored through compromise and negotiation. Armed coercion, he declared, would be "destructive of republican liberty." Clinging to the doctrine of state sovereignty, Vallandigham reflected the view of many northern Democrats, especially the poorer ones of the lower Midwest, an area originally settled by southerners. They wanted the Union preserved as much as they disliked blacks and feared abolition. When the war started in 1861, many of them turned to "Valiant Val" to express their fears.

"BLUFF BEN"

Politically, Benjamin Franklin Wade also was a product of his early environment. Born in 1800 in western Massachusetts to old Yankee stock, he was a descendant of the New England Puritan tradition. Although the Wades were poor farmers, their Protestant faith instilled in them the value of education. Thus Benjamin was taught to read the Bible by his mother, the daughter of a Congregational minister. As a young man, he rejected his parents' emphasis on formal religion, but he could not escape the effects of his Puritan upbringing. He approached life as a struggle between right and wrong and believed that compromising on fundamentals was tantamount to sin. Those who disagreed about such matters were not merely misguided but evil. Society, moreover, was capable of moral improvement. Thus Wade was as committed to the righteous exercise of government power as Vallandigham was opposed to it. That attitude dovetailed perfectly with the economic changes he noticed while growing up. As cotton mills and other businesses sprang up in New England after the War of 1812, the entire area seemed to benefit from more jobs and greater commerce. When he later backed government support for industry, he did not forget the favorable impact of these enterprises on his boyhood environment.

Wade's Puritan background influenced him in other ways, too. Industriousness, he believed, was a virtue and idleness a sin. To earn his keep, the ambitious young Wade hired himself out to other farm families. Later, he worked as a laborer on the construction of the Erie Canal in upstate New York. And when his family moved to northeastern Ohio in 1821, he worked as a farmer and drover and even taught school for a while. Driven to succeed, he set his sights on becoming a lawyer, so he began studying law under a local attorney. In 1828, he was admitted to the bar.

Wade was a natural Whig, as were many of the other settlers in northeastern Ohio. With their backing, in 1837 Wade won election to the state senate in a landslide. The young legislator sometimes broke with his party on policies such as subsidies for corporations that he believed favored business interests too much. Otherwise, he was a staunch Whig. He favored tariffs for industry and shared many Whigs' views about slavery. To Wade, slavery was not just an economic issue but a moral wrong.

By the early 1840s, Wade was married with two children. Meanwhile, he continued to serve in the state legislature and developed a lucrative law practice. In 1847, he was elected to a judgeship. Three years later, when Congress passed the Fugitive Slave Act, he was catapulted onto the national stage. Passed as part of the Compromise of 1850, the act compelled northerners to assist southern slave catchers. Alleged runaways could now be taken into slavery solely on the sworn statement of a slave owner. Accused blacks had no right to testify for themselves in court. Wade declared that as a district judge, he would refuse to uphold the law. That position had a lot to do with his election by the state legislature to the U.S. Senate in 1851.

When Wade arrived in the Senate, he joined a small group of antislavery senators in attacking the Fugitive Slave Act. His firm antislavery views quickly established his reputation as a fearless radical. His debates with southerners were often characterized by blunt talk and taunts of his slaveholding colleagues. **[See Source 1.]** His outspoken manner soon earned him the nickname "Bluff Ben." Although he also earned the respect of his southern opponents, he fought them on slavery at every turn. Thus, when the Kansas–Nebraska Act opened the door to the westward expansion of slavery, Wade and his fellow antislavery Whigs joined the new Republican Party. By this time, he had adopted most of the Whig economic program as his own, including protective tariffs and federal funding for internal improvements such as roads and canals. As a Republican, he continued to promote these policies. At the same time, he continued to oppose policies that favored a particular industry or put business above all other interests. Most of all, he fought against the "sin" of slavery and the northerners and southerners in Congress who supported it.

Easily winning reelection in 1857, Wade soon established himself as a rising star in the new Republican Party. By 1860, he was a prominent member of the Senate and a Republican presidential candidate. Although he lost the nomination to Lincoln, when Lincoln won the election, Wade would have his day. Serving on the Senate committee that tried to head off secession, he opposed any compromise with the South. In late 1860, for instance, Senator John Crittenden of Kentucky proposed that 36°30′ north latitude, established as the boundary between slave and free territory in the Louisiana Purchase, be extended to the Pacific. Wade urged Lincoln to reject the so-called Crittenden Compromise. The Republicans, he believed, had been fairly elected on a platform to exclude slavery from the territories. They could not now ignore the majority will. Lincoln agreed, and the last hope for compromise between the North and South was gone.

Once the Civil War began, however, Wade was not pleased with his president. The moderate Lincoln was more concerned with repairing the Union than ending slavery. As the political leader of the Union, Lincoln knew that there was a wide range of opinions on slavery in the North, from those of radical abolitionists to those of slaveholders in the loyal slave states. He knew, too, that many Democrats sympathized with their southern brethren and feared the prospect of competing with black labor. Moving quickly to satisfy Wade and his supporters would only alienate northern Democrats such as Clement Vallandigham and their backers. And if most northerners did not stay committed to the fight for the Union, the North's tremendous advantages in resources and manpower would not matter. **[See Source 2.]**

Wade and other Radical Republicans, however, had high expectations. Mostly abolitionists, they wanted immediate emancipation of slaves and punishment for southern secessionists. They envisioned a complete social restructuring of the South after it was defeated. They believed that the government should redistribute plantation owners' land to former slaves, strip all Confederates of political rights, destroy the economic basis of the southern planter aristocracy, and replace that aristocracy with a more democratic and egalitarian social order. Serving as chairman of the Joint Committee on the Conduct of the War, Wade quickly emerged as a leader of the Radical Republicans. The Union war effort in 1861 had proved disastrous, and the Radicals used this oversight committee to challenge Lincoln's conduct of the war. Indeed, it would be their main weapon in the battle to shape the Union's wartime policies. For Wade and other leaders of the faction, including Thaddeus Stevens, Wendell Phillips, and Charles Sumner, Lincoln was being too cautious. When he delayed emancipation and supported Democratic generals, they were outraged.

Lincoln's support for General George McClellan was especially outrageous to Wade. A longtime Democrat, the general had taken command of the Army of the Potomac following the disastrous Union defeat at Bull Run in July 1861. Wade had joined the many Washington residents who went to the battlefield to watch what they assumed would be the only battle of the war. In the midst of the ensuing rout, the enraged senator used his carriage to block the road back to the capital and threatened the retreating Union soldiers with his rifle. Now, as McClellan's overly cautious nature made him reluctant to fight, Wade stepped up the pressure on Lincoln. He even worked with Ambrose Burnside and other officers under McClellan to gather ammunition against the general. In return for the information, Wade would ignore charges that Burnside had moved too slowly at the Battle of Antietam in 1862.

Wade's attacks on McClellan reflected the Ohio senator's views about the proper way to conduct the war in general. He constantly badgered Lincoln to move faster, carry the fight to the South, and crush the rebellion quickly. At one point, he said that the president was not smart enough to lead the nation during the crisis and cynically noted, "I do not wonder that people desert to [Confederate president] Jeff Davis as he has brains; I may desert myself." When the Lincolns hosted a ball at the White House, Wade refused to attend and released to the press his brutal reply to the Lincolns' invitation: "Are the President and Mrs. Lincoln aware that there is a civil war? If they are not, Mr. and Mrs. Wade are, and for that reason decline to participate in feasting and dancing." Every action Lincoln took exposed him to Wade's withering scrutiny. Lacking military or administrative experience, the senator did not realize that the armies often could not have moved faster even if their leaders had ordered them to.

More than Lincoln's conservative conduct of the war, Wade and other Radicals were concerned with the administration's foot-dragging on slavery. The Radicals urged Lincoln to abolish slavery as the first step toward the dramatic reform of American society. They called for full and immediate emancipation, land redistribution, and political rights for freedmen. As Union armies won victories and occupied portions of the South, Lincoln carried out a much more moderate plan. First, Union generals administered no clear policy of abolition. Some commanders, such as John C. Frémont, pursued their own policies for emancipation by freeing the slaves in occupied territories. The Radicals applauded such efforts and were dismayed when Lincoln overturned military emancipation. Only a person who came from "poor white trash," Wade sneered, would reverse emancipation. Soon rumors of the president's negotiations with southern Unionists in the conquered territories of Louisiana and Arkansas flew about the capital. One claimed that Lincoln had struck a bargain that would bring those states back into the Union and preserve slavery. Wade fully believed such rumors. Lincoln's next annual message to Congress, he declared, would include a recommendation "to give each rebel who shall serve during the war a hundred and sixty acres of land." Beneath the sneers and sarcasm, Wade and his allies worried that Lincoln had sold them out.

In fact, the president was walking a political tightrope. He had to try to keep the slaveholding border states—Missouri, Kentucky, Maryland, and Delaware—in the Union. The loss of these strategically placed states would be a major blow to the North's war effort. Lincoln himself acknowledged the strategic importance of these states when he declared that he would *like* to have God on his side, but he *must* have Kentucky. Any bold approach toward emancipation might well force it and the other border states right out of the Union. Furthermore, white racism made emancipation very unpopular in the North. Many northern workers did not like slavery because they agreed with Hinton Rowan Helper and other antislavery agitators that it degraded free labor (see Chapter 12). At the same time, they did not want to compete with free blacks for jobs and land.

Lincoln also had an eye on the complicated constitutional and legal questions surrounding emancipation. Could the government abolish slavery legally? If so, which branch of the national government had the power to do so? If the state governments had sovereignty over the matter, how could the Republicans convince state leaders to carry out emancipation? Would slave owners have to be compensated financially for the freedom of their workers? If so, where would the money come from?

Whatever Wade and the Radical Republicans thought about the matter, Lincoln knew that emancipation was a complex and dangerous issue. Thus, when he finally did move against slavery, it was in a hedged and halfhearted way. Lincoln's Emancipation Proclamation, which went into effect in 1863, pertained only to slavery in rebellious territory. In other words, it excluded the loyal slave states and those areas in Confederate states already under the control of Union forces. It freed only those slaves behind enemy lines, where the Confederates were not about to carry out Lincoln's order.

Wade and his fellow Radicals saw the Emancipation Proclamation as more evidence of Lincoln's conservatism. They were not any happier with his proposed plan for Reconstruction of the defeated Confederate states. Lincoln called for each state to create a new government after only a small fraction of its male citizens swore allegiance to the United States. Fearful that Democrats would gain control of the reconstructed states under the president's plan, Wade offered an alternative. With Congressman Henry Davis of Maryland, he introduced legislation requiring a majority of citizens in former Confederate states to take such an oath. Although the Wade–Davis bill passed in Congress, Lincoln vetoed it. The bill's authors promptly issued the Wade–Davis Manifesto, a heated denunciation of Lincoln's policies. **[See Source 3.]**

The manifesto was one of the Ohio senator's greatest political blunders. The majority of northerners agreed with Lincoln that the Civil War was above all a crusade to preserve the Union. They approved his moderate course on slavery and his plans to bring the rebellious states back into the Union as quickly as possible. Thus many of them reacted with disgust to the manifesto. Moderate Republicans began to suspect that the Radicals wished to divide the party. If a Democrat were elected in 1864, they reasoned, the Radicals could rid themselves of the South once and for all. The Democrats looked as if they were heading for a victory in the fall elections, and if they carried the day, there might be a negotiated peace with the South after all.

"EXACT AND EQUAL JUSTICE"

Moderate Republican fears about a negotiated peace backed by the Radicals did not seem far-fetched in 1864. By then, war weariness across the North created a groundswell of Democratic support. The leaders of the Democratic resurgence were Vallandigham and his fellow Peace Democrats. These Copperheads were convinced that Lincoln's war policies were destroying American liberty. Lincoln had extended federal power at the expense of the states and individual citizens. Early in the war, he had acted without congressional approval, unilaterally mobilizing the country for war. They believed that he had inappropriately moved at the federal level against slavery. And, they charged, he had assumed dictatorial powers. In 1861, he had suspended the writ of habeas corpus,[*] taking away the constitutional right of citizens to a speedy trial. Although the Constitution

---

[*]*Habeas corpus:* The legal right of jailed persons to be brought before a court to determine whether they should be charged with a crime or released.

allowed the writ to be suspended during times of rebellion or invasion, congressional leaders argued that only the legislative branch had the authority to do so. Thus Lincoln was extending his executive powers beyond constitutional bounds. In fact, when the chief justice of the Supreme Court had ruled that Lincoln's suspension of habeas corpus was unconstitutional, Lincoln had simply ignored the ruling.

The president had also declared martial law and subjected "disloyal" persons to imprisonment. As a result, perhaps as many as thirteen thousand people were detained, many of them for long periods. They were never brought to trial, and the government never presented evidence against them. Many of them were guilty of demonstrating Confederate sympathies or opposing administration policies. At one point, Union forces even arrested thirty-one Maryland state legislators to prevent them from voting for the state to secede. Meanwhile, the administration's draft policy forced citizens to serve in the army. It also allowed those who could afford to do so to buy their way out of service or hire another man to take their place for three hundred dollars. The rich were exempt from military duty, while the poor had to fight.

In Vallandigham's view, the administration's financial policies took tyranny even further. Lincoln raised taxes to pay for the war. He even instituted an income tax that was later found to be unconstitutional. He reorganized the currency system through the establishment of a national bank and the introduction of paper money not backed by gold. A national bank and paper money had long been supported by the old Whig Party, to which Lincoln had belonged. They also were part of the Republican Party platform. Now the president argued that such measures were necessary to conduct the war. To Lincoln, crushing dissent, drafting poor men to fight the war, raising taxes, and creating an economic climate favorable to business were all part of his plans to win the war. To Vallandigham and many other Democrats, it seemed that he was using the conflict as a way to enact policies favorable to business interests. They argued that these moves only proved that Lincoln was power hungry and oppressive.

Already by 1862, Vallandigham's fiery oratory and relentless criticism of Lincoln had made him the most prominent Peace Democrat. His slogan, "The Constitution as it is, the Union as it was," became the rallying cry for antiwar protesters across the country. As the war continued and the casualties mounted, Vallandigham found a receptive audience. He roused his supporters with slashing attacks on Lincoln's suspension of civil liberties and his tax policies. With the Union war effort bogged down by late 1862, Vallandigham's oratory grew more heated. Appealing to the racist sentiments of northerners, the Copperhead leader declared that Lincoln's policies would bring a flood of blacks to the North. The South, he asserted, could not be conquered. The only trophies of war that the North had to show for its efforts were "defeat, debt, taxation, sepulchers ... the suspension of *habeas corpus,* the violation ... of freedom of the press and of speech." Lincoln and his cronies had "made this country one of the worst despotisms on earth." The Republicans had made the war for Union a war for abolition, he cried, and what had it accomplished? "Let the dead at Fredericksburg and Vicksburg answer," he declared.
[See Source 4.]

With the cry "Rich man's war, poor man's fight," Vallandigham also attacked the draft with great effect. Quick to sense the unfairness of Lincoln's policy, many workers and farmers responded favorably to Vallandigham's slogan. Republicans, in turn, were quick to blame Vallandigham for helping to stir up draft resistance. Some even blamed him for the New York draft riot in 1863. Sparked by the Lincoln administration's draft, the riot left 120 people dead and resulted in millions of dollars' worth of property damage. It also exposed the racial and ethnic tensions in northern society. Much of the rioters' violence, like "Valiant Val's" rhetoric, was directed against blacks. And most of the rioters were workers and immigrants—people generally receptive to his message. The charge that Vallandigham had incited this violence, however, was far-fetched. **[See Source 5.]**

Yet even for Benjamin Wade and other Radical Republicans, Vallandigham's rhetoric and actions proved too much. To counter the Peace Democrats' growing support, Wade publicly declared Vallandigham a traitor. The Ohio Democrat's "every breath," he argued, was devoted to the destruction of the republic. Vallandigham, Wade charged on the Senate floor, was a member of the Knights of the Golden Circle, a secret prosouthern organization dedicated to helping the Confederacy via sabotage. A number of knights had been arrested for treasonous activities, and Vallandigham could not afford to let Wade's charges go unanswered. On the floor of the House of Representatives, he responded. Vallandigham opened his speech by reading Wade's slanderous charges and then shouted out at the top of his lungs, "Now, sir, here in my place in the House, and as a Representative, I denounce—and I speak it advisedly—the author of that speech as a liar, a scoundrel, and a coward. His name is Benjamin F. Wade!" **[See Source 6.]**

Republican attempts to discredit Vallandigham continued, but Wade's charges of treason would not stick. In fact, Vallandigham's popularity grew as Union armies suffered more setbacks on the battlefield. In 1863, he delivered a series of antiwar, antiadministration, anti-Lincoln speeches that enraged the Republicans. Already Wade's old friend Ambrose Burnside, now serving as military governor of Ohio, had issued various orders to clamp down on Copperhead activity. In May 1863, he ordered Vallandigham's arrest. The Ohio representative was charged with "publicly expressing ... his sympathies for those in arms against the Government of the United States, declaring disloyal sentiments and opinions, with the object and purpose of weakening the power of the Government in its efforts to suppress an unlawful rebellion."

Vallandigham was tried by court-martial, convicted, and sentenced to a term in a military prison "during the continuance of the war." While cries of outrage swept the Democratic areas of the North, Vallandigham's attorneys appealed his case. The federal courts refused to overturn the decision because the judges could not decide whether the government had been justified in its action against him. Later, the Supreme Court decided in Ex parte *Vallandigham* in 1864 that it could not hear the case because it had no jurisdiction to hear appeals from a military commission. His legal options were exhausted, but not his political chances. From behind bars, Vallandigham managed to rally his supporters to continue their efforts. In fact, his arrest only validated Vallandigham's arguments that the Lincoln administration was indeed tyrannical. Imprisoned, he was now a martyr and a symbol of the injustices of "Mr. Lincoln's War."

To head off the political damage already suffered in the Vallandigham case, Lincoln and his cabinet decided to exile him to the South. Released from prison shortly after his arrest, he was carried to Confederate lines in Tennessee. Although southerners received him warmly, they did not want him to stay. They realized that he had more value as a Copperhead than as a Confederate. After a month in the South, he made his way to Canada, where he continued to lead the Peace Democrats from exile. Then he secretly returned to Ohio in defiance of federal authority. While he campaigned publicly for George McClellan, the Democratic nominee for president in 1864, the Republicans conveniently ignored his presence. Vallandigham's actions were in vain, however, for the election was ultimately decided on the battlefield. When General William T. Sherman captured Atlanta in September, flagging Union spirits were revived and Democratic hopes for electoral victory shattered. Lincoln and the Republicans won reelection that fall, and Union armies won the war the following spring.

In the end, Vallandigham and the Copperheads lost. Their hopes for a Union restored on prewar terms were dashed. After the war, Vallandigham attempted unsuccessfully to rejuvenate his political career. Returning to his law practice, he again proved his superb legal abilities. His fiery oratory continued to mesmerize juries. His courtroom dramatics, however, finally killed him. In 1871, while defending a man accused of murder, Vallandigham argued that the victim had actually shot himself by accident. The famous attorney planned to make his case by dramatically reenacting the scene. While demonstrating for his colleagues what he intended to do in the courtroom, he shot himself fatally with a pistol he mistakenly thought was unloaded.

For a time, it seemed that Wade and the Radicals had won. During the presidency of Lincoln's successor, Andrew Johnson, they seized control of Reconstruction. Wade hoped that Congress would now help ensure blacks' economic security and political equality. The Confederates would finally be punished. During congressional Reconstruction, many former Confederates did lose their political rights, and freedmen won the right to vote. Wade's dream of a radical restructuring of southern society, however, was never fulfilled. Most blacks were impoverished and never got the chance to purchase their own land. Left in dire economic circumstances, they were politically vulnerable. In time, resurgent southern Democrats would find it easy to strip them of their voting rights and impose a rigid racial caste system on them.

Long before then, Wade experienced his own defeat. He knew that voting rights for blacks were unpopular in Ohio even after the Civil War, but he would not waver from his belief in "exact and equal justice for all men without reference to color, condition, or race." Instead, he enthusiastically "waved the bloody shirt" of the Civil War by reminding voters about pro-Confederate Democrats like "the bold, convicted traitor" Clement Vallandigham. By 1867, however, Wade found that such tactics would not work. Ohio voters elected a Democratic legislature that year. When the legislature in turn elected a Democratic senator, Wade's political career was over. After leaving the Senate in 1869, he returned to his law practice and became involved in railroad building. He lived until 1878, long enough to see Reconstruction overturned and his hopes for "exact and equal justice" for blacks dashed. In the end, Wade had to wonder whether he or Vallandigham had actually accomplished more as a result of "Mr. Lincoln's War."

·PRIMARY SOURCES·

Source 1: *Benjamin Wade Assaults a Southern Colleague* (1854)

In 1854, the Kansas–Nebraska Act proposed to resolve the issue of slavery in Kansas and Nebraska by letting the settlers there decide whether or not to allow slavery. In debates in the Senate, Benjamin Wade blasted the bill and colleagues who supported it. What does this attack on a senator from North Carolina reveal about Wade's approach to politics? Why do you think this sort of attack would have appealed to many northerners by 1854?

SOURCE: "Benjamin Wade Assaults a Southern Colleague' (1854). Originally from CONGRESSIONAL GLOBE, 33d Cong., 1st sess., 1854, appendix, p. 313

There was one argument made by the Senator from North Carolina, which struck me as exceedingly singular. He has set forth all the beauties of the patriarchal institution, as he calls it, to show the affectionate relation existing between him and his slaves, with whom he grew up from boyhood, with whom he was intimate and familiar, and whom he pronounced the best friends he had upon earth. He said, "Do you want to make us hard-hearted? Now sir," said he, "[i]f I can better my condition and the condition of my slaves by going into Nebraska, where the soil is better, and where we will have a better supply of all things, in the name of God, do you want to stand forth and prevent me?" Did anyone notice the force with which he urged that appeal? So wedded was he to the idea that he could not exist anywhere without his old friends, as he called them, and yet he could not take his old "mammy," as he called her, who nursed him and brought him up to manhood, into that Territory. Why? Notwithstanding these intimate relations, he could not take her there, because he could not have the right to sell her when he got there. There could not be any other reasons for it; for, most assuredly, if he wanted to take his affectionate old mammy there and give her her freedom, there would be nothing in the way, either in a slave law or anything else.

Source 2: Abraham Lincoln, *Letter to Horace Greeley* (1862)

In this letter to Republican newspaper editor Horace Greeley, Lincoln explains his view of the Civil War. What does Lincoln identify as the paramount issue of the war? How do you think Wade and Vallandigham would have responded to Lincoln's views regarding the Union's primary aim in the war?

Dear Sir

I have just read yours of the 19th addressed to myself through the *New-York Tribune.* If there be in it any statements, or assumptions of fact which I may know to be erroneous, I do not, now and here, controvert them....

As to the policy I "seem to be pursuing" as you say, I have not meant to leave any one in doubt.

I would save the Union. I would save it the shortest way under the Constitution. The sooner the national authority can be restored, the nearer the Union will be "the Union as it was." If there be those who would not save the Union unless they could at the same time *save* slavery, I do not agree with them. If there be those who would not save the Union unless they could at the same time *destroy* slavery, I do not agree with them. My paramount object in this struggle *is* to save the Union, and is *not* either to save or to destroy slavery. If I could save the Union without freeing *any* slave I would do it, and if I could save it by freeing *all* the slaves I would do it and if I could save it by freeing some and leaving others alone I would also do that. What I do about slavery and the colored race, I do because I believe it helps to save the Union; and what I forbear, I forbear because I do *not* believe it would help to save the Union. I shall do *less* whenever I shall believe what I am doing hurts the cause and I shall do *more* whenever I shall believe doing more will help the cause. I shall try to correct errors when shown to be errors, and I shall adopt new views so fast as they shall appear to be true views.

SOURCE: Abraham Lincoln, "Letter to Horace Greeley" (1862). Originally from NEW YORK TRIBUNE, August 25, 1862.

I have here stated my purpose according to my view of *official* duty; and I intend no modification of my oft-expressed *personal* wish that all men every where could be free. Yours,

A. Lincoln

Source 3: Benjamin Wade and Henry Davis, *The Wade-Davis Manifesto* (1864)

In the following excerpt from the Wade–Davis Manifesto of August 5, 1864, Senator Benjamin Wade and Congressman Henry Davis attack President Lincoln's veto of the Wade–Davis bill. What arguments do they use against Lincoln?

We have read without surprise, but not without indignation, the Proclamation of the President of the 8th of July....

The President, by preventing this bill from becoming a law, holds the electoral votes of the rebel States at the dictation of his personal ambition.

If those votes turn the balance in his favor, is it to be supposed that his competitor, defeated by such means, will acquiesce?

If the rebel majority assert their supremacy in those States, and send votes which elect an enemy of the Government, will we not repel his claims? ...

Seriously impressed with these dangers, Congress, *"the proper constituted authority,"* formally declared that there are no State governments in the rebel States, and provided for their erection at a proper time, and both the Senate and the House of Representatives rejected the Senators and Representatives chosen under the authority of what the President calls the free constitution and government of Arkansas.

The President's proclamation *"holds for naught"* this judgment, and discards the authority of the Supreme Court, and strides headlong toward the anarchy his proclamation of the 8th of December inaugurated....

That judgment of Congress which the President defies was the exercise of an authority exclusively vested in Congress by the Constitution to determine what is the established government in a State, and in its own nature and by the highest judicial authority binding on all other departments of the Government....

A more studied outrage on the legislative authority of the people has never been perpetrated.

Congress passed a bill, the President refused to approve it, and then by proclamation puts as much of it in force as he sees fit, and proposes to execute those parts by officers unknown to the laws of the United States and not subject to the confirmation of the Senate!

The bill directed the appointment of Provisional Governors by and with the advice and consent of the Senate.

The President, after defeating the law, proposes to appoint without law, and without the advice and consent of the Senate, *Military* Governors for the rebel States!

He has already exercised this dictatorial usurpation in Louisiana, and he defeated the bill to prevent its limitation.... The President has greatly presumed on the

SOURCE: Benjamin Wade and Henry Davis, "The Wade-Davis Manifesto" (1864).

forbearance which the supporters of his Administration have so long practiced, in view of the arduous conflict in which we are engaged, and the reckless ferocity of our political opponents.

But he must understand that our support is of a cause and not of a man, that the authority of Congress is paramount and must be respected, that the whole body of the Union men of Congress will not submit to be impeached by him of rash and unconstitutional legislation, and if he wishes our support, he must confine himself to his executive duties—to obey and execute, not make the laws—to suppress by arms armed rebellion, and leave political reorganization to Congress.

If the supporters of the Government fail to insist on this, they become responsible for the usurpations which they fail to rebuke, and are justly liable to the indignation of the people whose rights and security, committed to their keeping, they sacrifice.

Let them consider the remedy for these usurpations, and, having found it, fearlessly execute it.

Source 4:   Clement Vallandigham, "The Great Civil War in America" (1863)

In this excerpt from his speech before the House of Representatives on January 14, 1863, Clement Vallandigham condemns the war effort. What arguments does he use to attack the war? How do his attacks on Lincoln's war policies compare to Benjamin Wade and Henry Davis's arguments in Source 3?

Money and credit, then, you have had in prodigal profusion. And were men wanted? More than a million rushed to arms! Seventy-five thousand first, (and the country stood aghast at the multitude,) then eighty-three thousand more were demanded, and three hundred and ten thousand responded to the call. The President next asked for four hundred thousand, and Congress, in their generous confidence, gave him five hundred thousand, and, not to be outdone, he took six hundred and thirty-seven thousand. Half of these melted away in their first campaign, and the President demanded three hundred thousand more for the war, and then drafted yet another three hundred thousand for nine months.... And yet victory strangely follows the standard of the foe. From Great Bethel to Vicksburg, the battle has not been to the strong. Yet every disaster, except the last, has been followed by a call for more troops, and every time, so far, they have been promptly furnished. From the beginning the war has been conducted like a political campaign, and it has been the folly of the party in power that they have assumed, that numbers alone would win the field in a contest not with ballots but with musket and sword. But numbers, you have had almost without number—the largest, best appointed, best armed, fed and clad host of brave men, well organized and well disciplined, ever marshaled. A Navy, too, not the most formidable perhaps, but the most numerous and gallant, and the costliest in the world, and against a foe, almost without a navy at all. Thus, with twenty millions of people, and every element of strength and force at command—power, patronage, influence, unanimity, enthusiasm,

SOURCE: Clement Vallandigham, "The Great Civil War in America" (1863). From CONGRESSIONAL GLOBE, 37th Cong., 3d sess., 1863.

confidence, credit, money, men, an Army and a Navy the largest and the noblest ever set in the field, or afloat upon the sea; with the support, almost servile, of every State, county, and municipality in the North and West, with a Congress swift to do the bidding of the Executive, without opposition anywhere at home, and with an arbitrary power which neither the Czar of Russia, nor the Emperor of Austria dare exercise, yet after nearly two years of more vigorous prosecution of war than ever recorded in history, after more skirmishes, combats and battles than Alexander, Caesar, or the first Napoleon ever fought in any five years of their military career, you have utterly, signally, disastrously—I will not say ignominiously—failed to subdue ten millions of "rebels," whom you had taught the people of the North and West not only to hate, but to despise. Rebels, did I say? Yes, your fathers were rebels or your grandfathers. He, who now before me on canvas looks down so sadly upon us, the false, degenerate, and imbecile guardians of the great Republic which he founded, was a rebel. And yet we, cradled ourselves in rebellion, and who have fostered and fraternized with every insurrection in the nineteenth century everywhere throughout the globe, would now forsooth, make the word "rebel" a reproach. Rebels certainly they are; but all the persistent and stupendous efforts of the most gigantic warfare of modern times have through your incompetency and folly availed nothing to crush them out, cut off though they have been, by our blockade, from all the world, and dependent only upon their own courage and resources.... But money you have expended without limit, and blood poured out like water. Defeat, debt, taxation, sepulchers, these are your trophies. In vain, the people gave you treasure, and the soldier yielded up his life. "Fight, tax, emancipate, let these," said the gentleman from Maine, [Mr. Pike,] at the last session, "be the trinity of our salvation." Sir, they have become the trinity of your deep damnation. The war for the Union is, in your hands, a most bloody and costly failure. The President confessed it on the 22nd of September [with the promulgation of the Preliminary Emancipation Proclamation] solemnly, officially, and under the broad seal of the United States. And he has now repeated the confession. The priests and rabbis of abolition taught him that God would not prosper such a cause. War for the Union was abandoned, war for the negro openly begun, and with stronger battalions than before. With what success? Let the dead at Fredericksburg and Vicksburg answer.

Source 5:   *Scene of New York City Draft Rioters Lynching an African American* (1863)

Anti-draft rioters in New York City in 1863 frequently targeted African Americans. What does this image reveal about the depth of racial animosity in the North during the Civil War? Given Vallandigham's opposition to the draft, which allowed well-to-do citizens to buy their way out of military service, what does this source suggest about at least one possible source of Vallandigham's political support in the North?

SOURCE: http://hd.housedivided.dickinson.edu/node/40651; originally from *Illustrated London News* (1863).

THE RIOTS IN NEW YORK : THE MOB LYNCHING A NEGRO IN CLARKSON-STREET.—SEE PAGE 142.

A New York City Draft Riot victim

Mary Evans Picture Library Ltd/AGE Fotostock

Source 6:   *Clement Vallandigham Attacks Benjamin Wade* (1862)

In response to an attack by Benjamin Wade, Clement Vallandigham denounced Wade on the floor of the House of Representatives. As a result, a Wade ally from Ohio introduced an unsuccessful resolution of censure against Vallandigham. What do Vallandigham's remarks reveal about his situation as a dissenter during the Civil War? What do they reveal about Vallandigham himself?

Mr. Chairman, I have waited patiently for three days for this the earliest occasion presented for a personal explanation.

In a speech delivered in this city the other day—not in this House—certainly not in the Senate—no such speech could have been tolerated in an American Senate—I find the following:

"I accuse them [the Democratic Party] of a deliberate purpose to assail, through the judicial tribunals and through the Senate and the House of Representatives of the United States, and everywhere else, and to overawe, intimidate, and trample under foot, if they can, the men who boldly stand forth in defense of their country, now imperiled by this gigantic rebellion. I have watched it long. I have seen it in secret. I have seen its movements ever since that party got together, with a colleague of mine in the other House as chairman of the committee on resolutions—*a man who never had any sympathy with this*

SOURCE: "Clement Vallandigham Attacks Benjamin Wade" (1862). From CONGRESSIONAL GLOBE, 37th Cong., 2d sess., 1862, 1828–29, 1830.

Republic, but whose every breath is devoted to its destruction, just as far as his heart dare permit him to go."

Now, sir, here in my place in the House, and as a Representative, I denounce—and I speak it advisedly—the author of that speech as a liar, a scoundrel, and a coward. His name is Benjamin F. Wade....

Now, in the first place, I deny that I have violated any rule. I took a paper, and read from a printed speech that which related to me personally, and which contained a foul and infamous libel which the utterer knew, at the time, to be false and slanderous. He, the member from Ohio, talk now, indeed! of the opprobrium of the epithets, "liar," "scoundrel," and "coward"! Does he not know that the word "traitor" enters here now covered ten times over with the leprosy of reproach; and am I to sit in this Hall unmoved while that epithet is insinuated against me, in all its taint and foulness, by a member of the Senate, it may be, where I have no chance to meet and hurl it back on the spot as it deserves? Am I to bear it calmly any longer, uttered by any responsible person? I tell you, nay. And when I choose to meet and brand it as a man and as a gentleman should meet and brand it, am I to be called in question here and the first offender go acquit? Sir, I referred to the man, not to the Senator. My manner of allusion was in accordance with ancient parliamentary usage; and if the member from Ohio had known anything about parliamentary usage, he would have known that.... I said nothing for which I could properly be called to order in debate....

But I scorn to stand upon that point alone. If what I said has been out of order, let the member from Ohio go to the Senate first and there vindicate the violated obligations of parliamentary decorum. Is it disorderly for a member of this House to refer to a member of the Senate, and yet exactly in order for a Senator to denounce a member of this House ... as "a man who never had any sympathy with this Republic, and whose every breath is devoted to its destruction, just as far as his heart dare permit him to go?" And has the member from Ohio no holy indignation against a Senator who has thus wantonly, and in violation of all parliamentary law, slandered a Representative in this House? Sir, let him go to the Senate, where those false words were uttered, if they were uttered in the Senate, and let him see to it that that body shall first vindicate its obligations to the members of this House, before he dares to call me to a reckoning for words spoken in retort here. How does he know that the words spoken by me had reference to a Senator? But no; suppose they had, what of it? Was not the retaliation just what he deserved? Could anything less have expiated the offense? Sir, I spoke of him as Benjamin F. Wade, an individual, a citizen of my own State, and made no allusion to him as a Senator....

I have not finished the sentence. Whenever Benjamin F. Wade shall take back the false and slanderous accusation which he has made against me, I will take back the language I have applied to him; but not before.

QUESTIONS TO CONSIDER

1. How would you compare Clement Vallandigham's and Benjamin Wade's political views? How do you account for the differences? What were the most important influences shaping each man's outlook?

2. Some historians have argued that Vallandigham was a traitor to the Union cause, while others view him as a loyal and legitimate political opponent. Which view do you think is correct? Why?

3. Wade was one of the most radical politicians of his time. What was so radical about his views? What threat did they pose to Abraham Lincoln during the Civil War?

4. Wars often result in the narrowing of civil liberties. The Civil War was no exception. Do you think Lincoln was justified in dealing with Vallandigham as he did? What do the careers of Vallandigham and Wade reveal about the political pressures confronting Lincoln during the war? Do you see any parallels regarding the issue of civil liberties during the Civil War and in our own time?

FOR FURTHER READING

Frank L. Klement, *The Limits of Dissent: Clement L. Vallandigham and the Civil War* (New York: Fordham University Press, 1998), provides a balanced study of Vallandigham's role in the war.

Mark E. Neely Jr., *The Fate of Liberty: Abraham Lincoln and Civil Liberties* (New York: Oxford University Press, 1991), offers a Pulitzer Prize–winning study of Lincoln's constitutional policies that offers a sympathetic view of his actions.

Phillip S. Paludan, *The Presidency of Abraham Lincoln* (Lawrence: University Press of Kansas, 1994), provides a balanced interpretation of the constitutional issues confronting Lincoln.

Hans Louis Trefousse, *Benjamin Franklin Wade: Radical Republican from Ohio* (New York: Twayne Publishers, 1963), provides the classic biography of Wade.

15

Race and Redemption in the Reconstructed South: Robert Smalls and Wade Hampton

In the predawn hours of May 13, 1862, the small Confederate ship *Planter* made its way out of Charleston Harbor. As it steamed toward the ships blockading the South Carolina port, Union lookouts strained their eyes, then prepared to sound the alarm to open fire on the small vessel. Suddenly, one lookout spotted a white flag flying on the boat, and the Union ships held their fire. As the *Planter* came alongside, Union naval officers were shocked. No whites were on board. Instead, they saw only black men, women, and children, who were dancing, singing, and shouting for joy. When a Union officer boarded, a well-dressed black man stepped forward to address him. "Good morning, sir! I've brought you some of the old United States guns, sir!" Indeed he had. An armed Confederate vessel, the *Planter* contained a cargo of unmounted cannon and sixteen slaves who had captured the boat and escaped to freedom. The man who had organized the capture was the ship's pilot, a twenty-three-year-old slave named Robert Smalls.

The very next month in the Battle of Seven Pines, a forty-four-year-old Confederate Brigadier General named Wade Hampton led his brigade into an entrenched Union force near the Chickahominy River, east of Richmond, Virginia. Hampton and his men confronted a hail of Union fire. Half of his brigade fell dead or wounded. Hit in the foot, Hampton remained on his horse and under fire while a Confederate army surgeon extracted the bullet. After the battle, Confederate General Robert E. Lee, the new commander of the Army of Northern Virginia, cited Hampton in his official report. "General Hampton," Lee wrote, "... was remarkable for his coolness, promptness, and decided practical ability as a leader of men in difficult and dangerous circumstances. In these high characteristics ... he has few equals and perhaps no superior." In fact, Wade

Library of Congress, Prints & Photographs Division, [LC-DIG-cwpbh-03583]

Mathew Brady/Newscom

Robert Smalls   Wade Hampton

Hampton would go on by the end of the Civil War to establish a reputation on the battlefield that few commanders, Union or Confederate, could match.

Robert Smalls and Wade Hampton served bravely in the Civil War. Both men called South Carolina home and came to be involved in politics there in the period after the war known as Reconstruction. As political leaders, both would find themselves deeply embroiled in a struggle to determine the political fate of their state. And, as in the Civil War, they would fight for very different causes. A Republican representative from South Carolina, Smalls would support his party's efforts to reconstruct the South and guarantee political equality for the freedmen. A prominent planter and governor of the state, Hampton could never accept racial equality and in time would lead Democrats in overthrowing the Republican regime in South Carolina. Hampton and Smalls were only two of the millions of Americans who contributed to the Union and Confederate war efforts. Like so many other Americans, they did not agree about what should occur in the South when the war was over. For that reason, the stories of these two Civil War heroes may help us understand what many in South Carolina and beyond saw at stake in the fight over Reconstruction and why that battle ultimately turned out as it did.

"THE SMARTEST *CULLUD* MAN"

Little in Robert Smalls's background could have foretold his rise in life. In fact, he would rise from utter obscurity. He was born in 1839 in Beaufort, South Carolina, to a slave woman who worked as a domestic servant. His father was an unknown white man, although many believed that he was John McKee, his mother's master. John McKee died when Robert was six, and his son Henry sent Smalls to live with relatives in Charleston when he was twelve. He lived in the home of his master's sister-in-law, working as a waiter, a lamplighter, and a stevedore. Smalls was "hired out," meaning that he worked for wages. He kept some of his pay for himself and sent the rest to his master. This situation gave the young slave relative autonomy. He may even have had enough freedom to pursue an education during his years in the city. Smalls apparently taught himself to read and possibly attended for a few months a school run by one of Charleston's many black societies. Formed in violation of the South Carolina law that prohibited more than four slaves from assembling at one time, such societies often provided education and other services to the African-American community.

In 1858, Smalls married Hannah Jones, a hotel maid who was also a slave. He was nineteen; she was thirty-one. Smalls said he married Hannah because he wanted "to have a wife to prevent me from running around—to have somebody to do for me and to keep me." Slaves, of course, were not allowed to marry legally, but Smalls made a deal with his master. He would pay McKee fifteen dollars a month so that he could marry Hannah. Smalls made a similar deal with Hannah's master, paying him five dollars a month. This allowed the two slaves to keep enough money to support themselves and even have children. Smalls later agreed to purchase his wife and daughter for eight hundred dollars. When he fled the city in 1862, he had seven hundred dollars, having never paid any of the agreed-upon amount to his wife's owner. How he accumulated this sum and managed to keep his household running is difficult to imagine. His own wages as a deck hand in 1861 amounted to only sixteen dollars a month, and Hannah probably made no more than ten dollars a month as a maid, assuming that she continued to work after their marriage.

Somehow the little family managed to make it, probably due to Smalls's abilities as a trader. His position as a deck hand on the *Planter* allowed him even greater autonomy than his job on the docks. Traveling on the river and coastal steamer, Smalls was able to make regular visits to friends and associates in a wider area. He traded goods within the slave community and probably with whites as well. As a sailor, Smalls acquired valuable skills. He learned to handle the ship and eventually became a wheelman. (Actually, he was a pilot, a title white Southerners refused to give blacks.) When the Civil War offered him the opportunity to escape bondage, his skills, education, and position served him well. Smalls carefully planned the escape of his family and friends. One night when the ship's three white officers were on shore, he pulled off his plan in a dramatic fashion.

The theft of the *Planter* brought not only freedom but also an economic windfall. The northern press jumped on the story of Smalls's heroic action. *Harper's Weekly*, for instance, ran a picture of Smalls and an article on the "plucky Africans." One New York newspaper commented that few events during the Civil War "produced a heartier chuckle of satisfaction" than the theft of the *Planter*. The "fellow" behind the feat, it observed, "is no Small man." Given such favorable reaction, Smalls and his fellow hijackers were awarded a bounty by Congress for liberating the *Planter*. As leader of the party, Smalls got the largest share, fifteen hundred dollars. He continued to work as a pilot on the *Planter*, which was now operating as a troop transport for the Union. The ship shuttled men and supplies between the Sea Islands[*] off South Carolina and mainland areas

---

[*]*Sea Islands:* Low-lying islands off the coast of South Carolina and Georgia. Occupied early in the war by Union forces, the islands were home to a large number of blacks who worked on the rice plantations there.

occupied by Union forces. In addition, he piloted other ships, including some engaged in unsuccessful attacks on Charleston.

At the same time, Smalls worked to improve the condition of fellow blacks. In Union-occupied Beaufort, he engaged in fund-raising to assist freedmen with education and employment. He also traveled to New York during the war to raise awareness of the condition of the growing ranks of free blacks in the South. He had been sent north by freedmen in Beaufort County who were eager to help themselves rather than wait for charity or government assistance. Such efforts were widespread throughout the postwar South, but African Americans in Beaufort County became organized—and politicized— several years before those in most other areas. A highly concentrated black population, early occupation by Union forces, and a large number of black soldiers and white teachers and missionaries contributed to their efforts. Already in 1864, blacks in the area had expressed their political preferences by organizing a delegation to the Republican convention in Baltimore. Although the delegates could not secure official representation at the convention, they made it clear that they were ready to "fight for the Union [and] die for it" and that they also wanted the right to "vote for it."

Unfortunately, that right was not immediately forthcoming, even when the Civil War ended. When Andrew Johnson became president after Lincoln's assassination in April 1865, he promoted a Reconstruction plan that excluded blacks from politics. Committed to white rule in the South, Johnson wanted a policy that would bring the rebellious states back into the Union without a fundamental restructuring of southern society. Under his Reconstruction plan, white Southerners—often former Confederates—quickly reorganized state governments. By early 1866, southern state legislatures elected under the president's plan had passed Black Codes. These laws severely limited the rights of African Americans to own property, assemble, move about freely, and vote. Often they prevented interracial marriage and upheld labor contracts that favored white landowners. The Black Codes in South Carolina legalized harsh labor practices regarding blacks and placed severe restrictions on freedmen. At a convention in late 1865, South Carolina blacks protested the new laws. In an address to the state's whites, the convention demanded that blacks "be governed by the same laws that control other men." **[See Source 1.]**

For several years after the war, Smalls was more concerned with improving his own position than with getting involved in politics. Even before the war ended, he returned to Beaufort and opened a store. He did well enough to purchase his former master's house by paying the back taxes on it. In 1867, he purchased an eight-room building at a government tax sale and deeded it "to the Colored children" of Beaufort as a school. These actions are a measure of his status in the community. One observer, capturing the dialect of Sea Island blacks, noted that Smalls was "regarded by all the other negroes as immensely rich, and decidedly 'the smartest *cullud* man in South Carolina.'" Widely known, well-off, obviously intelligent, and self-possessed, Smalls was a natural leader in his community. His emergence as a prominent black politician during Reconstruction was almost inevitable.

"A HORDE OF BARBARIANS"

If nothing in Robert Smalls's background seemed to prepare him for fame and political fortune, virtually everything in Wade Hampton's marked him for both. Hampton was the oldest son of Wade Hampton II, a South Carolina planter and businessman and one the South's richest men. Though only one generation removed from his southern frontier roots, Wade Hampton II had established himself as a leader in the southern planter aristocracy. The Hampton seat was a sprawling plantation near Columbia, but the family owned other plantations in South Carolina, Mississippi, and Louisiana. A generation earlier, Wade Hampton I had settled in the back country, made a fortune, and went on to serve in the House of Representatives. By the late 1820s, he owned more than two thousand slaves, and his annual income from his Louisiana plantations alone was $100,000—a princely sum at the time. Wade Hampton III was born in 1818 into this world of wealth and privilege—made possible, of course, by the South's slave system.

Hampton's upbringing reflected the family's circumstances. He attended a private academy, where he received a classical education, then enrolled at South Carolina College (now the University of South Carolina) at the age of fourteen. Graduating in 1836, he went on to study law. At the age of twenty, he married Margaret Preston, the daughter of a prominent Virginia family. Meanwhile, he had also gained a valuable education elsewhere. As a young man, Hampton learned something about plantation management on the family's vast holdings in South Carolina and Mississippi. He also took to the outdoors. Both his father and grandfather were skilled sportsmen, and at an early age, he became an accomplished horseman and experienced hunter. It was later said that Hampton had killed as many as eighty bears on his hunting expeditions, sometimes with nothing more than a knife. Maturing into a powerfully built six-footer, he had learned skills that would help win him a reputation on the battlefield and in time make him in the minds of many South Carolinians a natural leader of a white supremacist counterassault on the state's Reconstruction government.

Befitting a man of his station, Hampton would also gain political experience. In 1852, he took a seat in the South Carolina assembly and six years later moved to the state senate. By then South Carolina was a hotbed of growing secessionist sentiment. Whites in the Palmetto State were literally surrounded and outnumbered by their black slaves. Naturally insecure, they had long been hypersensitive to any action they perceived as harmful to their interests or that weakened their "peculiar institution." In 1832, South Carolina had sparked the Nullification Crisis when it declared a new federal tariff of 1832 null and void. As the sectional crisis of the 1850s intensified, Robert Barnwell Rhett and other "fire eaters" easily stoked secessionist sentiment in the state. Wade Hampton was not one of them. A generation earlier, Hampton's father had fallen into the Whig camp, as had many business-minded Southerners who valued the bonds (and commercial ties) of Union. Hampton inherited this Whig orientation—and views that were moderate for his time and place. In fact, he spent late 1860 at his Mississippi plantations, which had just produced a generous cotton crop. Removed from his home state's fervor, Hampton greeted the news of its secession with no enthusiasm.

Hampton's loyalties, though, lay with South Carolina. When the Civil War began with the firing on Fort Sumter, he resigned his seat in the senate and enlisted as a private in the state militia. Despite his lack of military experience, the governor immediately commissioned him as a colonel. Then Hampton formed and partially financed "Hampton's Legion," a unit more than one thousand strong made up of infantry, cavalry, and artillery. Reassigned that summer to the Confederate army, Hampton's unit saw combat at the First Battle of Bull Run, where he was wounded the first of five times during the war. As the war progressed, Hampton's bravery and skill as a horseman earned him increasing respect and additional promotions. At the Battle of Fredericksburg in 1862, he led cavalry raids behind Union lines, capturing both prisoners and supplies. At the Battle of Gettysburg the next year, he led a cavalry attack against Union forces, received multiple wounds, and was taken back to Virginia in an ambulance. After returning to action and receiving command of the Cavalry Corps, he went on to defeat Union general Philip Sheridan's cavalry in 1864 during the Overland Campaign in Virginia and never suffered a defeat during the remainder of the war. He ended the war as a lieutenant general in the Confederate cavalry service—a rank shared only with future Ku Klux Klan founder Nathan Bedford Forrest.

Hampton was a hero by war's end. His unwavering commitment to the Confederate cause, however, had exacted a high price. Among his losses, Hampton counted one of his two sons. Much of his wealth was gone, consumed by war or used to supply his soldiers. While laying waste to large swaths of Confederate territory, General William T. Sherman's forces destroyed Millwood, Hampton's childhood home near Columbia, which had also been reduced, according to one Northern journalist, to "a wilderness of ruins." Finally, of course, Hampton's slaves—one of his biggest assets and the very foundation of the family's wealth, power, and social position—had been freed. As a female acquaintance told the South Carolinian diarist Mary Boykin Chesnut, "General Hampton is home again. He looks crushed."

Hampton's attitude reflected the feelings of many former Confederates. For a brief time at war's end he had contemplated guerrilla action against the victorious Union forces. He even toyed with the idea of leaving the country for Mexico or Brazil. Hampton decided to stay and rebuild his fortunes. Like many former Confederates, though, he was unable to accept fully the implications of the Union's victory. In fact, he believed that Andrew Johnson had no constitutional authority to remake the state governments of the defeated South. In a speech to a mixed audience of whites and blacks in late 1865, he declared that slavery had been destroyed "by a single despotic stroke of the pen." And, of course, Hampton shared the racial views of most whites as well. He would warn his black listeners not to "think, because you are free as the white people, that you are their equal, because you are not."

Hampton would have no direct role in the government that emerged under Andrew Johnson's plan for Reconstruction. That plan excluded former Confederate political and military leaders from participation in the political reconstruction of the former Confederate states without an individual pardon, which Hampton likely did not earn until 1872. Yet he was a natural political leader in the minds of many white South Carolinians. Thus, when the Johnson-appointed provisional governor called a convention to reorganize the state government, Hampton was elected as a delegate. Later that year, many voters again defied the prohibition against participation by former Confederates when they nearly elected him governor over his own protests. Such defiance did not bode well for the smooth reconstruction of South Carolina.

In fact, the Johnson plan had laid down minimal conditions for the political reconstruction of former Confederate states. Aside from excluding from politics former Confederate leaders without a presidential pardon, it required states to ratify the Thirteenth Amendment prohibiting slavery, invalidate Confederate debt, and repudiate secession. Black voting, of course, played no role under the Johnson plan, and the new governments that arose in South Carolina and other former Confederate states virtually ignored the political and economic aspirations of the freedmen. In South Carolina, the new legislature enacted a Black Code that severely restricted the freedom of blacks, forcing the federal military commander in the state to invalidate it. In the end, Johnson's terms proved quite acceptable to Hampton and most other whites in the South. At the same time, the results of Johnson's plan created ample cause for alarm elsewhere. Fearing that former Confederates sought to overturn the results of the war, Congress refused to seat representatives and senators elected under the president's plan and thereby acknowledge the new governments' legitimacy.

In the face of growing Republican outrage over presidential Reconstruction, Hampton stepped forward to express support for a beleaguered Johnson. Speaking for the white leadership in late 1865, he advised South Carolinians to overlook Johnson's lack of constitutional authority to remake the state's government and accept the terms laid down by the president, including an end to slave labor. South Carolinians, he declared, should support Johnson "so long as he manifests a disposition to restore all our rights as a sovereign state." In a public letter to the president the next year, Hampton declared gratitude that Johnson had prevented "life itself" from being "utterly crushed out of our unfortunate country." He also pointed to evidence of the "bitterest and most vindictive hatred" harbored by northern Republicans against the South: the creation of the "hydra-head monster" known as the Freedmen's Bureau[*] and the decision to send black troops into the state, "pouring into our whole country a horde of barbarians." **[See Source 2.]** Speaking to Confederate veterans in the fall of 1866, Hampton chastised the North for failing to live up to its word by refusing to seat the delegates elected to Congress under Johnson's plan. Responding to his speech, the *New York Times* declared that "complaints of a breach of faith are utterly without foundation." Going further, one northern journalist who traveled through the South after the war singled out Hampton as an "exemplar" of white Southerners' "proud and domineering spirit." **[Sec Source 3.]**

Such accounts fed growing northern alarm about the southern state governments set up under Johnson's plan. They also helped rally the Radical Republicans[*] to action. In 1866, Congress passed the Fourteenth Amendment and submitted it to the states for ratification. The amendment extended citizenship to African Americans, barred former Confederates from holding office, and penalized states that did not allow blacks to vote by reducing their representation in Congress. All but one of the former Confederate states rejected the amendment (although it was ratified in 1868). James Orr, then governor of South Carolina, expressed the sentiment of many southern whites when he declared that blacks were "steeped in ignorance, crime, and vice" and should not be allowed to vote. This resistance to the wishes of Congress further angered many northerners, who now believed that Johnson and the southern politicians were overturning the Union's victory in the war. In late 1866, therefore, Republicans made big gains in the congressional elections, and the Radicals in Congress seized the initiative. Early the next year, they passed the first of the Reconstruction Acts,[*] which overturned the governments established under Johnson's plan and imposed military rule on most of the former Confederate states. Under the watchful eyes of the military, the freedmen would be registered to vote, new state constitutions drafted, and new elections held. In South Carolina and across the South, Republicans were swept into power.

As these events unfolded in South Carolina, Hampton emerged as a leading spokesman for the state's alarmed whites. At the same time, he began to take a more conciliatory approach, conceding that *some* blacks should be allowed to vote. "We can control

---

[*]*Freedmen's Bureau:* A temporary bureau established by Congress in 1865 to provide assistance to the freedmen and oversee abandoned lands in the South.

[*]*Radical Republicans:* Those Republicans who wanted the abolition of slavery, an extension of citizenship to former slaves, and punishment of Confederate leaders. After the war, the Radicals believed that Reconstruction could not be achieved without a restructuring of southern society.

[*]*Reconstruction Acts:* Acts passed by Congress in 1867 and 1868 that divided former Confederate states into five military districts, subjected them to martial law, and gave military commanders the power to register voters and oversee elections.

and direct the negroes [*sic*] if we act discreetly," he wrote to a white associate in 1867, "and in my judgment the highest duty of every Southern man is to secure the good will and confidence of the negro [*sic*]. Our future depends on this." Any attempt by white South Carolinians to appeal to black voters, however, was destined to fail. The overwhelming majority of freedmen were in no mood to be led by the state's traditional white leaders, especially when Hampton and other prominent Democrats repeatedly endorsed white supremacy.

In fact, as the career of Robert Smalls illustrates, the overturning of South Carolina's Johnson government finally gave the freedmen an opportunity to assert themselves politically. After helping form the Beaufort Republican Club in 1867, Smalls received its nomination as a delegate to the state's constitutional convention. Meeting early in 1868, the convention brought together 124 delegates, 78 of whom were black. Although one South Carolina newspaper charged that the black delegates were "misguided as to their true welfare," South Carolina's new constitution was revolutionary for the South and reflected the concerns of the state's black majority. It called, for instance, for state assistance to help people in "their homeless and landless condition." It declared that "no person shall be deprived of the right of suffrage for non-payment of the poll tax."[*] It abolished segregation. The delegates also recognized that the maintenance of a government "faithful to the interests and liberties of the people" depended "in great measure on the intelligence of the people themselves." Thus, following a resolution offered by Smalls, the constitution provided for free elementary schooling for all children.

Submitted to South Carolina's now largely black electorate, the new constitution was overwhelmingly approved. Shortly after that, new elections brought Republicans to power. Responding to these events, the state Democratic Party's executive committee, chaired by Hampton, issued *The Respectful Remonstrance on Behalf of the White People of South Carolina*. It contained a litany of objections to Republican rule in the state, including the enfranchisement of all black males and the disenfranchisement of former Confederate office holders. "The superior race," it declared, "has been made subservient to the inferior." Protest, though, is all that Hampton could do by the end of 1868. His political rights were still not fully restored and Republicans were in control. Like many other white Democratic leaders across the South, he retreated from politics. For a number of years, Hampton focused on repairing his tattered finances. His labor force needed to be reestablished under new terms. He was badly in debt, crops were poor, and he had lost some of his Mississippi property. As he had earlier written in despair to a Virginia relative, "The war was full or sorrows and griefs to me, but peace has been worse."

"MASSACRED IN COLD BLOOD"

While Hampton withdrew, Robert Smalls's career continued to embody the hopes that many freedmen placed in Reconstruction. In 1868, Smalls won a seat in the lower house of the legislature—the only one in the reconstructed South made up of a majority of black legislators. In fact, the majority of the state's legislators were ex-slaves. Smalls and the other freedmen often deferred to whites and the better-educated freeborn blacks, but Smalls continued to fight for issues that affected his black constituents. He served on a

---

[*]*Poll tax:* A tax established in many southern states as a requirement for voting in order to discourage blacks from casting ballots.

commission "to establish and maintain a system of free common schools" and sponsored a bill to enforce the Civil Rights Act of 1866, which granted the same civil rights to all persons born in the United States. He also served on a panel that investigated the intimidation, even murder, of Republican voters in the state during the 1868 election.

Smalls devoted much of his energy in the legislature to mundane issues that benefited his constituents in Beaufort County. He championed the construction of roads, railroads, government buildings, and docks in his district. He mobilized voters with brass bands and torchlight parades, and he knew how to arouse them with passionate rhetoric. He called on black voters to "bury the democratic party so deep that there will not be seen even a bubble coming from the spot where the burial took place," and he vowed to "pour hot shot into the ranks of traitors." At the same time, his financial support of the widow and family of his former master built up the goodwill of many whites in the county. All these efforts paid off, as Smalls built a political machine* based on the loyalty of his constituents. As one observer put it, "The men, women and children seem to regard him with a feeling akin to worship." Although Smalls was not highly educated, another noted, he was "a thoroughly representative man among the people" and had "their unlimited confidence." That confidence was evident in 1870, when he handily won election to the upper house of the state legislature. Smalls sat in the state senate for four years and then in 1874 won election to the U.S. House of Representatives. Mobilizing his Beaufort County machine, he swamped his opponent by a margin of more than four to one.

Taking his seat in Congress in 1875, Smalls continued to mind the needs of his South Carolina constituents—white and black. In 1876, for example, Smalls fought a minor battle over federal control of the Citadel, the military school in Charleston that had been seized by the national government during the war. The takeover of the school had upset many white South Carolinians, and Smalls demanded that the secretary of war at least pay rent to the city of Charleston for use of the grounds. As in the state legislature, however, much of his energy was devoted to the passage of bills concerning such mundane matters as appropriating funds for the maintenance of harbors. Although such work was not glamorous, Smalls recognized its importance for his district's well-being.

At the same time, Smalls worked to protect black workers. Labor disputes were a frequent source of friction between the freedmen and white landowners, especially in South Carolina's rice producing low country. In 1876, laborers on Combahee River plantations walked off their jobs, demanding higher pay and cash wages. The strike eventually produced a confrontation between armed whites and the strikers that likely would have led to bloodshed but for Smalls's intervention. After failing to receive the support of Republican authorities, the planters eventually gave in to laborers' demands—an outcome that no doubt reinforced their desire for a change in government.

Smalls was at the height of his power, but troubling developments beyond his own district had already begun to undermine Reconstruction. The bastion of anti-Reconstruction whites, the Democratic Party had made a remarkable comeback elsewhere in the South by the early 1870s. In fact, by the time Smalls first took his seat in Congress in 1876, the Democrats had a majority in the House of Representatives for the first time. About two-thirds of the Democrats in the House were southerners, and eighty of them were veterans of the Confederate military. Calling themselves Redeemers,* these

---

Political machine: A type of political organization that often dominated city and state politics in the late nineteenth century. The bosses who ran these machines often built up support by dispensing favors to constituents.

Redeemers: Conservative white Democrats who vowed to save, or redeem, the South from Republican rule.

southern Democrats launched a violent assault against Republican rule. As white terrorist organizations such as the Ku Klux Klan and the Red Shirts used violence and even murder to intimidate Republican voters, the Democrats began to regain political control in one state after another.

South Carolina was a particularly fertile field for the growth of vigilante groups. Although whites were able to join the state militia there, it had become an all-black force. White South Carolinians responded by flocking into the Ku Klux Klan and numerous "rifle clubs." Often founded by former Confederate officers, these clubs were usually nothing more than armed bands of night riders. The inevitable result was a rising tide of violence, mostly committed by whites against blacks. In 1870 and 1871, Congress passed the so-called Ku Klux Klan Acts,* which gave the president the power to suspend the writ of habeas corpus* in areas of armed insurrection. After federal agents arrested more than five hundred white South Carolinians across nine counties, a congressional committee investigated the bloodshed in 1872. One of its witnesses was Wade Hampton, who had spent much of his time out of South Carolina but remained visible enough in the state to still be one of its "natural" leaders. Hampton suggested that blacks had intimidated other blacks who wanted to vote for Democrats, but denied any knowledge that Democrats in the state were using violence to suppress black voting. **[See Source 4.]**

Smalls, on other hand, knew that without the protection of federal troops white vigilante groups would be free to terrorize black voters and eventually overthrow Republican control of the state. His fears were well-founded. By 1876, whites in South Carolina had organized about three hundred rifle clubs, with twenty-four in mostly black Beaufort County alone. In one particularly gruesome incident that summer in Hamburg (now North Augusta), South Carolina, a mob of about a thousand armed whites surrounded a black militia unit and murdered a number of militiamen after they surrendered. As one newspaper put it, they "were shot down like rabbits." In the face of such assaults, Smalls fought to save what was left of Reconstruction. Shortly after the massacre, he unsuccessfully attempted to amend a force reduction bill, arguing that no military forces should be withdrawn from South Carolina "so long as the militia of that State … are assaulted, disarmed, and taken prisoners, and then massacred in cold blood by lawless band of men." **[See Source 5.]**

South Carolina Democrats, meanwhile, did not rely solely on violence to battle Republicans. They had also launched a vocal propaganda campaign against the alleged corruption and mismanagement of the Republican-controlled state government. As with the Reconstruction governments in other states, South Carolina's legislature had made large expenditures to help rebuild the war-torn South. Increased spending on a shrunken, war-ravaged tax base made these Republican regimes inviting targets. So did the presence in them of northerners, who were derisively called carpetbaggers.* The Redeemers railed against the wasteful excesses of "carpetbag" governments that, they said, had spent once responsible states to the brink of bankruptcy. Most of all, though, the Redeemers played

---

Ku Klux Klan Acts: Passed in Congress in 1870 and 1871, these acts resulted from overwhelming evidence of widespread white terrorism against blacks. They gave the president new powers to put down such violence, including the detention of whites.

Habeas corpus: The legal right of jailed persons to be brought before a court to determine whether they should be charged with a crime or released.

Carpetbaggers: The label applied by white southerners to northerners in the South during Reconstruction. The term was used to suggest that these "Yankees" carried their worldly goods in their carpetbags (suitcases) and therefore had no roots in the community. Because some of the northerners were involved in Reconstruction politics, the label also implied that they were corrupt—that is, out to enrich themselves at the public's expense.

on the deeply held racism of the white southerners. "Ignorant" blacks, they charged, had been taken advantage of by grasping "Yankees," and the result was a disgraceful riot of incompetence and theft. With its black-majority legislature, South Carolina was especially vulnerable to this charge. In 1874, *New York Tribune* reporter James Pike wrote an influential book titled *The Prostrate State: South Carolina Under Negro Government,* in which he referred to the actions of the legislature as a "shocking burlesque upon legislative proceedings" and to the black legislators themselves as an "uncouth and untutored multitude."

"NOTHING MORE TO DO WITH HIM"

These developments did not bode well for Smalls or Reconstruction. They set the stage, though, for Wade Hampton to lead the Democratic "redemption" of South Carolina, one of only three states where Republicans were still in control. As white Democrats became more assertive, prominent members of the state's Democratic Party turned to Hampton to accept its nomination for governor in 1876. Running against the incumbent Republican, Hampton enjoyed the backing of less "respectable" whites: the Red Shirts and members of Democratic rifle clubs, who frequently disrupted Republican rallies and intimidated black voters with whippings, assaults, and murders. **[See Source 6.]** Even as he promised blacks equal treatment under his administration and distanced himself from the "type of South Carolinian ... who killed negroes [sic] without provocation," Hampton tolerated widespread violence against blacks during the election, perhaps the bloodiest in the state's history. To mobilize white voters, many of whom had not voted since Republicans took control of the state, he even went on a triumphal tour of the state accompanied by hundreds of armed supporters.

Like the presidential election that year, the election for governor in South Carolina ended in a deadlock with disputed votes on each side. For six months, the state had two legislatures and two governors. The deadlocked presidential election of 1876, however, gave Hampton and his supporters their opening. The Democratic candidate, Samuel J. Tilden, won the popular vote, but twenty electoral votes in the Deep South were in dispute. When a special commission appointed by Congress met to resolve the issue, it awarded all twenty electoral votes—and the presidency—to the Republican candidate, Rutherford B. Hayes. The Democrats lost the presidency by one electoral vote, but they had gained something, too. Although Republicans retained control of the presidency, Democrats were able to end the protection provided to blacks by federal troops in the remaining Republican states in the South. Without it, the Republican governments in South Carolina, Florida, and Louisiana were doomed. In 1877, Hampton became the undisputed governor. At the same time, the Democratic Redeemer assembly named Benjamin Butler, the man who led the white assault in the Hamburg massacre, the state's new U.S. senator. With the so-called Compromise of 1877,[*] conservative Democratic rule was restored across the South. Reconstruction was over.

The meaning of Hampton's victory quickly became clear, especially for blacks. Although Hampton appointed freedmen to some minor state offices and for now they

---

[*]*Compromise of 1877:* The political deal struck between Republicans and Democrats to break the deadlocked presidential election of 1876. In exchange for keeping control of the presidency, Republicans agreed to end military protection for Republican voters in three southern states, thereby ensuring an end to Reconstruction across the South.

maintained the right to vote, Redemption proved disastrous for blacks. What protection federal force had provided to safeguard their civil rights was gone. Intimidation, voter fraud, and gerrymandering left the Republican Party in shambles. It was the same across the South. As one black Southerner put it, "Every state in the South had got into the hands of those who kept us as slaves."

After winning control of the state, Hampton and the Democrats in South Carolina moved to purge Republicans from important offices. One way was to prove the corruption of the prior Republican regimes. In his second term in Congress, Smalls became a prime target of their investigations. While serving in the state senate, he had chaired the Printing Committee, which oversaw the government's printing contracts. Now the Democrats accused him of accepting a bribe in connection with those contracts. Smalls said that he was innocent, but he was convicted by a jury and sentenced to three years in prison "with hard labor." He appealed the verdict before the state supreme court and lost, but the Democratic governor pardoned him when the Republicans promised to drop their investigation into Democratic election fraud. In reality, Smalls probably had overstepped the bounds of legality, but the evidence was scanty, others also were involved, and his crime paled in comparison to those committed by other politicians of the day. It was obvious that Smalls had been a political target and that the Democrats wanted control of his congressional district.

The Democrats had not seen the last of the determined Smalls, however. In 1878, he ran for reelection to Congress. As they had done throughout the South, the Democrats influenced the election by frightening voters away from the polls. Smalls lost, but he was undeterred. Two years later, he ran for Congress again. Despite all their advantages, the Democrats realized that it would be a close race. To counter Smalls's popularity among black voters, the Democrats stuffed the ballot boxes. The fraud was so obvious that Smalls was awarded the victory when he challenged the results. By the time he took his seat, however, his term was almost over. To ensure their victory when Smalls ran again in 1882, the Democrats in control of the state legislature redrew the boundaries of his congressional district so that he was unable even to win the Republican primary. Denied the nomination, he would regain his seat in 1884 when the Republican winner died in office and a party convention selected him to finish out the term. Later that year, he was reelected. The Democrats were still determined to have his seat, however, and in 1886 they once again resorted to violence, tossing out Republican ballots and forcing black voters away from the polls to defeat Smalls for good. Appointed a collector of customs for the port of Beaufort when the Republicans won the presidency in 1888, he served in that position on and off until 1913, one of the few black officeholders in the South. Until the day he died in 1915, however, he was convinced that Reconstruction had been a failure.

Meanwhile, Wade Hampton's political career had also been cut short. He won a second term as governor in 1878, but days after his reelection as governor in 1878, the state assembly named him to the U.S. Senate. There he continued in his role of spokesman for the South during two terms, even if it meant defending the Ku Klux Klan from northern attacks. His popularity, though, would not last. Hampton had won office with the support of less "respectable" upcountry whites who did not often share the gentry's paternalistic attitude toward blacks. Ironically, he lost office when the forces of racial violence that he had ridden into office turned on him. In 1890, the upcountry followers' of Benjamin Tillman, a populist, anti-black Democrat who had played an important role in the Hamburg massacre in 1876, launched a race-baiting campaign for control of the South Carolina government. As hard times hit southern farmers in the late nineteenth century, the Tillmanite campaign revealed a class divide within the "solid" Democratic South. The "natural" leader Hampton became one of the Tillmanites' targets, and in

1890, they denied him a third term in the Senate. Hampton's political career was over. He went on to serve as a U.S. Railroad Commissioner for five years and then spent his remaining days at home in South Carolina.

Like Smalls, Hampton never doubted that Congressional Reconstruction was a failure. For Smalls, of course, it had failed by abandoning the freedmen; for Hampton, Congressional Reconstruction should never have happened at all. If judged by the second-class legal status of the freedmen and their economic and political condition, surely it *had* failed. In 1877, most blacks remained impoverished and tied to the land. By the time Hampton died in 1902, South Carolina and most other southern states had legally stripped the freedmen of the right to vote and hammered into place a rigid system of racial segregation enforced by lynching and other forms of violence. In South Carolina, this racial caste system stood as the ultimate bitter fruit of the Hampton-led redemption of the state. There and beyond, the predication of one publication had come to pass. "The Negro," The *Nation* magazine had declared in 1877, "will disappear from the field of national politics. Henceforth, the nation, as a nation, will have nothing more to do with him." Addressing that legal and political abandonment would be left for future generations. Only in the civil rights era of the next century would their efforts bear fruit. Then, in a "second Reconstruction," the nation began to finish the work of the first.

•PRIMARY SOURCES•

Source 1:   Zion Presbyterian Church, *"Memorial to the Senate and House of Representatives"* (1865)

The freed people of the South were at the heart of Reconstruction. In this document, African Americans from Zion Presbyterian Church in Charleston, South Carolina, present a list of demands to the U.S. Congress. What do these demands reveal about the people's desires? What does the tone of this document suggest about those who wrote it and, in particular, the position in which they found themselves at the time?

Gentlemen:

We, the colored people of the State of South Carolina, in Convention assembled, respectfully present for your attention some prominent facts in relation to our present condition, and make a modest yet earnest appeal to your considerate judgment.

We, your memorialists, with profound gratitude to almighty God, recognize the great boon of freedom conferred upon us by the instrumentality of our late President, Abraham Lincoln, and the armies of the United States.

"The Fixed decree, which not all Heaven can move,
Thou, Fate, fulfill it; and, ye Powers, approve."

We also recognize with liveliest gratitude the vast services of the Freed-men's Bureau together with the efforts of the good and wise throughout the land to raise up

SOURCE: Reprinted in James S. Allen, RECONSTRUCTION: THE BATTLE FOR DEMOCRACY, 1865–1876 (New York; International Publishers, 1937), appendix, pp. 228–229; originally from South Carolina African Americans' Petition, November 24, 1865.

an oppressed and deeply injured people in the scale of civilized being, during the throb-bings of a mighty revolution which must affect the future destiny of the world.

Conscious of the difficulties that surround our position, we would ask for no rights or privileges but such as rest upon the strong basis of justice and expediency, in view of the best interests of our entire country.

We ask first, that the strong arm of law and order be placed alike over the entire people of this State; that life and property be secured, and the laborer free to sell his labor as the merchant his goods.

We ask that a fair and impartial instruction be given to the pledges of the govern-ment to us concerning the land question.

We ask that the three great agents of civilized society—the school, the pulpit, the press—be as secure in South Carolina as in Massachusetts or Vermont.

We ask that equal suffrage be conferred upon us, in common with the white men of this State.

This we ask, because "all free governments derive their just powers from the consent of the governed"; and we are largely in the majority in this State, bearing for a long period the burden of onerous taxation, without a just representation. We ask for equal suffrage as a protection for the hostility evoked by our known faithfulness to our country and flag under all circumstances.

We ask that colored men shall not in every instance be tried by white men; and that neither by custom nor enactment shall we be excluded from the jury box.

We ask that, inasmuch as the Constitution of the United States explicitly declares that the right to keep and bear arms shall not be infringed and the Constitution is the Supreme law of the land—that the late efforts of the Legislature of this State to pass an act to deprive us of arms be forbidden, as a plain violation of the Constitution, and unjust to many of us in the highest degree, who have been soldiers, and purchased our muskets from the United States Government when mustered out of service.

We protest against any code of black laws the Legislature of this State may enact, and pray to be governed by the same laws that control other men. The right to assemble in peaceful convention, to discuss the political questions of the day; the right to enter upon all the avenues of agriculture, commerce, trade; to amass wealth by thrift and in-dustry; the right to develop our whole being by all the appliances that belong to civilized society, cannot be questioned by any class of intelligent legislators.

We solemnly affirm and desire to live orderly and peacefully with all the people of this State; and commending this memorial to your considerate judgment.

Thus we ever pray.

Charleston, S.C. November 24, 1865
Zion Presbyterian Church.

Source 2: *Wade Hampton Protests to the President* (1866)

Acting as a spokesman for the white South, Wade Hampton wrote Andrew Johnson a widely read letter in August 1866 that expressed his views about Reconstruction under the president's plan. What are his chief complaints about Reconstruction? What does the tone of this letter suggest about

SOURCE: Charles E. Cauthen, ed., FAMILY LETTERS OF THE THREE WADE HAMPTONS, 1782–1901 (Columbia: University of South Carolina Press, 1953), pp. 124–125, 128–129, 130–131, 139–140.

*the willingness of Hampton or other former Confederate leaders to accept political or social changes in
the South under Reconstruction?*

[W]hilst we acknowledge to their fullest extent our obligations to you, we think, that
owing to the misrepresentations of the true condition and feelings of the Southern people made to you by interested and mischievous parties, you have not exercised all the
power in your hands, to restore to the South as fully and as speedily as might have
been done peace—quiet and the inestimable rights of civil government. We do not at
all question, Mr. President, your earnest disposition to extend to us all these blessings
and to bring back the South to the Union with all her rights as well as all her duties
intact and unimpaired. Nor are we insensible of the great difficulties which have met
you at every step, nor of the bitter opposition which *fanaticism* has arrayed against you,
in your efforts to accomplish this laudable purpose. You have given too many unequiv-
ocal evidences of your ardent desire to bring about this result, for us to doubt either the
earnestness of your wishes or the sincerity of your convictions upon this vital point. And
if your efforts have not been crowned with the success they deserve and if the hopes and
expectations of the South have been disappointed, we attribute these results to no fault of
yours, but solely to the inherent difficulties of your position and to that malignant spirit
of fanaticism, which demands as the price of reunion, the complete degradation and the
absolute ruin of the South....

The close of the war—or to speak more accurately—the cessation of active hostilities, found the South in the conditions I have but feebly portrayed. Clothed in sack-
cloth and ashes, with her desecrated fanes and her desolated hearths on all sides, she had
to commence life anew. If stern Justice demanded that she should be punished, surely
that Justice should have been tempered by mercy. The North professed to fight solely
for the reestablishment of a fraternal union. When the sword was sheathed, what policy
could so well have effected this result as conciliation. Look back, Mr. President at the
events which have marked this, to the South, most bitter and mournful year and say if
the retrospect shows one effort made to conciliate her—one act of legislation that is not
calculated to gall and irritate her—or one evidence that the dominant party at the
North does not still cherish towards her, feelings of the bitterest and most vindictive
hatred. The very first act of *peace*, consisted in pouring into our whole country a horde
of barbarians—your brutal negro troops under their no less brutal and more degraded
Yankee Officers. Every licence was allowed to those wretches and the grossest outrages
were committed by them with impunity. Their very presence amongst us at such a
time, was felt as a direct and premeditated insult to the whole Southern people. Confederate soldiers returning home, weary and travel-stained, were seized by these negro
soldiers, and the buttons of that grey jacket, under which perhaps was beating as heroic
and as patriotic a heart as ever gave *its all* to a bleeding country—were roughly and
ignominiously torn off. No armed foe being in the field, the great armies of the North,
waged active and honorable warfare against Confederate grey and its brass buttons! Noble occupation for brave soldiers! It at least brought them into nearer contact with
those hated emblems of Southern Soldiery, than they had ventured to assume, during
the past four years....

The next step in the process of reconstruction was quite as unfortunate as that of
garrisoning the South with negro troops. This was the establishment of that incubus,—
that Hydra-headed Monster, the Freedman's Bureau. When the North had given freedom to four millions of stolen slaves, it was hoped that this generous offering which she
had laid on the Altar of Liberty, would have terminated forever that baleful agitation of

the negro question, which has deluged the land with blood and has ruined the fairest portion of this continent. The South acquiesced in the decree—though she was so blind as not to see the justice of it—which by one despotic stroke of a pen stripped her of more than a moiety of her property and she promptly and honestly endeavoured to adapt herself to the new relations between the two races, which this decree had brought about. The Southern people, amongst whom the negro had lived for generations, naturally imagined that they were fully competent to direct, to instruct and to protect him. Humanity and interest, which so seldom point in the same direction, in this case impelled the South to do all in its power to fit the negro for his new condition. The strong, but paternal hand which had controlled him through centuries of slavery, having been suddenly and rudely withdrawn, the only hope of rendering him, either useful, industrious or harmless, was to elevate him in the scale of civilization and to make him appreciate not only the blessings, but the duties of freedom. This was the prevalent, I may say the universal sentiment of the South and that much more not been done to carry this sentiment into effect, is due solely to the pernicious and mischievous interference of that most vicious institution, the Freedman's Bureau....

I have endeavoured, Mr. President, to lay before you fully and frankly those points wherein the South regards herself as injured and wronged and it only remains for me to state what I believe to be the prevailing sentiments of the people. That they felt the keenest disappointment at the failure of their attempt to separate from the North, there can be no question, and that they regarded this failure as a great misfortune, I do not pretend to deny. But while they were almost unanimous in their feelings on these points, they were perfectly sincere in their acceptance of the terms upon which they surrendered. They accepted those terms in good faith—without reservation—and they were and are prepared to abide them to the letter. Upon the main question, that most materially affecting their interests—the abolition of slavery—I honestly believe there is no desire to reverse the decree which has gone forth. I do not think that they would remand the negro to slavery, if they had the power to do so without question. The negro, whilst he was a slave, was happy, useful, honest and industrious. But his unfortunate association with the Yankee, has corrupted him to such a degree that we should now be very loath to own him, or to be responsible for his rascalities. While he was *ours*, we did all in our power to ameliorate his condition, but since he has been withdrawn from our care, we feel no longer responsible for him, except as one who is to live amongst us and we turn him over willingly to those who imported him from Africa, sold him to us, and then stole him to make him free. We are perfectly aware what his fate will be, but we feel no longer responsible for it. I am sure that the Southern States would protect him and give him all the rights he is capable of enjoying, if he is left to their care. Northern interference has already entailed certain extirmination on the race and a continuation of that interference will but hasten the fulfillment of this doom....

Source 3: *A Northerner Assesses Southern Attitudes* (1866)

Sidney Andrews was one of a number of northern journalists and observers who traveled through the South during Reconstruction. Andrews, whose dispatches appeared in Boston and Chicago

SOURCE: Sidney Andrews, THE SOUTH SINCE THE WAR (Boston, Houghton Mifflin Company, 1971; originally published in 1866).

newspapers, spent considerable time in South Carolina and commented extensively on the conditions and attitudes he found there. How does he characterize the attitudes of what he calls the "ruling class" in the state? What impact do you think his reports would have on northerners?

The indifference which so many of the people feel and express as to the fate of the negro is shocking and to the last degree revolting to me. He is actually to many of them nothing but a troublesome animal; not a human being, with hopes and longings and feelings, but a mere animal, valuable, but altogether unlovable. "I would shoot one just as soon as I would a dog," said a man to me yesterday on the cars. And I saw one shot at in Columbia as if he had been only a dog,—shot at from the door of a store, and at midday! "If I can only git shet of 'em I don't care what becomes of 'em," said one of my two stage companions in the ride from Columbia to Winnsboro, while speaking of the seventy negroes on his plantation. Of course he means to "git shet of 'em" as soon as possible. There are others who will follow his example....

Education never was general in the State, and for the last two or three years it has been almost entirely neglected. The ignorance of the great body of the whites is a fact that will astonish any observer conversant with the middle classes of the North. Travel where you will, and that sure indication of modern civilization, the school-house, is not to be found. Outside half a dozen of the larger towns I have not seen a dozen in over six hundred miles of travel. A few persons express the hope that the Legislature will do something to set the College once more at work; but, generally speaking, the indifference of the masses to the whole subject of education is as startling as it is painful.

The negroes, on the other hand, though in a very ignorant manner, are much interested in the matter. They all seem anxious to learn to read,—many of them appearing to have a notion that thereby will come honor and happiness. Schools for their benefit have already been established at some of the principal points, and the intent of the Freedmen's Bureau is that there shall be at least one in each district before spring. The disposition of the whites toward the negro schools is not good, and in many localities the teachers would be subject to insult, and probably to outrage, but for the presence of the military....

Where there is such a spirit of caste, where the ruling class has a personal interest in fostering prejudice, where the masses are in such an inert condition, where ignorance so generally prevails, where there is so little ambition for betterment, where life is so hard and material in its tone, it is not strange to find much hatred and contempt. Ignorance is generally cruel and frequently brutal. The political leaders of this people have apparently indoctrinated them with the notion that they are superior to any other class in the country. Hence there is usually very little effort to conceal the prevalent scorn of the Yankee,— this term being applied to the citizen of any Northern State. Any plan of reconstruction is wrong that tends to leave these old leaders in power. A few of them give certain evidence of a change of heart,—by some means save these for the sore and troubled future; but for the others, the men who not only brought on the war, but ruined the mental and moral force of their people before unfurling the banner of Rebellion,—for these there should never any more be place or countenance among honest and humane and patriotic people....

In South Carolina there is very little pretence of love for the Union, but everywhere a passionate devotion to the State; and the common sentiment holds that man guilty of treason who prefers the United States to South Carolina. There is no occasion to wonder at the admiration of the people for Wade Hampton, for he is the very exemplar of their spirit,—of their proud and narrow and domineering spirit. "It is our duty," he says, in a letter which he has recently addressed to the people of the State,—"it is our duty to support the President of the United States so long as he manifests a disposition to restore all our rights as a sovereign State." That sentence will forever stand as a model of cool arrogance, and yet it is in full accord with the spirit of the South-Carolinians. The war has taught them that the physical force of the nation cannot be resisted, and they will be obedient to the letter of the law; but the whole current of their lives flows in direct antagonism to its spirit....

Prior to the war we heard continually of the love of the master for his slave, and the love of the slave for his master. There was also much talk to the effect that the negro lived in the midst of pleasant surroundings, and had no desire to change his situation. It was asserted that he delighted in a state of dependence, and throve on the universal favor of the whites. Some of this language we conjectured might be extravagant; but to the single fact that there was universal good-will between the two classes every Southern white person bore evidence. So, too, during my trip through Georgia and the Carolinas they have generally seemed anxious to convince me that the blacks behaved well during the war,—kept at their old tasks, labored cheerfully and faithfully, did not show a disposition to be lawless, and were rarely guilty of acts of violence, even in sections where there were many women and children, and but few white men.

Yet I found everywhere now the most direct antagonism between the two classes. The whites charge generally that the negro is idle and at the bottom of all local disturbance, and credit him with most of the vices and very few of the virtues of humanity. The negroes charge that the whites are revengeful, and intend to cheat the laboring class at every opportunity, and credit them with neither good purposes nor kindly hearts. This present and positive hostility of each class to the other is a fact that will sorely perplex any Northern man travelling in either of these States. One would say, that, if there had formerly been such pleasant relations between them, there ought now to be mutual sympathy and forbearance, instead of mutual distrust and antagonism. One would say, too, that self-interest, the common interest of capital and labor, ought to keep them in harmony; while the fact is, that this very interest appears to put them in an attitude of partial defiance toward each other. I believe the most charitable traveller must come to the conclusion that the professed love of the whites for the blacks was mostly a monstrous sham or a downright false pretence. For myself, I judge that it was nothing less than an arrant humbug.

Source 4:   *Wade Hampton Testifies before a Congressional Committee* (1871)

In 1871, a Joint Congressional Committee took testimony in South Carolina regarding conditions in the state under Congressional Reconstruction. In this excerpt, Wade Hampton is questioned by the Republican chairman, Senator John Scott of Pennsylvania, and Democratic representative Philadelph Van Trump of Ohio. In particular, they ask Hampton about the violence against blacks and about his views regarding blacks in the state. What does this source reveal about Hampton's attitudes? Do you think he was a credible witness, or that this testimony reflects what Sidney Andrews, the author of the previous source, called "a proud narrow, and domineering spirit"?

SOURCE: U.S. Congress, Report of the Joint Select Committee to Inquire into the Condition of Affairs in the Lake Insurrectionary States, vol. 4, South Carolina, (Washington, D.C.: Government Printing Office, 1872), pp. 1222–1223, 1227–1228, 1235–1236).

By Rep. Van Trump:

QUESTION.   Is it your opinion then, general, or not, that negro suffrage unrestricted
by education, and general participation with the white race in State
legislation, and the holding of civil, State, and local offices, culminating
in a hostile supremacy on the part of the inferior race, is a decided
failure in South Carolina, as now exhibited?

ANSWER.   Yes, sir, I think it is.

QUESTION.   In your intercourse with the people of South Carolina and the South
generally, have you observed any marked or systematic hostility among
any considerable part of the white population against a fair and reasonable system, honestly administered, of education for and among the
negroes as a separate class?

ANSWER.   No, sir; I think the people are very much impressed with the propriety
of educating them, and would willingly give all the aid in their power
to do so. I mean the white people generally, as a class. Of course, there
are violent men in all parties.

QUESTION.   Notwithstanding these sectional—and I mean by sectional, portions of
the State—notwithstanding these sectional exhibitions of lawlessness,
and the violations of law, have you ever known a single instance in
South Carolina, since the war, of resistance to the service of legal
process?

ANSWER.   No, sir; it has never come under my observation at all.

QUESTION.   Then, in your opinion, is the reason why these violences, committed
by men in disguise, are unpunished, because the offenders cannot be
identified or discovered, or is it a laxity in the administration of law, or
imperfection in the process of law, by which these men in disguise
escape?

ANSWER.   I really do not know as to that all. I know nothing of these outrages
except what I have seen in the papers, and how any one made his
escape I do not know. But I think it would be very difficult to identify
any men who disguise themselves as I am told they have done in more
than one case.

QUESTION.   What is your opinion, as a citizen of South Carolina, and noticing
these things as far as you can notice them, as to this organization called
the Ku-Klux organization?

ANSWER.   As far as I know, I have never seen any man that was identified with that
organization, if one exists. I have never been approached upon the
subject at all, and I do not know that there is an organization of that
kind at all. The outrages have been committed, I have no question, for
that I have been stated; but whether this is done by any organization
extending through the State or merely from some local outbreak, I do
not know; but I am inclined to think it is the latter....

By the Chairman:

QUESTION.   In the counties where these outrages exist, if they go to the extent of
taking negroes out of their beds and whipping them to the number of

one hundred and fifty or two hundred persons in a county, within five or six months, is it your idea that such a state of things could grow into toleration if the public sentiment of the leading men condemned it, and was actively at work to repress it?

ANSWER. I do not know. In the first place, while I have never heard of outrages committed to anything like that extent in any county, I should not think that punishment to as great an extent as that could be administered without a large number of persons being engaged in it, certainly.

QUESTION. Have you any idea that any portion of the democratic organization in this State is silently acquiescing in such a state of things, with the idea that it will ultimately, by the terror produced upon the colored people, prevent them from exercising the elective franchise?

ANSWER. No, sir. I do not believe that it was intended, or has ever been tried as a system extensively, to intimidate the colored vote. That is my honest conviction; I have never seen it, and I know I have heard always in this committee that we should never resort to anything of the sort, but try, on the contrary, to enlighten them. The only instances of intimidation—at least, I have no doubt the great majority of instances of intimidation in this State, as far as the colored population are concerned, have come from men of their own race, acting against those who voted, or wanted to vote, against the radical ticket. I have seen that myself. I saw two instances in which a deliberate attempt was made to murder colored people for no other reason in the world than because they expressed a desire of going with the democratic party.

QUESTION. Was that openly made?

ANSWER. Yes, sir; openly. One was over at Aiken, where there was a meeting during the presidential contest, and an old man—a very excellent man—a colored man, who had always borne a good character, was president of a democratic club—a negro club. He went over there and made a speech. I was sitting in the hotel when the meeting was over, and he was walking back, with two others, to get on a train; a large crowd followed him; we did not apprehend anything serious, but when they approached him, one man stepped out of the crowd and struck him with a large stick, knocking him down. General Butler[*] was present, and it was with great difficulty that we prevented a fight on the spot. A great many men were there, highly excited, and they procured arms, and for a few moments it was imminent that there would be a fight between the whites and the blacks.

QUESTION. Were there no arrests made after that occurrence?

ANSWER. No, sir. The other occasion was in the fall, at Charleston. General Butler was candidate for lieutenant governor. He asked me to speak, and I said a few words. They called on a colored man to speak. He got up on the stand, when some one in the crowd threw a large rock

---

[*]*General Matthew C. Butler:* General Butler, who served in the Hampton Legion during the Civil War, would be Hampton's colleague in politics for many years.

at him on the stand. It was thrown from the negroes, and there again we came very near having another collision....

QUESTION. One question I am prompted to ask by some sentiments which I have found in this State, and I ask for your opinion in regard to them. Is it your belief that the people of South Carolina will continue to yield obedience to the State government if the present majority of negro voters continues the republican party in power, or will the existing discontent increase and involve a contest between the races?

ANSWER. I am very much at a loss to pronounce an opinion upon that. I have been very much afraid of a collision—so much so that I wrote a letter to President Grant some years ago on that subject....
In that letter I remember expressing my fears that there would be a collision of the races in the State. Those fears are not yet removed; and that has been the main reason why I have deprecated rousing any antagonism between the two races. What would be the result, I do not know. I do not believe that the white people can now, or will, live under a rule where persons so entirely ignorant, so venal, so corrupt, have the management of their State government. I do not see how it is possible. I think they will bear as long as they can, but there will be a point beyond which they cannot bear.

QUESTION. In that very point of view I put the question, for it is one of great interest, certainly a perplexing one, and you being so much better acquainted with the state of sentiment among the white people than it is possible for the committee to be, I wish to know if the present negro majority continue the republican party in power, do you believe there will be submission, or will the feeling, which you have described, culminate in resistance to the State government?

ANSWER. If it was merely the negro majority to continue, I do not think it would produce a conflict. In other words, if they were to choose good men and have the government administered economically, I think the people would submit and bear it, in the hope that peaceful remedies and agencies would eventually restore their rights—the rights of the white people. But if they go on as they have been going on, taxing the State to this enormous extent, and being so venal and corrupt as they unquestionably are, for there can be no doubt of it. I have been told that no measure of any importance passes the legislature without the members being bought up regularly; that it is a notorious thing that money is placed upon the desks before them by parties who want measures carried through, and they are not paying any taxes themselves, but impose these enormous taxes, and that they have an exaggerated opinion of their power as they do have. I am afraid it may end in a collision. The negro has an exaggerated opinion of his own power. You gentlemen do not know the negro at all, and there is the great difficulty. You all think the negroes are actuated by the same feeling as the white men, but that is a mistake. I do not pretend to say why it is but they are not. They have been dependent for a long time; they have no provision; they have no forethought at all; they are content to live from hand to mouth; they do not pretend to lay up anything; they are very credulous; they have an exaggerated opinion of their own power. I have known them to express the opinion, and I have no doubt they have the idea, that but for them the southern cause would have been successful; that they were the parties to whom success was due. I have heard them say so; that it was not until their aid was called for. More than once I have heard them express that opinion; that the Federal Army was triumphant, and they believe that they are strong enough, not only to defeat all the southern people, but all the northern people combined with them. I am not speaking of the more intelligent ones, but of the great mass of laborers. I have had a great deal to do with the negroes. I have spoken very kindly to them always, and all the negroes that I have living with me now, or the larger number of them, are my old slaves. I talk very freely with them. I give them the best advice I can. They talk very freely to me: and either they tell very wonderful lies or have been badly informed. I will give you one instance. My property was taken possession of by some hanger-on of the Federal Army while I was out of the way. He had hands there. When I went back after the war, I proposed to make a contract with them. They came up to see me. They went down to see this man, who had moved away, and came back and asked me for the truth. They said this man, who had been in the Federal Army and had worked them, had told them that if they hired to me they would all be branded and be put back into slavery for five years. I said, "Are you fools enough to believe that!" A man answered, "I don't know; this man told us so." I asked them, "Did I ever tell you a lie in my life!" They said, "No sir; you never did." I assured them it was not so. They actually told me that.

Source 5:   *Representative Robert Smalls Protests the Withdrawal of Federal Troops* (1876)

In the face of rising vigilante action against blacks in South Carolina, Robert Smalls introduced an amendment to a bill in Congress that would have reduced federal military forces in the state. What does Smalls's testimony reveal about the threat to Republican rule in the state? How would you compare the letter in this source to the appeal to Congress a decade earlier in Source 1?

I offer the amendment which I send to the desk. The clerk read as follows:

Add to the first section the following:

Provided, That no troops for the purposes named in this section shall be drawn from the State of South Carolina so long as the militia of that State peaceably assembled are assaulted, disarmed, and taken prisoners, and then massacred in cold blood by lawless bands of men invading that State from the State of Georgia.

I hope the House will adopt that proviso as an amendment to the bill. As I have only five minutes I send to the desk a letter published in one of the newspapers here from an eye-witness of the massacre at Hamburgh [*sic*], and I ask the Clerk to read it.

SOURCE: Congressional Record, 44th Congress, 1st sessions, 1876, 5, pt.5: 4641–42.

The Clerk read as follows:

The origin of the difficulty, as I learn from the best and most reliable authority, is as follows: On the Fourth of July the colored people of the town were engaged in celebrating the day, and part of the celebration consisted in the parade of the colored militia company. After marching through the principal streets of the town, the company came to a halt across one of the roads leading out of the town. While resting there two white men drove up in a buggy, and with curses ordered the company to break ranks and let them pass through. The captain of the company replied that there was plenty of room on either side of the company, and they could pass that way. The white men continued cursing and refused to turn out. So the captain of the militia, to avoid difficulty, ordered his men to break ranks and permit the buggy to pass through....

Late in the afternoon General M. C. Butler, one of the most malignant of the unreconstructed rebels, rode into the town, accompanied by a score of well-armed white men, and stated to the leading colored men that he came for the purpose of prosecuting the case on the part of the two white men, and he demanded that the militia company should give up their arms and also surrender their officers. This demand the militia was ready to comply with for the purpose of avoiding a difficulty if General Butler would guarantee them entire safety from molestation by the crowd of white desperadoes. This Butler refused to do, and persisted in his demand for the surrender of the guns and officers, and threatened that if the surrender was not immediately made he would take the guns and officers by force of arms. This threat aroused the militia company to a realizing sense of their impending danger, and they at once repaired to a large brick building, some two hundred yards from the river, used by them as on armory, and there took refuge. They numbered in all about forty men and had a very small quantity of ammunition. During this time, while the militia were taking refuge in their armory the white desperadoes were coming into the town in large numbers, not only from the adjacent county of Edgefield, but also from the city of Augusta, Georgia, until they numbered over fifteen hundred well-armed and ruffianly men, who were under the immediate command and direction of the ex-rebel chief, M. C. Butler. After the entire force had arrived, the building where the militia had taken refuge was entirely surrounded and a brisk fire opened upon it. This fire was kept up for some two hours, when, finding that the militia could not be dislodged by small arms, a messenger was sent to Augusta for artillery. During all this time not a shot had been fired by the militia-men. The artillery arrived and was posted on the bank of the river and opened fire on the building with grape and canister.

[An attempt to interrupt reading fails.]

The militia now realized that it was necessary to evacuate the armory at once. They proceeded to do so, getting out of a back window into a cornfield. They were soon discovered by the ruffians, and a rush was made for them. Fortunately, by hiding and hard fighting, a portion of the command escaped, but twenty-one were captured by the bushwhackers and taken immediately to a place near the railroad station.

Here a quasi-drumhead court-martial[*] was organized by the blood-hunters, and the last scene of the horrible drama began. It must now be remembered that not one of the twenty-one colored men had a pistol or gun about them. The moment they were captured their arms were taken from them, and they were absolutely defenseless. The orderly sergeant of the militia company was ordered to call the roll, and the first

---

[*]*Drumhead court-martial:* A court-martial held in the field for the purpose of trying offenses during military operations.

name called out to be shot in cold blood was Allan T. Attaway, the first lieutenant of the company, and holding the position of county commissioner of Aiken County, in which county Hamburgh is situated. He pleaded for his life, as only one in his position could plead, but his pleading were met with curses and blows, and he was taken from the sight of his comrades and a file of twelve men fired upon him. He was penetrated by four balls, one entering his brain, and the other three the lower portion of his body. He was instantly killed and after he was dead the brutes in human shape struck him over the head with their guns and stabbed him in the face with their bayonets. Three other men were treated in the same brutal manner. The fifth man when taken out made a dash for his life, and luckily escaped with only a slight wound in his leg.

In another portion of the town the chief of police, a colored man named James Cook, was taken from his house and while begging for his life brutally murdered. Not satisfied with this, the inhuman fiends beat him over the head with their muskets and cut out his tongue.

Another colored man, one of the marshals of the town, surrendered and was immediately shot through the body and mortally wounded. He has since died....

Are the southern colored citizens to be protected or are they to be left at the mercy of such ruffians as massacred the poor men of Hamburgh? Murdered Attaway was a man of considerable prominence in the republican party of the county. He was a law-abiding citizen, held a responsible office, and was well thought of by very many people. The other murdered men were good citizens and have never been known to infringe the law. The whole affair was a well and secretly planned scheme to destroy all the leading republicans of the county of Aiken living in Hamburgh. M. C. Butler, who lost a leg while fighting in the ranks of the rebels, and who is to-day the bitterest of Ku-Klux democrats, was the instigator of the whole affair and the blood-thirsty leader of the massacre. He boasted in Hamburgh during the fight that that was only the beginning; that the end should not be until after the elections in November. Such a man should be dealt with without pity or without hesitation. The United States Government is not powerless, and surely she will not be silent in an emergency like this, the parallel of which pen cannot describe. In this centennial year will she stand idly by and see her soil stained with the blood of defenseless citizens, and witness the bitter tears of women and children falling upon the murdered bodies of their loved ones? God forbid that such an attitude will be assumed toward the colored people of the South by the "best Government the world ever saw." Something must be done, and that quickly, or South Carolina will shed tears of blood and her limbs be shackled by democratic chains.

What I have written in this letter are facts which I vouch for entirely, and are not distorted in any degree. It's a "plain, unvarnished" narration of painful and horrible truths.

Source 6:   *Instructions to Red Shirts* (1876)

During the campaign for governor of South Carolina in 1876, the Democratic Executive Committee of Edgefield County adopted a plan for the intimidation of Republican voters. Often referred to as the "Edgefield plan" or the "shotgun plan," it declared that every Democrat should be a member of

SOURCE: From Robert K. Ackerman, WADE HAMPTON III (Columbia: University of South Carolina Press, 2007).

Democratic club and that each club or of member should follow certain procedures to ensure a Republican defeat. What do these instructions reveal about the means the Hampton forces employed to bring about his election victory? What light do they shed on the Congressional testimony of Robert Smalls and Wade Hampton in the previous sources?

Each club should have a roster of every voter, white and black, in the township or region the club represented.

Every club member should be armed [the clubs often became synonymous with the rifle clubs]. The clubs should have a military organization and supplies for three days' action.

The clubs should demand that at least one of the three election managers be a Democrat.

The clubs should have a representative present when the votes are counted and demand a duplicate of the results.

The clubs should send a committee to Columbia with the duplicates to ensure an accurate count by the State Board of Canvassers.

Every club should provide transportation for voters to the polls.

The clubs should be alert to prevent underage blacks from voting and to prevent multiple voting.

Every Democrat should control the vote of one black, either by intimidation, by purchase, or by keeping him from voting.

Democrats should attend every Republican meeting to demand a division of time to challenge their statements, call them liars, cheats, or thieves.

Democrats should realize that argument serves no purpose with blacks; they can only be influenced by fear and cupidity ("treat them so as to show them you are the superior race and that their natural position is that of subordinates to the white man").

Clubs should let it be known that they will hold radical leaders responsible for any bloodshed, any house burnings, and voting irregularities.

Members of the county executive committees will visit the area clubs.

There should be five mass meetings in the counties, concentrating on July and August.

The counties should choose good candidates, preferring native whites to carpetbaggers.

There will be no financial assessments until the cotton harvest.

All transactions should be secret.

The clubs should enroll boys from age sixteen and up.

The watch word would be "Fight the devil with fire."

Organize black Democratic clubs or pretend to have organized such clubs.

The uniform is the red shirt.

QUESTIONS TO CONSIDER

1. What does the career of Robert Smalls reveal about the goals of blacks at the end of the Civil War? To what extent were they fulfilled under Congressional Reconstruction?

2. How would you account for the triumph of Wade Hampton and the Democrats in South Carolina in 1876? What would have to have changed to prevent the triumph of the Redeemers in that state and elsewhere in the South?

3. Based on the essay and sources in this chapter, what role do you think the racial or other attitudes of white southerners played in determining the way Reconstruction turned out? Which of Hampton's arguments do you think whites outside the South would have found most appealing?

4. Robert Smalls and Wade Hampton likely never met one another. If they had, what do you think each would have said to the other to attempt to get him to see his point of view regarding Congressional Reconstruction in South Carolina? What would have Smalls emphasized about its accomplishments? What would have Hampton said about its failures?

FOR FURTHER READING

Robert K. Ackerman, *Wade Hampton III* (Columbia: University of South Carolina Press, 2007), offers a recent and largely sympathetic biography of Hampton.

Eric Foner, *Reconstruction: America's Unfinished Revolution, 1863–1877* (New York: Harper & Row, 1988), offers a synthesis of the Reconstruction era. Foner argues that Reconstruction provided opportunities for reform that were not taken and correctly places African Americans at the center of the story.

Edward A. Miller Jr., *Gullah Statesman: Robert Smalls from Slavery to Congress, 1839–1915* (Columbia: University of South Carolina Press, 1995), provides a useful biography of the African-American leader.

Kenneth M. Stampp, *The Era of Reconstruction, 1865–1877* (New York: Random House, 1965), remains a starting point for studies that present Reconstruction as a positive and successful policy.

Richard Zuczek, *State of Rebellion: Reconstruction in South Carolina* (Columbia: University of South Carolina Press, 1996), offers a thorough examination of the politics of Reconstruction in the Palmetto State.